The Real Retirement Crisis

The Real Retirement Crisis

Why (Almost) Everything You Know About the US Retirement System Is Wrong

Andrew G. Biggs

AEI PRESS

Publisher for the American Enterprise Institute

WASHINGTON, DC

ISBN-13: 978-0-8447-5081-1 (Hardback)
ISBN-13: 978-0-8447-5082-8 (Paperback)
ISBN-13: 978-0-8447-5083-5 (Ebook)

Library of Congress Control Number: 2025930153

Jacket design by Claude Aubert. Author image by Kelly Armijo. Jacket image by Kovalova Ivanna, AI generated. Adobe Stock Images.

A=I PRESS

Publisher for the American Enterprise Institute
for Public Policy Research
1789 Massachusetts Avenue, NW
Washington, DC 20036

Printed in the United States of America

Contents

1

Retirement Realities

A Google search on the phrase "retirement crisis" finds 22,800 mentions in print and online news media. I regret to say that I've read most of them. "A Generation of Americans Is Entering Old Age the Least Prepared in Decades," says an award-winning *Wall Street Journal* story.[1] "Bankruptcy Booms Among Older Americans," the *New York Times* tells us.[2] "Social Security benefits have lost one-third of their buying power since 2000," the *Washington Post* reports.[3] "Half of Older Americans Have Nothing in Retirement Savings," says *Bloomberg*, citing a research report from the US Government Accountability Office.[4] "Retirees risk running out of money a decade before death," *Bloomberg* again tells us, this time relying on research from the World Economic Forum.[5] "U.S. Heading from Retirement 'Crisis' to Retirement 'Catastrophe,'" says financial planning website ThinkAdvisor, citing a report from the firm Allianz.[6]

As Captain America says in the Marvel movie, "I can do this all day."[7] Truly, barely a day goes by when I don't read something apocalyptic about retirement. But every headline printed above, all of which are from major media sources, is wrong. And I don't mean subtly wrong or wrong by virtue of some technicality. I mean just wrong, as in, the opposite of correct.

Yet as much as people claim that Americans no longer read, they certainly have digested the retirement crisis narrative as expressed in the news media. In a 2021 survey by the National Institute on Retirement Security, the research arm of the defined benefit pensions industry, two-thirds of Americans said they believe the nation faces a "retirement crisis," with 30 percent of respondents "strongly agreeing" with that statement. Only 16 percent disagreed, with just 3 percent strongly disagreeing.[8] In a 2017 Vanguard survey, 56 percent of near retirees agreed with the statement "I believe there is a national retirement crisis."[9] In 2023, a "runaway majority" of 89 percent of Americans agreed in an American Advisors Group survey that yes, there is a "retirement savings crisis."[10]

Evidence of Americans' concern over retirement savings adequacy is not difficult to find. A 2023 survey conducted by the American Advisors Group found 89 percent of Americans worry that the country is in the grips of a "retirement crisis."[11] A 2021 survey commissioned by the National Institute on Retirement Security found that

> more than two-thirds of Americans (67 percent) say the nation faces a retirement crisis. More than half (56 percent) are concerned that they won't be able to achieve a financially secure retirement. Some 68 percent say the average worker cannot save enough on their own to guarantee a secure retirement. And 65 percent of current workers say it's likely they will have to work past retirement age to have enough money to retire. ... The vast majority of Democrats (70 percent), Independents (70 percent) and Republicans (62 percent) agree that the nation faces a retirement crisis.[12]

In 2023, 61 percent of Americans surveyed by Allianz Life responded that they feared running out of money in retirement more than they feared death.[13] A 2017 survey by Vanguard finds that a majority of Americans, both near retirees (59 percent) and recent retirees (54 percent), believe the country faces a "retirement crisis."[14] In a 2015 survey conducted by the Transamerica Center for Retirement Studies, 44 percent of near retirees feared lacking sufficient savings to last a full retirement.[15] Among retirees, 44 percent each feared a costly stay in a long-term care facility or that Social Security would run short of money.

In a 2022 survey conducted by the financial consulting firm WTW, "69% of U.S. employees surveyed recognize they are not saving enough for retirement."[16] In a 2021 survey conducted by the Principal Financial Group, just 49 percent of respondents expressed "confidence in living comfortably in retirement."[17]

These findings above match those from Gallup: In 2021, only 53 percent of working-age Americans expressed confidence in attaining a comfortable retirement.[18] Sixty-one percent of Americans tell Gallup they worry "a great deal" or "a fair amount" about the Social Security program, which is the largest source of income for most seniors.[19]

When it comes to retirement, Americans are worried.

Our elected officials, in their way, have responded to those concerns. Ninety percent of Democratic members of the House of Representatives cosponsored the Social Security 2100 Act, legislation that would not only maintain but expand Social Security benefits, for rich and poor retirees alike—at a multitrillion-dollar cost in terms of increased payroll taxes on poor, middle-class, and high-income Americans. Many states have moved to establish automatic individual retirement account (IRA) plans, which would set up IRAs for every worker and automatically enroll employees in those plans. Likewise, in 2022, Congress instituted a $100 billion-plus bailout of underfunded multiemployer pension plans, which are retirement programs for unionized employees in the trucking, mining, and other industries.

Some of these plans are helpful—others debatable or unwarranted. But there is a larger point: Retirement savings are not free.

Saving more for retirement isn't like eating healthier or exercising more, in which you're pretty much better off regardless. Increasing Social Security payroll taxes by over one-third to expand benefits across the board would affect households' take-home pay and the government's ability to fund other programs such as health, education, and infrastructure. Social Security may be the federal government's largest program, but it's not the only one. The federal government does have goals other than taking more money from young (mostly poorer) people and giving it to older (mostly richer) people.

Likewise, if we push low-income workers to save more, such as through auto IRAs, they'll have a greater amount of money in retirement but less money today to buy a home, pay for college, or just put food on the table.

Those are personal costs. But there may be economic costs as well. Recently, the Penn Wharton Budget Model group used a sophisticated economic model to simulate the effects of the most popular congressional Social Security expansion plan versus a reform plan that balances Social Security by progressively reducing benefits, raising the retirement age, and paying lower cost-of-living adjustments.

In the Penn Wharton Budget Model, gross domestic product in 2050 was 7 percentage points lower under the Social Security expansion plan than the benefit cuts plan because raising taxes to pay higher Social Security benefits reduces incentives to both work and save.[20] Even at half that size, these would be major economic effects.

All of which is to say that how we judge the adequacy of Americans' retirement savings matters a great deal, both in our roles as individuals planning our finances and as citizens considering how our government should allocate its resources.

A central thesis of this book is that Americans have done a much better job of saving for retirement than is currently assumed. Despite the gloomy coverage in the news media and scaremongering from interest groups and politicians, Americans are doing nearly everything that would ordinarily be advised to improve their income security in old age. More Americans are saving more for retirement than ever before in US history. They are working more at older ages, and they are delaying claiming Social Security.

The incomes seniors receive are at record highs across the income distribution, while poverty in old age is at record lows. And retirement savings for working-age Americans are at record levels for every age, income, education, and racial and ethnic group. The news headlines may claim one thing, but the data show another.

If there is a retirement crisis facing the United States, it comes from a different source. While household personal savings for retirement have moved upward, there has been a worrying increase in governmental ledgers—but this increase is for the multitrillion-dollar unfunded liabilities of government retirement plans, which range from the federal Social Security program to pensions for schoolteachers and local government employees. In the US and around the world, the vast majority of the so-called retirement savings gap derives from governments failing to fund their retirement benefit obligations, not from households failing to save adequately on their own.

If the true "retirement crisis" in the United States is on the government side, why do news media and political discussions depict the popular narrative so differently? Why can news reporters and policymakers not grasp what is in the data? I see two explanations.

The first and more reasonable explanation is that retirement planning is complex and scary. Anyone preparing for retirement must decide how much to save, how to invest their savings, when to retire, and how to draw down their savings in old age. It's a complex, mathematical task, and you get only one shot at it. It's not surprising then that Americans are worried about retirement.

As we'll see, those worries usually aren't realized. Even if most current seniors are doing fine, those same people were pessimistic about their retirement prospects when they were in their working years. A lot of the worry about retirement planning is unavoidable, but media and policy discussions certainly shouldn't make things worse.

Second, there aren't strong incentives for many people to tell a more realistic story about the state of retirement savings. The news media don't have the incentive. Which headline would you click on: "Americans Entering Old Age the Least Prepared in Decades" or "Americans' Retirement Savings, Incomes Have Never Been Higher"? One of those headlines is true, and one came from an actual newspaper report.

The financial industry doesn't have the incentive to tell a positive story. What are the chances your favorite mega-investment firm will tell you you're saving *too much* for retirement? If a pharmaceutical company ran advertisements stating that you may have an ailment for which it happens to offer a treatment, you would at least consider that this is how the pharmaceutical company makes its living. That usually doesn't occur in discussions of retirement planning.

Politicians don't have the incentive to tell you the real story, if only because no one would believe them. But it goes beyond that. Political progressives tend to be more skeptical of private-sector solutions to problems like retirement. Obviously, those concerns aren't completely unwarranted; there *are* Americans who don't save for retirement as they should and end up regretting it when they grow old.

Public policy can help address these shortcomings in various ways. And yet, too often, instead of evidence-based policymaking, we sometimes end up with policy-based evidence-making. That is, once elected officials have decided on a policy position—for instance, 401(k)s don't work or Social Security should be expanded—they may close their minds to any evidence that fails to support that position. I have seen it many times when I have given testimony before congressional committees: Members of Congress have their talking points, written on three-by-five cards. I could provide an infinite stream of hard data showing that their retirement crisis narrative doesn't hold true, but the chances of changing minds are slim.

But there are two stories about retirement in America, and in this book, I tell the second one. That's the story that's drawn from hard data and peer-reviewed research. A big part of my job in writing this book is simply to act as a Greek-to-English translator between the facts, figures, math, and Greek letters that show up in economic research on retirement savings and the plain English that an ordinary reader reasonably demands when presented with an argument.

I start by explaining how economists think about retirement planning, which is usually in the framework of what's often called the "life-cycle model" of spending and saving. That model, which predicts how individuals try to maximize the welfare and well-being that their incomes will generate over their lifetimes, is in some ways highly intuitive and in other ways not. But the life-cycle model can provide insights into the US retirement savings environment that one would ordinarily not obtain.

These insights certainly will not come from the news media, which, as I show in following chapters, often report what appears to be the precise opposite of the truth regarding retirement savings and retirement incomes. Those insights also won't come from advocacy organizations, where policy positions dictate the evidence that will be presented, not the other way around.

And those insights often won't even come from financial planners, who one might ordinarily assume would translate best practices derived from economics into the everyday practices that dictate how we prepare for retirement. In a 2022 study titled "Popular Personal Financial Advice Versus the Professors," a Yale economist James Choi compares recommendations from the most popular personal finance advisers in books, television, and radio to what mainstream economics research says about these same topics.[21]

In some ways, celebrity financial advisers' advice is more practical in focusing on simple rules that will stand up to procrastination and a lack of willpower. But in other ways, common financial advice is directly contrary to what economists would consider to be prudent planning.

For example, celebrity financial planners often recommend that every person save the same share of their salary for retirement—12 to 15 percent is the going rate—every year through their career. This is far from what economics would recommend, and, fortunately, it's far from what most Americans actually do. As we will see, individuals often follow what textbook economics would recommend, even if they have never read an economics textbook or they would be criticized by celebrity financial planners for what they're doing.

Throughout this book we see a US retirement system that defies the odds. A system that matches up surprisingly well to what economic theory recommends. A system that has been improving over time. A system that compares well to other developed countries. A system that, for all of Americans' worries along the way, ends up with seniors overwhelmingly satisfied with their financial security in old age.

But we also see a range of pitfalls, small and large. Government policymakers commonly must set Social Security and retirement policy relying on data on retirement plan participation and retirement incomes that bear little resemblance to the truth. State and local governments manage multitrillion-dollar public employee pensions under accounting rules that are almost unique in the retirement world, rules that dramatically downplay the costs of these plans and dramatically increase incentives for excessive risk-taking.

Indeed, as I show, the real "retirement crisis" is not in household savings, which have increased dramatically over the years. Rather, the crisis lies in government retirement programs that, almost uniformly, governments refuse to adequately fund. Countrywide and indeed worldwide, the retirement savings gap is mainly a government pension funding gap.

So I discuss and propose solutions to underfunded public-sector pensions and the even larger challenge of Social Security reform. These solutions, however, must go well beyond merely making these plans solvent for coming decades. In fact, the only way to convince Americans to accept the sacrifices and challenges involved with making Social Security in particular solvent is to simultaneously make the program work better. That demands looking at why we have Social Security in the first place and how a Social Security program for the 21st century would look different from the plan that was instituted in the early 20th century.

This book is unlike most on retirement. It is not a personal financial planning book, though I think many ordinary Americans would benefit

from understanding the insights that economics brings to retirement savings issues. It is not a book on the history of Social Security or other retirement savings plans, though I do refer to how the history of what happened
and what people were thinking at the time often differs from how we
understand those events today. This also is not a book specifically for prac-
titioners, even if I think there is much here that they will find new and
interesting. I present the details of tax rules or the Social Security benefit
formula only as needed to illustrate the topics I explore.

Throughout this book, I present facts, insights, and arguments that I
have found compelling over a career working in retirement policy. Many
are fascinating, counterintuitive, inspiring, or sometimes even infuriating.
I hope that readers completing this book come away feeling the same.

PART I

2

What's Your Retirement Number?

You can't be too rich or too thin. But can you save too much for retirement? One would think not, given that everywhere we see messages encouraging us to save more. Less isn't more when it comes to retirement savings. More is more.

Now, obviously that's an overstatement. Even the most devoted purveyor of claims that America faces a "retirement crisis," which can be averted only through dramatic legislation to expand Social Security and overhaul private retirement savings plans, would admit that in theory it's possible to save too much for retirement.

And if you are looking for that theory, it's called the "life-cycle hypothesis" or the "life-cycle model" of spending and saving. The life-cycle model grew out of the work for economists Albert Ando and Franco Modigliani, who first published the framework for the hypothesis in 1963.[1] The life-cycle model has been expanded and amended in the decades since to become what is called a "workhorse" model in economics—a go-to way of thinking about spending and saving decisions whose usefulness and applicability need no longer be questioned.

The life-cycle approach has dominated economists' thinking about retirement saving and many other issues for the past half century. It provides insights that otherwise are absent in most discussions of retirement saving and potentially informs what lawmakers should do to facilitate retirement security through Social Security, private retirement plans, and other policies yet to be implemented.

But by first walking through common, albeit flawed, ways of thinking about retirement savings, we can better understand what the life-cycle model adds to the picture.

How Not to Think About Preretirement Savings

"Americans' Magic Number for Retirement Rises to $1.27 Million," reported the financial website SmartAsset, based on Northwestern Mutual's "Planning & Progress Study 2023."[2] *US News & World Report* cites "long-held advice . . . that a client who has accumulated $1 million would be able to live comfortably for the remainder of their life."[3] A 2022 Transamerica survey found that most Americans believed they could comfortably retire with savings of $1 million.[4] A 2023 Charles Schwab survey of account holders found that "on average, workers think they need $1.8 million saved for retirement."[5] The only problem, CNBC's reporting added, is that 96 percent of Americans hold less than $1 million in assets.

Other advice is a bit more flexible. Fidelity Investments recommends that you should have retirement savings by the end of your career equal to 10 times your final salary.[6] Some experts, like the prominent retirement economist Teresa Ghilarducci, argue that it's better to have 20 times your final salary.[7] So higher-income households must save more for retirement than low earners need to. Still, at least there's a single number we can rely on.

But even this isn't right. Social Security is the foundation of retirement income for the vast majority of Americans. Social Security's benefit formula, however, is progressive: The lowest earners might receive a benefit equal to 80 percent of their preretirement earning, while high earners might receive just a 30 percent "replacement rate." If we all target the same "savings-to-salary" ratio at the end of our careers, low earners would end up with a higher income in retirement than they had while working. That doesn't make sense.

Here's the reality: There's no single number that tells you how much you'll need to save for retirement. No single dollar figure. No single multiple of final salary. No single replacement rate of preretirement earnings. It won't surprise you to hear that I think much of the financial advice you'll read online or hear from financial planners' TV or radio shows isn't of great quality.

What's more important to understand is what people are trying to do when they save for retirement, which is far more complex and interesting than hitting some single number thrown out in a financial column in your local newspaper. This book is informed by what economic theory and analysis of data have to say about how Americans should and do save for retirement. So it's worth starting with some discussion of what that economic perspective means.

Economics is about how individuals make choices to maximize their welfare under conditions of scarcity and uncertainty. Yes, that's a mouthful, but it contains a lot of insights.

We all want more stuff. And we want our receipt of that stuff to be guaranteed, not risky. But we can't have everything we want, and economics is fundamentally about how we address those trade-offs. And those trade-offs are everywhere, omnipresent in our lives and our decision-making.

For instance, we all wish we had higher incomes. A higher income brings more of all the material things we wish for—whether it's luxuries such as a bigger house, a flashy car, and fashionable clothes or the ability to send your kids to college, take care of an ailing relative, or support a local charity. It's the rare person who says they want less rather than more of these. And to get more of these, we need more of one thing: money.

And yet, in reality, nearly all of us *could* have higher incomes, but we choose not to. We could work longer hours at our main job, pick up a second job, or switch to a higher-paying but less enjoyable occupation. We could also switch to a job that, while carrying various sorts of risks, would pay a higher salary; think of a stockbroker or a salesmen on commission or a deep-sea fisherman working *The Deadliest Catch*. Maybe a higher income doesn't seem so attractive after all, if the alternative is getting snagged on a giant fishhook.

Why don't we make those changes, if we all want higher incomes? It's because higher incomes aren't all we want. We also want free time—the so-called labor-leisure trade-off between money and time to do other things, including enjoy the money we've earned. We want satisfying work and to avoid dangerous or unpleasant jobs. We want certainty in our incomes rather than incomes that fluctuate. More income is better, all other things equal. But all other things usually *aren't* equal. Economics is about the process of making the best of our trade-offs.

Saving for retirement is one part of that process of optimizing our choices amid numerous trade-offs. Sure, we all wish we had more retirement savings because it leads to higher incomes in old age. And when wealth falls into our lap, such as when we win a prize, receive an inheritance, or watch the stock market rise, everyone is happy.

But having more retirement savings isn't the same as saving more for retirement. And, barring winning the lottery, saving more is really the decision we face. While "savings" is a noun designating the money sitting in your bank or retirement account, "saving" is a verb, designating an action in which people choose to spend less today to have more money in the future. That is to say, saving—the verb—isn't about having more so much as it is about consuming less. If you spend less today, the savings you build are simply a by-product of that lower spending. Cut your spending, and watch your bank account grow.

Saving more for retirement means sending a greater share of our current income to our retirement account and a smaller share to other things, in particular those we can purchase in the here and now, which we just admitted we all want more, not less, of. So again, retirement saving involves trade-offs.

How much to save for retirement also depends on how we decide to handle uncertainty, particularly with how we invest our money. We would all prefer our retirement income to be guaranteed against investment risk, to be protected against inflation, and to last as long as we live rather than potentially running out. That's one reason people cite for liking traditional defined benefit pensions, which may offer all those desired outcomes. They protect the employee against market risk associated with investing their savings, generally (at least in the public sector) provide cost-of-living adjustments to protect against inflation, and offer a benefit that's guaranteed to last as long as the employee lives.

But providing all those advantages is expensive. Sure, we could invest our savings only in guaranteed, inflation-protected US Treasury bonds and buy so many of them that there would be little risk of running out of money. But that would demand that we save an enormous share of our present income for retirement, which denies us more of what our income could buy us today. Again, it's about trade-offs.

When individuals invest for retirement on their own, such as through 401(k)s and individual retirement accounts, their choices reflect those trade-offs. Employees saving for retirement through a 401(k) typically take a balanced approach rather than shifting entirely in one direction or the other. By investing part of their contributions in stocks, which have higher expected returns, they can generate the same level of future retirement income with a lower rate of contributions today. That leaves more money to spend elsewhere.

But most savers don't invest entirely in stocks, even though that would reduce their current contributions even further. The reason is that an all-stock portfolio carries a lot of risk, even over the long term, and that would lead to uncertainties in their future retirement incomes that the typical person finds unacceptably high. Again, trade-offs. It's always about trade-offs.

Of course, investment risk is just one uncertainty we face; risks abound as we think about preparing for retirement. While we all hope for a long life full of around-the-world cruises and exotic holidays, the downside of such luck is having to pay for it all. Paying for a long and opulent retirement means less money while we're young.

Worse yet, we're not guaranteed to have that long life in good health. Many people pass away much younger and so need less in old age. Saving assiduously for a retirement that doesn't happen leaves money on the table that could have been used for other things. It's enough to make your head spin. Which is why, in practice, we often choose to overlook some of the smaller risks to focus on the larger task.

Simply put, the statement "more retirement savings is better" considers only half the problem, because we also think that more income to spend today is better and savings and spending are the opposites of each other.

There May Not Be a Number. But There Is a Theory.

Economists have given a great deal of thought to—and won a few Nobel Prizes for—analyzing just these kinds of questions. Most prominently, the economist Modigliani won the Nobel Memorial Prize in Economic Sciences in 1985 for what is called the life-cycle theory (or model or hypothesis) of saving and spending, which gives us insights into how individuals save for retirement and how those individual decisions can affect saving and spending in an entire economy. Today, the life-cycle model "is the standard way that economists think about the intertemporal allocation of time, effort and money."[8] It provides a mental framework onto which an analyst can frame a question or fit facts gathered along the way.

The life-cycle model states, in simple terms, that when people decide how much to spend today, they are not thinking only of today. They also think about the future and how much money they will have available to them in future years. The life-cycle model doesn't assume we can see the future. But its key insight is that spending and saving decisions are made today in light of our expectations and preferences about the future. Most people aren't irrational hand-to-mouth consumers who spend every penny they take in. They think about the future and plan accordingly, if imperfectly.[9]

More precisely, the life-cycle model holds that people will choose to spend, save, or borrow in such a way as to maximize the discounted present value of the expected marginal utility they derive from spending their money over their lifetime. That's a lot to process. But if we break it up, we can see the insights the life-cycle theory delivers.

First, what is "utility"? That's just a fancy way of referring to the satisfaction, happiness, or welfare that we obtain, in this case, from spending money. We previously said that people don't want to simply maximize their incomes or their retirement savings, because those involve significant trade-offs. But individuals *do* wish to maximize their utility, because utility is a value that takes those trade-offs into account. An individual's "utility function," the mathematical equation that an economist might set up to help analyze different choices, might factor in labor versus leisure, risk versus uncertainty, or a pleasant job versus an unpleasant one.

Simply put, we arrange our spending and saving to make ourselves as happy as we can be throughout our lives. Who can argue with that? So when people sometimes claim that "economists know the price of everything but the value of nothing," they're wrong. The workhorse economic theory of retirement saving isn't based on money, but happiness.

But what's "marginal utility"? That's the welfare we derive from the final dollar we spend at any given time. By looking at the final dollar of spending at any given time, we focus on whether that particular dollar produces more utility if we spend it today versus saving it and then spending it at some other time of our lives. If we maximize the marginal utility of our spending over our lives, no dollars spent in any given year would produce more happiness if we spent them in some other year.

Marginal utility plays into the life-cycle model because not every dollar of spending produces the same level of utility. For instance, if my income this year doubled, the utility I derive from it would also increase—but it wouldn't double. The reason is what economists generally refer to as "diminishing marginal utility." That simply means that the more you consume of something, the less any additional consumption will make you happy.

That first slice of pizza you ate today? Fantastic! The third slice? Maybe not so good. The fifth slice you'd have to force me to eat. But if you could turn today's fifth slice of pizza into tomorrow's first, you'd end up happier overall. In general, diminishing marginal utility means that we'll attempt to spread our spending more evenly over time rather than spending a lot in one year and a little in another.

It's also common to assume that our capacity to derive utility from spending is the same at all points in our lives. Put more technically, while we always assume that the marginal utility of spending declines, we often go further in assuming that the *rate* at which marginal utility declines is the same over our lives. A so-called utility function is a mathematical representation of how much happiness we get from spending a given amount of money. If people employ the same utility function at every time of their lives, that will tend to push them toward spending the same amount of money every year.

We touch on that assumption later, which can be important in thinking about how spending evolves in retirement. If the marginal utility we derive from spending a given dollar is different at different points of our lives, we may not actually choose to spend the same amount each year. This can have important implications for how our desired income evolves over retirement.

What does the present value part refer to? In reality, it is about two things. First, people tend to prefer to enjoy things today rather than put them off to the future. Ordinary people call that impatience, but economists quantify that impatience into what they call our rate of time preference. It's not the same for everyone.

Some people prefer to consume things today, while others are willing to defer gratification for a long time. Time preferences, in particular the willingness to defer gratification, are extremely important for what we commonly think of as success in life. But for our purposes, we're taking time preferences as a given: Some people want to consume more now. Others are happy to wait until later. Both will design their retirement savings plans around those preferences.

But there's a second factor. If we put aside money today, we can earn interest on those savings, which gives us even more money to spend in the future. So our impatience in wanting things today is offset by the interest paid on the money we choose not to spend.

In economics, it's common to assume that, at least on average, the interest rate on savings is equal to the average rate of time preference. This also points toward spending about the same every year. But, as we will see, there is research that calls this assumption into question, particularly when interest rates are extremely low.[10]

What does the "expected" part of the life-cycle model refer to? Well, much of what we do in life—particularly in retirement savings—is uncertain. Will I maintain the same job for the rest of my career? Will I lose my job or become disabled and unable to work? Will I receive any investment returns on my savings? Will Social Security benefits be cut, or can I count on everything that I've been promised? We simply don't know many things, many of which happen to be important.

We can think more clearly about this uncertainty in two ways. First, people generally prefer certain outcomes to uncertain ones. Economists refer to this as "risk aversion." So if two investments offer the same average returns but one is risky while the other isn't, we'll tend to choose the less risky investment. Of course, when people make these choices, it affects the price of the investment such that, over time at least, prices for stocks or bonds reflect both the expected return on the investment and the risk that actual returns may turn out to be different from expectations.

Often people focus on the different rates of return that tend to be paid on safe or risky investments. But a mathematically equivalent way of thinking about that is to say that people are willing to pay less for risky investments than for safe ones. It's the low price investors are willing to pay for risky investments like stocks that cause them to have higher average returns. As we'll see, a big mistake, made especially in the public sector, is to think about an investment's potential return without thinking carefully about the risk attached to it.

Second, the expected utility we derive from some uncertain future dollar amount isn't the same as the utility we'd derive from the expected dollar amount. That's confusing, so let's run through an example. Imagine you invested $100 today and plan on holding it for 10 years. Let's also imagine that after 10 years there are only two possible outcomes: Your investment might have doubled in value to $200, or it might have gained no value and still be worth only $100. So the expected future value of your investment—that is, the possible future values of $100 and $200 weighted by their probability of occurring—is $150.

But the expected utility we place on our investment isn't the utility we derive from being able to spend $150. Rather, it's the average of the utilities of the two possible outcomes of our investment. That is, it's the average of the utility we'd derive from being able to spend $100 and the utility we'd derive from having $200 to spend.

That average will be lower than the utility we'd gain from a $150 investment outcome due to diminishing marginal utility of money: The first dollar we can spend is more valuable to us than succeeding dollars, so the utility of $200 isn't twice that of receiving $100. This aspect of things will matter when we start thinking about investing in risky assets, whether it's individuals saving for retirement in 401(k) accounts or governments investing to fund their employee pension plans.

These aspects of the life-cycle model and financial economics explain why people invest in safe assets such as bonds even if risky assets such as stocks tend to produce higher returns over time. When we think about investing in safe versus risky assets, it's much like the trade-off between consuming today and consuming in the future. We shift our savings between safe, low-returning investments such as bonds and risky, high-returning investments such as stocks until the expected utility we derive from the total portfolio is maximized—meaning that we can't increase our utility by shifting dollars from either bonds to stocks or stocks to bonds.

These assumptions simplify the reasoning and produce a cleaner result. If we assume that (1) a person's rate of time preference is the same as the interest rate they can earn on their savings, (2) the marginal utility they derive from spending is the same throughout their lives, and (3) they know their life expectancy with certainty, then they will choose to borrow and save such that they can spend the same amount every year of their adult life, from the time they start work throughout their retirement.

In the early years of a person's adult life, when their earnings tend to be low, they may borrow through credit cards, student loans, or a mortgage to afford a better lifestyle than their current income could provide. (See Figure 1.) Once their career starts to pick up and their earnings rise, the person will shift from borrowing to saving, such as by paying off past debts and starting to put aside money for retirement. The higher their income rises over time, the greater the share of their income the person is likely to save.

As they approach retirement, their wage income will decline and eventually cease. But their spending will remain the same, with the loss of wage income made up for by drawing down their savings. So even if a household's income follows a hump-shaped pattern from early life through retirement, their spending will remain reasonably constant over time.

I illustrate this concept in Figure 1. I use figures from the Social Security Administration's Office of the Chief Actuary to estimate the amount that a typical worker earns each year of their life. I assume this person began working in 1970 and retires at age 67 in 2016. Their earnings are shown in inflation-adjusted dollars. I also assume that this person will survive until age 85 and that they can receive an inflation-adjusted interest rate of 3 percent on their savings. I then calculate that their lifetime earnings, plus interest, would be sufficient to sustain a steady annual spending rate of about $31,000.

Now, to be clear, these figures are stylized. Household spending actually does change over people's lifetimes, for reasons we will explore in future chapters. But the key concept, that people borrow and save to maintain a steadier standard of living over time than their annual incomes would allow, is widely accepted.

The Exceptions to the Model

The life-cycle model has many exceptions, and economists have gradually factored them in. For example, some people might wish to leave an

Figure 1. Stylized Income and Spending over the Life Cycle

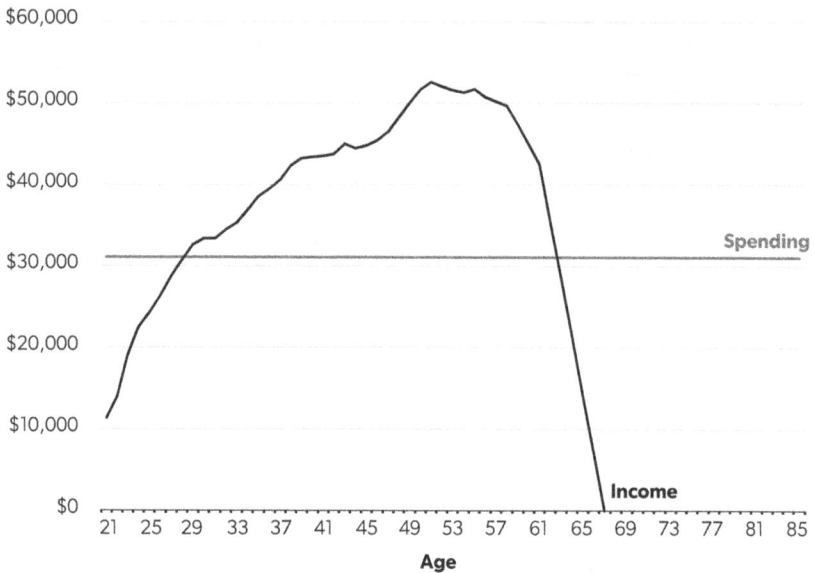

Source: Author's calculations from Social Security Administration data.

inheritance for their children rather than spend all their savings on themselves. Some might wish to act in certain ways but aren't able to. Young people with lower salaries might want to borrow against their future earnings so they can enjoy a higher standard of living while young but poor. But if no one will lend to them, they're unable to do that.

Likewise, experts aren't clear on how the life-cycle model interacts with children entering a household. Does the entire household smooth its consumption over time, such that parents spend less when they have kids living at home, or do parents smooth their own consumption while letting household spending rise and then fall as children enter and then leave the household? The answer can have important implications for how much parents might need to save for retirement.

But, big picture, the life-cycle model corresponds with our basic intuitions about spending and saving. It's a lot to process in one sitting, and economists like to layer on a lot of math, but, taken step by step, much of the life-cycle approach is just common sense.

While financial planners often recommend rules of thumb that don't match the life-cycle model, such as saving the same percentage of your salary every year of your life, much of conventional financial planning does match the life-cycle model's predictions. It's common for financial planners to recommend that retirement savers aim to achieve a 70 percent replacement rate in retirement, meaning their retirement income will replace 70 percent of their salaries just before retirement.

The 70 percent figure starts with the assumption that we wish to spend the same amount in retirement as we did while working—just as the life-cycle model predicts—but then subtracts out costs that tend to be lower in retirement, such as taxes, mortgage payments, work-related costs, and retirement saving itself. So even if households planning for retirement don't explicitly optimize under a formal life-cycle approach, their intuition and rules of thumb in retirement planning more or less accord with it.

The life-cycle model makes several important predictions regarding human behavior and retirement policies set by the government. For instance, if a person inherits a sum of money, they're not likely to spend it all at once. They might splurge a bit at first, but in general, they'll tend to draw down their newfound wealth more or less evenly in the years that follow their inheritance. They'll spend a bit more and save a bit less than they otherwise would.

The same goes for government policies. If the government decided to reduce retirement benefits such as Social Security, many of us would at least attempt to save a bit more or work longer before we retired. Likewise, if Social Security benefits were increased, people might save less for retirement.

There's a fair amount of research on these types of questions, some of which I look into in later chapters. And while it doesn't conclude that every person will in every circumstance do what a simple interpretation of the life-cycle model predicts, the overall results tend in that direction. This means that when lawmakers change policies, they should anticipate that people's behavior might change in response.

Now, we know this won't always happen. Human beings aren't nearly as predictable as a mathematical model, and we all do things for our own complicated reasons. Behavioral economics studies the ways in which human beings' actions may diverge, often predictably, from what a perfectly rational actor might do.

Moreover, even if we wanted to do precisely what the life-cycle model says we should, sometimes it's hard to figure out. Economists testing theories using the life-cycle model sometimes use what are called "dynamic programming methods," in which a computer model works its way through a seemingly infinite array of choices regarding spending levels, portfolio allocations, investment returns, longevity, and so forth, running countless calculations over many hours or days to find an optimal strategy. That's more sophisticated than most financial planners' calculations—and far beyond what the typical person does. So we often rely on simplified strategies that capture the basics of the life-cycle model's implications without working out every detail.

But again, life is about trade-offs. There are significant costs in money, time, and headaches to constantly updating our assumptions and optimizing our choices. Many of us simply rely on rules of thumb that will at least get us in the ballpark of where we would like to end up. And sometimes close enough is fine. If we look at surveys of retirees regarding their happiness and financial security, those rules of thumb seem to work fairly well.

In the following chapters, I discuss a number of issues. Why do so many analysts claim that America faces a retirement crisis of inadequate incomes? How do these claims hold up? How does the US compare to other countries regarding retirement savings and retirement income security? How have retirement incomes changed over time? How much money will you need to live comfortably in retirement?

How do children affect your need to save for retirement and your ability to do so? How does work fit into your retirement plans? What are your chances of running out of money in old age? How are government-sponsored retirement programs, such as Social Security and public-sector pensions for government employees, faring? How might these programs be reformed?

But all this must start with an understanding of why we save for retirement in the first place. Retirement saving isn't a goal we maximize, so that more is always better, but rather a tool we employ to ensure a steady standard of living over time that will maximize the happiness we derive from whatever level of lifetime income we have been blessed with.

3

How Much Is Enough?

One might think that a book assessing the adequacy of Americans' retirement savings would start by tallying up the facts and figures regarding how much Americans have (or haven't) put aside for old age. But how much Americans have saved for retirement is actually not the most important or challenging question.

The more challenging and important question that retirement analysts think about and argue over is, "How much is enough?" In fact, our judgments regarding the effectiveness of the US retirement system, and whether Congress should undertake expensive and far-reaching steps to change Social Security and private savings plans, mostly come down to that question.

As discussed in Chapter 2, both mainstream economic theory and standard financial planning work from the premise that individuals generally wish to maintain their preretirement standard of living once they reach old age.[1] But people preparing for retirement rarely do so explicitly in the context of the life-cycle model, with its emphasis on, for example, smoothing the discounted marginal utility of consumption. That's far too complex for a typical person to handle.

In the real world, we rely on simplified methods and rules of thumb to approximate what the life-cycle approach would tell us. Replacement rates, which express retirement income as a percentage of preretirement earnings, are a common shorthand measure of how well a retiree can maintain their preretirement standard of living.

Moreover, replacement rates aren't simply used by individuals and financial planners; they also are a workhorse measure of retirement income adequacy used in many studies. For years, the Social Security Administration (SSA) has printed measures of Social Security benefit replacement rates in the annual trustees report. The Congressional Budget Office (CBO) similarly publishes Social Security replacement rates, albeit using a different measure than the Social Security trustees.

When prominent studies such as Boston College's National Retirement Risk Index (NRRI) conclude that Americans aren't saving enough for retirement, in practice, that means the NRRI is predicting that large numbers of future retirees will have replacement rates below the level the model's authors judge to be adequate. The NRRI, which is discussed in detail in a following chapter, projects households' future retirement resources, including Social Security, pension benefits, and savings. It then assesses whether these resources will be sufficient for retirees to maintain their preretirement standard of living.

As discussed in Chapter 2, the SSA states that "most financial advisors say that you will need 70 percent or more of pre-retirement earnings to live comfortably."[2] While stating that financial planners recommend a 70 percent replacement rate, the SSA goes on to say that "Social Security replaces about 40 percent of the average worker's pre-retirement earnings."[3] The claim that Social Security typically replaces only about 40 percent of an individual's preretirement earnings is a central feature of this chapter. That is because, despite replacement rates being ubiquitous in analyses of retirement income adequacy, there is no single agreed-on methodology by which to calculate replacement rates.

Traditionally, replacement rates were often measured relative to final earnings. As the Government Accountability Office stated, "Generally, [the replacement rate] is calculated as the ratio of retirement income in the first year of retirement to household income in the year immediately preceding retirement."[4] The so-called Greenspan Commission that helped craft the 1983 Social Security reforms that addressed a solvency crisis at the time defined replacement rates based on earnings immediately preceding retirement.[5] For example, a Social Security benefit paid at age 65 would be compared to total earnings as of age 64. For many years, replacement rates printed in the annual Social Security trustees report also were measured relative to final earnings.

While "final earnings" replacement rates are useful in certain cases, such as a long-term employee at a single firm, among the general population, earnings can vary significantly from year to year. Moreover, the life-cycle hypothesis in economics predicts that individuals will attempt to smooth consumption over many years, so economists tend to favor replacement rates that are measured relative to earnings over much longer periods. As the SSA's Dean Leimer pointed out, "Because lifetime earnings streams differ markedly between individuals, [final year] preretirement earnings are not representative of lifetime earnings positions. Thus, if a lifetime concept of the replacement base is desired, then earnings must be averaged over many years."[6]

Canadian researcher Bonnie-Jeanne MacDonald and her coauthors compared final earnings replacement rates to an alternative replacement rate designed to more closely capture a consumption-smoothing target. The researchers found a correlation of just 0.11, which indicates that final earnings replacement rates aren't necessarily a good shorthand measure for what individuals planning to follow the life-cycle model's predictions would wish to do.[7] Instead, in separate studies, Michael Boskin and John Shoven of Stanford University and Andrew Rettenmaier and Thomas Saving of Texas A&M University advocated measuring replacement rates relative to the inflation-adjusted average of lifetime earnings, which captures the potential expenditures of a typical worker over their entire working lifetime.[8]

But this is not how replacement rates are calculated in many of the most prominent statistics and studies of retirement income adequacy. For instance, recall the SSA's statement that, for a typical American, Social Security replaces about 42 percent of preretirement earnings. That figure is not calculated how financial planners and economists tend to calculate replacement rates. Nor are the replacement rates in the NRRI, which follows the SSA in using an alternative method.

In contrast to financial planners, who often use final earnings replacement rates, and economists, who favor replacement rates calculated relative to some long-term average of inflation-adjusted earnings, the SSA's actuaries calculate replacement rates differently. Social Security benefits for a new retiree in a given year are effectively compared to earnings for workers in the labor force in that same year, *not* to retirees' own preretirement earnings. How this happens is explained presently.

The approach of comparing retirees' incomes to non-retirees' incomes represents the relative financial statuses of different age groups in the population but does not convey information regarding how well seniors can maintain their own preretirement standard of living and should not be portrayed as doing so. Unfortunately, that is precisely what has happened.

So it is important to clarify how replacement rates are calculated and what these calculations signify.

Moreover, the SSA methodology for calculating replacement rates is sensitive to the rate of economy-wide wage growth, such that measurements of total retirement income replacement rates, inclusive of both Social Security benefits and other sources of income, will vary over time based on the rate of wage growth that is assumed for future years. Higher real wage growth would result in future retirees appearing to be less able to support themselves in old age. The SSA approach can provide a misleading viewpoint of changes over time in households' ability to maintain their standard of living in old age.

Measuring Social Security Replacement Rates

It makes sense to walk through how the SSA calculates replacement rates, which is a far more involved process than one might expect. To start, I build an illustrative worker's earnings using figures produced by the SSA. I then calculate that worker's Social Security benefits and replacement rate.

The SSA publishes factors that, for each age from 21 through 65, express the probability that a person of that age will be employed and their average earnings contingent on being employed. Multiplying the two factors produces expected earnings by age. For instance, at age 21, individuals are reported to have an 82.3 percent probability of working and, contingent on working, have earnings equal to 28.3 percent of the national average wage. Expected earnings at age 21 are reported as 23.3 percent of the average wage. The same process can be applied to produce earnings at every age, and then benefits are calculated based on these earnings.

To simulate Social Security replacement rates for an average-wage worker, I applied the SSA factors to generate an age-earnings profile for an individual born in 1956 who begins working at age 21 and retires in 2023 at the normal retirement age (66 years and eight months). That stylized average-wage worker would receive an annual benefit of about $25,013.

If we assume that working-age individuals tend to smooth their consumption from year to year and that retirees wish to maintain the standard of living they enjoyed during their working years, then a reasonable Social

Security replacement rate would compare the initial benefits an individual receives at retirement age with the inflation-indexed average of that same individual's career-long preretirement earnings. Adjusted for inflation, this stylized worker's earnings from age 21 through age 66 average $41,030 annually. Given the $28,013 benefit at retirement, this produces a replacement rate relative to career-average earnings of 61 percent.

Many workers are unable to smooth their standard of living early in their career due to the inability to borrow against their future earnings. This lowers their potential consumption earlier in their careers relative to what they could attain later. For this reason, it may be reasonable to compare Social Security benefits to the final 35 years of inflation-adjusted earnings before retirement.

Since earnings tend to rise over a worker's career, comparing benefits to the final 35 years of inflation-indexed earnings produces a Social Security replacement rate of 53.9 percent of preretirement earnings. If a typical worker hopes to achieve a 70 percent total retirement income replacement rate, Social Security benefits would cover approximately three-quarters of the total amount the retiree needed.

According to the 2023 Social Security trustees report, Social Security pays a medium-wage worker retiring in 2023 at their normal retirement age a benefit equal to just 42.6 percent of their preretirement earnings.[9] What accounts for the 11 percentage point difference between the trustees' figure and the 53.9 percent replacement rate for an average worker calculated above? The answer encompasses several steps.

First, the SSA methodology increases the value of an average worker's earnings each year by 21.6 percent. Due to Social Security's progressive benefit formula, benefits don't increase proportionately, and the replacement rate declines to 50 percent. Next, the SSA adjusts the stylized worker's past earnings for national average wage growth rather than for the typically lower rate of inflation. This step applies only to measuring replacement rates, not to calculating benefits. Since wage-indexed earnings are higher than inflation-indexed earnings, this reduces the replacement rate to 43 percent. Finally, SSA calculates replacement rates not based on the final 35 years of earnings but on the highest 35 years of earnings, a step that reduces their calculated replacement rate to just 42.6 percent.[10]

The important question is, "What does all this mean?" For a stylized medium earner retiring in a given year, the SSA replacement-rate methodology effectively equates that worker's career-average preretirement earnings—that is, earnings that took place over four decades or so—with the average wage of employees working *in that year*. For example, according to the SSA, a medium-wage worker retiring in 2023 is taken to have had preretirement earnings over their career averaging $66,207.[11] This figure supposedly representing average earnings in the past slightly *exceeds* the SSA's reported figure of a $66,147 average wage of a worker employed in 2023.

A replacement rate that compares the Social Security benefits of individuals retiring in a given year to the earnings of workers in the labor force in that same year is philosophically and quantitatively different from comparing a new retiree's Social Security benefit to their own past earnings.[12] A replacement rate is calculated in which nothing is being replaced, or, rather, the SSA calculation assumes that retirees wish to replace earnings they never actually had. In reality, the SSA calculation compares a retiree's Social Security benefit to the salary of a working-age person who may be decades younger and have much higher real earnings than the retiree ever had.[13]

There is a significant difference between the 53.9 percent replacement rate calculated relative to the final 35 years of inflation-adjusted earnings for a worker with average earnings to the 42.6 percent replacement rate based on the average of the highest 35 years of wage-indexed earnings for a stylized worker whose annual earnings are 21.6 percent above the average. Again, assuming that a retiree required an income equal to 70 percent of their preretirement earnings, Social Security benefits would be sufficient to provide an average worker with 77 percent of that total required income in the former case but only 61 percent in the latter.

There are two explanations for the different approaches to calculating replacement rates. The first is based on differing economic philosophies. The second is based on a practical intent to maintain a long-used factoid regarding the adequacy of Social Security retirement benefits.

Both the economic perspective based on the life-cycle hypothesis and practical financial planning advice accept the premise that most individuals seek to smooth their standard of living from year to year and, more specifically for this case, from work into retirement. Based on these premises, replacement rates calculated relative to the inflation-adjusted average of preretirement earnings provide information on Social Security benefits' ability to maintain the purchasing power that retirees enjoyed during their working years.

By contrast, advocates of calculating replacement rates relative to wage-indexed career-average earnings argue that retirees do not target the ability to maintain their preretirement standard of living but instead wish for a standard of living that keeps up with the standard of living enjoyed by working-age households. The SSA's actuaries state that wage-indexing career-average earnings

> effectively equates earnings levels over time relative to the standard of living of workers of the day. As the standard of living rises over time, using wage indexed career-average earnings brings the average up to date to the standard of living at the end of career.[14]

The NRRI also employs wage-indexed earnings in setting target replacement rates to measure the adequacy of total retirement incomes. Alicia Munnell, one of the NRRI's authors, states:

> When constructing the NRRI targets, my colleagues and I made a conscious decision to assume that households had a preference for a standard of living that increased during their working lives at the rate of economy-wide wage growth. This assumption reflected our belief that households care not only about their absolute standard of living, but also about their relative standard of living.[15]

The problem with this assumption is that it is at odds with economic theory, empirical evidence, and the practice of financial planning.

The Social Security trustees initially raised concerns regarding wage-indexed replacement rates in 2013, stating that the SSA actuaries' "method of calculation produces percentages that may differ significantly from those that would be produced by comparing benefits to these representative workers' recent average earnings levels or to other more common measures of pre-retirement income."[16] The trustees' concerns drew in part on my 2008 work with the SSA's Glenn Springstead. Using a microsimulation model of Americans newly retiring in 2005, we found that for the middle quintile of lifetime earners, Social Security benefits replaced 56 percent of the inflation-adjusted average of lifetime earnings, 64 percent of the average of earnings in the five years before benefit claiming, and 47 percent of wage-indexed career average earnings.[17]

These results presented a wide range of plausible figures. Based on such concerns, in 2014 the trustees eliminated replacement rates from their annual report.

The trustees' removal of replacement rates from their annual report prompted various government agencies to more deeply consider how replacement rates are calculated and used. None of these independent evaluations appeared to support the practice of estimating the adequacy of Social Security benefits by comparing those benefits to wage-indexed career-average earnings, as had been the practice in the years leading up to 2014.

In a 2016 review of replacement-rate methodology, the Government Accountability Office wrote:

> Economists broadly agree that a conceptual benchmark measure for adequate retirement saving is an amount that will . . . allow a household to maintain its pre-retirement standard of living into retirement. . . . The goal of the target replacement rate may be to replace earnings right before retirement or to smooth consumption over a retiree's life.[18]

It does not mention seeking to maintain the standard of living of workers in the labor force at the time the individual is retired.

In 2014, the CBO stated that "indexing earnings to prices . . . better captures the real amount of resources available to a worker over his or her lifetime, whereas indexing earnings to wages . . . may overstate those amounts."[19] In a more wide-ranging 2019 review of replacement rates, the CBO noted:

Other measures, known as *Social Security replacement rates*, are used to determine the extent to which benefits enable retirees to maintain their preretirement standard of living. . . . Price adjustment [of career-average earnings] is generally used to compare the purchasing power of retirees' benefits with the purchasing power of their own earnings when they were still working; wage adjustment is used to compare the purchasing power of retirees' benefits with the purchasing power of earnings of workers who are currently in the labor force.[20] (Emphasis in original.)

Similarly, in 2012 the SSA's Patrick Purcell noted that

Social Security bases retired-worker benefits on the worker's earnings through age 60 indexed to national average wages. . . . For purposes other than calculating Social Security benefits, however, past earnings [for the calculation of replacement rates] are more commonly indexed to prices.[21]

All this is consistent with the origins of the life-cycle hypothesis, in which Albert Ando and Franco Modigliani noted that their model "starts from the utility function of the individual consumer: his utility is assumed to be a function of *his own* aggregate consumption in current and future periods."[22] (Emphasis added.) Neither mainstream economics nor financial planning is typically concerned with keeping up with the Joneses, while the SSA's measures of replacement rates embed that assumption deeply in the methodology.

There appeared to be no such reflection by the 2023 trustees, who returned replacement rates to the annual report entirely unchanged from prior methodology with no reference to the 2013 removal and no explanation for reversing the 2013 trustees' decision.

A second, more practical objective may better explain why the Social Security actuaries and trustees adopted a replacement-rate methodology that differs from those financial planners, economists, or government agencies use. Before 2002, the SSA measured replacement rates as many financial planners do: "as a percentage of earnings in the 12-month period preceding retirement."[23] Replacement rates for a stylized medium-wage worker who earned the national average wage every year of their career hovered about 40 percent of preretirement earnings. These figures are the source of the common perception that Social Security typically replaces about 40 percent of preretirement earnings.

Over time, the SSA became concerned that the stylized steady-earnings patterns used to illustrate replacement rates did not closely resemble actual workers participating in Social Security. First, the national average wage as measured by the SSA is contingent on working, but most individuals do not work every year of their career. Second, actual average workers tend to have a hump-shaped age-earnings profile, such that they earn less than the national average early in life, slightly more than the average at the peak of their careers, and less than the average wage as they approach retirement.

In 2000, C. Eugene Steuerle and his coauthors from the Urban Institute cited SSA analysis finding that the SSA actuaries' stylized worker who was assumed to earn the national average wage over a full working career would have average annual preretirement earnings 51 percent higher than a typical worker in the middle quintile of the population.[24] To address these issues, the SSA's actuaries used administrative data on age-specific earnings and employment probabilities to generate hypothetical workers with more realistic lifetime earnings profiles.[25] However, using these more accurate age-earnings profiles would have produced final earnings Social Security replacement rates for a typical worker considerably higher than the well-known 40 percent figure.

In response, the SSA first altered its measure of preretirement earnings from final earnings to the highest 35 years of wage-indexed earnings, then it further increased annual earnings by almost 22 percent to calibrate the resulting replacement rates to match the roughly 40 percent figure produced using the previously stylized worker who earned the national average wage each year. In other words, in designing the new medium-scaled earner used to illustrate Social Security benefits and replacement rates, the result was predetermined.

Replacement-Rate Methodology and the "Retirement Crisis"

Issues with the SSA replacement-rate methodology extend further when it is applied to calculating replacement rates based on total retirement incomes. While the SSA actuaries and trustees do not calculate total retirement income replacement rates, other analysts in the SSA have often adhered to the actuaries' methodology for their own studies.

As discussed above, the SSA approach to calculating replacement rates will make retirement income adequacy appear lower by assuming that retirees wish to match the incomes of workers at the time of their retirement rather than maintain their own, generally lower, preretirement standard of living. But, in combination with the Social Security trustees' assumptions for real wage growth, the SSA replacement-rate methodology also will cause the future of retirement security to appear worse than the present, precipitating fears that Americans face a retirement crisis of inadequate incomes in old age.

Recall that, so long as national average wage growth exceeds inflation, wage-indexed career-average earnings will always be higher than inflation-indexed earnings, so wage-indexed replacement rates will always be lower than inflation-indexed replacement rates. But the gap between wage-indexed and inflation-indexed career earnings grows larger when the assumed rate of real wage growth increases. And that appears to be what is occurring with projections of future retirement incomes.

Perhaps the most credible study predicting a significant decline in retirement income adequacy came from the SSA in 2012.[26] Authored by Barbara Butrica and Karen Smith of the Urban Institute and Howard Iams of the SSA, the study used the most advanced and detailed model of the population and retirement income sources available, the SSA's Model of Income in the Near Term (MINT). That study projected that future seniors will have significantly lower replacement rates than past retirees did, with a larger share of future retirees with incomes below 75 percent of their preretirement earnings. Updated unpublished projections produced for the author using a more recent iteration of the MINT model continue to produce similar results.

The SSA study calculated that the median American senior who was born during the Great Depression era of 1926 to 1935 had a total retirement income equal to 95 percent of their wage-indexed career average earnings. Thirty-five percent of seniors born during the Depression era had a retirement income replacement rate under 75 percent, a measure designed to capture the share of seniors with inadequate retirement incomes.

Moving forward to Generation X, born from 1966 to 1975, the SSA MINT model projects that the median Gen X retiree will have a wage-indexed replacement rate of only 84 percent, with 43 percent having replacement rates below 75 percent. In simple terms, that is the so-called retirement crisis.

But the SSA projection that future retirees will have lower retirement income adequacy than past and present seniors entirely depends on using the SSA actuaries' methodology for calculating replacement rates. That same 2012 SSA study also published replacement rates measured relative to career-average *inflation-adjusted* earnings, which I argued are a more reasonable measure of retirement income adequacy. And those inflation-adjusted replacement-rate figures project that Americans' retirement income security will actually *improve* slightly.

Depression-era birth cohorts had a median inflation-indexed replacement rate of 109 percent of their preretirement earnings, with 26 percent of seniors having replacement rates below 75 percent. That's a more encouraging baseline picture. Even more importantly, by the time the Gen X birth cohorts retire, the median senior will have a replacement rate of 110 percent of their inflation-adjusted preretirement earnings, with only 25 percent having replacement rates below 75 percent.

In other words, using a more plausible measure of replacement rates that is more consistent with economic theory and financial planning methods, retirement income security is improving rather than declining.

The factor that accounts for the difference between projected wage- and inflation-indexed replacement rates is that the Social Security trustees report assumes higher rates of real wage growth for the future than occurred in the past. To explore this, I created two stylized lifetime earnings patterns using the SSA actuaries' scaled medium earner. The first is born in 1930 and is designed to represent the Depression-era birth cohorts, while the second is a Gen Xer born in 1970. Each begins working at age 21 and works through age 64. For each stylized worker, I calculate both the inflation-adjusted average and the wage-indexed average of the final 35 years of earnings and compare the two.

For the stylized worker born in 1930, their wage-indexed career-average earnings are 2 percent larger than their inflation-adjusted earnings. Thus, if the worker had a 70 percent total retirement income replacement rate when measured in inflation-indexed terms, their wage-indexed replacement rate would be about 69 percent, a difference of slightly over 1 percentage point.

For the stylized earner born in 1970, however, their wage-indexed career average earnings exceeded their inflation-adjusted earnings by 23 percent. If that earner had a total retirement income replacement rate of 70 percent when measured in inflation-adjusted terms, their wage-indexed replacement rate would be only 57 percent, a difference of 13 percentage points.[27]

Higher national average wage growth throughout the Gen X cohorts' working careers would tend to widen the gap between wage-indexed and inflation-indexed replacement rates. But much of the increase in wage growth over the Gen X cohorts' careers is the result of the trustees' projections, not of having experienced unusually high real wage growth to date.

From 1992 to 2020, the national average wage increased at a real annual rate of 0.9 percent; from 2020 to 2035, when the stylized Gen Xer born in 1970 would reach age 65, real wage growth is assumed to average 1.4 percent annually. So, at least in part, the retirement crisis projected by the SSA's MINT model is due not merely to the employment of an inappropriate replacement-rate methodology but also to projections of real wage growth that could turn out to be different.

The authors of the 2012 SSA study understood this, writing that the widening gap between wage- and inflation-indexed replacement rates was "a result of differential real wage growth between cohorts."[28] The authors did not take the point further, which is unfortunate because the broad question the paper explored—whether Americans face declining or roughly steady preparation for retirement—appears to hinge on it.

That the Social Security trustees assume higher real wage growth for the future than the economy has experienced in the past may surprise those who follow Social Security policy, as it has often been argued that the Social Security trustees' economic assumptions are pessimistic.

For instance, the Economic Policy Institute's Christian Weller and Edith Rasell stated, "The [trustees] report continues to be based on pessimistic assumptions about the future economy."[29] Likewise, economists Dean Baker, Brad DeLong, and Paul Krugman referred to "the pessimistic projection of the Social Security trustees that very long run labor productivity growth will average 1.6 percent a year."[30]

However, Social Security's finances care about the growth of wages, since wages are taxed to pay benefit and wage growth is factored into the tax and benefit formulas in numerous ways. And real wage growth, while obviously dependent on the growth of productivity, also depends on changes in other factors such as the labor share of gross domestic product and the wage share of total compensation.

Regardless, the Social Security trustees assume future wage growth that is healthy relative to what Americans have experienced over the past half century. And yet, ironically, that optimistic assumption for real wage growth creates the pessimistic conclusion that future American seniors face a retirement crisis of inadequate incomes and savings.

How Much Is Enough?

A great deal hinges on households' and policymakers' judgment of the adequacy of US retirement savings. If Americans fear a retirement crisis of inadequate incomes in old age, they may increase the amounts they save today, forgoing alternative uses of those funds. Likewise, if policymakers fear a significant shortfall in future retirement incomes, they may choose to expand Social Security, the revenues necessary for which would then be unavailable for other governmental purposes.

Discussion of retirement income adequacy often hinges on issues such as whether employees are offered a retirement plan at work, the rate at which employees participate and contribute, and labor supply at older ages and Social Security–claiming ages. All those issues are of course important.

And yet, at least based on the SSA's projections of future retirement incomes, our judgment of future seniors' retirement income adequacy depends not on answering the question "How much?" but rather, "How much is enough?" That is, whether we think Americans face a retirement crisis or an improvement in their retirement income adequacy depends less on what we think about how much we're saving for retirement and more on how much we think households *need* to save for retirement.

Specifically, the discussion here shows that the same projected levels of retirement income can lead to dramatically different assessments of retirement income adequacy depending on whether income adequacy is defined as maintaining one's own preretirement standard of living versus maintaining a standard of living that rises with the wages of workers then in the labor force. Only the former is a true measure of retirement income adequacy in the conventional sense that financial planners or economists think of things, while the latter is premised on a relative income approach in which individuals are assumed to wish to keep up with the Joneses.

Moreover, keeping up with the Joneses—in this case, with the wages of employees in the labor force at the time an individual is retired—grows more difficult when the rate of economy-wide wage growth is higher. The SSA's projections of a significant decline in median retirement income replacement rates and increase in the share of seniors with low replacement rates is entirely driven by the assumption that seniors desire an income that rises along with national average wages. If retirees are instead assumed to desire an income that allows for a similar standard of living that they enjoyed before retirement, a standard that is more consistent with financial planning and the life-cycle hypothesis in economics, retirement income adequacy is found to improve in future decades.

PART II

4

The Weak Evidence for America's
"Retirement Crisis"

To kill an error is as good a service as, and sometimes better
than, the establishing of a new truth or fact.

—Charles Darwin, letter to Alexander Stephen Wilson

One view regarding Americans' retirement saving that is both embraced
by majorities of ordinary citizens and seemingly backed by overwhelming research is that retirement savings are inadequate for US households to maintain their preretirement standard of living in old age. With
public opinion surveys showing that nearly nine in 10 Americans believe
our country faces a retirement crisis of inadequate savings for old age and
numerous studies reaching similar conclusions, anyone arguing against
claims of a retirement crisis faces a steep hill to climb.

In a February 2023 public opinion survey of 1,500 Americans age 60 to 75
fielded by the American Advisors Group, 89 percent of respondents agreed
the United States faces a retirement crisis.[1] A 2021 survey conducted by
the National Institute on Retirement Security (NIRS) found 67 percent of
US adults of all ages agreeing that the country faces a retirement crisis.[2] A
2015 survey by Vanguard Research found 59 percent of near retirees and
54 percent of retirees agreeing "there is a national retirement crisis."[3]

Ordinary citizens' pessimistic views regarding retirement savings are
seemingly backed by decades of research concluding that working-age
Americans lack the savings to maintain their standard of living as they
shift from work into retirement. And yet, contra Joseph Stalin's apoc-
ryphal quote, quantity does not have a quality all its own when it comes
to research.

In this chapter, I look at eight studies dating back to 2002, each of which
concludes that the retirement savings of US households are in some way

inadequate. These studies use various data, methods, and assumptions and set different bars for sufficiency of retirement income resources. What they share is arriving at pessimistic conclusions regarding US retirement savings. I conclude that none of these studies conclusively points to a significant problem facing future cohorts of retirees.

Following the assessment of existing studies, I present data that suggest two points. First, current US retirees do not face anything approaching a retirement crisis. Second, the current working-age households are in many ways better prepared for retirement than current seniors were at similar ages in the past.

Indeed, fears of significant retirement income shortfalls are overstated. While some share of future seniors are likely to have inadequate incomes to maintain their preretirement standard of living, it is far from clear that the share of underprepared retirees will be larger in the future than it is at present. Moreover, the share of future retirees with incomes below some absolute standard, such as the federal poverty threshold, is likely to decline significantly.

Studies of Retirement Savings Adequacy

In this section, I review the methodology of a number of studies that conclude that Americans have significantly under-saved for retirement. Some of these studies are recent, while others date back more than two decades. Similarly, some studies have received greater public, media, or academic attention than others. Nevertheless, all contribute to the perception among citizens and policymakers that future Americans face significant retirement income shortfalls. I begin with two studies by Edward Wolff and John Gist.

"Retirement Insecurity: The Income Shortfalls Awaiting the Soon-to-Retire," authored by Wolff and published by the Economic Policy Institute (EPI), was one of the earliest of the retirement crisis studies. Wolff's research, the EPI declared, delivered "troubling news for millions of Americans now nearing retirement age."[4] The study, which focused on individuals age 47 to 64 in 1998, projected that more than 40 percent of those households would retire on less than half their preretirement income and nearly 20 percent would have retirement incomes below the poverty line.

Because it is an early study, we can test Wolff's predictions today. The 47- to 64-year-olds analyzed by Wolff are currently in the heart of retirement. The official poverty rate for Americans age 67 to 84 in 2022 was not Wolff's predicted 20 percent but just 8.6 percent, down from 10.2 percent in 2002.[5] Unofficial measures of poverty, such as deriving incomes from IRS administration data and analyzing the expenditures of seniors, show even lower levels of poverty in old age.

In retrospect, it appears that Wolff's projection that 40 percent of retirees would be unable to replace half their preretirement earnings also was unduly pessimistic. An IRS analysis of tax return data from 1999 through 2010 found that fewer than 10 percent of Americans approaching retirement at the turn of the century retired on less than half their preretirement earnings.[6] These are a group similar in age to those examined in Wolff's study.

A potential reason that Wolff overstated financial insecurity among current retirees is that, while the study projected forward Social Security benefits and defined benefit pensions, it failed to model future accruals in defined contribution retirement accounts.[7]

This shortcoming appears to be shared with a 2013 study by Gist, which concludes that "the evidence strongly suggests that early boomers may be the last generation on track to exceed the wealth of the cohorts that came before them and to enjoy a secure retirement."[8] However, that study "project[s] the anticipated wealth that individuals and families may have upon retirement given *current* income levels and wealth accumulation," so it is not surprising that younger generations that more heavily rely on defined contribution retirement plans tend to fare more poorly than those closer to retirement.

The Retirement Security Projection Model. The Employee Benefit Research Institute (EBRI) maintains the Retirement Security Projection Model (RSPM), which projects a variety of retirement income sources, including Social Security benefits, 401(k) and individual retirement account (IRA) balances, defined benefit pensions, and housing equity. The most recent iteration of the EBRI's RSPM projects that 43 percent of working-age Americans are at risk of having inadequate incomes in retirement. The total projected retirement savings shortfall under the EBRI's model as of 2018 was $4.4 trillion.[9]

The RSPM establishes a target level of retirement spending for each household by first placing the household within a broad income class and then using Consumer Expenditure Survey data to calculate the mean level of household expenditures for households with incomes in that range. The broad income classes include retirees with incomes less than $20,000, those with incomes between $20,000 and $40,000, and those with incomes above $40,000.

However, setting retirement spending targets based on mean spending in a broad income class can cause some otherwise well-prepared households to appear underprepared for retirement. For instance, every household with incomes between $20,000 and $40,000 has a retirement spending target based on the mean of households in that income rate, which presumably would be close to that of a household with an income of $30,000. This implies that roughly half the households—those with incomes between $20,000 and $29,999—would be required to maintain the expenditures of a household with an income up to 50 percent higher than their own. The application of a single retirement expenditure target to households with different levels of preretirement incomes would tend to exaggerate the share of households at risk of running short of resources in old age.

We can test this supposition using early iterations of the RSPM model. In 2003, the RSPM projected that

> America's elderly face an income shortfall between 2020 and 2030 of at least $400 billion. . . . This shortfall is between the amount required for the elderly to afford basic expenditures for the remainder of their life and the income and benefits they are actually projected to have.[10]

The $400 billion projected shortfall is a present value calculated as of 2003; if we assume that the EBRI used a nominal discount rate of 6 percent, the 2023 value of the projected shortfall would approach $1.3 trillion. While we currently are only four years into the 2020s, there is little evidence that current retirees face anything like such shortfalls.

As is discussed in following sections, elderly incomes are at record-high levels across the income distribution, poverty in old age has declined significantly over the past several decades, and self-reported levels of financial security are high. Thus, the RSPM model may have a skew that causes it to understate the level of retirement preparedness of working-age households.

At the same time, unlike some other models that project a significant worsening of retirement income security for future cohorts of seniors, the RSPM projects that the share of adequately prepared households is similar across different age cohorts. As of 2019, the EBRI model projected that 57.8 percent of Americans then age 60 to 64 could maintain an adequate income throughout retirement. Among Americans age 30 to 35, the youngest cohorts modeled by the EBRI, 57.9 percent were projected to have adequate retirement incomes. The best-prepared age group comprised those age 45 to 49 in 2019, in which 60.6 percent were projected to have an adequate income throughout retirement.

Thus, while the EBRI RSPM predicts an income shortfall for current retirees that appears to significantly overstate that group's financial problems, the model also projects no significant worsening in the retirement income adequacy of future cohorts of Americans. If one does not see a retirement crisis among current seniors, the RSPM model should not lead one to believe that future seniors will face such a crisis.

NIRS (2012 and 2020). NIRS is the research arm of the defined benefit pensions industry, with a particular emphasis on government employee pensions. NIRS has published a series of studies concluding that Americans are vastly under-saving for retirement. The most prominent NIRS study, authored in 2013 by Nari Rhee, is titled "The Retirement Savings Crisis: Is It Worse Than We Think?"[11]

The short answer to NIRS's rhetorical question is "Yes, indeed." Rhee concludes that 84 percent of US households at the time were falling short of reasonable retirement savings targets. The total "retirement savings gap," the report concluded, may reach $14 trillion. The *New York Times* reported that "the report lends weight to the longstanding criticisms of the increased reliance on individual savings in the United States retirement system."[12]

But the NIRS report makes several methodological assumptions that may reasonably be questioned. First, it assumes that households should begin saving for retirement at age 25. By contrast, economist Jason Scott and his Stanford University coauthors, in a 2023 study published in the *Journal of Retirement*, find that the life-cycle model suggests that saving may optimally be put off until the late 30s or early 40s.[13] Using the NIRS benchmark, working-age households that follow the life-cycle model's saving recommendations would be considered under-saving in every year of their careers, even if on the day of their retirement they ultimately achieved NIRS's target level of assets.

Second, the NIRS study treats Social Security as if it pays a uniform replacement rate to all beneficiaries when, in fact, Social Security's progressive benefit formula provides higher replacement rates to lower earners.[14]

Third, Rhee assumes that the entire funding gap for defined benefit pensions, which the Federal Reserve's Financial Accounts of the United States reports exceeded $6.5 trillion in 2022,[15] will be resolved through benefit reductions. This a puzzling choice for an organization that advocates for traditional pensions as a safer way to prepare for retirement. More important, it is at odds with a history in which participants in underfunded defined benefit pensions, both in the public and private sector, tend to be paid the vast majority of their accrued benefits.[16] With these and other methodological choices left unresolved, it is difficult to draw hard conclusions from the study.

A more recent NIRS study from 2020, by Tyler Bond and Frank Porell, examines the income sources for seniors and their reliance on Social Security benefits in old age.[17] The study, as the *Washington Post* reported, concluded that Social Security "is the only income source for 40 percent of retirees over the age of 60,"[18] a contention repeated by CNBC, *Forbes*, and other media sources.

Bond and Porell rely on the Census Bureau's Survey of Income and Program Participation (SIPP), which asks respondents of their various sources of income. From the SIPP data, the authors conclude that "40.2 percent of older persons received income only from Social Security."[19]

One methodological choice that may drive the study's results is how the authors define seniors. Bond and Porell define their population as Americans age 60 and over who work fewer than 30 hours per week.

This definition reduces the sample of retirees with earned income while increasing the sample of disabled workers, who heavily depend on Social Security. This shifts the results considerably.

The Social Security Administration's (SSA) Irena Dushi, Howard Iams, and Brad Trenkamp used SIPP to analyze all Americans 65 and over, finding that only 19.6 percent received at least 90 percent of their total incomes from Social Security.[20] That's less than half the share of retirees that NIRS claims, and the SSA study measures dependence using a lower bar— 90 percent of total income rather than NIRS's 100 percent.

Other recent analyses of retiree incomes using IRS data, which are considered more accurate than household surveys, find even lower reliance on Social Security benefits. Dushi and Trenkamp find that only 13.8 percent of Americans 65 and over in 2016 received 90 percent or more of their income from Social Security.[21] Similarly, Adam Bee and Joshua Mitchell of the US Census Bureau find that 12.2 percent of the 65 and over population in 2012 received 90 percent or more of its income from the program.[22] Thus, news headlines to the contrary, it is far more reasonable to conclude that the share of seniors who wholly depend on Social Security for income in old age is in fact small.

Moreover, Porell and Bond's own calculations fail to support the study's conclusions. Of the group classified as "Social Security income only," making up 40.2 percent of their sample, the median Social Security benefit is $14,280 per year, while the authors calculate a median total income of $17,652 per year. This implies that the typical retiree in a group that ostensibly has no income other than Social Security in fact receives 19 percent of its income from sources outside the program. Such statistics, as tantalizing as they may be to the news media, simply do not hold up to scrutiny.

The Elder Index. The Elder Index is a project of the Center for Social and Demographic Research on Aging at the University of Massachusetts Boston.[23] The Elder Index first establishes a minimum level of income necessary to cover basic needs in different areas of the United States and then estimates the percentage of senior households with incomes insufficient to meet that threshold. The Elder Index in 2015 concluded that 41 percent of all seniors nationwide were economically insecure. According to the Elder Index, 53 percent of single retirees nationwide and 27 percent of retired couples cannot "cover basic needs . . . including shelter, medical care, food, and transportation."[24] The Elder Index's findings have received approving coverage in the *New York Times, Washington Post, USA Today,* and elsewhere.

But the Elder Index defines "basic needs" in such a way that substantial levels of economic insecurity are nearly impossible to avoid. The Elder Index assumes that economic security for a senior requires an income sufficient to maintain, among other things, the median cost of housing in their area of residence, the mean level of health care expenses, and the mean expenditures on transportation. By definition, at least half of current seniors will spend less than these amounts; in the case of health care spending, which is highly skewed, far more than half may spend less than the mean amount. I discuss health costs in retirement in greater detail in Chapter 10.

The Elder Index in fact defines something closer to being "middle class" in the population age 65 and older, and, again by definition, not every senior can attain that relative standard of living. But the Elder Index does not define a true minimum standard of living that one should expect every retiree household to be able to attain.

National Retirement Risk Index. The National Retirement Risk Index (NRRI) is a project of the Center for Retirement Research at Boston College. The NRRI began in 2006 and has been updated in subsequent years.[25]

The NRRI starts with data on household earnings and assets from the Federal Reserve's Survey of Consumer Finances. The NRRI then projects working-age households' current earnings and future retirement incomes to calculate their retirement income "replacement rates," representing retirement income as a percentage of preretirement earnings. Target replacement rates vary by income, with lower-income retirees requiring a higher replacement rate. If the household's projected replacement rate falls short of a target level by more than 10 percentage points, that household is considered "at risk" of an inadequate income in retirement. Using this approach, the NRRI found as of 2012 that 53 percent of working-age Americans are saving inadequately for retirement and that the total retirement savings shortfall reaches $6.6 trillion.[26]

It is impossible to assess the validity of the NRRI's projections for two reasons. First, the various publications based on the model provide insufficient documentation such that the model can be replicated. Second, NRRI publications provide insufficient output such that the model's projections of core outputs, such as average Social Security benefits or retiree household incomes, could be compared to projections from other models. In the nearly two decades since the NRRI was developed, no detailed methodological description of the model has been released.

However, we do know several things about the NRRI. First, the authors of the NRRI state that the model's replacement rates are calculated relative to career-average earnings that are first adjusted upward to account for the growth of national average wages. These wage-indexed preretirement earnings will exceed inflation-adjusted average earnings by upward of 20 percent, thereby reducing the replacement rates the model measures for retiree households and increasing the share of households that are deemed to have insufficient savings.

As discussed in the prior chapter, the NRRI's use of wage-indexed earnings in the replacement-rate calculation is based on an assumption that

> households had a preference for a standard of living that increased during their working lives at the rate of economy-wide wage growth. This assumption reflected our belief that households care not only about their absolute standard of living, but also about their relative standard of living.[27]

This view is reminiscent of economist James Duesenberry's 1949 relative income hypothesis, in which individuals' spending decisions take into account not only their own resources but a desire to keep up with the Joneses.[28] While not unreasonable as a conjecture, most research has concluded that the life-cycle model better reflects how individuals and households act in practice and relative income approaches play no role in contemporary retirement planning or research on retirement savings adequacy. In other words, the use of wage-indexed replacement rates relies on an empirical assumption that almost no one in the retirement research or policy world accepts.

The NRRI also omits several significant sources of income in old age. In a 2018 assessment of retirement savings adequacy in Australia, economist John Burnett and his coauthors note a

> severe shortcoming of existing assessments of retirement savings adequacy is the focus on retirement savings accounts, such as 401(k) accounts in the United States (U.S.), sometimes additionally taking into account government pensions. The retirement income of the majority of individuals and households is, however, drawn from a wider set of sources that includes property and financial assets other than retirement savings accounts. Thus, many existing assessments of savings adequacy likely paint an imperfect picture of adequacy.[29]

The NRRI is subject to these criticisms, as it does not consider the full range of income sources available to seniors.

First, the NRRI replacement rates do not include earnings in retirement, which in the 2019 Survey of Consumer Finances made up 23 percent of the incomes of the entire 65 and over population. The NRRI's justification is that earnings do not continue throughout retirement, which of course is true. But earnings earlier in retirement allow seniors to defer the drawdown of their retirement savings, and data indicate that retiree households draw down savings more slowly than would be anticipated if they spent down savings immediately upon retirement.

Earnings in retirement might explain that slow depletion of savings. If earnings make up about one-quarter of the incomes of the over-65 population and the average life expectancy past 65 is assumed to be 20 years, this implies that retirees could defer drawing down their assets for about five years in retirement, increasing the income available to them by one-quarter.

Other retirement income models, such as the SSA's Model of Income in the Near Term, include earnings in old age as part of replacement-rate calculations. One response might be that earnings after age 65 should not be counted because individuals who continue to work are not truly retired. If so, however, then the NRRI should not continue to assume that individuals retire and begin drawing down their savings at age 65.

Again, if earnings make up roughly one-quarter of income past age 65 and life expectancy as of age 65 is about 20 years, then on average the NRRI should assume a retirement age and onset of asset drawdown of 70. That would change the picture for retirement income adequacy considerably. For example, the NRRI's authors found in a 2012 analysis that delaying retirement from age 65 to 70 would reduce the share of Americans at risk of inadequate retirement incomes from roughly half to about 15 percent.[30] The authors state that "five years of additional work would solve the problem for the bulk of the population," but on average that is what the NRRI already should be assuming.

Second, the NRRI does not project the value of nonfinancial assets, such as a farm or small business, and does not include the income derived from those nonfinancial assets. In the 2019 Survey of Consumer Finances, farm, business, and other nonfinancial income make up 13.5 percent of the total incomes of households age 65 and over. Perhaps more important, for the roughly one-fifth of senior households that report receiving any farm, business, or other nonfinancial income, income from those sources makes up nearly one-third of their total incomes.

These amounts substantially exceed the total incomes that such households receive from combined Social Security benefits and private retirement plans. Many of these households are likely counted in the NRRI as having inadequate incomes due to the NRRI's exclusion of income from nonfinancial assets.

Third, the NRRI excludes transfer income, which can include government welfare programs such as unemployment insurance, food stamps, Temporary Aid for Needy Families, and Supplemental Security Income and payments such as alimony and child support. While only about 19 percent of the over-65 population received transfer income, according to the Survey of Consumer Finances, for those who did, such transfer payments made up nearly one-fifth of their total incomes. While many households that receive transfer payments in retirement also may have received such payments before retiring, many government welfare programs ease eligibility requirements for seniors. Once again, this exclusion of significant sources of income, even for a modest segment of the population, would tend to increase the share of Americans deemed to have inadequate incomes in old age.

Fourth, the NRRI assumes that Americans retiring after the Social Security trust funds are projected to be exhausted will be subject to significant benefit reductions. At the time the NRRI was first written, the combined Social Security trust funds were projected to remain solvent until 2040; the current projection from Social Security's trustees is solvency to sometime in 2033. The NRRI assumed that households reaching age 65 before insolvency would receive their full scheduled Social Security benefits throughout their retirement, while those retiring after insolvency would receive a 30 percent benefit reduction. This is not a literal interpretation of current law, in which all beneficiaries would be subject to reductions when the trust funds ran dry.

Moreover, in today's context, when prominent political leaders from both main parties oppose any Social Security benefit reductions, it appears unrealistic that households retiring after the currently projected insolvency date would be subject to large, across-the-board benefit cuts. Therefore, the retirement prospects of Americans turning age 65 after Social Security's projected insolvency (they would currently be in their 50s) are likely to be brighter than is portrayed in the NRRI.

In short, there is good reason to suppose that the NRRI sets the bar for retirement income adequacy too high and excludes from its calculations sources that currently provide over one-third of the incomes for households over age 65. Given the lack of documentation and validation of the model, there is no reason to take its projections as authoritative.

The World Economic Forum. A 2019 study from the World Economic Forum (WEF), titled "Investing in (and for) Our Future," predicted that across the world, retirees were likely to run out of money a decade or more before they died.[31] This study generated news headlines around the world, contributing to a growing perception of a worldwide retirement crisis. "The size of the gap is such that it requires action" from policymakers, employers, and individuals, report coauthor Han Yik noted in a *Bloomberg* article.[32]

The WEF study estimates how long the savings of a typical retiree would be sufficient to maintain an income equal to 70 percent of their preretirement earnings. With regard to the United States, the study calculates that the average 65-year-old American has sufficient savings to cover only 9.7 years of retirement income out of a nearly 20-year expected retirement.

However, the WEF study assumes the entire 70 percent replacement rate must be funded from the retiree's own savings, ignoring any other sources of retirement income. As the report states, "These outcomes exclude any other benefits, such as corporate defined benefit pensions or government benefits such as social security."[33] While data to precisely estimate the effects of this assumption are not available, we can approximate. The Congressional Budget Office estimates that Social Security provides members of households born in the 1950s and retiring around 2020 with benefits equal to an average of 50 percent of their inflation-adjusted pre-retirement earnings.[34]

If so, personal savings must replace only 20 percent of preretirement earnings to maintain a target 70 percent replacement rate. If the WEF finds the average American can afford 9.7 years of retirement at a 70 percent replacement rate out of their own savings, this implies that their savings could replace 20 percent of their preretirement earnings for 34 years, extending at least one decade past their life expectancy. Again, this is an example of a study that generated headlines, in this case worldwide, but whose conclusions founder when more reasonable assumptions are applied.

The Government Accountability Office. The Government Accountability Office (GAO) also generated newspaper headlines in 2019 with its finding that nearly half of older Americans—48 percent of those age 55 and over in 2016—"have no retirement savings."[35] Senator Bernie Sanders and others commonly cited this claim as evidence of Americans' poor retirement savings and the need to expand Social Security benefits. Yet both the GAO's factual claim, that many households nearing retirement have no savings, and the implications of that factual claim are questionable.

The GAO report, which relies on data from the Federal Reserve's Survey of Consumer Finances, counts as retirement savings only balances in retirement accounts such as 401(k)s and IRAs. This is contrary to the practices of national income accounting, in which accrued benefits in traditional defined benefit pensions are counted as household retirement assets. Moreover, excluding benefits owed by traditional pensions dramatically reduces the share of households deemed to be saving for retirement. For instance, nearly the entire governmental workforce in the United States is offered a defined benefit pension, yet public-sector employees who have no balances in a retirement account on top of that pension are deemed to lack retirement savings.

If you designate as retirement savings both retirement account savings and eligibility for a traditional pension benefit, the share of older Americans with retirement savings stood at 68 percent in 2019. And the share of older Americans with retirement savings in 2019 had increased from 64 percent in 1989. In other words, the prevalence of retirement savings is both higher than the GAO headline claimed and improving rather than declining.

Moreover, one should not necessarily jump to the conclusion that the remaining households without savings face insufficient resources in retirement. In 2019, the mean annual household earnings of households nearing retirement age (age 55 through 64) that lacked either a retirement account balance or a defined benefit pension was $24,293, equal to about 30 percent of the mean earnings of all households in this age group. This is an income group that is likely to receive high replacement rates under the progressive Social Security benefit formula and thus has little need (or ability) to save for retirement outside of Social Security.

In addition, even many households that reach retirement without a pension or retirement account are not necessarily unprepared to support themselves in old age. In 2019, the mean income of households age 65 to 74 that lacked any retirement plan was $38,614. In 2010, the mean earnings of households age 56 to 65—the same birth cohorts examined as retirees in 2019—was $39,639 in 2019 dollars. Thus, at the mean, even recent retirees who lacked any explicit retirement plan had incomes equal to 97 percent of their incomes just before retirement.

Disaggregation of the incomes of retiree household members who lack a formal retirement plan indicates that, while doubtless many have low income due to low earnings before retirement, others may be farmers or small-business owners who effectively saved for retirement through their business rather than via an explicit retirement plan. Even this group of retirees that lacks any formal retirement plan does not appear unduly reliant on Social Security, which provides 40 percent of their total

Table 1. Incomes of Recent Retiree Households That Lacked a Retirement Plan, 2019

	Dollars (2019)	Percentage of Total
Business and Farm Income	7,772	20%
Interest and Dividend Income	393	1%
Social Security and Pensions	15,568	40%
Earnings	10,161	26%
Transfer Income*	2,408	6%
Capital Gains	2,548	7%
Total Income	38,850	100%

Source: Author's calculations from the Survey of Consumer Finances.
Note: The sample includes respondents age 65 to 74 in 2019 who reported lacking both a retirement account and any eligibility to a traditional pension benefit. * This includes unemployment benefits, alimony, child support, Temporary Assistance for Needy Families, food stamps, Social Security Income, and other payments.

average incomes, or transfer payments, which provide only 7 percent. (See Table 1.)

In 2023, the GAO made an additional successful bid for news headlines. "Only one in 10 low-income workers between the ages of 51 and 64 had any retirement savings in 2019," the *New York Post* reported, citing "a troubling report recently published by the US Government Accountability Office."[36] CBS News had similar concerns: "Millions of older workers are nearing retirement with nothing saved."[37]

But the latest GAO report introduced an additional sleight of hand: In addition to measuring only retirement account balances, not eligibility for traditional pension benefits, the GAO included in its analysis of workers' retirement savings many Americans who aren't actually workers. In fact, in the lowest-income quintile of age 51 to 64 households in 2019, the group in which the GAO claimed nearly no one had retirement savings, two-thirds of households did not have any member earning even a single dollar of wages. This is important because, as economist Teresa Ghilarducci noted, retirement savings "come from earnings. They don't come from inheritances, they don't come from gifts—they come mainly from earnings."[38] It shouldn't be surprising, therefore, that in an income group in which just one-third of households have anyone working, not many would have retirement accounts.

In sum, it's easy to conclude that many workers aren't saving for retirement if we include people who aren't working and exclude traditional pensions, which remain a significant source of retirement income for many. But here is a more realistic figure, using the same Survey of Consumer Finances data for 2019: If we look at all households age 51 to 64 that are earning more than $20,000 (roughly the poverty level for a household of two people), 80 percent have retirement account savings or have accrued traditional pension benefits. Even among households with total earnings between just $20,000 and $40,000, 49 percent had a formal retirement plan.

The Pew Charitable Trusts. "Limited savings could lead to a cumulative additional cost to the federal government of $964 billion between 2021 and 2040," with another $334 billion foisted onto state governments.[39] That is the conclusion of a 2023 study from the Pew Charitable Trusts. Pew presents a seemingly compelling argument: Americans aren't saving enough for retirement, which will force more seniors onto welfare programs for the elderly. So government should push lower-income Americans to save more for retirement. That worrying message received unquestioning coverage from mainstream media outlets such as CNBC, *Forbes*, and *Bloomberg*; trade journals like *Pensions & Investments*; and even the National Conference of State Legislators, which pushed the report out to its members.[40]

I admire much of Pew's work, but this report makes a fundamental error in what it means to save enough for retirement. Both economics and financial planning assume that people wish to maintain the same standard of living in old age as they had during their working years. Since the cost of living declines in retirement, the SSA says that retirees can maintain their preretirement lifestyle with an income equal to about 70 percent of their preretirement earnings.

This perspective matters for Pew's analysis in several ways. First, a person who is poor during their working years will likely end up poor in retirement, even if they save optimally. They're making the most of their limited resources. And most poor retirees who qualify for the means-tested benefits Pew discusses had low earnings over their lifetime; we know this based on their low Social Security benefits, which are calculated from their lifetime earnings.

Seniors accessing means-tested welfare benefits in retirement isn't a problem of insufficient savings; it's a problem of being poor—throughout life, not just in old age. Indeed, poverty tends to *decline* as households shift from their working years into retirement, which is the opposite of what you would expect to see if low-income Americans were saving too little.[41]

On top of that, Pew sets an extraordinarily high standard for an "adequate income" in retirement. Having "less than $75,000 in annual income," Pew states, "indicates financial vulnerability."[42] To whom?

In 2018, the median 65 and over household had an income of $55,610, according to the US Census Bureau[43]—making them the richest retirees in US history and the richest retirees in the world, based on Organisation for Economic Co-operation and Development data. A retiree household with Pew's threshold $75,000 annual income could adequately replace preretirement earnings of around $108,000, based on the 70 percent replacement rate rule of thumb. In the Federal Reserve's Survey of Consumer Finances, median annual earnings for working-age households in 2019 were just $57,000. In other words, the Pew study recommends a retirement income roughly twice what a typical household would need.

Moreover, no retiree with a $75,000 annual income receives welfare benefits. Medicaid, food stamps, and other programs are aimed at seniors with much lower incomes, generally around the poverty threshold of around $18,000 for two seniors. So when Pew states, "The average income shortfall in retirement among vulnerable older households in 2020 was $6,740, which will increase state spending for Medicaid and other assistance programs,"[44] I don't think that's correct.

Falling short of a $75,000 retirement income doesn't get you anything. It's falling short of poverty that does. And poverty in old age isn't rising.

To address this alleged retirement savings shortfall, Pew recommends that every worker who isn't currently offered an employer-sponsored retirement plan be automatically signed up for an IRA. I'm fine with that. The retirement plan coverage gap is a lot smaller than people think, but there's no reason every employee shouldn't have access to one.

But let's be clear what Pew also is arguing: that low-income Americans should save more to disqualify themselves from welfare benefits in old age. Truly low-income households might lose every dollar of additional savings to lower government benefits in retirement. I don't think a financial planner in good faith could recommend that a low-earning household do what Pew is advocating.

Moreover, if we wished to trim $90 billion out of annual federal spending dedicated to retirees, as Pew appears to think is important, why not reduce Social Security benefits for the richest retirees? By 2040, the maximum annual retirement benefit will top $55,000 in today's dollars, up from an already-high $49,930 in 2024. Middle- and high-income retirees are where the real money is and where poverty isn't. Why not start there?

But there is some good news: Pew's baseline projections of rising dependence on welfare benefits in old age are likely incorrect. In other words, its entire concern may be mistaken. The best projections—from the SSA, using a sophisticated microsimulation model developed over nearly three decades—are that old-age poverty will decline in coming decades.

The SSA projects that in 2030, 3.24 million seniors will have sub-poverty-level incomes. By 2050, that number will rise marginally, to 3.31 million, but this is entirely due to rising numbers of retirees. The actual poverty rate among seniors is projected to fall from about 5 percent to around 4 percent. After 2050, both the poverty rate and the raw number of retirees are projected to decline.

Other projections tell a similar story. For example, the Congressional Budget Office projects that from 2021 to 2032, the number of seniors receiving Medicaid benefits will barely change.[45] Overall participation in Supplemental Nutrition Assistance Program benefits will fall, although the Congressional Budget Office does not break down projected participation by age.[46] While detailed projections for other transfer programs are not available, there is no reason to believe the broader trend will be much different. Rising incomes and falling poverty will *reduce* dependence on welfare programs in old age.

The Vanguard Retirement Outlook. One of the most recent additions to the retirement readiness studies comes from a research team at the investment giant Vanguard. Released in late 2023 with exclusive coverage from the *Wall Street Journal*,[47] "The Vanguard Retirement Outlook: A National Perspective on Retirement Readiness" reaches sobering conclusions: The typical retiree will have an income roughly one-quarter less than they will need to maintain their preretirement standard of living.[48]

Among lower-income Americans, the picture is even worse: Vanguard projects that low-income seniors will have retirement incomes nearly one-third below what they'll need. As with most media coverage of retirement readiness, that summary is about all the typical person will read.

But they should dig deeper, because a study's conclusions depend on its assumptions. Vanguard's is a technical study, so, unfortunately, most of the explanations are technical. But they're worth reading if you care about retirement savings adequacy in the US.

To start, there's the question of how much people wish to spend after retirement. Vanguard assumes that retirees wish to spend the same amount every year, from the age they retire until they die. That sounds reasonable. Except the Vanguard authors themselves acknowledge, "In reality, as [RAND Corporation economists] Michael Hurd and Susann Rohwedder note, consumption falls as people age."[49]

In fact, Michael Hurd and Susann Rohwedder show that annual spending declines by roughly 50 percent from age 65 to age 90, even when health care spending is included.[50] Vanguard's steady-spending assumption matters to its results: On average, a household would need to save nearly 50 percent more to finance steady expenditures in retirement than to afford a more realistic path of spending.

Second, Vanguard assumes that all retirement spending must be financed from Social Security benefits, retirement plans, and other financial assets. In fact, Federal Reserve data show that over-65 households receive only about 60 percent of their incomes from those sources. About 23 percent comes from earnings in retirement, and another 14 percent comes from farm or business income. Another 3 percent of their incomes comes from transfer benefits, such as welfare or alimony payments. All in, over one-third of the average retirees' income is missing in Vanguard's study. Add that income back, and the picture presumably changes quite a bit.

Third, Vanguard judges a household to have saved adequately if its income is enough to maintain its target income over 90 percent of investment return and longevity outcomes. That's a pretty conservative assumption. For instance, while Vanguard assumes a mean investment return of about 5.8 percent over the long term, the 10th percentile long-term return would be only around 3.5 percent.

Similarly, while a typical 65-year-old might live to around age 85, the 90th percentile of longevity means surviving to age 95, about one-half longer. Combine low investment returns with a long life, and, yes, financing retirement will be difficult. But again, 90 percent of the outcomes will be better than what Vanguard projects.

There may well be more on the technical side, but it's worth doing a simple gut check. Vanguard projects that lower-income households, those at the 25th percentile of income distribution, will fall far short of being able to maintain their preretirement standard of living. But if we look at low-income retirees *today*, we don't see anything like what Vanguard is predicting.

In a 2023 study, economists Peter Brady and Steven Bass of the Investment Company Institute used IRS data to track households' incomes as they shifted from work into retirement, following them from age 55 through 72.[51] Brady and Bass show that for households at the 25th percentile of the income distribution at age 55, average annual incomes do not drop *at all* between age 55 and 72. For the Vanguard projections to be plausible, retirement incomes need to fall off a cliff in the near future. Vanguard itself argues that retirement savings adequacy is actually improving, meaning future retirees should be somewhat better off than today's.

There are simply too many methodological problems with Vanguard's retirement readiness outlook to let its conclusions keep you awake at night.

It's Not All Bad News

A theme of this chapter analyzing model-based projections of retirement income security is twofold. First, these models tend to set the bar excessively high for what retirees themselves would consider adequate. Second, in certain cases, modeling assumptions would cause future retirees to appear less prepared than current retirees even if the two were equally able to maintain their preretirement standard of living.

Not every model-based projection of retirement income security reaches such pessimistic conclusions. A prominent 2006 study by University of Wisconsin economist John Karl Scholz and his coauthors concluded that "fewer than 20 percent of households have less wealth than their optimal targets, and the wealth deficit of those who are undersaving is generally small."[52] That study, unlike most of those cited earlier, was subjected to peer review, published in a well-regarded academic journal, and won the 2007 Teachers Insurance and Annuity Association of America–College Retirement Equities Fund Paul A. Samuelson Award for Outstanding Scholarly Writing on Lifelong Financial Security.

More recent work by Hurd and Rohwedder reached similar conclusions using different methodologies.[53] They track the spending patterns of seniors throughout retirement then project whether households approaching retirement will have sufficient resources to maintain a similar spending path. They find that 71 percent of Americans nearing retirement have sufficient resources, though with significant differences across groups. For instance, 89 percent of college-educated married households were found to have sufficient savings, versus only 29 percent of single women with less than a high school education.

Updated projections from Hurd and Rohwedder published in 2023 confirmed these results and presented additional details.[54] Overall, 68 percent of individuals age 66 to 69 in 2016 had sufficient resources to assure an at least 95 percent chance of maintaining their standard of living throughout retirement. However, there remained differences among groups.

Single individuals were far less likely to be prepared (51 percent) than married individuals (81 percent). Individuals with less than a high school education (48 percent) were less prepared than those with a bachelor's or graduate degree (81 percent). And whites (76 percent) were better off than blacks (44 percent) or Hispanics (50 percent).

Part of the racial gap in retirement preparation is likely driven by differences in marriage rates: While 63 percent of white 66- to 69-year-olds in 2016 were married, only 37 percent of black and 44 percent of Hispanics were married. Interestingly, data experiments in which retirees were assumed to reduce spending by 10 percent brought only modest increases in the share of 66- to 69-year-olds with adequate resources. What this would appear to indicate is that, while most households appear to have adequate retirement savings, the shortfalls in savings where they exist may be deep.

In addition, as discussed elsewhere, the Urban Institute's Barbara Butrica and Karen Smith and the SSA's Iams project that future seniors will have retirement income replacement rates, measured as sustainable income in old age as a percentage of the inflation-adjusted average of preretirement earnings, that are similar to those received by past and present retirees.[55]

In sum, the research evidence for a true "retirement crisis" in which most Americans will fall short by a substantial margin of an adequate retirement income is weak. The number of studies cannot make up for a lack of quality, and each of the numerous studies cited earlier contains significant shortcomings that undercut their gloomy conclusions. Other, relatively optimistic studies receive little attention in discussions of retirement savings adequacy. So it is not surprising that policymakers and the news media conclude that the US retirement system is not working.

In the chapters that follow, I turn to the data on retirement savings and incomes in the United States. These data tell a compelling and far more encouraging story.

5

Mind the Gap: Retirement Plan Coverage and Participation

Are enough Americans saving for retirement? To answer that, we first need to know how many Americans are saving for retirement in the first place. Believe it or not, in many cases, we do not know. Various data show anything from a yawning retirement plan coverage gap to the vast majority of employees having access to a retirement plan through their employer.

In this chapter, I review claims, data, and evidence on retirement plan participation in the United States over the past half century, focusing especially on the shift in the private sector from traditional defined benefit plans to defined contribution retirement accounts, the most popular of which is the 401(k) plan.

Let's Start with the Conventional Wisdom

A reader of a typical newspaper account would likely conclude that many US workers aren't even offered the opportunity to save for retirement and many of those who are don't take it up. According to the AARP, "Just over half of all workers in the United States do not have access to a retirement plan at work."[1] Among low-income and minority workers, retirement plan coverage is even lower.

Teresa Ghilarducci, a professor of economics at the New School for Social Research and one of the nation's most widely quoted experts on retirement savings, goes further: "Retirement plan coverage has been falling for 20 years, even before the Covid-19 recession." Barely one-third of US workers participate in a retirement plan at work, according to Ghilarducci. "Even when the economy was doing well at the end of 2019, only 36% of workers age 25–64 had a retirement plan at work (a fall in coverage rates from 41% in 2015)."[2]

"All data sources," Ghilarducci and her coauthors write, "show that the shift from traditional defined-benefit pensions to the cheaper and employer-friendly 401(k) plans over years has not resulted in an increase in retirement plan coverage for workers, leaving large portions of workers without access to retirement plans."[3] "Employers can't provide retirement plans. Let's stop pretending they can," Ghilarducci argues.[4] She proposes, in conjunction with expanded Social Security benefits, replacing employer-based 401(k)s with a government-sponsored savings program to which all employees would be mandated to contribute, with the government providing a guaranteed rate of return on plan balances.[5] Whatever the merits of Ghilarducci's proposal, and it has some, its rationale bears closer examination.

But these concerns are not restricted to more progressive-leaning retirement analysts. The politically moderate Pew Charitable Trusts argues that the retirement coverage gap will lead to "insufficient retirement savings," which "will significantly affect every state and the federal government over the next 20 years, resulting in increased public assistance costs, reduced tax revenue, decreased household spending and standards of living, and lower employment."[6]

An economic analysis commissioned by Pew projected that the retirement plan coverage gap could lead to $1.3 trillion in additional welfare costs for the federal government and the states as underprepared seniors fall back on income-based welfare programs.[7] Closing the retirement plan coverage gap by establishing state-run automatic individual retirement account (IRA) plans would generate significant savings for taxpayers. Once again, the policy solution may not necessarily end up a bad one. But we also want to know the true depth and breadth of the problem the policy is designed to address.

To answer that question, I apply three questions to the worrying figures mentioned. First, are they correct? Do they accurately represent the share of Americans who have access to a retirement plan and are actively preparing for retirement, over and above what they can expect to receive from Social Security?

Second, how have retirement plan participation rates changed over time? How did the decades-long shift from traditional defined benefit pensions, under which the employer guaranteed a fixed benefit in retirement, to defined contribution retirement accounts, in which employees bear the investment risk, change access to workplace retirement plans?

Third, what percentage of households *should* be saving for retirement at any given time? Should retirement policy aim for a 100 percent retirement plan participation rate, or is it better for individuals not to be saving in some cases?

Where the Numbers Come From

The seemingly dire retirement plan participation rates I have cited are largely drawn from the US government's Current Population Survey (CPS). The CPS is the federal government's most prominent household survey, and its data are used to calculate a number of figures that Americans regularly encounter in the newspaper, such as the unemployment rate, the poverty rate, and income inequality.

A household survey is more or less as it sounds. A Census Bureau employee contacts an adult household member. Among many other questions, Americans are asked whether they are offered a retirement plan at work and whether they participate in such a plan. The household member, called the respondent, answers.

Indeed, those figures look grim. Figure 1, drawn from the CPS, shows the percentage of both private-sector workers who state they are offered a plan at work and participate in that plan and additional workers who say their employer offers a plan but they either were not covered by the plan or otherwise did not participate. In 1980, 52 percent of US workers said they participated in a workplace retirement plan, and an additional 6 percent of workers stated their employer offered a plan but they did not participate.

Overall, 58 percent of workers said their employer offered a plan. By 2022, retirement plan coverage as recorded in the CPS had dropped to 41 percent, with only 34 percent of employees stating they participated. In other words, just one-third of private-sector workers are saving for retirement. The numbers don't lie. Or do they?

There are good reasons to conclude that retirement plan participation rates are dramatically higher than the figures cited by proponents of the retirement crisis narrative. The problem with the CPS's survey data on

Figure 1. Coverage and Participation in Workplace Retirement Plans, Employees Age 21–64

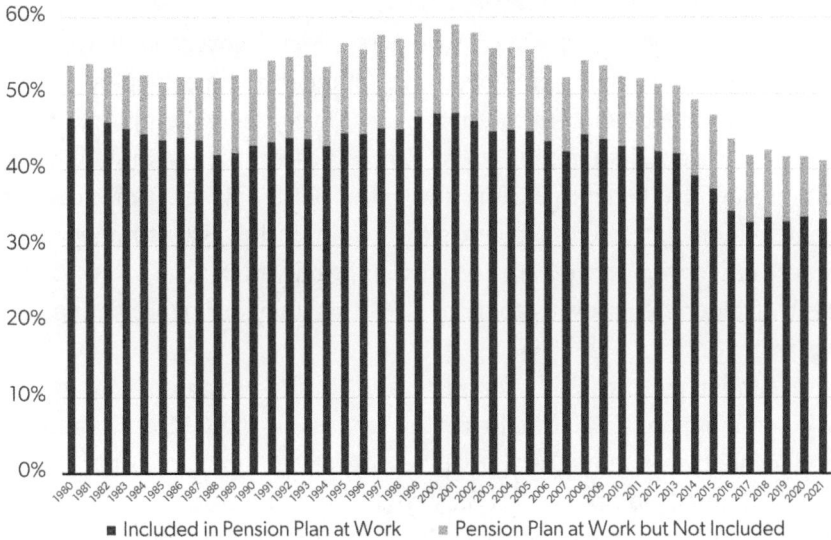

■ Included in Pension Plan at Work   ▪ Pension Plan at Work but Not Included

Source: Author's calculations from Current Population Survey data.

retirement plan coverage is simply that many people appear to answer the questions incorrectly. While seemingly difficult to believe, researchers have long understood that Americans make errors when reporting their retirement plan access, participation, or pension type in surveys.[8]

On reflection, it's easy to imagine people making a mistake. Perhaps they don't understand what their employer offers, they misunderstood the question, or they just answered too quickly. Remember that the pension question is only one of more than 200 questions in the CPS. Many survey respondents probably just want to finish it.

Still, this could easily come down to a dueling-experts debate, with one side saying one thing and another saying the opposite. I admit that, as someone on the optimistic side of the retirement crisis debate, it's a bit convenient for me to respond to negative data on retirement plan coverage by saying, "The data are wrong."

So it is worth highlighting some examples that an ordinary reader can understand. These examples show the CPS producing estimates of retirement plan coverage that can be proven incorrect. We do this by look-ing at CPS responses by employees with whom we can independently ver-ify if they are covered by a retirement plan.

The easiest group to check would be federal government workers. All federal government employees, including part-time employees, are enrolled in one or more retirement plans. Every federal employee hired since 1987 is enrolled in the Federal Employees Retirement System, a tra-ditional defined benefit pension, and in the Thrift Savings Plan, a defined contribution retirement account similar to a 401(k). So retirement plan access and coverage are both 100 percent. And yet, in 2022, only 60 per-cent of federal employees told the CPS that they are participating in a retirement plan!

A similar pattern holds for state and local government employees. We can compare these employees' responses to the CPS to what state and local governments themselves report to the Bureau of Labor Statis-tics's National Compensation Survey (NCS). For full-time state or local government employees in 2021, the NCS finds 99 percent retirement plan coverage and 88 percent participation.[9] Yet in the 2021 CPS, only 71 percent of full-time state and local government employees tell the CPS they're offered a retirement plan at work. And just 65 percent said they actually participate.

A third example shows how unreliable data actually can feed into pub-lic policy decisions. Oregon has established the nation's first state auto IRA program, called OregonSaves. Auto IRAs are designed to address the retirement plan coverage gap by automatically enrolling employees who lack a workplace retirement plan in an IRA set up for them by the state.

When OregonSaves was being debated, consultants for the state used CPS data to estimate that in 2014, slightly over one million Oregon private-sector employees lacked access to a retirement plan at work.[10] CPS data for 2022 show a similar figure. On this basis, OregonSaves was passed into law and established a rolling deadline for employers of differ-ent sizes to register their employees with the program. By May 15, 2019, all employers with 10 or more employees were required to register their workers with the program if the employer did not offer a workplace retirement plan.[11] By November 15, 2019, all employers with five or more employees were required to register with OregonSaves.

As of 2022, CPS data reported over 713,000 Oregon employees working for firms with 10 or more employees who lacked access to a workplace retirement plan. The CPS does not identify firm sizes of between five and nine employees, so these workers—who should have been enrolled in OregonSaves by the end of 2019—are not included in these figures. But as of September 2024, OregonSaves had only 130,000 active accounts, a small fraction of what might have been expected based on CPS data.[12]

This is not to say that state auto IRA programs are a poor idea. University of Oregon economist John Chalmers finds that OregonSaves serves a low-income population with high rates of job turnover that would be difficult for employer-based plans to serve on a cost-effective basis.[13] (In Chapter 17, I argue for a federal version of such a plan.) The dramatic difference in figures between the number of employees the CPS data stated had no retirement plan access at work and a state-run plan that mandated automatic enrollment for such workers is strong evidence that the CPS data should not be relied on to gauge the adequacy of retirement plan coverage in the private sector.

What Do Other Data Tell Us?

We can easily see both the broad differences and the trends by comparing two data sources for the same set of individuals: employees working at private-sector businesses with 500 or more employees. Even in 2010, significant differences in participation rates were reported in the CPS versus the NCS.

In the CPS for 2010, only 51 percent of employees at large firms reported that they participated in a retirement plan. In the NCS, large businesses reported that 75 percent of their employees were participating in a retirement plan—a gap of 24 percentage points. But, beginning with the CPS survey redesign in 2014, reported participation rates fell precipitously, declining to 43 percent for large businesses by 2022 (Figure 2). This implies that, in over little more than a decade, about 3.5 million workers at the largest Americans employers lost their pensions. Whatever the CPS data might claim, Americans would have likely heard about this newsworthy event.

Figure 2. Retirement Plan Participation Rates, Businesses with 500 or More Employees

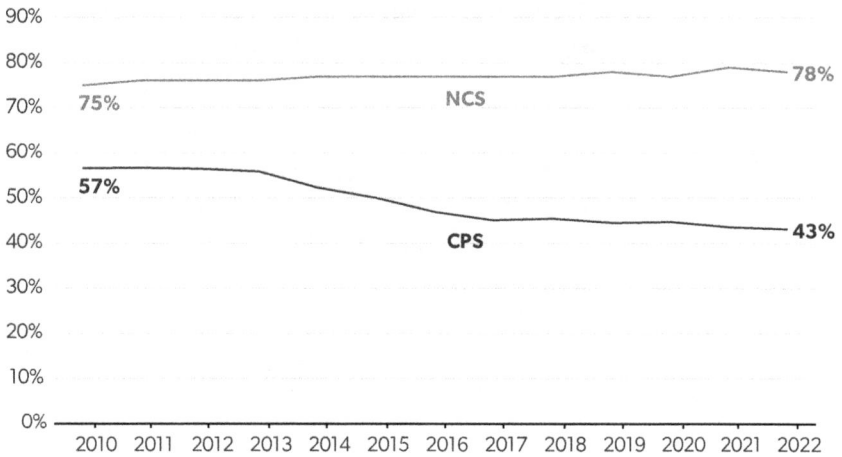

Source: Author's calculations from Current Population Survey data.

But perhaps those lost pensions never made the news because they never occurred. In the NCS, retirement plan participation rates at businesses with 500 or more employers increased, from 75 percent in 2010 to 78 percent in 2022.

Another dataset, from the Department of Labor, contradicts the CPS directly. The Department of Labor regulates private-sector pensions. Each year, employers with retirement plans must submit to the Labor Department what is called Form 5500. One might assume that an employer reporting details of their retirement plan to their regulator on a legally binding government document would show greater accuracy than would an ordinary citizen answering off the top of their head one question out of over 200 asked in the CPS.

Form 5500 contains a variety of data, including the number of "active participants" covered by the plan. The Department of Labor's definition of active participants is actually misleading: It refers to the number of employees who could participate in the plan, not the number who actually are participating. So, active participants more accurately tracks the number of employees with access to a retirement plan. But even here, the Labor

Department's data show a much more encouraging picture than does the CPS data that news stories rely on.

In 2022, according to CPS data, 35.9 million employees of private-sector firms had access to a retirement plan. Out of the 120.9 million private-sector workers reported in the CPS, 29 percent are reported to have a pension plan at work. The remaining workers either work for an employer that does not offer any retirement plan or the employer offers a plan but the employee is not eligible. (For instance, newly hired workers sometimes have to wait before they can participate.)

By contrast, the Department of Labor reports that 103.9 million private-sector employees had access to a workplace retirement plan in 2022.[14] Out of a total private-sector workforce as reported by the Federal Reserve Board of 130.3 million, this results in a private-sector coverage rate of 79.7 percent.

Now, the Department of Labor's figure may slightly overstate the true number of employees who are covered by retirement plans since its data double count the small number of employees who have access to more than one employer-sponsored retirement plan. But it is almost impossible to conceive that the CPS data showing low and declining retirement plan coverage in the United States are accurate given what a variety of other data sources indicate. And yet, those CPS data generate concerns over a "retirement crisis."

Are People Really Answering a Simple Question Incorrectly?

It may be hard to accept that so many Americans, asked a simple question of whether they're offered a retirement plan at work, consistently answer incorrectly. But my contention that the CPS data are wrong is backed by an interesting study conducted by the Social Security Administration (SSA).

Two SSA researchers, Irena Dushi and Howard Iams, matched individuals' responses to a household survey question regarding retirement plan participation to those same individuals' IRS tax records, which confirm whether the employee is enrolled in a retirement plan.[15] That household survey was the Survey of Income and Program Participation (SIPP), which is generally regarded as being more reliable than the CPS.

The SSA researcher found reporting errors in both directions. Some workers reported having a retirement plan when they did not. However, an even larger number reported not being offered a plan when tax records actually showed they were. Fifty percent of full-time workers in 2006 reported having access to a retirement plan at work. But examination of those employees' IRS W-2 forms revealed that in fact 66 percent had access to a 401(k) or other retirement plan. Likewise, while only 34 percent reported participating in a retirement plan, tax records showed that 46 percent were actually taking part.

The SSA researchers found that "the participation rate in DC (defined contribution) plans is about 11 percentage-points higher when using W-2 tax records rather than survey reports."[16] While other factors may account for differences in retirement plan coverage reported in household surveys versus employer or government datasets, reporting errors by survey respondents doubtless play a significant role.

But the problem is more than just response error. The CPS has always produced lower rates of retirement plan access than employer surveys such as the NCS. But in recent years, the gap has widened. That widening gap likely derives from changes to the CPS itself.

The CPS went through a survey redesign for the 2014 survey. In that year, both the old and new versions of the survey were given to some households, allowing researchers to assess whether changes in certain results were due to changes in households' own circumstances or how the questions were asked. The Employee Benefit Research Institute's (EBRI) Craig Copeland analyzed the changes, showing that they resulted in an immediate 2.6 percentage point reduction in the share of employees stating that they worked for an employer that offered a retirement plan. Declines in reported plan access were higher for full-time workers and public-sector employees.[17]

The EBRI has repeatedly drawn attention to this issue, warning that "relying on [the CPS] to understand trends in [retirement plan] coverage is dangerous and misleading at best."[18] Nearly every retirement analyst is aware of the problems associated with the CPS survey redesign, yet these doubly flawed figures are nevertheless trotted out to portray a US retirement system in disarray.

However, the Census Bureau introduced new supplementary questions to the CPS in 2019 that allowed EBRI researchers to construct what they believe to be a more accurate measure of retirement plan participation. As part of the CPS survey questions regarding income, respondents were asked if they received interest income from retirement accounts and, if so, from what type of account. Since receipt of interest income from a retirement account presupposes ownership of such an account, Copeland was able to adjust existing CPS data to capture this new information. These adjustments closed about two-thirds of the gap in reported participation between the CPS and the NCS.

For instance, in the CPS for 2018, only 46 percent of private-sector workers employed at businesses of 500 or more employees reported participating in a retirement plan, versus 78 percent of employees as reported in the NCS. EBRI's adjustments to the CPS incorporating newly introduced questions increased the 2018 reported participation rate to 68 percent. A substantial gap remains, presumably attributable to continued reporting error or other causes, but the participation gap shrinks considerably in all age, income, and education groups.[19]

What Higher-Quality Data Tell Us

Having concluded that CPS data on retirement plan access aren't high quality, it is worth looking at other data sources that might provide a more accurate picture.

The NCS gathers data from employers rather than employees. This has some downsides, because the NCS provides much more limited demographic data on workers themselves. For example, the NCS includes data such as employees' broad earning level, whether the employee is full-time or part-time or a member of a labor union, and the region of the country in which the business is based. But the NCS does not include other common variables in household surveys, such as race, education, marital status, and the number of children.

Table 1, which is drawn from the NCS, shows retirement plan coverage and participation rates by several employee and job characteristics, including full- or part-time status, earnings level, and the number of employees at the establishment at which the employee works.[20] Among full-time employees, 78 percent had access to a retirement plan, and

62 percent participated. In contrast, only 41 percent of part-time employees had access to a retirement plan, with 21 percent participating. This is perhaps not unexpected, given that part-time jobs are lower paid and often more transient.

Lower-paid workers are also less likely to participate in retirement plans. Only 44 percent of employees in the lowest-paid 25 percent (or "quartile") of the workforce were offered a retirement plan on the job; of this group, barely half (23 percent) participated. This perhaps indicates lower demand for retirement plans relative to other pay or benefits, particularly given that lower-paid employees receive higher replacement rates from Social Security.

Among the highest-paid quartile of the private-sector workforce, 90 percent of employees had access to a retirement plan, and 79 percent participated. This again makes sense, because higher-paid employees have a greater need to save for retirement given the lower replacement rates they receive from Social Security. Nearly nine in 10 highest-quartile employees who are offered a retirement plan participate.

Retirement plan coverage also varies considerably by establishment size. Small establishments with fewer than 50 employees are less likely to offer a retirement plan, with only 52 percent coverage. By contrast, 91 percent of establishments of 500 or more employees offer a retirement plan. Variation in coverage by establishment size is likely related to the fixed costs of establishing and maintaining a retirement plan, which are more affordable for larger businesses. The difference does not appear to be driven principally by employee demand; variation in participation rates contingent on coverage rises with establishment size, but not dramatically so.

As we saw earlier, one way around the demographic limitations of employer surveys is to match household survey responses from individuals to their IRS tax records, which retains the demographic richness of household surveys while eliminating the response error on retirement plan coverage that plagues most survey data. Unfortunately, for confidentiality reasons, this approach is generally available only within government agencies and, even then, under closely prescribed conditions.

In 2015 research that matched responses from the SIPP to IRS data showing retirement plan participation, Dushi, Iams, and Jules

Table 1. Access to and Participation in Workplace Retirement Plans, as Reported by Employers

	Access	Participation
Full-Time	78%	62%
Part-Time	41%	21%
Salary Level		
Lowest Quartile	44%	23%
Second Quartile	68%	48%
Third Quartile	79%	63%
Highest Quartile	90%	79%
Establishment Size		
1 to 49	52%	35%
50 to 99	70%	51%
100 to 499	80%	60%
500 or More	91%	79%

Source: US Bureau of Labor Statistics.

Lichtenstein found that 75 percent of full- or part-time private-sector workers were offered a retirement plan in 2012 and 61 percent participated. Among employers with 100 or more workers, 87 percent of employees were offered a retirement plan, and 71 percent participated.[21] Compared to surveys such as the CPS, these figures present a major difference in how many Americans are saving for retirement. Yet such figures go almost unreported in the news media.

We also can look to IRS data, which in theory should be more accurate than either employer or employee survey responses. However, the publicly available IRS figures have even greater limitations on demographic details than employer surveys such as the NCS do.

While dating back only to 2008, the IRS figures show that from 2008 to 2018, the share of all Americans with wage income who are participating in a retirement plan rose from 49.4 percent to 52.8 percent, a promising increase given that it occurred over only a single decade.[22] Over that same period, the CPS reported a decline in participation among all workers with positive earnings from 31.1 percent to 25.5 percent.

Who Should Be—and Is—Saving for Retirement?

In discussions of the US retirement system, there is an implicit assumption that every person should be saving for retirement at every point during their adult life—or even *before* their adult life. The well-known financial planner Ric Edelman has proposed establishing retirement accounts for newborns, with contributions coming from the federal government.[23] Proposals for auto IRA plans established by state governments often derive from the same assumption: If you're not saving, you should be. And to be clear, the main objects of such proposals would be low-income Americans, who save for retirement at significantly lower rates than middle and high earners do.

I think the desire to get everyone saving often comes from a moral standpoint rather than a financial one. Saving is, by definition, the willingness to defer gratification today to reap the benefits tomorrow. In most other contexts, we think of the willingness to defer gratification as a sign of moral character: the student who studies instead of going out to a party or the weight-conscious person who defers dessert to improve their health. And that's fine as far as it goes.

Yet that's not how economists view retirement saving, and it's really not how ordinary Americans or policymakers should either. In the life-cycle model, saving is a tool. Saving is used to shift resources from today to some time in your life when those resources could be more valuably used. Borrowing does the opposite, shifting money from a future time when it will be less valuable or useful to the present time when it can be used more profitably.

The life-cycle model predicts that individuals will borrow and save in ways that will tend to produce a smoother standard of living over their lifetime. And, specifically, they won't choose to make themselves poorer when they're poorer to be better-off when they're well-off. Instead, they'll do the opposite.

A 2021 syndicated column by the financial reporter Jill Schlesinger gave me the springboard to consider these points. The column stated what it called a dismal fact: "The median retirement savings balance for the bottom 50 percent of American families is $0."[24] That certainly does sound dismal. And, as a factoid, it's true: I turned to the Federal Reserve's Survey of Consumer Finances, and, indeed, the factoid appears correct. If I look at the bottom 50 percent of working-age households by income in 2019—those with incomes below $64,000 in that year—the median retirement account balance is in fact $0.

But on second thought, what does it really mean? Should Americans at the median of the bottom half of the income distribution be saving for retirement? To be clear, the median of the bottom half of the income distribution is the 25th percentile, meaning this household has an income that's below that of 75 percent of other US households. In 2019, their median household earnings were $22,124, they were typically married, and they had on average half a child living at home. Should this household really devote a substantial chunk of its $22,000 annual salary toward saving for retirement?

That's especially true when we consider that this household, and every other working household in the US, actually is saving for retirement via Social Security. Of the 12.4 percent total Social Security payroll tax, 10.6 percentage points are devoted to the retirement portion of the program. According to the Congressional Budget Office in 2021, Social Security will replace about two-thirds of preretirement earnings for a household at the 25th percentile of the earnings distribution.[25] Given that financial planners say that a retirement income equal to 70 percent of a person's preretirement earnings is usually enough, this household may be doing pretty much what a financial adviser or an economist would tell them to do.

Another way to think of a low-income household's de facto savings through Social Security is to calculate their *effective* contribution to the program. A worker's effective contribution to Social Security isn't just the formal amount they pay in, but that amount adjusted for Social Security's progressive benefit formula. The Congressional Budget Office estimates that a worker in the middle of the bottom half of the earnings distribution will receive benefits equal to about 1.9 times the taxes he or she pays in.[26] That's due to Social Security's progressive benefit formula.

This means that a low-wage worker's effective contributions are a lot higher than what they're actually paying in. With a 10.6 percent contribution rate and a "money's worth ratio" of 1.9, this implies that a low-wage earner will receive benefits equal to what they might receive if they had contributed 20.1 percent of their earnings to a retirement account invest-ing in government bonds. So that's how they're already preparing for retirement, and out of their $22,000 household salary, we expect them to save more? It just doesn't make sense.

A team of economists affiliated with Stanford University recently for-malized this insight with regard to retirement savings. They set up a com-puterized life-cycle model in which people tried to maximize the lifetime utility (or welfare) they derive from their incomes. And the way they do that is by borrowing and saving, shifting money from one part of their life to another. Economist John Scott and his coauthors show that, in the con-text of a life-cycle model, most young or low-income individuals *shouldn't* be actively saving for retirement.[27]

> Under realistic assumptions, the life-cycle model implies that most young people should not save for retirement. First, high-income workers tend to experience wage growth over their careers. For these workers, maintaining as steady a standard of living as possible therefore requires spending all income while young and only starting to save for retirement during middle age.[28]

Young people seem to have that part of the model down.

"Second, low-income workers, whose wage profiles tend to be flat-ter, receive high Social Security replacement rates, making optimal sav-ing rates very low."[29] Again, if Social Security already will replace most of your preretirement earnings, it doesn't make sense to save a great deal—especially if you are likely to be financially pressed in other areas.

The authors show that low savings are optimal for young and lower-income individuals even if their employer offers a matching contri-bution to their 401(k) plan.

At any given time, a big chunk of the population is either young or poor and therefore probably shouldn't be saving for retirement. For instance, let's assume that the lowest-earning fifth of the population, who the Congressional Budget Office says will receive a Social Security benefit equal to about 80 percent of their preretirement earnings, shouldn't be saving. If their earnings rise, they can start saving, but for now, it makes sense to rely on Social Security and devote their limited incomes to just getting by.

Likewise, about one-quarter of the adult population is under age 35, when the life-cycle model typically might recommend for retirement saving to begin. So that group shouldn't be saving either, even if it makes sense to start saving later in life. The intersection of these age and income groups makes up about 44 percent of the adult population. That's a lot of people who rationally shouldn't be saving.

The IRS data can be useful in looking at these questions.[30] The data, drawn from the IRS's Statistics of Income dataset, allow us to break down retirement plan participation by both age and earnings level. To illustrate, I start with taxpayers between age 45 and 54. This age group, in the logic of the life-cycle model, clearly should be looking to save for retirement. But within this group, we wish to eliminate those with low earnings who might be better off relying solely on Social Security.

I start with people earning $25,000 or less in 2017, who made up about the bottom quarter of the earnings distribution at that age. Of all people earning $25,000 or more in 2017, the IRS data show that 73 percent were participating in a retirement plan in that year. That's hardly a shabby level of participation.

Table 2 provides more detail, showing that retirement plan participation rates follow the life-cycle model in rising with both age and earnings. For instance, at age 26 to 34, only 50.9 percent of all individuals with earnings participated in a retirement plan. And among low-earning individuals in that age range, participation rates are even lower. For instance, only 28.2 percent of those age 26 to 34 and earning between $15,000 and $20,000 were saving for retirement.

But as age and earnings increase, so do retirement plan participation rates. For instance, 61.9 percent of all individuals age 45 to 54 in 2017 were participating in a retirement plan. And if we look at high earners with salaries of $100,000 or more, roughly nine in 10 were saving for retirement. The results shown in Table 2 are in line with what the life-cycle model would predict. Low earners and younger households are often saving for retirement in a textbook fashion, even if financial columnists and other well-intentioned but not well-informed commentators chide them for doing so.

Table 2. Retirement Plan Participation Rate by Age and Earning Level, 2017

Earning Level	Age Range				
	26–34	35–44	45–54	55–64	65+
All Earners	50.9	57.8	61.9	61.7	42.0
Under $5,000	8.8	11.7	11.7	17.0	14.8
$5,000–$9,999	14.9	16.0	18.5	20.4	18.1
$10,000–$14,999	22.0	22.1	26.0	27.6	27.9
$15,000–$19,999	28.2	28.3	33.4	37.0	35.0
$20,000–$24,999	33.8	35.1	38.9	45.1	41.1
$25,000–$29,999	47.1	44.3	49.6	53.6	46.8
$30,000–$39,999	57.5	56.9	58.5	63.8	54.0
$40,000–$49,999	64.9	65.6	67.5	69.0	59.8
$50,000–$74,999	73.4	73.2	75.2	76.8	67.5
$75,000–$99,999	80.7	80.4	82.4	84.1	75.1
$100,000–$199,999	96.7	84.4	86.4	86.4	76.8
$200,000–$499,999	**	88.9	89.8	89.4	77.7
$500,000–$999,999	**	91.7	91.8	89.3	76.1
$1,000,000 and Over	**	89.9	91.9	87.9	75.0

Source: Internal Revenue Service, "Table 1.5. All Returns: Sources of Income, Adjustments, and Tax Items, by Age, Tax Year 2020 (Filing Year 2021)," 2021, https://www.irs.gov/statistics/soi-tax-stats-individual-income-tax-returns-complete-report-publication-1304-basic-tables-part-1.
Note: ** Denotes insufficient sample size to generate figures without violating confidentiality rules.

Retirement Saving at the Household Level

Ordinarily we think about retirement savings by individual employees, because individuals tell their employer whether to sign them up for a 401(k). Moreover, much of the best data apply to individuals.

But the real economic unit is the household, which is generally made up of two spouses or partners. Households coordinate their activities in numerous ways, including saving for retirement. Unfortunately, IRS figures for married couples are not detailed but can still provide useful insights.

The IRS reports that, among spouses filing taxes jointly in 2017 in which both partners had wage income, 81.4 percent of couples had at least one partner participating in a retirement plan. In 35.4 percent of cases, only one spouse was participating in a workplace retirement plan, while in the remaining 64.6 percent of couples, both members participated. Since married couples tend to be both older and higher income, this again is evidence of retirement savings patterns matching with what the life-cycle hypothesis might predict.

A 2013 SSA analysis of household survey responses matched to IRS tax records by Dushi and Iams produced similar results. They found that 80 percent of couples had at least one spouse participating in an employer-sponsored retirement plan.[31]

And one spouse participating could be enough, so long as they contribute at a sufficiently high rate. In 2023, the annual limit for tax-deferred contributions to 401(k) plans was $22,500. If a couple, each earning $75,000, desired to save 10 percent of its earnings, that could be accomplished with an annual 401(k) contribution of $15,000, well under the contribution limit. For households at most income levels, the annual 401(k) contribution is high enough that one spouse could contribute enough to generate adequate retirement savings for both.

Figures regarding couples' participation rates raise a noteworthy point regarding retirement plan access. If 81 percent of couples had at least one spouse participating in a retirement plan, this implies that more than 81 percent of couples have at least one spouse with access to a retirement plan at work. The publicly available IRS data report only retirement plan participation, not whether a couple is offered a retirement plan on the job. But if, for instance, we assume that 90 percent of couples that are offered a plan will have at least one of the spouses participate, this implies that 89 percent of couples have access to a retirement plan at work.[32]

A US Treasury Department study, while slightly dated, provides additional insights on retirement plan participation at the household level. Treasury Department economists David Joulfaian and David Richardson used IRS data to analyze "the wage-earning population that could realistically be expected to set aside some amount of the labor compensation for retirement saving."[33] Unlike the figures above, Joulfaian and Richardson detailed the retirement plan participation rates of households by earnings level. They found, for instance, that 88 percent of households with combined earnings above about $75,000 in 2022 dollars were participating in an employer-sponsored retirement plan.

All this shows that most Americans who should be saving for retirement are in fact saving for retirement. This is not the conclusion one would draw from reading pessimistic media coverage of a retirement savings issues.

Was There a "Golden Age" of Traditional Pensions?

As we think about the share of employees who are covered by a retirement plan today, it also is worth considering pension coverage in the past. There has been a dramatic decline in pension access from decades past, and many pessimistic assessments of the current state of the US retirement system look back fondly on a time when traditional pensions were a reliable source of income for most seniors.

Once again, however, this remembrance is not the reality of times past. In fact, traditional pensions in the private sector often were like a rare animal spotted in the wild, fleetingly visible but then disappearing when you looked closer.

Data presented by Joshua Gotbaum, the former head of the Pension Benefit Guaranty Corporation, show that in 1950, about 20 percent of the private-sector workforce participated in a traditional defined benefit pension.[34] A small additional percentage of employees would have had some form of retirement savings account, such as a profit-sharing plan. But at that time, 401(k) plans did not exist.

By 1960, Gotbaum's figures show, participation in traditional pensions had increased to about 33 percent of the labor force, and by 1975, defined benefit pension participation peaked at about 39 percent of private-sector workers. Following the 1975 peak, participation in private-sector traditional pensions steadily declined. By 2020, only 11 percent of private-sector employees participated in a traditional pension.

Simply put, these data show there never was a time when the majority of private-sector workers could look forward to receiving a guaranteed pension benefit in retirement.

But there is an even more important point: Merely participating in a traditional pension plan did not in any way guarantee that one would receive a meaningful benefit from that plan. Even as participation in traditional pensions never topped 39 percent of the workforce, strict vesting rules meant that most workers formally participating in a defined benefit plan would not end up collecting a meaningful benefit.

Before the Employees Retirement Security Act (ERISA) of 1974, which established the current federal regulation of defined benefit pensions, these plans often required up to 15 years in a job before an employee qualified for any benefits. An employee might collect a pension only if they retired from that job, meaning a worker who left or lost a long-standing job before retirement could end up with nothing. These details usually are missing from wistful accounts of the days of traditional pensions.

In seeming contradiction to today's rose-colored glasses, a 1972 NBC news exposé labeled defined benefit pensions "the broken promise."[35] In that Peabody Award–winning documentary, NBC interviewed ordinary citizens who found that what is today often portrayed as the "gold standard" of retirement plans often left them with nothing.

> Unidentified Man: I figured I'd had twenty-three seniority built up, possibly less, up until I was in my forty years sometime at least before I retired and then to look back and see it all flowing away. Everything that you had planned on. Just seems like a waste of time.

> Unidentified Woman: There must be thousands of them, maybe millions of them, that's getting the same song and dance that my husband's got. When they reach their time for retirement, there is no funds to pay them.

> Unidentified Man: This man Hoffa on there retired with a 1.7 million-dollar lump sum pension. And I can't get three hundred dollars a month out of them on there for my retirement.

> Unidentified Man: Where does all this money go that's been paid into these pensions?[36]

The answer to the latter interviewee's questions is "Not always to retirees." That's what made traditional pensions affordable and attractive to employers.

Strict vesting requirements prevented most nominal pension participants from qualifying for a benefit in retirement. A 1972 study by the
Senate Labor Subcommittee found that between 70 and 92 percent of
employees who participated in a traditional pension failed to receive
any benefit from that plan.[37] Other pension participants found that they
received far less than they had expected.

Low coverage rates and strict vesting help explain why a 1962 SSA
survey of new retirees found that just 11 percent of all new retirees
received any sort of private-sector pension benefit.[38] Even by 1981, only
27 percent of new retirees received a private retirement plan benefit.
Even among the richest quarter of retirees, barely half received a private pension benefit. And just 9 percent of new retirees in the bottom
half of the income distribution received *any* benefit from a private pension plan in 1981.[39]

The idea that defined benefit pensions constituted a golden age of
retirement security for most Americans, much less the lower-earning
workers who need help the most, is simply belied by the data.

Why Did Traditional Pensions Go Away?

The standard story regarding the decline of traditional pensions is that
employers offered workers these plans until Congress introduced 401(k)s
in 1978, which freed employers from the cost and risk of guaranteeing
employees' benefits in old age. From that point, the race to the bottom
had begun.

Certainly, the fact that 401(k)s had lower administrative costs and fewer
legal obligations made them attractive to businesses, although Bureau of
Labor Statistics data do show that actual contributions by employers to
employee retirement plans did not decline as traditional pensions faded
and 401(k) retirement accounts took their place.

But there's clearly more to the story, since coverage by traditional pensions began to decline before the 401(k) was even introduced, much less
became a common option for most employees. Moreover, as we have seen,
401(k) coverage has risen substantially higher than defined benefit coverage, even at its peak.

The principal cause of the decline in traditional pension coverage was ERISA, which tightened federal regulation of defined benefit pensions. ERISA came about in response to the types of concerns raised in the 1972 NBC documentary, which included both a small number of high-profile pension insolvencies and the more widespread problem of strict vesting requirements preventing many pension participants from receiving a retirement benefit. ERISA strengthened funding requirements, forcing employers to put aside more funds to cover future pension benefits. It also liberalized vesting requirements, which increased pension costs by making more employees eligible for benefits.

Of course, making employers expand the share of employees entitled to benefits and more fully fund those benefits made defined benefit pensions more expensive. And that explains why participation in traditional pensions peaked in 1975, just one year after the passage of ERISA. By 1985, defined benefit pension coverage had declined by about 5 percentage points, with another 10 percentage point decline by 1995. Over time, existing employers began shifting employees to alternative retirement plans, while most newly formed businesses did not establish traditional pensions to begin with.

Traditional pensions made sense to employers so long as they did not need to offer benefits to all their employees and they didn't need to fully fund the benefits they had promised. But once looser vesting requirements broadened the share of employees who were entitled to a benefit and stricter funding rules required increased employer contributions, the true costs of traditional pensions became clearer.

A 2013 study by Copeland found that the vesting rate—defined as the percentage of workers who were entitled to a benefit from their retirement plan—nearly doubled from 24 percent in 1979 to 43 percent in 2012. According to Copeland, "This increase is largely due to the increased number of workers participating in defined contribution retirement plans (such as 401(k) plans), where employee contributions are immediately vested, and faster vesting requirements in private-sector pension plans."[40] But, of the two retirement plan types, only 401(k)-type plans have proved sustainable.

Once sponsors of defined benefit plans were forced to broaden the net of eligible employees and better fund those expanded benefit liabilities, the value that pensions created in terms of attracting and retaining employees weakened relative to offering higher salaries or enhancing other benefits, such as health coverage. Exacerbating this change on the employer side were evolving employee dynamics: Workers placed less value on guaranteed benefits and greater value on the portability of benefits between jobs.

This was not simply a case of employees changing their minds. Rather, as the Federal Reserve Board's Stephanie Aaronson and Julia Coronado found, the private-sector economy was changing such that industries and sectors where employees tended to value portability increased in size while traditional sectors where defined benefit pensions had been predominant receded.[41]

But this is not to imply that employers shifting away from traditional pensions meant that employers reduced their support for workers' retirement savings. The Bureau of Labor Statistics Employer Costs for Employee Compensation dataset shows that employer contributions to employee retirement plans remained steady at about 5 percent of employee wages from 1986 through 2022.[42]

Thinking About the Decline of Traditional Pensions

A former Department of Labor official, Seth Harris, wrote that "over time, as more and more employers sought to avoid mounting pension liabilities, 401(k) plans became more popular and pensions began to disappear." Using statistics showing that private-sector workers increasingly participate in 401(k)s rather than traditional pensions, Harris concluded: "The result is a retirement crisis, with millions of Americans approaching the end of their working lives with little or no retirement savings."[43]

Harris expresses a common viewpoint. Indeed, concerns over future retirement income shortfalls are often tied to the decades-long shift from traditional defined benefit plans to defined contribution retirement accounts such as 401(k)s. "Traditional pensions have become much less common, and individuals are increasingly responsible for planning and managing their own retirement savings accounts, such as 401(k)s," wrote the Government Accountability Office in 2017. "Many households are ill-equipped for this task and have little or no retirement savings." If no action is taken, it warned, "a retirement crisis could be looming."[44]

But again, let's be clear: This talk of a *transition* from defined benefit pensions refers to a form of retirement saving whose participation peaked nearly a half century ago and which, even at that peak, left six in 10 private-sector workers not participating and an even greater share without any accrued benefits.

The reality is that traditional pensions were never a strong factor in the private sector. Comparisons to state and local government employee pensions illustrate what bit players private defined benefit pensions always were. To show this, I rely on data from the Federal Reserve's Financial Accounts of the United States.[45]

For both the private sector and state and local government, I divide total accrued pension benefit entitlements in a given year by the number of employees in that year, producing the value of accrued pension benefits per employee (Figure 3). Now, this is not a perfect measure, because I lack data on the number of retirees who also are owed benefits by these pension systems, but the per-employee accruals give a flavor of the relative frequency and generosity of traditional pensions in the public and private sectors.

For instance, in 1950, 3.6 million workers were employed in state and local government. In that year, state and local pensions had total benefit liabilities of about $226 billion (in inflation-adjusted 2021 dollars). That equals $61,844 in accrued benefits per state and local government employee. In the private sector in 1950, there were 41 million workers, and private defined benefit pensions had $225 billion in accrued liabilities.

In other words, accrued liabilities in private-sector defined benefit plans were almost precisely the same as in state and local government plans even as the private sector employed over 10 times as many Americans. Accrued pension benefits per private-sector employee were only $5,480. Accrued benefits per state and local government employee exceeded private-sector benefits per worker by a factor of 11.3 to one.

From 1947 to 2021, accrued defined benefit pension benefits per worker in the state and local sector never exceeded the private pension benefits per worker by a ratio of less than 6.7 to one, which occurred in 1985. After 1985, as defined benefit plans receded in the private sector, the ratio of accrued benefits per worker increased to a 2021 value of 18.5 to one.

Figure 3. Ratio of Accrued Traditional Pension Benefits per Worker, State and Local Sector to Private Sector

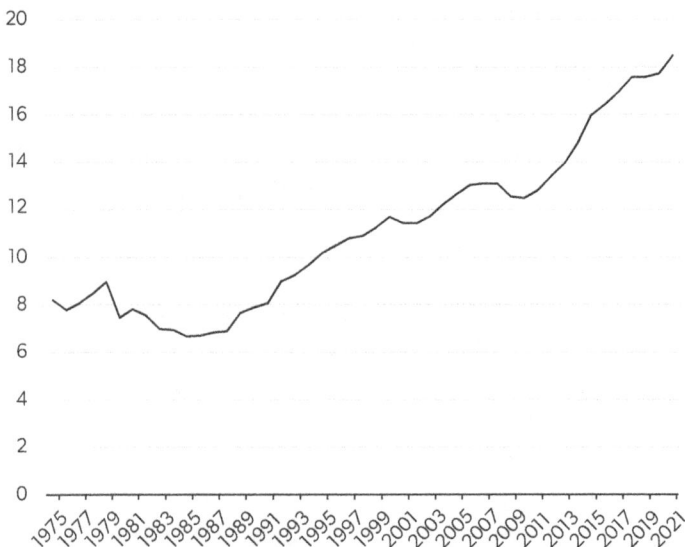

Source: US Federal Reserve Board, Financial Accounts of the United States, 2023, https://www.federalreserve.gov/feeds/z1.html.

The 6.7-to-one ratio of accrued benefits per worker in 1985 can provide us with some insight into the adequacy of traditional pensions in the private sector when those pensions were at their strongest. Let us assume that defined benefit pensions in the state and local government sector provided employees with an adequate but not exorbitant income in retirement. If so, then even at their peak, private-sector defined benefit pensions provided an average private-sector worker with only around 1/6.7th—or just 15 percent—of what would count as an adequate retirement income. That was never going to work. In every other year, the adequacy of private-sector defined benefit pensions would have been even lower.

For the typical private-sector worker, 401(k)s did not replace traditional pensions because there was no traditional pension to replace. Rather, 401(k)s offered a retirement plan and built savings where

Table 3. Annual Payments from Defined Benefit Pension Plans, 2021 US Dollars (Billions)

	Benefit Payments	Share of Total	Share of Workforce
Private Sector	$267	34%	85%
State and Local Government	$351	45%	12%
Federal Government	$162	21%	3%
Total	$780	100%	100%

Source: US Bureau of Economic Analysis, National Income and Product Accounts, Supplemental Tables.

previously little had existed. While the SSA's survey of new retirees in 1980–81 showed only 43 percent receiving benefits from either a private sector or government employee pension, researchers from the Investment Company Institute found that, in 2017, 75 percent of retirees received a benefit from such a plan.[46]

Even today, data from the National Income and Product Accounts show that private-sector defined benefit pension plans pay out only one-third of the total benefits from traditional pensions, with the remainder being paid from federal or state and local government employee plans. And this is despite private-sector employees making up about 84 percent of the total workforce, a share that has remained steady over the past several decades (Table 3).

Twenty-one percent of traditional pension benefits are paid to retired federal employees, who today make up only 3 percent of the labor force. State and local government pensions, which enrolled about 12 percent of the workforce, distributed 45 percent of total defined benefit pension payments.

These data show that 401(k)s don't need to replace defined benefit pensions. They need to replace only the roughly one-third of the traditional pension benefits that currently are being paid to private-sector retirees. Can they do it? This is discussed in the follow chapter, but I believe the evidence shows that they can.

Summing Up

The data presented here lead to several conclusions. First, claims that retirement plan coverage is low and declining in the private sector rely on household surveys that have been shown to generate faulty data. More reliable data from employers and government show high and rising access to retirement plans in private-sector jobs.

Second, retirement plan participation rates largely follow the life-cycle model's predictions, such that participation increases with age and earnings level. Younger and lower-earning individuals may rationally defer saving until their age or income rises. But most Americans who reasonably should be saving for retirement appear to be doing so.

Third, the transition from traditional defined benefit pensions to defined contribution retirement accounts appears to have expanded opportunities for Americans to save for retirement. There was never a time when the typical private-sector worker had access to a defined benefit pension. The introduction of 401(k)s provided retirement savings opportunities for many workers who had no previous option to save.

In the following chapter, I discuss whether those savings, along with other sources of income in retirement, are sufficient for retirees to maintain their preretirement standard of living.

6

What Has Happened to Retirement Savings?

In this chapter, I consider two things: sav*ing*, the verb, denoting how much Americans set aside for retirement out of each paycheck, and sav*ings*, the noun, which represents the total amount we have accumulated for retirement, including interest on our contributions. The conventional wisdom has it that we have too little of either. Not enough Americans participate in retirement plans; when they do, they don't contribute a big enough share of their salary. As a result, they approach retirement with little or nothing set aside for old age.

These claims are backed by factoids, some of which I examine in detail in this chapter. These isolated slices of data are often compelling at first glance. And the typical media reporter, member of Congress, or newspaper reader often doesn't go much beyond a first glance before reaching a conclusion and moving on to other things. Yet, as we will see, some of these persuasive factoids, when properly understood and interpreted, point toward precisely the opposite conclusion that their purveyors intend.

How Much Are We Putting Away for Retirement?

The conventional way to think about retirement plan contributions is as a percentage of workers' salaries. This makes sense for several reasons. First, for many workers, that's how they specify their own contribution, and if their employer offers a match, it also usually is calculated on a percentage-of-salary basis. Second, contributions as a percentage of salary allow for comparability over time. As working-age Americans' earnings increase over time, we'll need to save more if we want to replace those lost earnings with savings once we retire. Expressing contributions as a percentage of salary captures those changes.

Through much of this chapter, I present retirement plan contributions as a percentage of employee wages and salaries. Figure 1 relies principally

Figure 1. Private Retirement Plan Contributions as a Percentage of Employee Wages and Salaries (Including Wages of Nonparticipating Workers)

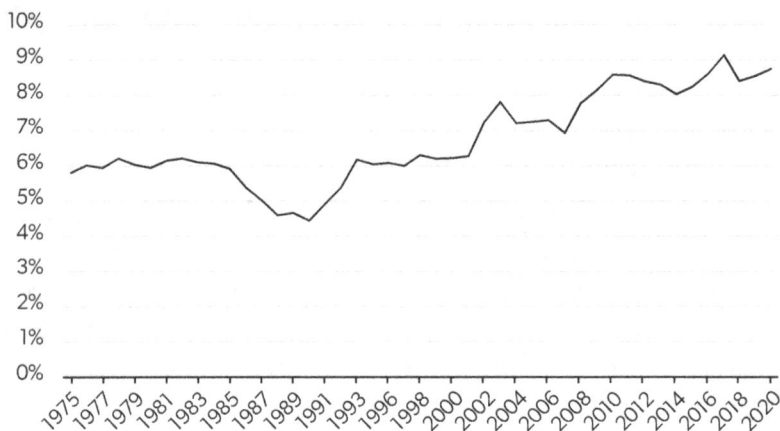

Source: US Department of Labor; and US Bureau of Economic Analysis.

on data from the US Department of Labor, which regulates private-sector retirement plans. Since 1975, the Labor Department has gathered data on private defined benefit and defined contribution retirement plans in its annual Private Pension Plan Bulletins, from which Figure 1 is derived. Figure 1 shows total contributions to private-sector retirement plans by both employers and employees, represented as a percentage of total private-sector wages and salaries (which are drawn from the Bureau of Economic Analysis). Wages and salaries included in the calculation of Figure 1 include those of nonparticipating employees, meaning the contribution rate for employees contingent on participating in a retirement plan would be higher.

The Labor Department data show that total retirement plan contributions remained steady at about 6 percent of employee wages from 1975 through about 1997. The one aberration was a decline in contributions to about 4.5 percent of wages that began in 1985, with recovery to previous levels by 1993. That temporary reduction in contributions was entirely among defined benefit plans and was driven by declining inflation and interest rates in the 1980s.

Beginning in the mid-1990s, retirement plan contributions as a percentage of employee wages began a long increase that may yet to have leveled off. From total contributions of 6 percent of wages and salaries in 1995, contributions to private retirement plans increased to 7.3 percent of employee wages in 2005, 8.3 percent in 2015, and 8.8 percent in 2020. In the final five years of data, from 2016 through 2020, the total private retirement plan contribution rate averaged 8.7 percent of employee wages. Relative to the average contribution rate of 5.6 percent of wages from 1975 through 1994, the 8.7 percent contribution rate from 2016 to 2020 represents a 55 percent relative increase in contributions.

This increase in contributions to retirement plans since 1975 is doubly remarkable given the increase in the Social Security tax rate over that same period. Since 1975, the combined Social Security tax rate has increased from 9.9 percent of earnings to 12.4 percent of earnings. Yet during the same period in which combined employer and employee Social Security taxes increased by 2.5 percentage points, employers and employees increased their retirement plan contributions by an additional 3 percent of earnings.

Consider also contributions solely to defined contribution plans, as 401(k)-style accounts have become the predominant savings vehicle for private-sector employees over the past several decades. As in Figure 1, the contribution rates shown in Figure 2 are not contribution rates for employees who participate in defined contribution plans. Rather, the dollar value of total defined contribution plan contributions is divided by the dollar value of all private-sector wages and salaries, including the wages and salaries of employees who participate in a defined benefit plan and no retirement plan at all.

The Bureau of Economic Analysis calculates for the National Income and Product Accounts total contributions to all retirement plans in all sectors, including private businesses and the federal, state, and local governments (Figure 3). The figures are collected in somewhat different ways than the Labor Department data discussed earlier and extend back only to 1984.

Nevertheless, the National Income and Product Accounts data show significant and rising contributions to employee retirement plans. Again, these contribution rates are calculated against all employee wages and salaries, not merely those of participating employees. Thus, contribution

Figure 2. Defined Contribution Pension Contributions, Percentage of All Private-Sector Wages (Including Wages Subject to Defined Benefit Plans and Wages of Nonparticipation Workers)

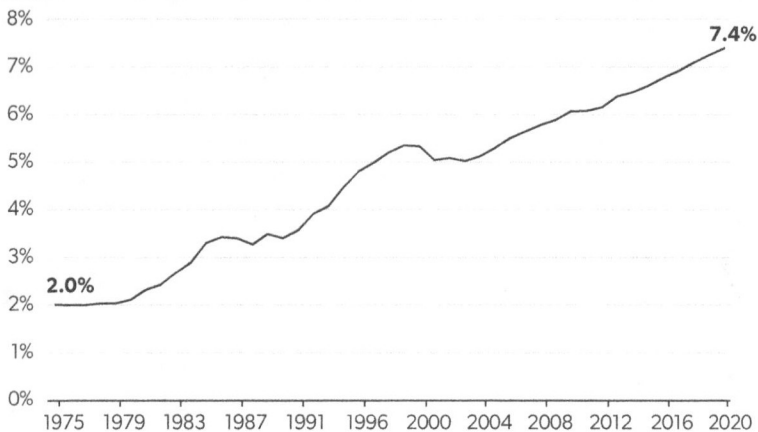

Source: US Department of Labor.

Figure 3. Retirement Plan Contributions as a Percentage of Wages and Salaries, Including Salaries of Employees Not Participating in a Retirement Plan, All Sectors

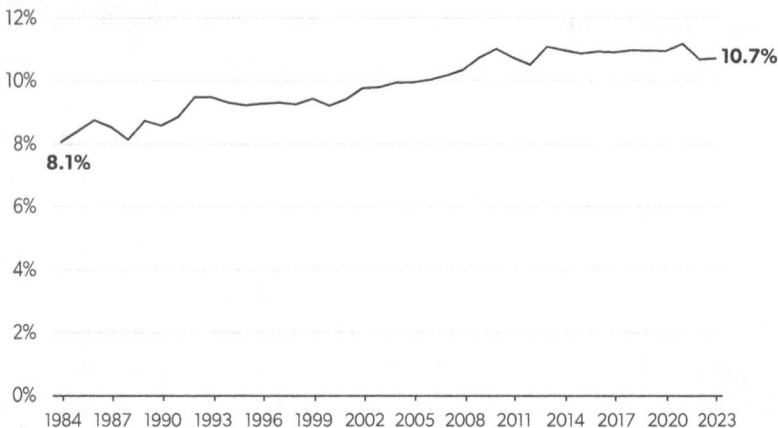

Source: National Income and Product Accounts.

rates for employees who do participate in a plan would be higher than the figures shown here.

How Much Are Different Individuals Contributing?

The numbers in Figures 1–3 show aggregated contributions, but it also is worthwhile knowing what employees of different types are paying into their retirement plans. Unfortunately, government data often are not helpful in this regard. As we've seen, household surveys provide a wealth of demographic information regarding Americans, but the numbers reported in those surveys often are inaccurate. The federal government does provide accurate and useful data on total contributions to retirement plans, as previously discussed, but these data cannot be broken down to provide details on different categories of employees.

However, data from retirement plan administrators can be helpful, albeit with caveats. The massive financial firm Vanguard publishes an annual volume, *How America Saves*, providing details on the contribution patterns of different participants in 401(k)s and other retirement plans managed by Vanguard.[1]

Vanguard is one of the largest 401(k) providers in the United States. It manages over 1,700 plans covering 4.5 million employees, with nearly $200 billion in assets. At the same time, the employees covered by Vanguard plans have above-average incomes, with the median eligible employee having an annual salary of $74,000. Thus, while Vanguard's figures are likely typical for the types of Americans who are actively saving for retirement, they would not be representative of the total US workforce.

Table 1, drawn from *How America Saves*, breaks down contribution rates as a percentage of employee wages by both income and age. Contribution rates include employee contributions and employer matching contributions, when available. As discussed in Chapter 4, the life-cycle model predicts that active saving for retirement should increase with income and age, and the Vanguard figures confirm that.

In Vanguard-managed plans, the average contribution rate rises from 7.6 percent of salary for employees earning less than $15,000 annually to 13.9 percent of pay for employees earning $150,000 or more. Contribution

Table 1. Contribution Rates, by Income and Age

Annual Salary	Percentage of Salary
Less Than $15,000	7.60%
$15,000–$29,999	6.80%
$30,000–$49,999	8.60%
$50,000–$74,999	10.60%
$75,000–$99,999	12.00%
$100,000–$149,999	13.20%
$150,000 or More	13.90%

Age	Percentage of Salary
Younger Than 25	8.10%
25–34	10.70%
35–44	11.10%
45–54	11.70%
55–64	12.90%
65 or Older	12.70%

Source: Data from Vanguard, *How America Saves 2023*, 2023, https://corporate.vanguard.com/content/dam/corp/research/pdf/how_america_saves_2023.pdf.

rates similarly rise with age, from 8.1 percent of salary for employees under age 25 to 12.9 percent of pay for employees age 55 to 64.

Are Americans Saving Enough?

An appropriate question to ask is whether the contribution rates detailed previously are enough—which is difficult to answer. Any specific household's retirement saving needs are unique, and there is no one-size-fits-all formula.

However, it is easier to answer a different question: Are current rates of retirement saving enough, *on average*? The "on average" element allows for a degree of simplification that can provide us with at least an approximate idea of how much a given household should set aside to meet a given retirement savings goal.

In a 2019 study published by the Pension Research Council, I set up a model to judge how much employees at different earnings levels should save for retirement.[2] The model analyzes retirement savings needs for five different wage levels of earnings, which are adopted from stylized earners that the Social Security Administration (SSA) uses to illustrate benefit levels. No analysis of household retirement savings adequacy can work if it first doesn't factor in Social Security benefits, which vary across the earnings spectrum.

So-called very low–wage earners have career-average annual earnings equal to 25 percent of the national average wage. The low-wage earners have average annual earnings equal to 45 percent of the average wage. These two worker types make up approximately the bottom two quintiles of the lifetime earnings distribution and are those policymakers would likely be most concerned with (Table 2).

Medium- and high-wage earners make an average of 100 percent and 160 percent of the national average wage over their careers, respectively. A maximum-wage earner makes the maximum salary subject to Social Security taxes every year of their career. The maximum taxable salary in 2024 is $168,600.

In the model, each worker is assumed to participate in Social Security and saves as necessary to achieve a certain target retirement income replacement rate, which equals their total retirement income including Social Security as a percentage of their preretirement earnings. Preretirement earnings are represented by inflation-adjusted average earnings from age 45 to 60. Based on a study by Robert Myers, who served as chief actuary to the SSA, I selected target replacement rates ranging from 90 percent of preretirement earnings for the very low–wage earner to 60 percent for the maximum-wage earner.[3]

For each worker type, I first calculated a Social Security benefit payable at the normal retirement age, which I converted to a replacement rate of average earnings from age 45 to 60. These Social Security replacement rates, netted out against the target replacement rate for total retirement incomes, left a residual amount that workers would need to save on their own. For each worker, I calculated the level of annual income needed to achieve the target replacement rate, the lump sum as of retirement age needed to provide that level of income through retirement, and

Table 2. Target Replacement Rates, Retirement Savings, and Preretirement Saving Rates

	———SSA Stylized Earnings Level, ——— Retiring at 66 in 2015				
	Very Low	**Low**	**Medium**	**High**	**Maximum**
Social Security Replacement Rate (%)	87	63	47	39	29
Target Replacement Rates (%)	90	83	75	67	60
Required Replacement Rate from Personal Savings (%)	3	20	28	28	31
Assumed Longevity at Age 66 (Years)	15	17	20	23	25
Target Savings as Multiple of Age 65 Earnings	0.6	4.0	6.6	7.5	6.2
Target Saving Rate as Percentage of Age 30–65 Earnings (%)	0.4	2.6	4.4	4.9	6.4

Source: Andrew G. Biggs, "How Much Should the Poor Save for Retirement? Data and Simulations on Retirement Income Adequacy Among Low-Earning Households," in *Remaking Retirement: Debt in an Aging Economy*, ed. Olivia S. Mitchell and Annamaria Lusardi (Oxford University Press, 2019).

the percentage of earnings from age 30 through 65 that each worker type would need to save. I assumed that workers earn a 5.7 percent real annual return on their savings before retirement and a 0.8 percent real return in retirement.

The resulting required saving rates were extremely low, at least relative to conventional wisdom. For instance, to achieve a total retirement income replacement rate of 90 percent, the very low–wage earner would need to save 0.4 percent of their earnings from age 30 through 65; the low-wage earner, 4.0 percent; the medium-wage earner, 4.4 percent; the high-wage earner, 4.9 percent; and the maximum-wage earner, 6.4 percent. Even when I increased expected lifespans in retirement by 20 percent or reduced assumed investment returns, target saving rates for most earners remained below those recommended by many investment advisers.

For lower earners, the reasons for low required savings are straightforward. First, low earners receive higher Social Security replacement rates than many realize. The very low earner receives a Social Security benefit equal to 82 percent of earnings from age 45 through 60, leaving only a small residual to finance on their own. The low earner receives a 63 percent Social Security replacement rate, versus a target total retirement income replacement rate of 83 percent.

I also factored in differential mortality by income, with adjustments derived from a Government Accountability Office review of recent literature.[4] For instance, while the medium-wage earner is assumed to live for 20 years past retirement age, a very low earner could be expected to live only 15 years. A maximum-wage earner, by contrast, could expect to survive an additional 25 years.

Calculations such as these help reconcile survey data showing the vast majority of retirees feel financially secure with the fact that few Americans did or do save at the rates of 12 to 15 percent of wages that financial advisers and firms like Vanguard recommend. Social Security replaces a larger share of a worker's preretirement earnings than many believe, thanks to misleading SSA replacement rates that are discussed in Chapter 4. And as we see in Chapter 10, spending in retirement is generally lower than most rules of thumb would have an American saving for retirement believe.

When all is said and done, the increasing amounts that Americans put away for retirement out of each paycheck are, on average at least, likely to be enough for them to maintain their standard of living in old age.

What Has Happened to Total Retirement Assets?

Saving is a verb, the act of setting aside money today to spend tomorrow. As seen earlier, Americans today are saving more for retirement than ever before. Savings, by contrast, are the accumulations over time of the amounts set aside, plus interest. What has happened to those amounts?

Once again, we can look at retirement savings in total and on a more granular level. We start with the total amounts, which are tracked regularly by the Federal Reserve via the Financial Accounts of the United States, which compiles data on financial transactions and assets and liabilities throughout the US economy. Figure 4 tells the story of rising retirement savings. It is based on employer-sponsored retirement plans in all sectors

Figure 4. Retirement Plan Assets as a Percentage of Total Wages and Salaries

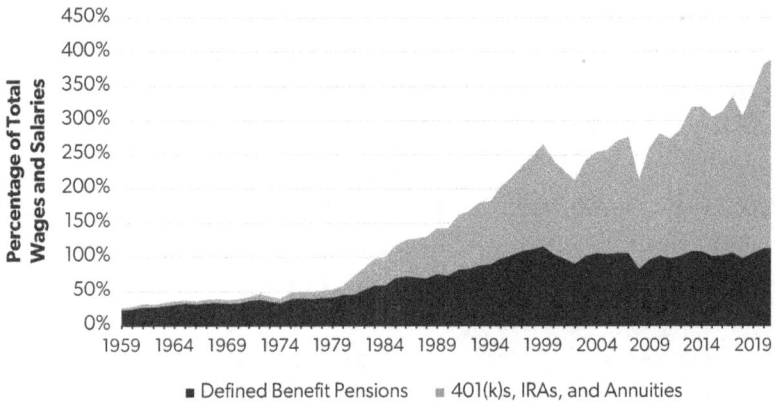

Source: Federal Reserve Board; and US Bureau of Economic Analysis.

of the economy—the private sector, the federal government, and state and local governments. Social Security is not included in these figures.

Figure 4 represents balances in two types of retirement savings: first, employer-sponsored defined benefit plans and second, employer-sponsored defined contribution plans, individual retirement accounts (IRAs), and annuities. IRA balances are merged with 401(k)s because most IRA balances are built from rollovers from 401(k) plans when employees change jobs, not from dedicated IRA contributions. Annuities are lumped in with IRAs by the Fed and are small relative to the other categories of savings.

Assets are represented not in nominal or inflation-adjusted dollars, but as a percentage of total wages and salaries. The logic is that retirement savings are accumulated to replace wages and salaries once a person stops working, so the ratio of savings to salaries captures that purpose.

Figure 4 is highly recommended for anyone who believes that the transition from defined benefit pensions to 401(k)s was bad for retirement savings. In 1959, when defined benefit pensions were pretty much the only game in town, total retirement plan assets were equal to only 26 percent of total wages and salaries. By 1978, when the regulation enabling 401(k) plans was written, total retirement plan assets had increased to 51 percent of total wages and salaries. By 1984, retirement plan assets had risen to 100 percent of wages and salaries; by 1995, to 200 percent; by 2013, to 300 percent; and by 2021, to 412 percent.

The turning point takes place around 1980. Defined benefit plan assets increase in two sectors: (1) the private sector, likely due to the Employee Retirement Income Security Act's (ERISA) requirement that sponsors better fund their obligations, and (2) the public sector, due to both improved efforts to fund and the rising generosity of public-sector pension benefits. So it is not as if defined benefit pensions played no role in rising retirement savings. But savings in retirement accounts simply exploded in the early 1980s, as both the IRA accounts created by ERISA in 1974 and 401(k)s began to grow.

Within two decades, retirement account assets exceeded savings in defined benefit plans. Today, defined contribution assets are 2.4 times greater than accrued benefits in defined benefit plans, even though defined benefit pensions continue to dominate in the federal, state, and local governments.

But however one might feel about defined benefit pensions versus 401(k)s, retirement savings are much higher in today's 401(k) world than in the past when defined benefit plans were the most common retirement plan available. Total savings set aside for retirement in 2022 were 8.5 times higher than in 1975, when participation in private-sector traditional pensions peaked, even after accounting for the growth of the wages that retirement savings must replace. Retirement savings have nearly doubled over the past two decades. It is almost impossible to square this increase in actual retirement savings against the common belief that, in the words of famed financial journalist Jane Bryant Quinn, "America's retirement savings system has failed."[5]

What If We Add Social Security to the Mix?

As I mention many times throughout this book, income in retirement comes from a combination of private retirement savings and Social Security. Looking at either without reference to the other doesn't give a complete picture.

While household retirement savings are skewed toward higher-income households, accrued Social Security benefits are tilted toward low earners.

Figure 5. Accrued Social Security Benefits and Private Retirement Savings

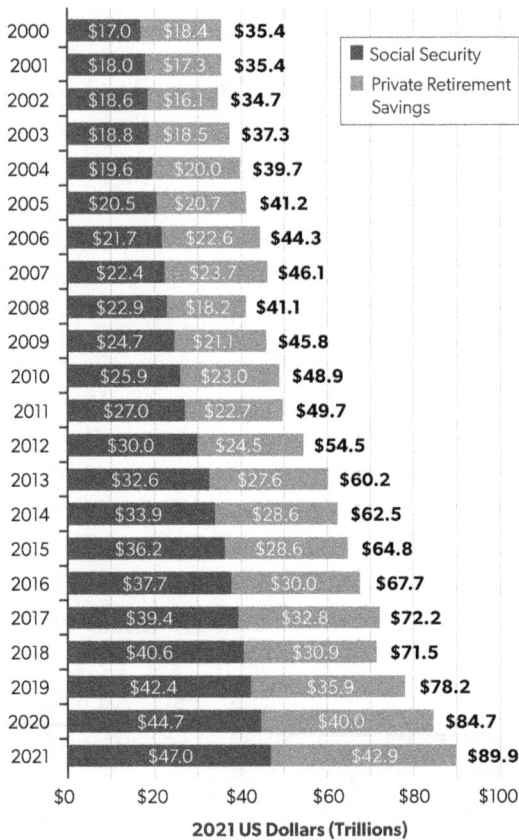

Year	Social Security	Private Retirement Savings	Total
2000	$17.0	$18.4	$35.4
2001	$18.0	$17.3	$35.4
2002	$18.6	$16.1	$34.7
2003	$18.8	$18.5	$37.3
2004	$19.6	$20.0	$39.7
2005	$20.5	$20.7	$41.2
2006	$21.7	$22.6	$44.3
2007	$22.4	$23.7	$46.1
2008	$22.9	$18.2	$41.1
2009	$24.7	$21.1	$45.8
2010	$25.9	$23.0	$48.9
2011	$27.0	$22.7	$49.7
2012	$30.0	$24.5	$54.5
2013	$32.6	$27.6	$60.2
2014	$33.9	$28.6	$62.5
2015	$36.2	$28.6	$64.8
2016	$37.7	$30.0	$67.7
2017	$39.4	$32.8	$72.2
2018	$40.6	$30.9	$71.5
2019	$42.4	$35.9	$78.2
2020	$44.7	$40.0	$84.7
2021	$47.0	$42.9	$89.9

2021 US Dollars (Trillions)

Source: Social Security Administration; and Federal Reserve Board.

Just as private retirement savings have increased substantially over time, so have the benefits Americans have accrued under Social Security. The SSA's actuaries produce an annual actuarial note that tabulates the value of accrued Social Security benefits—that is, benefits that Americans have earned but not yet received.[6]

The value of accrued Social Security benefits can be added to the value of private-sector retirement plans and household retirement savings such as IRAs to generate a value for total retirement savings (Figure 5). The SSA data series begins in only 2000, but even since then, total retirement

savings have increased: From 2000 to 2021, accrued Social Security benefits rose from $17 trillion (in constant 2021 dollars) to $47 trillion, a
177 percent increase.

Meanwhile, private retirement savings increased from $18.4 trillion to
$42.5 trillion, an increase of 131 percent. Total retirement savings con-
sisting of accrued Social Security benefits and private savings rose from
$35.4 trillion to $81.7 trillion in little over two decades. Each element of
total retirement savings is tilted toward a different segment of the income
distribution, but both have risen significantly.

OK, Retirement Savings Increased. But Just for the Rich?

One response to data showing that retirement savings have increased is
that all the gains have gone to high-income Americans. The Economic
Policy Institute's Natalie Sabadish and Monique Morrissey didn't take any
chances with subtlety: Their *Retirement Inequality Chartbook* was subtitled
How the 401(k) Revolution Created a Few Big Winners and Many Losers.[7]

Much of their case is simply pointing out that the rich save more for
retirement than the poor do, which, as we have seen, is true. But high-
income households would be expected to save more for retirement in
dollar terms simply because they have higher preretirement earnings to
replace in old age.

Moreover, as Wharton School of Business economist Olivia Mitchell
writes, "Social Security rules pay lower-wage workers much higher relative
benefits than higher-paid workers. . . . Maybe low saving rates are optimal
for the poor and middle class."[8] If a progressive Social Security benefit
formula makes it rational for very low earners to save little or nothing for
retirement, by virtue of benefits that replace a vast majority of their preretirement earnings, then the ratio of household retirement savings between
the rich and poor could be virtually infinite. This question is analyzed in
greater detail in the following section.

Here I explore a much narrower issue: Did retirement savings increase—
and for whom? The first question can be answered clearly in the affirma-
tive, as prior sections have shown. But the second question is much more
difficult to answer. The reason is that, while a number of datasets have

figures on the retirement account balances of different types of house-holds, many households did and continue to accrue benefits under tradi-tional defined benefit pensions.

As we've seen elsewhere, participants in federal, state, and local gov-ernment defined benefit plans continue to accrue benefits at a healthy pace, even if those plans' assets never seem to keep up. Moreover, even in the private sector, if we don't count accrued traditional pension benefits, then rising retirement plan balances will show an illusory increase in total household savings.

To get around these problems, I carried out a study in 2020 that started with the Federal Reserve's Survey of Consumer Finances, which measures household retirement account balances. I then grafted these data onto another Fed dataset, the Distributional Financial Accounts, which contains measures of accrued defined benefit pensions. When the two are combined, I have a measure of the household's total private retirement savings.[9]

I analyzed households in four different ways: by age, income, educational attainment, and race or ethnicity. To avoid creating any undue suspense, I will skip straight to the punch line: From 1989 to 2016, average retirement savings increased in every age, income, educational, and racial or ethnic group. Retirement savings increased whether measured in inflation-adjusted dollars or as a percentage of households' annual earnings.

Since we are focused on whether changes in the US retirement system over the past several decades have widened inequality of retirement sav-ings by income level, I reproduce here a table taken from that 2020 study. Table 3 measures retirement savings as a percentage of annual earnings, since the goal of saving for retirement is to replace lost earnings in old age. The question is whether households of different income categories increased their savings—and by how much.

The answer is that every quintile (or fifth) of the income distribution had higher savings relative to its income in 2016 than in 1989. But increases were not in any way uniform across the income distribution in a "the rich did better" or "the poor did better" kind of way. In the bottom fifth of the income distribution, where both incomes and savings are modest in dollar terms, average retirement savings nevertheless increased from 245 per-cent of annual incomes in 1989 to 377 percent in 2016. This is a 54 percent relative increase in retirement savings, meaning a household's ability to replace lost earnings increased by that percentage.

In the second quintile, which might be termed as the working poor, relative retirement savings increased by 47 percent. In the middle quintile, savings rose by 66 percent and by a much stronger 129 percent among the fourth quintile. This group might be considered the upper middle class, with average household incomes of about $87,000 in 2016.

Finally, the smallest relative increase in retirement savings was for the highest income quintile, where savings relative to average incomes increased by only 33 percent in relative terms. Of course, no one should worry about this group: They had high savings in 1989, 2016, and every year in between.

Moreover, one reason high-income households' savings rose relatively slowly compared to their annual incomes is that their incomes rose at a healthy pace over this period. There is no uniform story in the data by income, except that every income group appeared to be better prepared for retirement in 2016 than they were in 1989.

The same story is true when Americans are categorized by race, age, or education. Many people almost don't want to hear it, but we *are* better prepared for retirement today than in decades past.

In a 2019 study published by the Federal Reserve Board, two economists focused less on the growth of retirement savings than on their distribution. Specifically, John Sabelhaus and Alice Henriques Volz attempted to answer this question: "Are disappearing employer pensions contributing to rising wealth inequality?"[10] Sabelhaus and Henriques Volz modeled retirement account balances and accruals under defined benefit pensions for households age 50 to 59 in 1989 and 2016.

The authors found that both defined contribution balances and accrued defined benefit pension benefits are disproportionately held by the richest fourth (or quartile) of households. In 2016, 81 percent of retirement account balances were held by the richest quartile of households, along with 78 percent of accrued defined benefit pension benefits. In 1983, 76 percent of defined contribution account balances and 64 percent of accrued defined benefit pension benefits were held by the richest quartile. While defined benefit pensions appear to have become more regressive over time, in general, the differences between either pension types or over time are not large. Simply put, the rich hold most private retirement savings.

Table 3. Average Retirement Savings as a Percentage of Household Earnings (in 2016 Dollars)

| Year | Income Quintile | | | | |
	Bottom	Second	Middle	Fourth	Top
1989	245%	195%	209%	196%	404%
1992	311%	243%	221%	229%	440%
1995	419%	325%	254%	264%	427%
1998	286%	308%	292%	340%	492%
2001	299%	269%	257%	309%	438%
2004	279%	217%	298%	363%	443%
2007	439%	276%	312%	363%	462%
2010	444%	293%	336%	356%	497%
2013	453%	325%	385%	462%	564%
2016	377%	287%	348%	450%	536%
Percentage Change	54%	47%	66%	129%	33%

Source: Andrew G. Biggs, *Changes to Household Retirement Savings Since 1989*, American Enterprise Institute, May 8, 2020, https://www.aei.org/research-products/report/changes-to-household-retirement-savings-since-1989.

But, and this is the key to rebutting the "few big winners and many losers" narrative, Sabelhaus and Henriques Volz found that "the shifting pension landscape neither fueled nor dampened overall wealth inequality."[11] The composition of retirement savings changed considerably from defined benefit to defined contribution plans, but the distribution of retirement savings over different groups of Americans largely remained the same.

The Distribution of Household Savings and Social Security Benefits

The explanation for inequality in household retirement savings lies not in how we save—through defined benefit pensions or 401(k)s—but in *why* we save. Sabelhaus and Henriques Volz's 2019 study reveals a great deal about the interactions between Social Security benefits and the amounts that we save on top of Social Security.

In addition to measuring retirement account balances and accrued pension benefits, Sabelhaus and Henriques Volz calculated the future Social Security benefits that households had earned but not received. Analysts sometimes call this "Social Security wealth," which means the present value of the future Social Security benefits a person can expect to receive. As Sabelhaus and Henriques Volz write, "Social Security is the key to understanding retirement resources for most families."[12]

People don't save for retirement simply to save. If the life-cycle model is to mean anything, households participate in pensions or retirement accounts as part of a larger framework in which they wish to save neither too little nor too much, so that they can maintain their standard of living in old age without beggaring themselves while young.

The benefits households expect to receive from Social Security can and do play into these calculations. The key again is that Social Security is progressive, paying relatively higher benefits to relatively lower-income retirees. As the authors write, the "vast differences in [Social Security] income replacement rates are important for interpreting the distributional findings on employer-sponsored retirement . . . and suggests a completely different way to think about what retirement wealth really means to most families."[13]

A table from the Sabelhaus and Henriques Volz study is worth reprinting. Table 4 breaks down households into four quartiles of household wealth. As you might expect, households at different levels of wealth also have different levels of household incomes, ranging from $31,500 for the bottom quartile to over $400,000 for the highest. And they have different levels of both household retirement savings via retirement accounts or defined benefit pensions and accrued Social Security benefits.

Where these figures are illuminating is when they are expressed as a percentage of each household's preretirement income. For instance, the bottom wealth quartile of near retirees has practically no retirement savings: Their average balances of $6,500 are equal to just 20 percent of their annual incomes. But they had accrued average Social Security benefits equal to 510 percent of their incomes, producing total retirement wealth equal to 530 percent of their annual incomes.

Now, the mix of household savings and Social Security benefits is different as we move up toward the wealthiest households. But total retirement savings relative to preretirement incomes differ by far less. The households

Table 4. Retirement Wealth for Working Families Approaching Retirement (Age 50–59) in 2016

Wealth Quartile	Average Preretirement Income	Wealth (Dollars)			Wealth (Percentage of Preretirement Income)		
		Household Retirement Savings	Accrued Social Security Benefits	Total Retirement Savings	Household Retirement Savings	Accrued Social Security Benefits	Total Retirement Savings
1	$31,500	$6,500	$160,800	$167,300	20%	510%	530%
2	$57,800	$61,900	$262,100	$324,000	110%	450%	560%
3	$86,600	$342,800	$339,200	$682,000	400%	390%	790%
4	$408,200	$1,465,100	$489,300	$1,954,400	360%	120%	480%
All	$146,000	$469,100	$312,800	$781,900	320%	210%	540%

Source: John Sabelhaus and Alice Henriques Volz, "Are Disappearing Employer Pensions Contributing to Rising Wealth Inequality?," Board of Governors of the Federal Reserve System, February 1, 2019, https://www.federalreserve.gov/econres/notes/feds-notes/are-disappearing-employer-pensions-contributing-to-rising-wealth-inequality-20190201.html.

seemingly in best condition to maintain their preretirement earnings are in the third wealth quartile, a group with average preretirement incomes of $86,600. Their retirement savings were roughly equally split between private savings and accrued Social Security benefits, and the total equaled 790 percent of their annual preretirement incomes. At the top of the wealth distribution, households had savings equal to 540 percent of their preretirement incomes.

In short, we simply cannot think about the distribution of private retirement savings without first considering the progressivity of Social Security benefits. Differences in the dollar values of retirement savings are vast, but differences in households' abilities to maintain their standard of living from work into retirement are far narrower. And the function of a retirement system, at root, is to enable households to maintain their preretirement standard of living in old age. The US retirement system as a whole does not appear to do so unequally.

Factoids, however compelling, are no substitute for facts, for the full range of data and analysis that can inform us of how well Americans are preparing for retirement.

7

A Work in Progress: How Extended Work Lives Improve Retirement Income Security

In 1934, the French entomologist Antoine Magnan calculated that bees should not be able to fly. The aerodynamics were all wrong.[1] Bees, not knowing this, continued to fly anyway.

We've also heard for decades that Americans cannot work longer. Our health is too poor, our jobs are too strenuous, and age discrimination is too widespread for longer work lives to meaningfully contribute to boosting income security in retirement.[2]

Fortunately, Americans haven't listened. They have increased their labor force participation at older ages and delayed claiming Social Security benefits, helping contribute to record-high retirement incomes and record-low levels of old-age poverty. This is the story of how extended work lives have contributed toward more secure retirements.

The Financial Benefits of Longer Work Lives

Most discussion of retirement income security focuses on savings: getting employers to offer retirement plans, ensuring that employees sign up, figuring how much they should contribute and how to get them to do so, handling asset allocation issues and driving down fees, and then determining how savers should convert their lump sums into streams of income in retirement. All of that is important.

But perhaps even more important for retirement income security, research shows, is one simple question: At what age do you retire? Saving more during your working years increases your retirement account balance but does not increase your Social Security benefits or reduce the amount of time over which your savings must last.

By contrast, working longer also increases retirement account balances, via extra years of contributions and more time for balances to earn interest. But working longer also increases one's Social Security benefit due to the system's delayed retirement adjustment and reduces the number of years over which one's savings must last.

My American Enterprise Institute colleague Sita Nataraj Slavov and her coauthors have found that "delaying retirement by 3–6 months has the same impact on the retirement standard of living as saving an additional one-percentage point of labor earnings for 30 years."[3] That's an astounding difference based on only a modest delay in retirement.

Similarly, research has concluded that encouraging early retirement benefits was harmful to Americans' retirement income security. Early Social Security benefits were introduced in the late 1950s for women and early 1960s for men, and the availability of reduced benefits collected early led to early retirement and a decline in labor force participation at older ages.

Syracuse University economist Gary Engelhardt and his coauthors found that allowing early retirement benefits caused Americans to claim benefits 1.4 years earlier on average, which reduced benefits by 3 percent for the typical household and even more for low-income retirees. This resulted, the authors say, in "a large associated rise in elderly poverty and income inequality; the introduction of early claiming raised the elderly poverty rate by about one percentage point."[4]

The Evolution in US Retirement Ages

It's worth starting at the beginning, or at least the beginning of the data as they are available. While good data on employment by age do not begin until the early 1960s, we do have figures on the average age at which Americans claimed Social Security benefits back to when benefits were first paid in 1940.

In 1940, the average male claimed Social Security benefits not at the normal retirement age of 65 but at age 68.1; women on average claimed benefits at age 67.4.[5] (See Figure 1.) The idea that current Americans can't work longer is defied by the fact that in the past Americans *did* work longer. And this was when Americans' health and longevity were poorer, age discrimination was not prohibited, and jobs were more physically demanding.

Figure 1. Average Age of Social Security Benefit Claiming, by Gender and Year

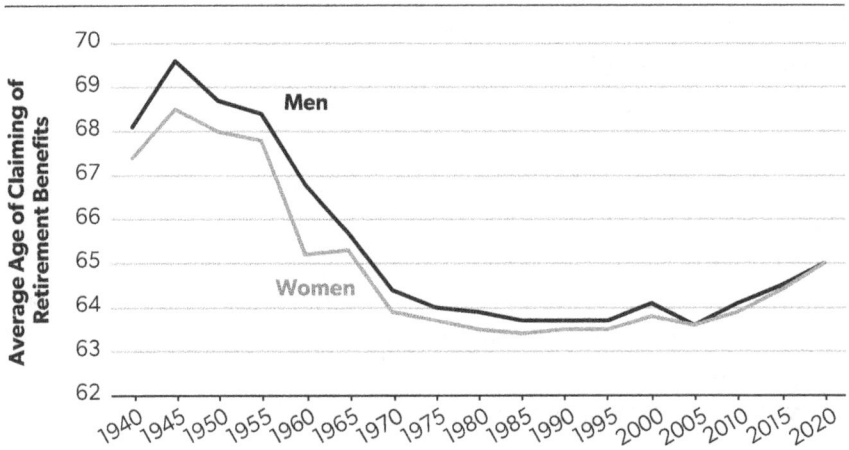

Source: Social Security Administration, *Annual Statistical Supplement to the Social Security Bulletin, 2023,* Tables 6.B, November 2023, https://www.ssa.gov/policy/docs/statcomps/supplement/2023/supplement23.pdf.

Americans delayed claiming benefits in the early years of Social Security's existence for two reasons. First, during Social Security's initial two decades of existence, you simply couldn't claim benefits before age 65. There was no early retirement yet. So mathematically, the average claiming ages for Social Security benefits almost had to be above 65 simply because 65 was the minimum age you could receive benefits.

Second, during its early years, Social Security levied a punitive earnings test on retirees who continued to work. Originally, the receipt of even a single dollar of employment income in a given month would lead to the loss of that entire month's benefits. It wasn't until the 1960 amendments to the Social Security Act were passed that something resembling the modern retirement earnings test emerged, with more revisions in the 1983 Social Security reforms. But the general point is that for much of Social Security's history, a senior had to effectively choose between work and Social Security. Interestingly, many continued to choose work.

However, once reduced early retirement benefits were introduced—in 1956 for women and 1960 for men—the game changed. From 1955 to 1970, the average claiming age for women fell from 67.8 to 63.9 years; for men, the average retirement age fell from 68.4 to 64.4. The average claiming age continued to decline, falling to 63.7 for men and 63.4 for women in 1985, and it remained in these areas for the following two decades.

However, in 2005, Americans began to claim Social Security later, perhaps in response to the gradual legislated increase in the normal retirement age from 65 to 67 that began in 2000. In 2005, both men and women claimed benefits at an average age of 63.6. By 2020, the average claiming age had increased to 65.1 for men and 65.0 for women. By itself, that roughly year-and-a-half delay in claiming Social Security increases the average benefit by about 15 percent and offsets about three-quarters of the benefit reduction that took place via the two-year increase in the normal retirement age legislated as part of the 1983 reforms. By 2022, the most recent data available, average claiming ages crept up again, to 65.2 for men and 65.1 for women, the highest levels since the mid-1960s.

Labor Force Participation

Early Social Security benefit claiming in turn led to a decline in labor force participation at older ages. In 1950, 87 percent of men age 55 to 64 were still in the labor force. By 1970, that declined to 83 percent, falling further to 67 percent by 1990.

For women, the effects were different, because the introduction of early Social Security benefits also coincided with the more general increase in women's labor force participation at all ages. For women age 55 to 64, the labor force participation rate in 1950 was only 27 percent, rising dramatically to 43 percent by 1970 and increasing slightly to 45 percent by 1990. In general, the mid-1980s were the low-water mark for labor supply at older ages, including near retirees age 55 to 64 and those age 55 and over.

Thus, for decades labor force participation at older ages had been declining, encouraged by the introduction of early Social Security benefits in the late 1950s and early 1960s and the general increase in the incomes of the elderly. From 1966 to 1986, the labor force participation rate of Americans age 55 to 64 fell from 62 percent to 54 percent.

But beginning in the mid-1980s, employment among older Americans began to increase. Social norms began to change, mandatory retirement

Figure 2. Civilian Labor Force Participation Rate, Age 55–64

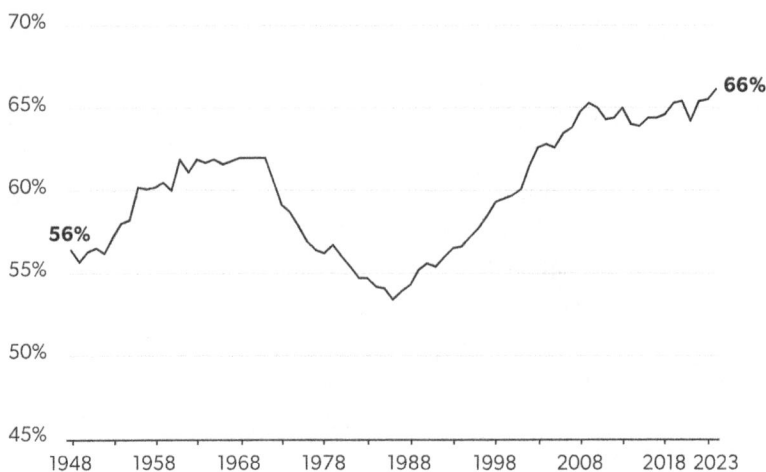

Source: US Bureau of Labor Statistics, Current Population Survey.

rules were relaxed or outlawed, and a traditional pension that punished longer work lives gave way to retirement accounts that rewarded continued work. By 2024, over 66 percent of Americans age 55 to 64 were participating in the labor force, the highest rates since data collection began in the late 1940s. (See Figure 2.)

And these haven't been poorly paid jobs. Despite the growing number of near retirees at work, the median earnings of working Americans age 55 to 64 in 2022 exceeded the median for all workers age 21–64 by about 11 percent.

It was during this period of rising labor force participation when efforts to encourage delayed retirement were discussed but often shot down.

The Prevalence of Physically Demanding Jobs

One common objection to claims that Americans can and should work longer is that too many older workers have physically demanding jobs that they cannot continue as they age. The historical increase in labor force participation at older ages, leading to record levels in 2022, belies this claim. But it is interesting to consider the common objection in greater detail.

The 1983 Social Security reforms, which gradually increased the normal retirement age from 65 to 67, mandated that the Social Security Administration (SSA) study Americans' ability to work longer, focusing on employees with physically demanding jobs.[6] After considering a range of possible definitions of physically demanding occupations, the SSA settled on occupations that required regularly lifting up to 50 pounds. By merging data from the *Dictionary of Occupational Titles*, which includes descriptions of job requirements, and the Current Population Survey, which includes annual data on Americans' occupations, the SSA was able estimate changes in the prevalence of physically demanding jobs over time.

The SSA found that the share of workers employed in physically demanding occupations declined from 20.3 percent in 1950 to 9.1 percent in 1980. Researchers at the Urban Institute updated these figures through 1996, finding a further decline to 7.5 percent.[7] Extrapolation of the annualized rate of decline to 2022 produces a predicted figure of 1.7 percent of 2022 US workers with physically demanding jobs, as defined by the SSA in 1986. (See Figure 3.)

This projected figure closely resembles data from a new Bureau of Labor Statistics dataset, the Occupational Requirements Survey (ORS). The ORS provides a reasonably similar question to the 1986 SSA study: Rather than asking whether an employee "regularly" must lift a given weight, the ORS asks whether an employee "frequently" lifts various weights.

Based on this wording, 1.1 percent of civilian workers in 2022 reported they must frequently lift between 25 and 50 pounds. Less than 0.5 percent of employees reported frequently being required to lift in excess of 50 pounds, implying that at most, about 1.6 percent of current employees satisfy the SSA's 1986 definition of having a "physically demanding job." If trends continue, which obviously is speculative, the share of employees with physically demanding jobs as defined by the SSA in 1986 could decline to 0.6 percent by 2040.

Obviously, a work requirement to lift a given weight is just one way in which difficult work conditions might be quantified. Richard Johnson and Gordon Mermin of the Urban Institute found that, from 1971 to 2006, the

Figure 3. Historical and Projected Share of the Workforce in Occupations Requiring Regular Heavy Lifting of up to 50 Pounds

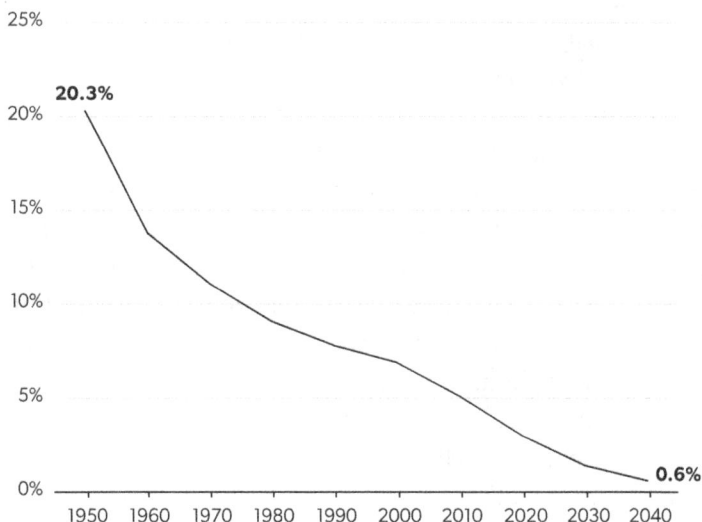

Source: Social Security Administration and Urban Institute through 2006; and author's calculations.

share of all jobs with difficult working conditions, such as outdoor work or high noise levels, fell from 32.1 percent to 24.8 percent, a 22 percent relative decline.[8] The share of jobs that involved either moderate or high physical demands fell from 56.5 to 46.0 percent, while the share with high physical demands such as strength and bending declined from 8.8 to 7.3 percent.

Writing separately, Johnson concluded that declining physical work demands in conjunction with improving health suggested that "more workers are now able to delay retirement and work until older ages than in the past."[9] Among workers age 55 to 60, Johnson found that

> the share of older workers facing virtually no physical demands on the job increased significantly in the 1990s. Nearly 2 out of 5 workers ages 55 to 60 reported in 2002 that their jobs almost never required much physical effort.[10]

Of course, physical requirements are not the only demands a job places on an employee. Mental demands have increased, and many service industry jobs—even if not intellectually challenging—require the employee to interact with the public in sometimes unpleasant or challenging ways. That said, compared to sheer physical demands, it is far less clear that older workers cannot meet cognitive or social needs. Moreover, since most job must impose some demands on employees, the decline of physically demanding jobs almost requires that other such demands must increase.

Some reports argue that far larger shares of Americans face physically demanding jobs. For example, Monique Morrissey of the Economic Policy Institute used the RAND Corporation's 2018 American Working Conditions Survey to conclude that 50.3 percent of older workers in 2022 had physically demanding jobs.[11] However, Morrissey produced a higher figure by loosening the SSA's criteria, such that a variety of job requirements causes an occupation to be deemed physically demanding.[12]

There are two problems with this approach. First, it renders comparisons over time meaningless, since there is no uniform measure of job demands. Second, claims that the majority of older workers are employed in physically demanding jobs undermines the claim that physical demands prevent extended work lives, since—as is discussed later—data show that Americans have extended their work lives significantly despite such conditions.

Workplace Injuries

Injuries and fatalities on the job, which can be taken as a proxy for demanding work conditions, also have declined. According to Bureau of Labor Statistics data, the rate of occupational illnesses and injuries in 2018 was only around one-quarter that of 1972.[13] (See Figure 4.) While a range of factors could be involved in this reduction, an obvious contributing factor would be a reduction in the physical demands of common jobs.

Figure 4. Incidence of Occupation Injuries and Illnesses

Source: US Bureau of Labor Statistics, Survey of Occupational Injuries and Illnesses, https://www.bls.gov/respondents/iif/.

Social Security–Claiming Ages

In 1960, the average male claimed Social Security at age 66.8. In 1961, Congress voted to allow men to claim reduced Social Security retirement benefits as early as age 62, to provide "a degree of protection if they find themselves unable to get work because of conditions beyond their control when they are nearing retirement age."[14] By 1965, the average male claiming age had declined to 65.7. The male claiming ages continued to decline, reaching age 63.7 by 1990. Patterns in claiming ages for women were similar.

Yet today, Americans are delaying claiming their Social Security retirement benefits. In 2022, men and women claimed Social Security retirement benefits an average of 1.5 years later than in 1990, collecting benefits at an average age of 65.1 and 65.2 years, respectively.[15]

Each year of delayed claiming results in an almost 7 percent increase in monthly Social Security benefits for as long as the person lives, along with higher benefits for their surviving spouse. The roughly 1.5-year delay in claiming benefits since 1990 offsets about three-quarters of the reduction in benefits that occurred via the gradual two-year increase in the normal retirement age from 65 to 67, which was legislated as part of the 1983

Social Security reforms. Delayed claiming is one reason the average Social Security benefit paid to a new retiree in 2021 was 36 percent higher after inflation than the average benefit received by a new retiree in 2000.[16]

Countering Objections

The data are now undeniable: If the conditions are right, Americans can and will extend their work lives, and they have been rewarded for doing so.

But one common response to these figures is that only high-income, highly educated Americans are able to delay retirement. Low earners, who are most at risk of poverty in old age, can't follow that same model, it is said. It is true that highly educated workers with less physically strenuous jobs face an easier time in extending their work lives. That pattern is not likely to change.

But over the past three decades, labor force participation among near retirees has risen most rapidly among the least-educated workers. Current Population Survey data show that from 1992 to 2019, employment rates for individuals age 62 to 65 who have only a high school diploma increased from 30 percent to 43 percent, which is a 45 percent relative increase in the share of that group that was still working. (See Table 1.)

By contrast, employment rates for the best-educated Americans with a master's degree or higher rose from 50 to 64 percent, a 28 percent relative increase. Across the educational spectrum, and despite the hurdles lower-income workers face, longer work lives have not been a story of the elite pulling away from the rest, but of the least well-off Americans starting to catch up.

Others might counter that lower-income Americans worked longer only because they had to—a Dickensian vision in which Americans, faced with stingy Social Security benefits, inadequate savings, and the threat of poverty in old age, had no choice but to work long past a decent retirement age.

And yet even this claim falls in the face of the data, discussed in greater detail elsewhere, which show that *retirees' incomes are at record highs* and *poverty in old age has never been lower*. Retiree incomes aren't simply higher on average, driven by a small number of high-income seniors while most other seniors did poorly. Census Bureau research shows that the median,

Table 1. Share of Individuals Age 62–65 Reporting Being "at Work," by Highest Level of Education

	High School	Some College or Associate	Bachelor's	Master's or Higher
1992	30%	33%	42%	50%
2019	43%	46%	56%	64%
Relative Change	45%	38%	34%	28%

Note: The relative change is the percentage working in 2019 divided by the percentage working in 1992, minus one.
Source: US Bureau of Labor Statistics, Current Population Survey.

or typical, retirees' income has never been higher. Incomes at the 25th and 75th percentiles of the income distribution, which might be taken to mark the lower and upper middle class, also have never been higher.[17]

And poverty in old age, which represents the incomes of the poorest US retirees, is at record lows. US seniors could have retired earlier and still enjoyed incomes that matched those of retirees from previous generations but instead chose to work longer and receive the highest incomes on record.

Thinking About Age Discrimination

Various research has shown that, when employers are presented with identical resumes with age as the only difference between two candidates, employers will often opt for the younger applicant.[18] This is, on its face, evidence of age discrimination.

Moreover, the evidence regarding how state laws against age discrimination have affected employment is conflicting. Some studies have found that state antidiscrimination laws provide a small bump up in employment at older ages.[19] Others have found the opposite: that antidiscrimination laws result in lower employment rates among near retirees.[20] The reasoning would be that antidiscrimination laws cause older employees to pose a risk to employers, who may then choose to avoid older workers.

Amid those conflicting findings, we should consider why age discrimination exists. One reason is that, at any given level of salary, older employees are likely to carry higher health care costs for the employer. Even if two employees' salaries are the same, an employer must pay more in total compensation for an older employee than a younger worker. This implies that the seemingly identical workers compared in resume tests are not identical in terms of employer costs. The policy that Medicare must be a secondary payer of health costs exacerbates this problem for employers of older workers.

Likewise, many employers invest in their workers via job training or other resources. A younger employee might remain on the job longer, giving more time for employer investments in employee human capital to pay off and therefore increasing the rate of return on such investments.

None of this is to say that we should abide or tolerate overt age discrimination. But it is to point out that older workers may come with certain costs or disadvantages, and policymakers should think of ways to offset them. For instance, any policies that work to reduce the high health care costs in the United States would disproportionately help older workers, who directly or indirectly bear more of that burden.

Job training for older employees, as has been proposed by several federal policymakers, could in theory help older Americans upgrade their skills to make them more attractive to employers. However, federal job training programs have a mixed record of success.[21] It may make greater sense for policymakers to attack the known obstacles to extended work lives more directly. I discuss some of these in the following sections.

Extended Work Lives Rarely Increase Lifetime Social Security Benefits

Despite the great progress that Americans have made in extending their work lives and enhancing their retirement incomes, there still are significant impediments to expanded employment at older ages. Social Security and Medicare are two such impediments.

The taxes we pay to Social Security and Medicare are termed "contributions," because in return for those taxes, we earn the right to future benefits.[22] To the degree that this link between taxes and benefits exists, Social Security and Medicare taxes would be viewed as deferred income, similar to 401(k) contributions, and should not discourage labor supply in the way that ordinary income taxes do.

It is well-known that an individual who delays claiming Social Security benefits receives an increased benefit when they eventually do choose to claim. This increased benefit is roughly "actuarially fair," meaning the discounted present value of lifetime benefits is approximately the same whether benefits are claimed at age 62, age 70, or any time in between.[23]

However, this rough actuarial neutrality pertains only to the delay in claiming benefits. Most people who delay claiming Social Security will continue to work in the meantime. And Social Security's benefit formula does not compensate delayed retirees for the additional taxes they paid in the meantime. This shifts those additional taxes from a contribution that will be returned later to a "pure tax" that is never returned.

Moreover, as I and my SSA coauthors showed in a 2009 study, most older Americans who choose to work longer receive little or no additional Social Security benefits in return for the additional taxes they pay.[24] This implies that, at the margin, Social Security contributions paid by near retirees should be considered a tax that deters work. There are two reasons for this.

First, Social Security benefits are based on a worker's highest 35 years of earnings. Earnings beyond that 35th year increase benefits only to the extent that they exceed the lowest of the 35 years already used in the benefit formula. Social Security's benefit formula actually worsens this effect, because before a year's earnings are inserted into the formula, they first are "indexed" for the growth of national average wages from the time the earnings took place to the year the worker turned age 60. This indexing makes it even less likely that new earnings occurring during delayed retirement would replace earnings already among the highest 35 counted in the Social Security benefit formula.

Social Security's trustees assume that national average wages will grow about 1.1 percent faster than inflation each year. As a result, for a year of new earnings to be higher in wage-indexed terms than earnings that took place, for instance, 40 years prior, the real, inflation-adjusted value of those new earnings must be about 55 percent higher than the value of the earnings 40 years prior.

Also, the new earnings must increase career-average earnings only to the degree that they exceed the wage-indexed value of those previous earnings. This makes it less likely that additional earnings near retirement will meaningfully increase Social Security retirement benefits.

Second, many women continue to receive an auxiliary Social Security benefit based on their husband's earnings. If a retiree's benefit is equal to less than 50 percent of their spouse's benefits, they are entitled to a supplemental benefit that will raise their total benefit up to 50 percent of the higher-earning spouse's benefit.

In cases in which a retiree receives a benefit based on their spouse's earnings record, additional work and earnings of their own—even if it increases their worker's benefit—would generally be offset by a lower supplemental benefit. As a result, their total benefit likely would not increase, particularly because—as detailed earlier—a retiree increasing their own benefit via delayed retirement is itself difficult.

The research I and my SSA coauthors conducted showed that the median individual who delayed retirement by one year and continued to work receives back only around 2.5 cents in additional benefits for each dollar of additional Social Security taxes they pay. Fewer than one in 10 near retirees who delay retirement receive additional Social Security benefits equal to the additional taxes they pay. For most individuals, delayed retirement would bring zero additional Medicare benefits, because Medicare benefits are conditional only upon qualifying, but beyond that they do not vary with the amount of taxes paid before retirement.

This implies that for most Americans nearing retirement, nearly all the 12.4 percent combined Social Security payroll tax is not a "contribution" for which benefits are received in return, but a "pure tax" on labor. The Medicare payroll tax, which for most earners is 2.9 percent of wages, already functions as a pure tax for most near retirees, since they already have attained the roughly 10 years of contributions necessary for benefit eligibility.

Various research has found that the labor supply of near retirees is particularly sensitive to tax rates, because—unlike middle-aged workers with mortgages and college to pay for—most near retirees face fewer direct financial pressures and have the option to claim Social Security.

In a 2009 study that relied on differences in state income tax rates, Lucie Schmidt of Williams College and Purvi Sevak of Hunter College found that a 10 percent increase in after-tax earnings would increase labor force participation by 7.5 percent among men and 11.4 percent among women.[25] These estimated labor supply elasticities are two to five times higher than the Congressional Budget Office assumes for the working-age population.[26] In other research, John Laitner and Dan Silverman of the University of Michigan found that eliminating the payroll tax at age 59 would cause individuals to delay retirement by an average of 1.1 years.[27]

And in a 2005 study, Eric French of the Federal Reserve Bank of Chicago found that a 10 percent increase in wages as of age 62 would dramatically increase work by seniors, sufficient to boost overall labor supply among workers of all ages by 1.1 percent.[28] Thus, Social Security's benefit formula likely reduces incentives for Americans to extend their work lives.

Some countries resolve this by ceasing collecting pension payroll taxes on older workers. For example, in the United Kingdom, the National Insurance contribution ceases once an individual reaches the state pension eligibility age. In Canada, the payroll tax to fund the Canada Pension Plan is optional beginning at age 65.

I have previously proposed reducing the Social Security payroll tax beginning at age 62 as part of larger reforms to ensure solvency and strengthen the safety net against poverty in old age.[29] Doing so would reduce revenues to the Social Security program—and increasingly so as Americans continue to work later in life. At the same time, to the degree that Americans worked longer because of reducing the payroll tax, revenues from federal income taxes, Medicare payroll taxes, and state income taxes would increase.

Lowering the payroll tax on older workers would reduce Social Security revenues, but individuals who continued to work would pay additional federal income and Medicare taxes. Using the parameters in French's 2005 study, I estimated in 2012 that eliminating the entire 12.4 percent Social Security payroll tax at age 62 would increase total lifetime labor supply by about 1.4 percent.

While a range of parameters needed to be assumed, I estimated that if state income tax revenues were included, the proposal would be roughly revenue neutral, while if state income taxes were excluded, increased federal income and Medicare taxes would offset about 90 percent of the cost to Social Security. That said, to keep Social Security whole would require transfers of general tax revenues to the program.

Moreover, the cost of an age-based payroll tax cut increases as labor force participation by retirees and near retirees rises, as it has and hopefully would continue to do. Nevertheless, an age-based payroll tax cut is one simple means of addressing Social Security's disincentives to delay retirement.

Medicare as Secondary Payer

Medicare plays an additional role in penalizing work at older ages. Medicare begins providing health benefits at age 65, except for seniors who continue to work in a job where the employer provides health coverage. In those cases, federal law designates Medicare as the "secondary payer," meaning Medicare covers only costs that are not covered under the employer's own plan. This policy saves Medicare money, but it also makes older Americans more expensive to hire.

Employers are not given the option to not offer health coverage to older workers, nor can they compensate older workers who opt out of employer-sponsored health coverage with higher wages. Either employers swallow those costs themselves, in which case seniors become less attractive to hire, or employers pass those costs on via lower wages to older employees, in which case work becomes less attractive to retirees. For a 65-year-old, the health costs that employers are forced to bear could reduce employee wages by 15 to 20 percent.[30] Some commentators have called for lowering the Medicare eligibility age from 65 to as low as age 50, which can make these circumstances even more complex.

Together, the implicit taxes presented by Social Security and Medicare can significantly lower either the availability of jobs for seniors or the wages that those jobs will pay.

Americans Have Already Defied the Predictions

There is no magic solution to further increasing work at older ages. Rather, Congress should simply work to keep the economy strong and the labor market vibrant while reducing government-controlled factors—such as health care costs and disincentives built into the Social Security and Medicare programs—that can make older workers less attractive to employers and work less attractive to America's near retirees.

At the same time, policymakers should recognize how far Americans have come in increasing labor force participation at older ages and delaying Social Security claiming, almost entirely without changes of policy dictated by Congress. The flexibility to delay retirement that is built into today's 401(k)s and other retirement accounts stands in contrast to the often sharp disincentives toward longer work lives embedded in the benefit formulas of traditional defined benefit pensions.

The shift from defined benefit to defined contribution plans seems not merely to have increased retirement plan coverage and boosted savings but enabled longer work lives as well. As we look to the future, we should not assume that Americans cannot work longer if given the incentive to do so.

PART III

8

The Cost of Bad Data Is
the Illusion of Knowledge

A sign of greatness is having attributed to you wise things you probably never said.[1] Thus, the physicist Stephen Hawking is reputed to have declared, "The greatest enemy of knowledge is not ignorance, it is the illusion of knowledge." Whether Hawking said it or not—and it appears the more likely answer is "not"—this aphorism readily applies to policy-makers' discussions of retirement incomes in the United States.

The most formidable hurdles to sensible, bipartisan steps to improve retirement security aren't the areas in which lawmakers are admittedly and understandably ignorant. Retirement is a complex issue, and elected officials cannot be experts in everything. Rather, the larger problem is the opinions in which lawmakers are confident but which, it turns out, simply aren't correct.

I have had the privilege, if not always the pleasure, of testifying before Congress many times regarding Social Security and retirement savings. In nearly every hearing, a member of Congress will say something along the lines of this statement from Representative John Larson, then the chairman of the House of Representatives Subcommittee on Social Security: "For nearly two-thirds of beneficiaries, Social Security represents the majority of their income. For more than one-third, it represents more than 90 percent of their income."[2] Similar statements can be found over time from, among many others, the National Academy of Social Insurance, which declares that "Social Security is the major source of income for older Americans. . . . For one in three (33 percent), it is all or nearly all of their income."[3]

For minority groups like blacks and Hispanics, nearly half of all retir-ees may be claimed to be entirely dependent on Social Security, at least according to the statistics cited by members of Congress, analysts, and activists. Figures like these understandably make it difficult to endorse reductions to Social Security benefits and indeed make a compelling case for expanding the program.

We see similar figures showing how poorly the US private retirement savings system is working. According to the most common federal government household survey—the Current Population Survey (CPS), administered by the US Census Bureau and the Bureau of Labor Statistics—only about one-third of current retirees receive *any* sort of benefit from a private retirement plan, such as a pension or 401(k). Moreover, despite continuing government efforts to expand retirement savings, this figure—in which the typical retirees receive nothing from private retirement plans—has remained more or less unchanged for decades.[4]

But, as discussed in earlier chapters, the quality of data on retirement incomes is poor, meaning that in many cases, figures stated for retiree incomes simply aren't correct.

Most analysis of retirement incomes relies on household surveys, in which retirees themselves respond to questions regarding various sources of income. While seemingly reasonable, many household surveys have difficulty accurately measuring the benefits that retirees collect from private retirement plans such as traditional pensions, individual retirement accounts (IRAs), and 401(k)s. In part, this is due simply to erroneous responses by survey respondents: While people tend to estimate their Social Security benefits fairly accurately, for whatever reason, they often make errors in describing how much they receive from private retirement plans.

But errors also arise due to the way in which these surveys define "income": In general, to be counted as income, money must be received regularly, such as from Social Security or a traditional pension. As-needed lump-sum withdrawals from retirement accounts are less likely to be included in most survey measures of income, even if they provide crucial resources in retirement. As US retirees have shifted from traditional defined benefit pensions that pay a regular monthly benefit check to retirement accounts, where retirees typically withdraw funds as needed, household surveys will increasingly understate retirees' true incomes.

To illustrate, I turn to data from the CPS. In 1979, 26 percent of Americans age 65 to 74 reported to the CPS that they received income from a private retirement plan. By 1986, the share of retirees receiving private retirement plan benefits rose to 33 percent. And in the following three and half decades, almost nothing changed: In 2018, only 34 percent of 65- to 74-year-olds reported receiving private retirement plan benefits.

Seemingly, progress on expanding retirement savings stalled over a third of a century ago, despite multiple pieces of federal legislation and regulatory changes designed to boost retirement savings. According to ostensibly credible federal government data, the typical retiree, then and now, receives nothing from a traditional pension, 401(k), 403(b) employer-sponsored plan, or IRA.

The lack of private retirement plan benefits seemingly makes retirees increasingly reliant on Social Security for income in old age. In 2010, according to the Social Security Administration (SSA), 36.3 percent of seniors received nearly all—90 percent or more—of their income from Social Security benefits, up from 30 percent in 1996 and 31 percent in 2000.[5] In other words, Americans have grown more reliant on Social Security even as the program's finances have become more precarious. The 401(k) revolution, it seems, had failed.

And yet, how can that be? As shown previously, savings in private retirement plans increased dramatically as 401(k) retirement accounts succeeded traditional defined benefit pensions. Moreover, the share of working women also has increased, which should have raised the percentage of retiree households receiving at least some income from a private retirement plan.[6] How could more retirees not be deriving more income from private retirement savings plans?

The answer, put bluntly, is that the data cited are simply wrong. The CPS does a poor job of measuring the benefits that retirees receive from private retirement plans, particularly drawdowns of retirement account balances. The CPS's measurement shortcomings have long underestimated retirees' incomes, but the CPS's errors have only grown larger as 401(k)s and IRAs have increasingly replaced traditional defined benefit pensions. How have these errors taken place?

The Faults with CPS Data

Over half a century ago, the SSA conducted a survey of the income of US retirees, asking seniors how much income they derived from various sources. While useful in many regards, the SSA was upfront in noting a key weakness in its 1968 study: The survey's results understated income from assets by more than half when compared to total asset income as reported to the IRS.

This error by itself reduced the survey's average annual incomes of retirees by more than 10 percent relative to what IRS figures showed.[7] While noting this error, which had been apparent to SSA researchers since an even earlier study published in 1963, the SSA study then went along its way. Six decades later, faulty survey data still shape how we view retirement income security in the United States.

Unfortunately, most other studies of retiree incomes since then have followed the same path as the early SSA studies: using flawed data to measure the financial well-being of retirees and, as a result, often coming to faulty conclusions. Today, for instance, we still read that over one-third of seniors rely on Social Security benefits for nearly their entire incomes, a statistic that while compelling, also is false and has been known to be false for decades. Efforts to correct these data have faced resistance, with the best explanation being that activists would be unhappy with any data that undercut their claims of a retirement crisis.

The key problem is one of definitions: Most government surveys seek to measure "money income," which is defined by the Census Bureau as "income received *on a regular basis*."[8] (Italics added.) Social Security benefits, traditional pension payments, or a paycheck from a job in retirement come every month; they are "regular" and thus are counted as income. Likewise, interest on savings or dividends from stock holdings also are paid regularly and should be counted.

But what about when a retiree draws down their savings as the funds are needed, be those savings either inside or outside a retirement account? Such irregular payments aren't "income" as far as the Census Bureau surveys are concerned. And so, for decades, these irregular sources of income have not been counted as parts of the incomes retirees can rely on in old age.

The effects of the mismeasurement of retiree incomes are widespread, because nearly all the information we commonly receive on retiree incomes comes from these household surveys, most commonly the CPS.

The results are shocking. The average incomes of US retirees, as measured by the US Census Bureau? Wrong. The official poverty rate for retirees? Wrong. The share of income that retirees receive from Social Security benefits? Wrong. The percentage of retirees who receive nearly all their income from Social Security? Wrong. The incomes that retirees receive from IRAs and 401(k)s? Wrong.

Fortunately, while the Census Bureau has strict definitions of what counts as income, the IRS isn't nearly so picky. The IRS doesn't care whether you get your income regularly or irregularly. It just cares that you pay your taxes. If you draw down your 401(k) as needed, that's income just the same as the pension or Social Security benefit check that arrives each month. However retirees might feel about this, the IRS's commonsense perspective helps shed light on how large the errors are in household survey measurements of retirement incomes.

In a 2012 *Wall Street Journal* op-ed, pension expert Sylvester Schieber and I pointed out that the CPS reported that in 2008 Americans age 65 and older collected about $228 billion in income from IRAs, employer-sponsored retirement plans, and annuities.[9] But for that same year, the IRS reported that Americans received about $568 billion from these same sources. This implies that official statistics, which are commonly used to portray Americans' supposedly inadequate retirement incomes and show that IRAs and 401(k) plans cannot work, in fact capture only about 40 percent of the benefits paid by these plans. These figures would seem to be relevant to discussions of retirement income adequacy and retirement policy overall.

But not to our critics, who seem wedded to the notion that personal saving for retirement just doesn't work. The Economic Policy Institute's Monique Morrissey wrote that our points seemed "politically driven" and "misleading" and, in any case, didn't amount to much.[10] Morrissey asked, "Is it true that some Census data underreports distributions from DC [defined contribution] plans and IRAs? Is this news? Does it matter?"

Her answers: "Yes, no, and not much." Keep moving, nothing to see here: It had long been recognized that the CPS understated retirement benefits, she wrote, but this was a significant problem in reporting incomes only for the extremely rich, who have more retirement account withdrawals to be understated. Put another way, "The long and short of this story," Morrissey wrote, "is that *one* measure of senior incomes understates the resources available to *some, mostly upper-income,* households."[11] (Emphasis added.)

And yet subsequent research conducted by the US Census Bureau shows that is not at all the case. In 2017, two Census economists, Adam Bee and Joshua Mitchell, leveraged the bureau's access to otherwise confidential IRS data on households' incomes.[12] Bee and Mitchell linked IRS data to responses from the CPS so that, for a variety of income sources, they could compare how much income seniors actually received to what they reported receiving in the CPS. They confirmed the suspicions raised in the Biggs-Schieber *Wall Street Journal* op-ed, and then some, while adding additional detail of their own.

Bee and Mitchell analyzed US households age 65 and over in 2012. To start, they found that the share of retirees actually receiving benefits from private retirement plans was far higher than previously assumed. In the CPS, only 37 percent of age 65 and over households in 2012 reported receiving any benefits from a private retirement plan. But in IRS data, 61 percent of seniors were shown to be receiving private plan benefits. This dramatic increase is simply the product of using more accurate data.

These increases in retirement benefit receipt were consistent across race lines, as shown in Table 1. For instance, in the CPS, only 35 percent of black households age 65 and over in 2012 were reported to have any income from a private retirement plan. But more accurate IRS data show that 55 percent of black seniors received private plan benefits in 2012. Increases were even larger among Asian and Hispanic retirees.

Receipt of retirement plan income also increased across income lines, albeit in less uniform ways. In the lowest fifth (or quintile) of total income, only 12 percent of seniors in 2012 were reported in the CPS as receiving retirement plan benefits. Retirement plan receipt increased only to 14 percent when using IRS data, a relatively modest 21 percent increase. (See Table 2.) This is not terribly surprising when one considers that households in the bottom income quintile had an average income of slightly less than $10,000, meaning they heavily depended on Social Security and Supplemental Security Income (SSI) benefits.

However, the largest increase in retirement benefit receipt revealed via the more accurate IRS data isn't at the top of the income distribution, as some critics presumed. Instead, the largest increases were in the *second* income quintile, where annual household incomes average at a modest $22,000. Only 24 percent of this group are reported to receive private

Table 1. Receipt of Retirement Plan Benefits by Race and Data Source, Households Age 65 and over in 2012

	CPS	IRS	Relative Increase
All	37%	61%	167%
White	38%	63%	168%
White, Non-Hispanic	39%	66%	167%
Black	35%	55%	161%
Asian	20%	38%	193%
Hispanic (Any Race)	20%	37%	187%

Source: Adam Bee and Joshua Mitchell, "The Hidden Resources of Women Working Longer: Evidence from Linked Survey-Administrative Data," in *Women Working Longer: Increased Employment at Older Ages* (University of Chicago Press, 2017).

Table 2. Receipt of Retirement Plan Benefits by Income Quintile and Data Source, Households Age 65 and over in 2012

	CPS	IRS	Relative Increase
Lowest	12%	14%	121%
Second	24%	47%	194%
Middle	42%	77%	182%
Fourth	53%	86%	162%
Highest	52%	83%	159%

Source: Adam Bee and Joshua Mitchell, "The Hidden Resources of Women Working Longer: Evidence from Linked Survey-Administrative Data," in *Women Working Longer: Increased Employment at Older Ages* (University of Chicago Press, 2017).

retirement plan benefits in the CPS, doubling to 47 percent using IRS data.

While receipt of retirement plan benefits did increase for the top income quintile when measured using IRS data, this increase was substantially smaller than for the second- and middle-income quintiles. The likely explanation is that households with higher levels of benefits from private plans are more likely to receive at least some in a form that the CPS counts as income and are more likely to have benefit receipt accurately reported in the CPS survey data.

The IRS data are more likely to capture unreported benefit receipt from retiree households with more modest incomes. IRS data also corrected reporting errors made outside the pension context, such as lower-income seniors confusing Social Security and SSI benefits.

Shining a New Light on Poverty in Old Age

Overall, more accurate data dramatically affected measured retirement incomes, and not merely for the rich. The median senior household income as reported in the CPS was $33,800, while the more accurate IRS data calculated a median income of $44,400, a 31.3 percent increase. For households age 65 and older at the 95th percentile of the income distribution, true incomes as measured in IRS data were 16.0 percent higher than as reported in the CPS survey response.

But for the median household, one right in the center of the income distribution, their income in IRS data exceeded their CPS-measured income by 30.3 percent. Even for retirees at the 25th percentile of the income distribution, meaning they are poorer than three-quarters of all retirees, their true incomes were 25.5 percent higher than in CPS data.

The Census Bureau study provides additional interesting and useful insights on poverty in old age. The more accurate IRS income data show substantially lower levels of poverty in old age than are presented in the official poverty figures based on CPS data. For 2012, official statistics based on CPS data showed that 9.1 percent of seniors had incomes below the federal poverty threshold. But using IRS data that more accurately track retirees' incomes, only 6.9 percent of seniors had incomes below the poverty threshold, a nearly one-quarter reduction in the number of Americans age 65 and over living in poverty.

The two Census Bureau economists also found that, contrary to decades-long claims that Americans are under-saving for retirement, the share of individuals living in poverty actually declines as Americans shift from work into retirement. Five years before claiming Social Security retirement benefits (denoted as time t in Figure 1), 5.5 percent of Americans had incomes that put them below the poverty threshold. By five years following retirement, only 3.6 percent of seniors had sub-poverty-level

Figure 1. Poverty Rate in Years Preceding and Following Social Security Benefit Claiming

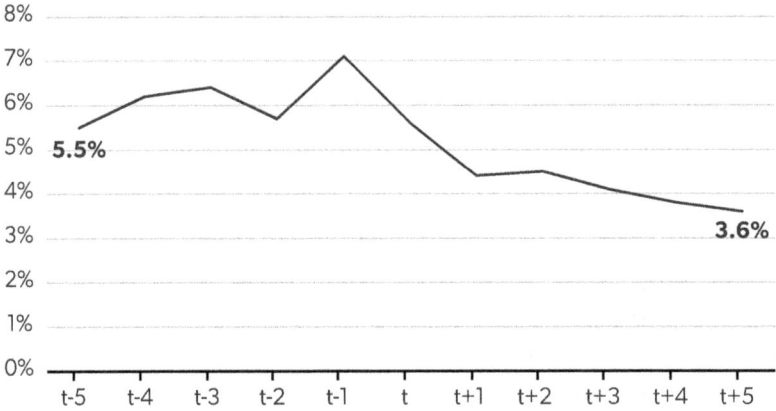

Source: Adam Bee and Joshua Mitchell, "The Hidden Resources of Women Working Longer: Evidence from Linked Survey-Administrative Data," in *Women Working Longer: Increased Employment at Older Ages* (University of Chicago Press, 2017).
Note: The "t" represents the age at which the person claimed Social Security benefits. For example, "t–2" is two years before claiming benefits, and "t+2" is two years after.

incomes. It is difficult to paint a picture where these low-income Americans should have saved more for retirement, given that their risk of poverty was higher before retirement than after.

Bee and Mitchell apply a similar analysis to individuals living above the poverty line. For individuals at the 25th, 50th, and 75th percentiles of the retirement income distribution, they present data on annual incomes up to five years following retirement and inflation-adjusted average pre-retirement earnings from 10 to 25 years before claiming Social Security. Table 3 presents these pseudo-replacement rates comparing incomes five years following retirement to average annual earnings at the same percentile five, 15, and 25 years before retirement.[13]

These are not true replacement rates, in that Bee and Mitchell compare the incomes of retirees at a given percentile of the earnings distribution to those of pre-retirees at the same percentile of the income distribution. A true replacement rate compares a retiree's income to their own preretirement earnings, which the figures presented by Bee

Table 3. Pseudo-Replacement Rates for Different Income Percentiles and Measures of Preretirement Earnings

	25th Percentile	Median	75th Percentile
Five Years Following	$24,100	$39,191	$60,904
10 Years Prior	$21,561	$39,086	$54,192
Pseudo-Replacement Rate	89%	100%	89%
15 Years Prior	$23,854	$40,992	$58,261
Pseudo-Replacement Rate	101%	96%	105%
25 Years Prior	$26,044	$41,928	$57,562
Pseudo-Replacement Rate	93%	93%	106%

Source: Adam Bee and Joshua Mitchell, "The Hidden Resources of Women Working Longer: Evidence from Linked Survey-Administrative Data," in *Women Working Longer: Increased Employment at Older Ages* (University of Chicago Press, 2017).

and Mitchell do not do. To the degree that retirees in a given income percentile resided in a different earnings percentile before retirement, their individual replacement rates could be lower or higher than the figures represented in Table 3.

While the specific figures differ between percentiles and measures of preretirement earnings, in all cases, the pseudo-replacement rates significantly exceed the 70 percent target rate financial planners often put forward. For instance, retirees at the 25th percentile of the income distribution had average annual incomes of $26,044. From five to 25 years before retirement, earnings at the 25th percentile averaged from $21,561 in the 10 years before retirement to $26,044 per year in the 25 years before retirement. Income in retirement equaled between 89 and 101 percent of inflation-adjusted average annual preretirement earnings.

For retirees with median incomes and at the 75th percentile of the income distribution, these pseudo-replacement rates were similar. This implies that retirees across the income distribution tended to substantially surpass the standard 70 percent replacement rate target.

Bee and Mitchell also found that poverty increases far less as retirees age than is generally supposed. In the CPS data used for the official poverty measure, the share of seniors living in poverty increases dramatically with

Table 4. Poverty Rates by Age, in Current Population Survey and IRS Data

	CPS	IRS
Age 65–74	7.9%	6.7%
Age 75–84	9.9%	7.0%
Age 85 and Over	12.2%	7.6%

Source: Adam Bee and Joshua Mitchell, "The Hidden Resources of Women Working Longer: Evidence from Linked Survey-Administrative Data," in *Women Working Longer: Increased Employment at Older Ages* (University of Chicago Press, 2017).

age, from 7.9 percent for seniors age 65 to 74 in 2012, to 9.9 percent for seniors age 75 to 84, and to 12.2 percent for seniors age 85 and over. This large increase over retirement seemingly buttresses the view that retirees may run short of money and lends support to policies such as higher annual cost-of-living adjustments for Social Security to boost benefits for the oldest retirees.

However, the more accurate IRS data Bee and Mitchell used show a much more muted increase in poverty. From age 65 to 74 to age 85 and over, the poverty rate increases only from 6.7 percent to 7.6 percent, a 13 percent relative increase as compared to the 54 percent relative increase in the CPS data. (See Table 4.)

Moreover, even this much smaller difference in poverty rates by age shown in IRS data may not be driven by retirees running short of money so much as by succeeding generations tending to be better off than the ones that preceded them. To illustrate, consider that in 2012, seniors age 75 to 84 had a poverty rate of 7.0 percent according to IRS data. But if we look at the poverty rate for Americans age 65 to 74 in 2002—the same cohorts of individuals—their poverty rate was almost precisely the same. Once again, this paints a far more positive picture of retirement income adequacy than one would guess given the presumption that a retirement crisis was well underway.

Reliance on Social Security

The IRS data used in the Census Bureau study also show that retirees are significantly less reliant on Social Security than is commonly claimed. While it is often stated that roughly two-thirds of retirees receive the majority of their income from Social Security benefits and one-third of retirees receive nearly all their income from Social Security, the Census Bureau analysis of IRS data showed different results. Only 42 percent of retirees receive half or more of their income from Social Security benefits, and only 12 percent of retirees receive 90 percent or more of their income from Social Security. This difference between the CPS and IRS figures occurs for two reasons.

First, as discussed earlier, the CPS data simply underestimate retiree household incomes. Second, when the SSA and others would calculate retirees' dependency on Social Security, they would do so on a household basis, presenting statistics in terms of "aged units" rather than individual seniors. (An "aged unit" is either a single senior or a married couple in which the husband is over 65 or the husband is under 55 and the wife is over 65.) Since couples tend to be less dependent on Social Security than single retirees are, this approach overstated the share of individual seniors who depend heavily on Social Security benefits in retirement.

One reason that administrative data show seniors to be less reliant on Social Security is that these data more accurately pick up the benefits retirees receive from private retirement plans, be they traditional defined benefit pensions or withdrawals from retirement accounts such as IRAs and 401(k)s. Among the 2012 seniors analyzed in the Bee and Mitchell study, only 44 percent are reported to have received private retirement plan benefits in the CPS. Yet IRS data show that 68 percent of seniors actually received such benefits. The true picture of Americans' retirement incomes is simply far more optimistic than is commonly portrayed.

Since the release of Bee and Mitchell's Census Bureau study in 2017, other research has confirmed their findings. In 2021, the SSA released an analysis by economists Irena Dushi and Brad Trenkamp that similarly matched IRS data to CPS survey responses. Using individuals age 65 and over in 2015, Dushi and Trenkamp found that rather than 8.7 percent of seniors with incomes below the poverty threshold, only 7.1 percent of seniors had sub-poverty incomes.[14] Simply using accurate data, some 800,000 seniors were removed from "poverty" that they were not experiencing in the first place. Dushi and Trenkamp also found that only 13.8 percent of seniors relied on Social Security for 90 percent or more of their income, barely one-third the share that is commonly claimed.

Other measures of poverty show even lower poverty rates for US seniors than those measured using IRS income data. The alternative approach is to measure not the money that seniors take in via income but the money that flows out via spending. This approach plausibly better captures the share of seniors who are *living* in poverty, as opposed to simply having sub-poverty-level incomes. The consumption poverty approach may capture resources that are not included even in IRS measures of income, such as informal gifts from friends or relatives, food stamps, Temporary Assistance for Needy Families, and certain other welfare benefits.

Bruce Meyer of the University of Chicago and James Sullivan of Notre Dame have produced a Consumption and Income Poverty Dashboard that uses Consumer Expenditure Survey data to measure the percentage of seniors who spend less than the federal poverty threshold.[15] Figure 2 compares this expenditure measure of poverty to the official federal poverty threshold based on income.

For most of the past 60 years, consumption poverty among the elderly has exceeded income poverty; that is, even if retirees had incomes above the poverty line, many did not spend an amount that exceeded the poverty threshold. In 1961, the earliest year for which household expenditure data are available, three-quarters of seniors reported spending an amount lower than the federal poverty threshold. In 2020, only 5.5 percent of Americans 65 and over spent less than the federal poverty threshold, a figure that is well below the 9.0 percent that the Census Bureau, using CPS data, calculates as having incomes below the poverty line.

Thus, currently only about one in 20 Americans age 65 and older truly live below the federal poverty threshold. Even this number is too high, and in later chapters, we examine ways to address poverty in old age. But these figures show how far retiree incomes in America have come, even over a period in which official data sources often show only scant progress.

Figure 2. Official Poverty Rate and Consumption Poverty Rate, Age 65 and Over

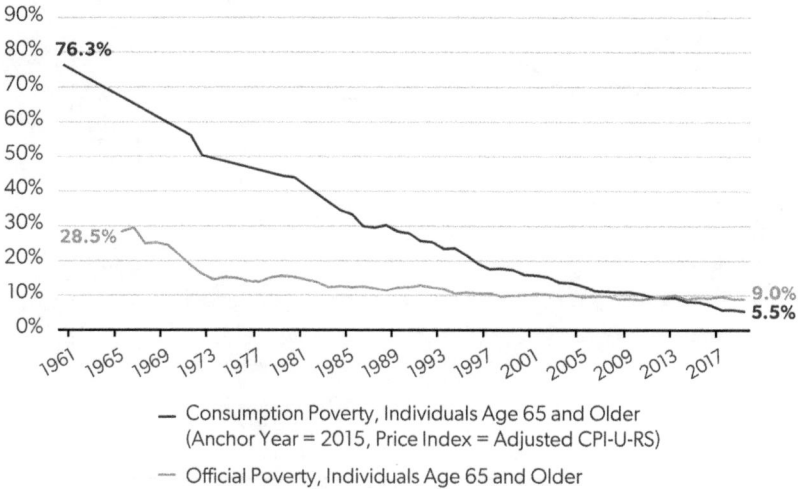

— Consumption Poverty, Individuals Age 65 and Older
(Anchor Year = 2015, Price Index = Adjusted CPI-U-RS)

— Official Poverty, Individuals Age 65 and Older

Source: University of Chicago, Harris School of Public Policy and Notre Dame University, Wilson Sheehan Lab for Economic Opportunities, "Consumption and Income Poverty Dashboard," 2022, http://povertymeasurement.org/dashboard.
Note: "CPI-U-RS" stands for Consumer Price Index for All Urban Consumers Research Series.

A Project to Provide Better Data

In an effort to provide higher-quality data consistently, the Census Bureau initiated the National Experimental Wellbeing Statistics (NEWS) project, "a project to create the most accurate estimates of household income and poverty" by combining household survey data with administrative data and other methodological improvements.[16] The first NEWS release in 2023 focused on data from 2018 and provided a much clearer picture of retiree incomes.

Interestingly, the data shortcomings discussed in this chapter have little effect on nonaged households. So the improved NEWS data showed almost no change in the incomes of households under age 65. And yet, for Americans age 65 and over in 2018, the results are truly startling: For householders age 65 and over, median household income is 27.3 percent

**Figure 3. Change to Household Income via More Accurate Data
Reporting, Age 65 and over in 2018**

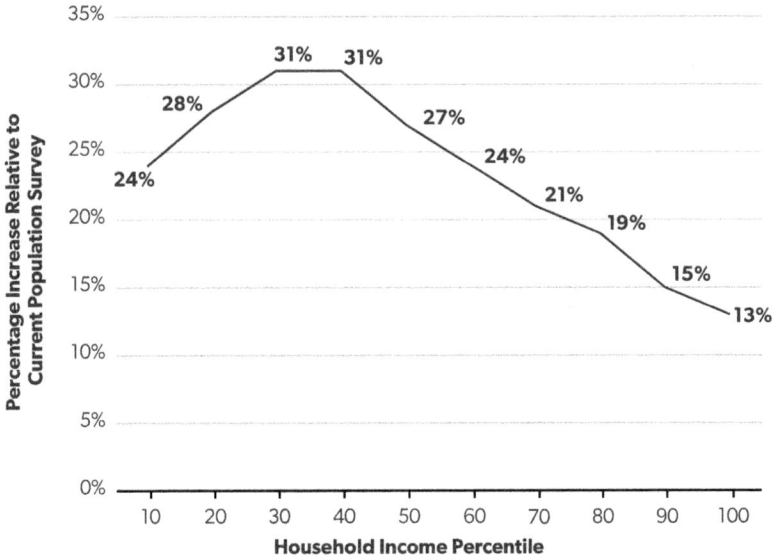

Source: US Census Bureau.

higher than in the survey estimate, and for people age 65 and over, poverty
is 3.3 percentage points lower than the survey estimate.

The median income of households age 65 and over in 2018 increased
from $43,700 as reported in the CPS and the American Community Sur-
vey to $55,610 in the Census Bureau's administrative data–augmented
NEWS data.

The Census Bureau's NEWS data are particularly good news for lower-
income retirees, whose incomes increase the most when measured using
accurate administrative data versus household survey responses. (See Figure 3.) For retirees in the bottom three quintiles of the income distribution, true incomes average 28 percent higher than is reported in household
survey data versus only a 16 percent average increase for seniors in the
highest three deciles of the income distribution.

It is difficult to understate the importance of these figures. For example, proposals to expand Social Security might increase the benefits of a

low-earning individual by perhaps 20 percent, most of which would be off-set by reduced benefits from the means-tested SSI program. So the net effect on seniors truly at risk of poverty would be modest.

By contrast, what the more accurate Census Bureau data show is that, without doing anything, incomes for the bottom decile of the retiree income distribution are 24 percent higher than previously thought. For the second and third deciles, which might be thought of as the working poor, incomes are 28 and 31 percent higher, respectively.

And yet, despite analysis showing conclusively the flaws in the most common household survey data on retirement incomes, to this day, data from the CPS dominate discussions of retirement income security. Members of Congress will still claim that one-third of seniors receive virtually all their income from Social Security, when the true figure is less than half that amount. And we still will hear about the inadequate number of seniors receiving benefits from private retirement plans.

And the flaws only grow worse over time, as a greater share of retirees come to rely on drawdowns of retirement account balances, which are not counted as income, versus regular monthly checks from traditional pensions, which are. As Mitchell put it in conversation, whether you think there is a retirement crisis, there is a crisis of retirement data.

9

Retiree Incomes: How Far We've Come

Private pensioners aren't begging on the streets, nor are they remotely likely to face that prospect.

—*New York Times*, January 4, 1978

What has happened to retiree incomes since the *New York Times* wrote those words over 40 years ago? Based on news coverage of retirement issues, one might think that since some past golden age of retirement, when everyone retired with a gold watch and a guaranteed monthly pension benefit, retirement security has gone to hell in a handbasket. But is that really true?

As shown in the previous chapter, the most commonly used data on retirement incomes, the federal government's Current Population Survey, is nearly useless for these purposes. It so severely understates the true incomes that seniors receive that it is not up to the task of assessing retirement income security over time. For this reason, I turn to administrative data that measure retirement incomes directly rather than via retirees' responses to survey questions.

The Congressional Budget Office (CBO) has produced detailed tabulations of data drawn from the IRS's Statistics of Income dataset.[1] The IRS data derive not from households' reports of their incomes on tax returns, which may be full of errors or understatements to reduce taxes, but from data provided to the IRS by the various parties that provide that income to retirees—employers, the Social Security Administration, investment firms, retirement plans, and so on.

This approach offers a far more accurate view of the incomes American retirees have received over time. The IRS doesn't care how you derive income from a pension, whether it be regular checks, a lump-sum payout, or some combination of the two. The IRS cares only about how much income you actually collect, and it's good at tracking those numbers via submissions from the retirement plans that issue the checks, not self-reports from the retirees who receive them.

A key disadvantage of the IRS data is that it is not possible to show incomes by race, gender, or other variables that are common in analyses of retirement incomes using household survey data. For that reason, the initial presentation here focuses on changes in average (or mean) retiree household incomes over time. Discussion of the distribution of retirement incomes, drawing on other sources, will follow.

Income in the CBO and IRS data includes three main components:

- Market income, which includes income from earnings, investments, private retirement plan benefits, employer health care contributions, employee contributions to retirement and other deferred benefit plans, and employer contributions to payroll taxes and unemployment insurance premiums;

- Social insurance benefits, which include Social Security, Medicare, unemployment insurance, and workers' compensation insurance benefits; and

- Means-tested benefits, which include Medicaid; the Children's Health Insurance Program; the Supplemental Nutrition Assistance Program, commonly referred to as "food stamps"; and Supplemental Security Income benefits.

Netted against these income sources are federal income taxes.

The CBO generally presents these figures in one of three groups. The first is market income, which consists of labor income; business income; capital income (including capital gains); income received in retirement for past services, such as pensions and retirement accounts; and other nongovernmental sources of income. The second is income before transfers and taxes, which includes market income plus social insurance benefits such as Social Security and Medicare. The third is income after transfers and taxes, which adds means-tested transfer benefits and deducts federal taxes.

The figures presented are all in 2018 inflation-adjusted dollars and are measured for households age 65 and above. Table 1 highlights the levels of

Table 1. Mean Incomes for Households Age 65 and over, 1979 and 2018

Year	Market Income	Income Before Transfers and Taxes	Federal Taxes	Means-Tested Transfers	Income After Taxes and Transfers	Average Tax Rate	Average Transfer Rate
1979	$34,100	$50,400	$9,100	$1,000	$42,300	18%	2.0%
2018	$72,200	$105,100	$15,500	$2,900	$92,500	15%	2.8%
Growth, Percentage	112%	109%	70%	190%	119%		
Growth, Dollars	$38,100	$54,700	$6,400	$1,900	$50,200		

Source: Tabulations of IRS Statistics of Income data by Congressional Budget Office, *The Distribution of Household Income, 2018*, 2021, https://www.cbo.gov/publication/57061.

each definition of income in 1979 and 2018, showing differences in both percentage and dollar terms.

In 1979, the average elderly-headed household—in which the head of household is age 65 or over—had a total market income of $34,100, measured in 2018 dollars. When social insurance benefits such as Social Security and Medicare are added, mean income rises to $50,400. The average retiree household in 1979 received means-tested transfer benefits worth $1,000, for an "average transfer rate" of 2.0 percent of income. The average retiree household in 1979 also paid $9,100 in federal taxes, for an average tax rate of 18 percent of income.

By 2018, mean market income for retiree households had increased to $72,200, an increase of 112 percent in real terms and $38,100 in dollar terms. Adding social insurance benefits raised mean retiree household income to $105,100. Means-tested transfer benefits nearly tripled from $1,000 to $2,900, rising from 2.0 to 2.8 percent of mean incomes. Average federal taxes rose to $15,500 per retiree household in 2019, but the average tax rate for retirees fell from 18 percent to only 15 percent of income.

The simple reality is that retirees are far better off today than they were in even the relatively recent past. Incomes measured using various definitions have more than doubled, while tax rates have fallen.

Table 2. Changes to Nonelderly Household Incomes, 1979 to 2018

	Average Market Income	Average Income Before Transfers and Taxes	Average Income After Transfers and Taxes
1979	$71,227	$73,125	$57,793
2018	$115,456	$119,013	$100,925
Growth, Percentage	62%	63%	75%
Growth, Dollars	$44,229	$45,888	$43,132

Source: Tabulations of IRS Statistics of Income data by Congressional Budget Office, *The Distribution of Household Income, 2018*, 2021, https://www.cbo.gov/publication/57061.

For comparison, it's worth calculating the same figures for nonelderly-headed households.[2] (See Table 2.) From 1979 to 2018, average market incomes for nonelderly households rose from $71,227 to $115,456, an increase of 62 percent (versus 112 percent for elderly-headed households). Once social insurance benefits are included, incomes before taxes and transfers rose by 63 percent (versus 109 percent for retirees). After adding means-tested transfer benefits and subtracting taxes, average nonelderly incomes rose to $100,925, a real increase of 75 percent from 1979.

Put another way, in 1979, the average retiree household had an after-tax-and-transfer income equal to 73 percent of that of nonelderly households. By 2018, average retiree household incomes were equal to 92 percent of the incomes of working-age households. Given that the cost of living tends to decline in retirement, the average retiree in the United States today likely has a higher standard of living than the average working-age American, a remarkable shift from the days when seniors were deemed to be eating cat food.

The CBO tabulations of IRS data also allow limited discussion of how income is distributed. The CBO provides data on fifths, or "quintiles," of the overall income distribution, which includes both elderly and nonelderly households. If retirees had the same incomes as the overall population, one would expect that about 20 percent of retirees would be in each of the five income quintiles. Yet in 1979, 32 percent of seniors had incomes in the lowest quintile of the overall income distribution, while just 16 percent were in the highest-income quintile. That is, retirees were twice as

Figure 1. Percentage of Households Age 65 and over in Each Quintile of the Overall Income Distribution, 1979 and 2018

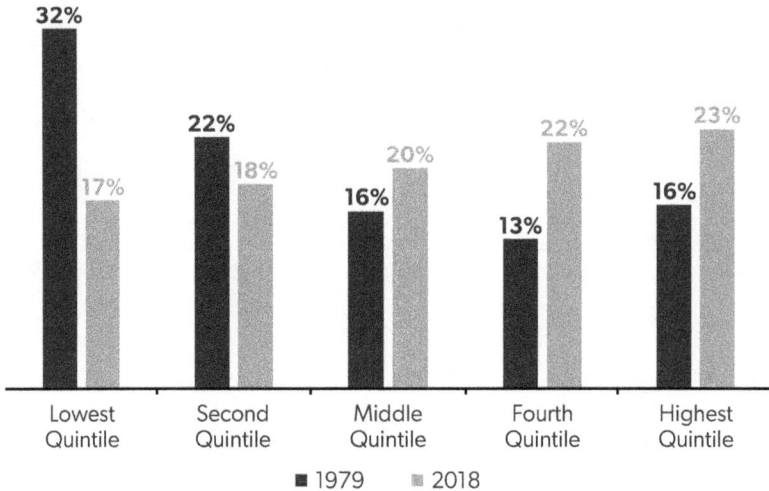

Source: Tabulations of IRS Statistics of Income data by Congressional Budget Office, *The Distribution of Household Income, 2018*, 2021, https://www.cbo.gov/publication/57061.

likely to be among the poorest Americans as they were to be among the richest. (See Figure 1.)

By 2018, however, the situation had changed dramatically: Only 17 percent of seniors had incomes in the lowest quintile, making them underrepresented among the poor, while 23 percent of those over age 65 had incomes in the highest quintile. Simply put, as recently as 1979, retirees were disproportionately low income, while today they are disproportionately upper income.

Other data support these conclusions and provide additional data. Two Census Bureau economists, Joshua Mitchell and Adam Bee, were allowed to match household survey responses to the respondents' tax returns, providing a much more accurate view of retirees' incomes.[3] (See Chapter 8 for more details on their work.) Bee and Mitchell's approach, which is difficult for nongovernmental researchers to view due to privacy concerns, shows that incomes have grown for all classes of retirees, from the poor to the rich.

Table 3. Median Household Incomes, Age 65 and Over

	1990	2015	Growth
25th Percentile	$19,817	$27,523	39%
Median (50th Percentile)	$37,800	$52,200	38%
75th Percentile	$63,853	$92,110	44%

Source: Adam Bee and Joshua Mitchell, "Do Older Americans Have More Income Than We Think?," *Proceedings. Annual Conference on Taxation and Minutes of the Annual Meeting of the National Tax Association* 110 (2017): 1–85.
Note: Figures are in 2015 inflation-adjusted dollars.

Looking from 1990 to 2015, Bee and Mitchell found that household incomes at the 25th percentile of the retiree income distribution, representing lower-income retirees, grew by 39 percent above inflation. (See Table 3.) At the median, representing middle-income retirees, household incomes increased by 38 percent in real terms. At the 75th percentile, representing the upper middle class, incomes grew by 44 percent. These figures show that growing prosperity among retirees has been widely shared.

It is worth considering how retiree incomes increased so much. As we have seen, income has many components—Social Security, pensions, earnings, and so on. What drove record-high incomes among US seniors? The answer is, roughly, everything. Returning to the IRS data tabulated by the CBO, we can view the growth of various sources of income for senior households.[4]

From 1979 to 2018, average Social Security benefits for the over-65 population rose from $12,300 to $20,400, a 66 percent increase over and above inflation. This increase is partly the result of Social Security's benefit formula, which raises the initial benefits paid to new retirees in line with the growth of economy-wide average earnings.[5]

But as large as the growth of Social Security benefits may appear, the percentage increase in inflation-adjusted Social Security benefits is the smallest among the major income groups. Average benefits paid from private retirement plans grew from $5,000 to $21,300 per household, a 326 percent increase. This increase is due to higher participation in private retirement plans and increased contributions to those plans.

Earnings in retirement grew by 128 percent, from $8,600 to $19,600. Higher earnings in retirement were driven by a rise in the labor force participation rate for over-65 Americans from 13 percent in 1979 to 18 percent in 2018 and higher dollar wages contingent on working.[6]

Average investment income, including income from business holdings, grew by 117 percent, from $19,700 to $42,800. Employer contributions for health, retirement plans, and payroll taxes, which are de facto income, increased by 486 percent, from $700 to $4,100. This increase was driven by higher rates of employment, higher health care contributions, and higher wages, which increase retirement plan contributions and payroll taxes. Means-tested transfers, unemployment, and workers' compensation insurance increased by 158 percent, from an average annual value of $1,200 to $3,100.

The dollar value of annual Medicare benefits increased by 224 percent, from $3,800 to $12,300. While it is unintuitive to think of Medicare benefits as income, they are counted as part of disposable income because they free up cash income for other uses. Average federal taxes increased from $9,100 to $15,500, but the 70 percent increase in taxes was, after Social Security benefits, the second slowest-growing factor affecting incomes. This increase in tax payments is noteworthy since, as shown earlier, the average tax rate on seniors' incomes dropped. Seniors are paying more federal taxes today because their incomes are so much higher.

These data undercut the narrative that it is only through Social Security benefits that seniors can maintain even a precarious financial existence in retirement. In fact, for the average retiree household, even a 66 percent increase in the real value of Social Security benefits over the past four decades has held back income growth since every other component of income has grown even faster. The benefits paid by private retirement plans grew by twice as much in dollar terms as Social Security benefits. Had private retirement benefits and earnings in retirement grown only at the 66 percent rate that Social Security benefits increased, total average retirement incomes in 2018 would have been 13 percent lower than the actual average income received by seniors in that year.

This discussion has been data heavy, but it leads to some surprising conclusions. Back when the *New York Times* editorial page spoke in 1978, seniors weren't as financially secure as the *Times* claimed: Americans over age 65 were still on average poorer than the rest of society. By 2018, however, that picture had changed significantly: Rather than being a disproportionately poor group, seniors are today a disproportionately rich one.

Further, the growth of retiree households' incomes has been led by the things many doomsayers said couldn't happen: more work in retirement and greater income from personal retirement savings. While Social Security benefits rose substantially in real terms, it was the slowest-growing component of retiree incomes over the past four decades.

Challenges remain, and obviously not every retiree today is financially secure. But anyone who adheres to a pessimistic view of the US retirement system and financial health of America's seniors is paying insufficient attention to the data.

10

Will I Run Out of Money? Tracking Spending in Retirement

Perhaps the greatest concern retirees have is running out of money in old age. As we saw in Chapter 4, some studies claim that the typical American will run out of money after 10 years of retirement, with another 10 years to go before they reach their life expectancy. Someone who approaches retirement with inadequate savings can save more and delay retirement, but a retiree who runs dry in old age has few options available. There seemingly is little room for error and many opportunities for things to go wrong.

And yet the data tell a different story. In fact, running out of money in old age is relatively rare, even in the face of late-in-life health care costs. The main reasons appear to be that household spending in retirement declines by significantly more than most people anticipate, household incomes decline by significantly less, and household wealth often does not decline.

The explanations are counterintuitive, given what we often read. To begin with, retirees are not spendthrifts; they tend to manage their assets conservatively. Moreover, while health care costs, including long-term care, may theoretically impose a crushing financing burden on retirees, in practice those costs tend to be modest, relatively rare, and focused on those who can most afford to bear them. In short, while many things could go wrong during retirement, for the vast majority of people, they don't.

Steady as She Goes?

So how do we reconcile different portrayals of retirement spending? It helps to start with the basic assumptions used in most analyses of retirement income adequacy. The simplest interpretation of the life-cycle model assumes that individuals wish to consume the same amount in every period of their life, both before and after retirement. Most financial planning advice follows the same path.

This doesn't mean that retirees would spend the same amount they did just before retirement, because the cost of living generally declines after retirement due to lower taxes, the cessation of work-related costs, potential downsizing of housing, and other factors. However, most analysts and financial planners tend to assume that once retired, households generally need the same income each year throughout retirement, after adjusting for inflation. Social Security cost-of-living adjustments, which increase benefits to account for the effects of inflation, implicitly assume the same thing.

Most analyses of retirement readiness also assume that retirees desire a constant income each year. Doing so is consistent with a simple interpretation of the life-cycle model of consumption and makes the math easier. For illustrative purposes, these analyses generally assume that retirees convert their savings to an inflation-adjusted annuity that pays the same amount every year throughout retirement. Even if we know that most retirees don't actually purchase annuities, this analytical device is assumed to provide a reasonable estimate of the steady income that retirees would desire. If that income falls below a given level, such as being able to replace 70 percent of a retiree's preretirement earnings, then the retiree is often deemed to have inadequate savings or other sources of retirement income.

Prominent studies such as the Center for Retirement Research's National Retirement Risk Index or the National Institute on Retirement Security's various studies on retirement savings conclude that Americans face a retirement crisis. All assume that retirees desire a steady income in old age to finance steady expenditures. So do more sophisticated retirement projection models such as the Social Security Administration's Model of Income in the Near Term and the Urban Institute's Dynamic Simulation of Income Model, even if they project a more encouraging picture of Americans' retirement prospects.

The Reality of Retirement Spending

While it's simple to assume that retirees wish to have a steady income throughout old age, that's not in fact how retirees actually spend. Various data sources across the US and other countries have found that household expenditures tend to *decline* as retirees age.

The RAND Corporation's Michael Hurd and Susann Rohwedder, building on over a decade of previous work, found that, contrary to conventional practice of retirement savings analysts, spending declines significantly in old age.[1] Hurd and Rohwedder, whose research was discussed in Chapter 4, used Health and Retirement Study data to track the specific spending patterns of retiree households from 2005 through 2019. They found that older retirees spend far less than new retirees do, even after including health care costs.

Although the degree of spending decline differs, a general pattern of lower spending is true for single retirees and married retirees, for more-educated and less-educated retirees, and for those with high levels of wealth and lower levels of wealth. By age 90, a retiree generally spends between 40 and 60 percent less than they did at age 65. These figures include costs for health care and long-term care.

As we will see, declining spending in old age is not unique to seniors in the United States. The question is: What explains it?

What Happens to Incomes?

Yale economist James Choi and his coauthors used IRS data to analyze how households' incomes change as they move through retirement.[2] IRS data are based on administrative filings from retirement plans, employers, governments, and other sources of income. Looking at the 1941 birth cohort, Choi and his coauthors show a median income at age 60 of $46,205. They show that by age 70, the median income falls only to $40,722, which is 88 percent of income at age 60. By age 76, income remains at 83 percent of age 60 levels.

More recently, Peter Brady and Steven Bass of the Investment Company Institute used IRS administrative data to track the incomes of Americans born in 1945 from 2000, when they were age 55, through 2017, when they reached age 72. Brady and Bass measured what they call "spendable income," which equals gross income minus amounts saved for retirement and paid in taxes.[3]

Brady and Bass found that the typical 72-year-old had a spendable income equal to 90 percent of what they received at age 55. Moreover, these spendable income replacement rates were higher for those who had lower incomes at age 55. For those in the bottom 25 percent of the income distribution at age 55, the typical replacement rate at age 72 was over 100 percent. In other words, they have more money to spend at age 72 than they did at age 55.

At the middle of the income distribution, the median replacement rate at age 72 was between 90 and 95 percent of income at age 55, while it was only for the top 10 percent of the income distribution at age 55 that replacement rates at age 72 fell below 80 percent. True replacement rates are likely even higher than those Brady and Bass reported because, in addition to declines in retirement saving and tax costs, housing payments, work-related costs, food costs, and other costs of living tend to decline in old age.

All this leads to an entirely counterintuitive result: Most retirees remain net savers, meaning they spend less than they take in. The Federal Reserve's Survey of Consumer Finances asks Americans whether in the previous year their spending exceeded, equaled, or fell short of their incomes. In the years immediately preceding retirement, when households are at the peak of their retirement savings efforts, it's not surprising that 58 percent of Americans report spending less than their annual incomes, with 28 percent spending about the same as they took in and only 15 percent spending more than their incomes. (See Table 1.)

What may be surprising is that this pattern continues nearly unchanged throughout retirement, when we would expect spending to exceed income by a substantial margin. By age 70 to 74, only 13 percent of households spent more than they took in, and even by age 90 to 94, fully 88 percent of households spent less than or the same as their incomes.

Other analysis adds detail to these findings. Economist David Love and his coauthors analyzed how retirees' savings changed over their retirements.[4] Instead of looking only at the dollar value of assets, they examined the income that retirees' wealth holdings could provide them over the years. They found that household wealth declines more slowly than remaining life expectancies, which means that the annual incomes retirees can provide for themselves increase rather than fall as they age. While not every household's wealth rises, retirees were more than twice as likely to

Table 1. Self-Reported Household Spending by Age

Age	Spending Exceeded Income	Spending Equaled Income	Spending Was Less Than Income
55–59	15%	28%	58%
60–64	15%	29%	57%
65–69	14%	30%	57%
70–74	13%	33%	54%
75–79	13%	35%	52%
80–84	13%	35%	52%
85–89	10%	40%	50%
90–94	12%	41%	47%

Source: Author's calculations from Survey of Consumer Finances, 1989–2019.

Table 2. Income, Spending, and Wealth, by Wealth Quintile, Retirees Age 65–70 in 2000

Wealth Quintile	Averages, 2000–10		Change in Financial Assets, 2000–10
	Income	Spending	
Bottom	$19,264	$23,814	$5,211
Second	$22,002	$24,221	$10,553
Middle	$32,610	$30,616	$32,726
Fourth	$39,442	$33,219	$72,109
Highest	$66,812	$43,325	$17,537

Source: Chris Browning et al., "Spending in Retirement: Determining the Consumption Gap," *Journal of Financial Planning* 29, no. 2 (2016): 42–53.

experience a large increase in their affordable annual income than they were to experience a large decline.

Likewise, in a study published in the *Journal of Financial Planning*, Chris Browning and his coauthors analyzed income, spending, and wealth for a group of 65-to-70-year-olds who retired in 2000.[5] Using data from the Health and Retirement Study, they followed 704 retirees from 2000 through

2010, tracking how much they received in income each year, how much they spent, and how their financial assets changed over that 10-year period.

The authors divided retirees into five groups, ordered by their wealth. Across all five wealth quintiles, average financial assets *increased* from 2000 through 2010. (See Table 2.) That is to say, after 10 years of retirement, most retirees had more financial assets than when they started.

Moreover, in the top three wealth quintiles, average annual spending didn't equal average annual incomes. In other words, most retirees weren't spending what they collected from Social Security, employer pensions, and other common income sources, much less spending down their savings. Among households in the bottom two wealth quintiles, spending exceeded incomes, but the increase in asset values was more than enough to cover the difference. Overall, the authors found that a retiree household with typical wealth could increase its annual spending by 8 percent over a 30-year retirement while still holding 40 percent of their financial assets in reserve against a health emergency or an extremely long lifespan.

Sudipto Banerjee, writing for the Employee Benefit Research Institute, found that "retirees generally exhibit very slow decumulation of assets."[6] Banerjee followed seniors over the first 18 years of their retirement and found that the median individual who began retirement with less than $200,000 in nonhousing assets spent down only about one-quarter of their assets. Retirees who started with between $200,000 and $500,000 spent down only 27.2 percent of their savings, while those with at least $500,000 in savings spent down less than 12 percent of their assets.

Looking at the lowest-wealth group, those with less than $200,000 in nonhousing wealth, about one-third spent down 80 percent or more of their assets within the first two decades of retirement. But a similar share of low-wealth retirees had increased their assets over that 18-year period. As Banerjee notes, "This is in sharp contrast with the predictions of models used to measure retirement security."[7]

These data, and others besides, establish that most retirees aren't coming close to running out of money. Contrary to the standard assumption that retirees will need to spend the same amount each year, retirees' spending drops considerably as they age. Moreover, while household survey data show a considerable decline in retirees' incomes as they grow older, more accurate IRS data show much higher incomes in old age. As a result, most retirees appear to not even spend their entire incomes, much less exhaust their savings.

As a result, today's retirees are likely to pass on trillions of dollars in wealth to their heirs, who will in turn retire with greater wealth than today's retirees had. According to the consulting firm Cerulli Associates, older Americans will transfer some $70 trillion between 2018 and 2042, of which $61 trillion will be passed down to their heirs;[8] Generation X alone is projected to inherit some $31 trillion. In earlier research, economist Jeffrey Brown and his coauthors found that a substantial number of retirees fail to spend down their retirement accounts and, if given the opportunity, would even avoid taking the minimum distributions required under tax law.[9]

The question is: Why? Why does spending fall even when both financial planning assumptions and simple economic theory indicate that we should wish to spend about the same from one year to the next?

Are Retirees Running Out of Money?

The most common explanation you might hear for declining spending in retirement is simple: Retirees reduce their spending when they realize they're running short of money. Behavioral economics tells us that many people are impatient and prefer to consume things today rather than having more in the future.

Likewise, many of us are financially illiterate and haven't planned carefully for retirement. In theory, many households could wake up after retirement and realize they're financially ill-prepared to support themselves over the next two decades or more. And for many years, that's what analysts thought.

Going back to the 1990s and early 2000s, compelling evidence appeared to show that, upon reaching retirement, Americans discovered they had inadequate savings and were forced to cut back on their standard of living. While we may not know the precise age at which we will retire, we are aware for decades before retirement of the need to set aside savings for old age. If individuals are rational planners and if they have available to them the tools to save for retirement, their standard of living at retirement should be similar to that immediately before retiring.

However, a series of studies initially appeared to find that households entering retirement dramatically reduced their spending, which the researchers assumed signaled that retirees suddenly realized they had not saved as much as they needed. Studies of both British and American households found sharp drops in spending at retirement. In particular, new retirees spent less on food—seemingly an essential purchase that households would scale back on only under the most adverse of circumstances.

This result was first found for new retirees in the US by economist Douglas Bernheim and his coauthors.[10] James Banks and his coauthors, writing of British retirees, stated, "We argue that the only way in which the life-cycle hypothesis could be reconciled with the remaining unanticipated dip in consumption would be with the systematic arrival of unexpected adverse information at the time of retirement"—such as that you had not saved enough to support yourself in old age.[11] Economists, with their presumption that *homo economicus* is forward-looking and fully rational, deemed this the "retirement consumption puzzle."

But later research solved that puzzle—and much more encouragingly. While retirees spent less on food, economists Mark Aguiar and Erik Hurst found, it wasn't because they ate less. Caloric consumption stayed more or less the same in old age. It was because retirees spent less money purchasing food at restaurants and more time preparing food at home.[12] In retrospect, this is easy to understand: While working, you might eat out at lunch or grab a meal after work, but in retirement, you can prepare a good meal at home at a lower cost. Retirees also can even pay less for an identical food item.

In a subsequent study, Aguiar and Hurst used price scanner data from grocery stores and time diaries showing how households spend their day.[13] They show that retirees spend more time shopping, but their reward for that is paying lower costs for precisely the same items as are purchased by pre-retiree households. Again, think of purchasing from a warehouse store or purchasing items where they are on sale versus paying a higher price at a convenience store. This money-for-time trade-off makes sense once a person has stopped working, and one could expect it to produce savings in various areas of expenditures, not merely food.

Other research tells a similar story. Rohwedder and her RAND Corporation colleagues looked at not merely how much retirees spend but what they spend their money on.[14] And the patterns of spending do not point toward resource constraints driving declining spending through retirement.

Consistent with other work, Rohwedder and her coauthors find that spending on transportation shrinks as a share of households' budgets from age 50–54 to age 85 and over. This makes sense if declining health makes it more difficult for retirees to drive on their own or if, as a younger observer might conclude, seniors just aren't as interested in driving a brand-new car. Spending on trips and vacations rises to a peak from age 65 to 69 then declines to less than half that level once retirees reach age 85. Again, health status plausibly explains these changes.

But if retirees were running out of money, one might expect that the first cuts would be to the most discretionary parts of their budgets, and nothing is more discretionary than gifts to charitable causes, friends and relatives, or others. Yet Rohwedder and her coauthors find that spending on gifts and donations more than doubles as a percentage of households' incomes from age 50–54 to age 85 and over. They conclude that for the majority of retirees, the decline in spending as they aged was more or less voluntary.

The Role of Health Care Costs

Even if retirees aren't running out of money, they might underspend early in their retirements out of a desire to build a buffer against health costs that might spring up late in life. The biggest fear many retirees face is high health care expenses, which—at least in news media articles—could easily lead to bankruptcy.

It would be surprising if health care concerns did not play a role, as studies by economist Mariacristina De Nardi and her coauthors conclude. They write, "The risk of living long and requiring expensive medical care is a key driver of saving for many higher-income elderly."[15] In this interpretation, comparing seniors' spending habits to their income and assets could produce a misleadingly positive view of their financial health in retirement, since low levels of spending earlier in retirement are driven by the need to conserve resources for later in life.

Imagine that retirees wished to spend the same amounts "on themselves" each year throughout retirement, meaning the same amounts for food, clothing, shelter, entertainment, and so on. Health care, by contrast, was thought of not so much as an ordinary consumption good but as a de facto tax that must be paid to be alive and kicking to enjoy food, clothing, and shelter. Moreover, retirees are aware that out-of-pocket health spending will be higher in old age than when they are newly retired. All this seems plausible.

And yet, how might spending patterns over retirement look under these assumptions? The answer is almost precisely the opposite of what we see in the data: Instead of total household expenditures beginning high and then declining, we would expect to see spending beginning low but then scaling up as health costs increase. That is, spending in non-health categories would remain roughly the same each year, but out-of-pocket spending on health care would increase year by year. Thus, while precautionary saving against late-in-life health costs obviously takes place, it does not seem sufficient to explain the broader pattern of spending in old age.

How Much Does Health Care in Retirement Cost?

It is worth taking a more detailed look at health costs in retirement. In a typical piece of news reporting, the *New York Times* reports on a Fidelity Investments estimate that a "65-year-old retiring this year can expect to spend an average of $157,500 on health and medical costs over a roughly 20-year retirement."[16] It is easy to see why such figures are newsworthy and why Americans preparing for retirement tremble at their sight.

And yet, there often is less to these figures than meets the eye. In 2021 data from the Consumer Expenditure Survey, households age 65 and over spent over $900 per year more on health care than Americans age 55 to 64. But, compared to 55- to 64-year-olds, seniors spent nearly $2,000 less per year on food, more than $4,000 less on housing, almost $3,800 less on transportation, and more than $6,000 less per year on contributions to Social Security and retirement savings plans. (See Table 3.) In other words, lower spending in various areas more than offsets rising expenditures for health care.

Moreover, the share of retirees' incomes spent on health care has barely increased since the mid-1980s. According to the federal government's

Table 3. Higher Health Spending in Old Age Offset by Lower Spending in Other Areas

	55–64 Years Old	65 Years and Older	Difference
Health Care	$6,093	$7,030	$937
Food	$8,419	$6,490	–$1,929
Housing	$23,007	$18,872	–$4,135
Transportation	$10,936	$7,160	–$3,776
Pensions and Social Security	$8,792	$2,371	–$6,421

Source: Consumer Expenditure Survey, 2021.

Consumer Expenditure Survey, in 1988, Americans age 65 and over spent 11.8 percent of their incomes on health care. In 2020, seniors spent an average of 12.8 percent of their incomes on health care.

Further, even this modest increase is sensitive to the year in which we begin and end measurement, since annual figures fluctuate from year to year. Overall, health spending as a percentage of incomes for the population age 65 and over increased by 0.02 percentage points per year from 1988 to 2020, a shockingly low rate of increase given what we read about health costs in retirement. Moreover, if household surveys significantly understate retirees' true incomes, as research discussed elsewhere confirms, then health spending as a percentage of actual retirement incomes is likely to be lower.

It is a similar story with long-term care costs, which are a plausible reason retirees might tend to underspend their savings. Long-term care, in particular nursing homes, produces costs that are theoretically nightmarish in size. In practice, however, long-term care costs tend to be more manageable. For instance, consider the following factoids presented by CNBC:

- About 70% of people over age 65 will need some form of long-term care before they die, per an analysis by the Urban Institute.

- The average annual cost of a private room in a nursing home was $102,000 in 2019, according to a survey by insurance company Genworth.

- Research by the Insured Retirement Institute found that 45% of boomers have no retirement savings and more than a quarter of those who do have less than $100,000.[17]

How can that *not* point toward a retirement crisis?

A 2017 study by Hurd and his coauthors provides some insight. Using data from the Health and Retirement Study, they followed members of households born between 1919 and 1923 over their retirement. Similar to other research, they found that significant numbers of retirees will need to access a nursing home in old age.

For the birth cohorts they examined, 56 percent of retirees used a nursing home, a higher rate of use than other studies have estimated. However, as they point out, that figure is highly skewed: Over half of retirees who used a nursing home stayed fewer than 10 nights in a nursing home over their entire retirement. (Working the math, this implies that across the entire retiree population, including those who never used nursing home care, 72 percent spent fewer than 10 nights in a nursing home.)

Among those who did use long-term care, a small number of retirees accounted for the vast majority of time in nursing homes. Seventy-five percent of retirees who needed nursing home care required fewer than eight months of nursing home care during their retirements. But 5 percent of retirees required four years or more in a nursing home.

Despite headlines declaring how much retirees might need to save to cover long-term care, the fact that nursing home costs are highly skewed—meaning that a small number of households spend a great deal on long-term care while the majority spend little or nothing—points toward this being a risk to insure against and not a cost to save for. Saving to self-insure against the unlikely but astronomical costs of a long-term stay in a nursing home is akin to saving to replace your home in case it burned down.

Moreover, the reality is that many Americans already are effectively insured for long-term care via Medicare, Medicaid, and other government programs. In the Hurd et al. study, 75 percent of retirees paid less than $1,000 toward long-term care, and 90 percent paid less than $20,000— again, over their full retirements, not per year. Ninety-five percent of retirees spent less than $47,000 on long-term care. Relative to earlier studies,

Hurd and his coauthors find that long-term care is more common and affordable than previously thought.

In a 2022 study, again using Health and Retirement Study data, Rohwedder, Péter Hudomiet, and Hurd looked at both the level and the distribution of out-of-pocket health costs in retirement.[18] Out-of-pocket health costs in the study include doctors' visits; hospitalizations; dental care; nursing home stays; in-home formal care; drugs, including over-the-counter medications; and other medical expenditures (in data from 2010 onward).

The study is designed to measure the risk that retirees will have to spend large additional amounts on health care in excess of the Medicare or private health insurance premiums they pay each month. The authors found that changes to health policies, such as the introduction of the Medicare Part D prescription drug benefit in 2006 and the Affordable Care Act passed in 2010, have increasingly shielded seniors from high health costs.

Rohwedder, Hudomiet, and Hurd find that "for the typical person, out-of-pocket health care expenditures are relatively modest."[19] For the median or typical senior, annual expenditures never exceeded $1,200 between 1998 and 2018 and in fact declined over that period, falling by 37 percent from 2004 through 2018. At the 95th percentile of out-of-pocket spending, representing the high end, annual per-person costs rose from $5,600 in 1998 to $11,100 in 2004 but then declined to $6,500 in 2018. In other words, much of the risk of crippling out-of-pocket costs that retirees fear has already been addressed.

Moreover, they find that health costs vary based on the retiree household's ability to pay.

> Those in poor health and with few resources often spend little OOP [out of pocket] because of Medicaid, even if their health care utilization is high. Those with substantial economic resources tend to spend a greater fraction of their overall spending on OOP health expenses (despite being in better overall health).[20]

In other words, the public health insurance system is working more or less as intended.

The three RAND economists also analyzed economic insecurity related to health care costs in old age, examining cases in which high health costs made it difficult for seniors to purchase medications or food. They found that economic insecurity due to health costs was lower among households age 65 and over than among households age 55 to 64. Moreover, contrary to what one might expect, health cost insecurity continued to decline with age.

> A consistent finding is that measures of distress are lower in the population 65 or older and the measures continue to decrease with advancing age. . . . For example, the rate of insecurity among single persons 80+ is 17 percentage points lower than among those 55 to 59.[21]

Now, this doesn't mean that long-term care or retiree health care costs in general aren't a problem, but they're mainly a problem for the government programs that pay most of the costs. For instance, the Congressional Research Service reports that in 2020, spending on long-term care and supports totaled $475 billion. But out-of-pocket spending by seniors on deductibles, copayments, and other costs covered only 13.5 percent of the total, equaling $64 billion.[22]

According to IRS data, the total income of Americans age 65 and over in 2020 was $2.55 trillion.[23] This means that seniors themselves devoted at most 2.5 percent of their incomes to long-term care costs—and likely less because some long-term care services are provided to Americans under age 65. Government programs such as Medicare and Medicaid covered about 72 percent of total costs, with the remainder covered by private insurers and other private providers. Long-term care, like much of health care in general, is indeed a financing problem, but for governments more than for households.

That the government finances so much of long-term care complicates the problems that Americans face in planning to finance whatever share of long-term costs they are likely to be responsible for. The problem is that the largest source of government funding for long-term care, Medicaid, is means-tested, providing benefits only to seniors with income and assets below given levels, including any private long-term care insurance.

A person who anticipates being below those thresholds should rationally make no effort to provide for long-term care, including private insurance. The existence of Medicaid acts as an implicit tax on the benefits provided via a private long-term care insurance policy, because many of those benefits could be received from Medicaid even if a policy was not purchased.

Economists Brown and Amy Finkelstein found that between two-thirds and three-quarters of the benefits provided through private long-term care insurance could otherwise be received through Medicaid, making private polices not cost-effective for many retirees.[24] The authors conclude that, even if the private insurance market were robust and policies were available at actuarially fair prices, the simple presence of Medicaid can act as a significant disincentive to insure against long-term care costs.

Many retirees may simply decide to chance it rather than pay substantial premiums for a private policy that may not provide much better protection than Medicaid does for free. In follow-on research, economist Leora Friedberg and her coauthors find that private long-term care insurance, even if offered on attractive financial terms, doesn't make sense for low- and middle-income retirees due to the protections already provided by Medicaid and other government programs.[25]

In 2017 research, economists James Poterba and Steven Venti looked at how the onset of specific health ailments affected retiree households' wealth.[26] This approach captures not only direct out-of-pocket health expenditure but also related effects that might affect a household's budget, such as the need for a spouse to cease working, travel costs related to health treatments, and home renovations to accommodate an infirm household member. Their results again highlight the role played by Medicaid and other needs-based providers of health care.

For instance, for a retiree with a net worth between $100,000 and $500,000, a stroke would reduce their net worth by $5,445. However, for a retiree with a net worth of less than $100,000, a stroke would reduce their wealth by only $1,058, while for a retiree with a net worth greater than $500,000, a stroke would cost them $14,952. In other words, while health care costs in retirement can be substantial, they also tend to be focused on retiree households that can most afford to bear them.

Moreover, many retirees hold a potential source of funds for nursing home care via their homes. Hurd and his coauthors find that women are much more likely to use long-term care than men are. Of female retirees, 64 percent use at least one night of nursing home care over their retirement, versus only 51 percent of men, and the mean number of nights of nursing home care is over twice as high for women as for men.

The reason appears to be that, because men have shorter average lives than women do, men are more likely to require long-term care during a period in which their spouse remains healthy. Men are more likely to receive care at home from their spouse. But by the time a female retiree is more likely to require long-term care, her spouse may have passed away, and, lacking others to care for her, a nursing home may be the best or only option available.

However, once the surviving spouse enters a nursing home, their home is no longer necessary and can be sold to help finance that care. This is not a perfect solution by any means, because it relies on average life expectancies for men and women and not every retiree is married or a homeowner. Moreover, some seniors wish to pass their home on as an inheritance rather than using it to finance their own nursing home care.

Nevertheless, the availability of home equity to serve as backstop financing for long-term care may help explain how most retirees can weather these costs even without having purchased a private insurance policy. Economist Thomas Davidoff finds that, while most retirees do not sell off their homes, they are more likely to do so when a household member enters a nursing home.[27] The option to access home equity if necessary may help explain how retirees can cover long-term care costs and why so few retirees purchase long-term care insurance policies.

How Do Retirees Spend in Other Countries?

We can also gauge the effects of health care costs on retirees' spending by looking at retirement spending patterns in countries where the government covers most health costs in retirement. And in those countries, retiree spending seems to follow a similar declining path to that seen in the United States.

In a 1992 study, economist Axel Börsch-Supan examined the spending habits of retirees in Germany.[28] Börsch-Supan found that retirees' savings do tend to decline between age 60 and 70. But after age 70, retirees tend to spend considerably less than their incomes would allow, such that they start rebuilding their wealth. From age 80 onward, typical German retirees save over 10 percent of their incomes. Economist Malene Kallestrup-Lamb and her coauthors used data on Danish retirees, finding that rather than spending down their wealth, nearly half increased their assets between age 68 and the time of their death.[29]

Fred Vettese, a Canadian actuary, finds that from age 53 to age 75, spending by Canadian households declines by over 40 percent.[30] European Commission economist Cesira Urzi Brancati and her coauthors focus on retirees in the United Kingdom.[31] Their study finds that spending begins to decline after age 70 and that by age 80, a typical British household spends 43 percent less than a household that is age 50.

Banks and his coauthors compare retiree spending in the US and the UK, concluding that the desire to protect against late-in-life health expenses likely explains part of US retirees' low spending relative to their retirement incomes.[32] But they find that, lacking the need to self-insure against health costs, the decline in spending among US retirees would be even larger. Retiree spending in the US drops by around 1 percent per year, versus a 3 percent annual decline in the UK. In other words, if US retirees had greater protection against late-in-life health costs, their spending would likely decline even more rapidly as they aged.

How Declining Health May Reduce Retiree Spending

However, another aspect of health may provide a fuller explanation. Recall that the life-cycle model discussed in Chapter 4 predicts that individuals will arrange their spending to equalize the marginal utility of consumption in each period, which is to say that the last dollar they spend at any given time would not produce a greater increment to their well-being if it were instead spent at some other time. If it did, they would either save or borrow to shift that dollar of spending to some other period when it would benefit them more.

The common follow-on conclusion that people will tend to spend the same amount every year depends on the assumption that individuals have the same utility function at every point in their lives. Having the same utility function means that the same amount of spending produces the same enjoyment of that spending, whenever it might occur.

But what if that's not true? Specifically, what if the marginal utility of household spending declines as the household ages, such that an additional dollar of spending would produce smaller increases in the household's well-being? If so, we would expect to see spending front-loaded to the beginning of retirement and then declining as people aged. In economic terms, while individuals may still wish to equalize the marginal utility of spending across different ages, as they grow older, their ability to derive utility from spending declines. And there is a commonsense explanation for why this might be.

It is common for financial planners to divide retirement into three stages. The first phase, the "go-go" years, starts early in retirement, when retirees are in good health, flush with money, and eager to spend it. A "young" retiree who is in good health would enjoy taking an around-the-world cruise with their spouse, for which they didn't have time while they were working.

The second phase, deemed the "slow-go" period, begins around age 75; at this point, retirees remain healthy, but everyday aches and pains might make certain activities less enjoyable. In the later "no-go" phase, beginning around age 85, infirmity prevents retirees from spending as much as they might, the loss of a spouse means they don't have someone to enjoy activities with, or they simply may derive more pleasure from spending time with their grandchildren than purchasing a new car.

In a 2013 study by Finkelstein and her coauthors, aptly titled "What Good Is Wealth Without Health?," the authors link health status to self-reported levels of well-being, their proxy for economic utility.[33] This link, they find, helps explain declining spending in old age. It also points to a lower need to save for retirement, by about 3 to 5 percentage points of preretirement earnings, compared to the assumption that retirees will spend the same amount each year as they age. Kallestrup-Lamb and her coauthors, looking at Danish retirees, also conclude that declining health may tend to reduce rather than increase household spending.[34]

Rohwedder and her coauthors, using new questions inserted into the Health and Retirement Study, analyzed how spending changes over retirement and, just as important, why it changes.[35] Retiree households were asked whether their spending declined over the prior six years, with the median household reporting an 11 percent decline in inflation-adjusted household expenditures. That part is relatively old news.

But the survey respondents were then asked *why* their spending fell, with choices including that fewer people were living in the household, the items they purchased became less expensive over time, they enjoyed spending less, and they could not afford to purchase as much. As retirees aged, they reported deriving less satisfaction from spending such as on eating out, traveling, purchasing new clothes, doing leisure activities, giving financial support to others, and acquiring new cars or home appliances.

In all these categories, spending from age 75 forward simply appears to produce less "utility" than when retirees were younger. If that's the case, then "young" retirees should spend more than the "old old," which is precisely what we see in the data.

Implications of Different Retirement Spending Assumptions

What we assume regarding retirees' assumed path of postretirement expenditures can significantly affect our assessment of the overall retirement savings adequacy of US households. For example, the Center for Retirement Research's National Retirement Risk Index holds that about half of working-age households are inadequately prepared for retirement. But that conclusion depends in part on the assumption that retirees wish to maintain a steady level of consumption throughout their remaining lifetimes and that an inability to maintain that level of spending may indicate an inadequate level of retirement resources.

The Center for Retirement Research's Alicia Munnell, Matthew Rutledge, and Anthony Webb reestimated levels of retirement income adequacy under an alternative approach in which retirees are assumed to desire higher levels of spending early in retirement and declining expenditures over time.[36] The authors found that the share of retirees deemed to be at risk of inadequate incomes in old age declined by about one-third when this single assumption regarding optimal spending patterns was changed. Those authors are themselves skeptical regarding whether retirees truly plan for declining spending as they age, but these figures show how important such an overlooked assumption can be.

Retirees are a diverse group, so no single explanation covers them all. Nevertheless, it does appear that fears of running out of money in old age are overstated. Most households spend much less in retirement than commonly thought, their incomes are substantially higher, and their savings tend to rise rather than fall.

Assumed patterns of spending throughout retirement can dramatically affect the amounts that households might need to save. Relative to the declining-expenditure patterns found in Hurd and Rohwedder, a steady-spending pattern beginning at the same initial level would require about 16 percent greater total retirement income resources over retirement.[37]

However, about two-thirds of retirement spending in that study was capable of being financed through Social Security benefits and traditional pensions, with only about one-third payable from wealth such as retirement account balances or other liquid savings. This implies that the typical household's liquid retirement savings would need to be about 47 percent higher under a steady-spending assumption than under the assumption that spending tends to gradually decline in retirement. It is easy to see how this single assumption can significantly affect how we assess the adequacy of Americans' retirement savings.

11

"A Crisis for Thee, but Not for Me": What Retirees Say About Retirement

There is little doubt that Americans worry about retirement, both their own and that of other Americans. People worry about a multitude of issues, and given the importance and uncertainty attached to retirement planning, some level of worry is natural. Yet concerns over retirement income adequacy seem to have gone well beyond that level. Most Americans today appear to believe that retirement planning constitutes not merely a challenge but a crisis.

What Do Retirees Really Think of Retirement Income?

As other chapters show, there is disagreement on what constitutes an adequate retirement income, based on a range of technical questions. While this disagreement can be narrowed, it cannot be eliminated. A second approach taken here is simply to ask retirees whether they believe their incomes are adequate to provide for a satisfactory standard of living. Questions that ask how a person's postretirement standard of living compares to their preretirement years can help us not only set a baseline as to where things stand today but also, through using historical data, look at how retirement income adequacy may have changed over time.

The Federal Reserve Board's Survey of Consumer Finances (SCF) is a workhorse dataset for financial researchers; it provides detailed information on households' income sources and assets. But the SCF also includes subjective questions by which Americans describe how they perceive their financial situations.

The SCF asks survey respondents to describe the adequacy of their incomes on a one-to-five scale, with one representing a "totally inadequate" income, three representing "enough to maintain one's standards of living," and five representing a "very satisfactory" income. Roughly

Figure 1. Self-Reported Adequacy of Retirement Incomes

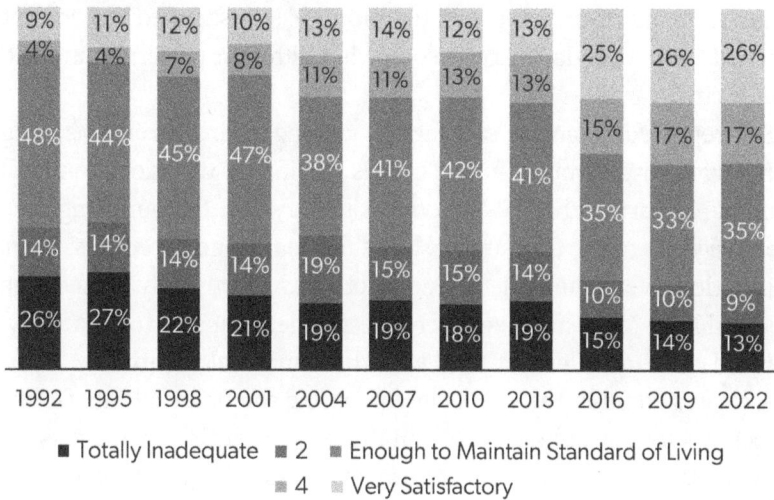

	1992	1995	1998	2001	2004	2007	2010	2013	2016	2019	2022
Very Satisfactory	9%	11%	12%	10%	13%	14%	12%	13%	25%	26%	26%
4	4%	4%	7%	8%	11%	11%	13%	13%	15%	17%	17%
Enough to Maintain Standard of Living	48%	44%	45%	47%	38%	41%	42%	41%	35%	33%	35%
2	14%	14%	14%	14%	19%	15%	15%	14%	10%	10%	9%
Totally Inadequate	26%	27%	22%	21%	19%	19%	18%	19%	15%	14%	13%

■ Totally Inadequate   ■ 2   ■ Enough to Maintain Standard of Living
■ 4   ▧ Very Satisfactory

Source: Survey of Consumer Finances.

speaking, we might categorize any response of three or greater as constituting an adequate retirement income, a response of two as slightly below the level needed to maintain one's preretirement standard of living, and a response of one as constituting a personal "retirement crisis." Figure 1 shows how Americans age 65 and over have answered these questions since 1992.

Even over the relatively short three decades from 1992 to 2022, the progress made in retirement income security is undeniable: The share of seniors indicating serious income deficiencies fell from nearly 26 percent to slightly over 13 percent. The share indicating that their retirement income was at least enough to maintain their standard of living—a baseline objective for retirement planning—rose from 61 to 71 percent. And the share of retirees indicating they live "very satisfactory" financial lives increased from just 9 percent to 26 percent. These data undeniably show that US retirees view their own income security as having increased dramatically over recent decades, much less relative to earlier periods such as the 1930s and 1950s.

The General Social Survey (GSS) focuses on qualitative assessments of various topics. The GSS asks respondents to describe their financial situation, ranging from "satisfied" to "more or less satisfied" to "not at all satisfied." The GSS data show a somewhat different pattern than the SCF figures cited earlier.

Self-reported financial satisfaction among retirees remains roughly stable from 1972 through 2018. There is significant variation from year to year, due in part to the GSS's modest sample sizes. But a moving average over five years of the GSS survey shows no clear trend in retirees' financial satisfaction over time. This is true whether we focus only on the highest reported level ("satisfied") or merge respondents answering that they are satisfied or more or less satisfied with their financial situation.

A clearer trend in the GSS is in comparing the financial satisfaction of US seniors to that of households on the verge of retirement, age 55 to 64. Near-retiree households in recent years expressed lower levels of financial satisfaction than did similarly aged households in the early 1970s. While responses again vary from year to year, the moving average of financial satisfaction responses for near retirees is downward.

From 2010 onward, Americans age 65 and over were 14 percentage points more likely than households age 55 to 64 to report financial satisfaction. There may be various reasons for these differences and reasonable responses to them, but the higher levels of self-reported financial satisfaction by retiree households would not ordinarily lead one to conclude that the US retirement system is not functioning well.

The Health and Retirement Study (HRS) asks survey respondents to compare their overall quality of life in retirement to the years just preceding retirement. The answer to this question obviously can account for changes in income and a range of additional factors such as increased amounts of free time and declining health. From 1992 to 1998, the share of seniors describing their retirement as "about the same" or "better" than the years immediately preceding retirement rose from around two-thirds to over four-fifths, remaining at roughly that level in the following years. Only about one-fifth described retirement as "not as good" as the years just before retiring.

The national polling firm Gallup asks a more specific financial question—namely, whether the person has "enough money to live comfortably."[1]

Note, this isn't merely a question about surviving or just getting by; it's about living in comfort. Nevertheless, nearly eight in 10 seniors indicate they have sufficient income to live comfortably, with little variation in results going back to 2002.

Moreover, in Gallup's survey, retirees consistently indicate significantly greater financial comfort than do working-age Americans. While about eight in 10 seniors report they have enough money to live comfortably, from 2002 through the most recent available data in 2015, only 67 percent of non-retirees reported being able to live comfortably. Again, these results would not point toward a need for working-age Americans to save more for retirement.

The Federal Reserve's Survey of Household Economics and Decision-making (SHED) asks a different set of questions. Respondents are asked, "Overall, which one of the following best describes how well you are managing financially?" Answers range on a four-level scale, starting with "finding it difficult to get by," "just getting by," and "doing okay" and ending with "living comfortably."[2] Table 1 shows results by age group for 2017.

Only 5 percent of Americans age 65 or over describe themselves as "finding it difficult to get by," which is half the level of the youngest age group (age 18 to 24). Moreover, self-described financial security improves almost continuously with age, a result that is directly contrary to the notion that younger Americans are spending too much and saving too little. Even if we look at households just approaching retirement, they are less financially secure than are retirees. Of households age 55 to 64, 70 percent describe themselves as either "doing okay" or "living comfortably," versus 79 percent of households age 65 and over.

The SHED data, while limited in duration, show an improvement in self-reported retirement income security from 2013 through 2022. In 2013, 12 percent of respondents age 65 to 74 described themselves as "finding it hard to get by," while 25 percent described themselves as "living comfortably." (See Table 2.) From 2013 to 2022, the share of seniors reporting they were "finding it hard to get by" declined to slightly over 4 percent, while the share "living comfortably" increased to 44 percent. In total, 82 percent of seniors in 2022 described their financial situations as either "doing okay" or "living comfortably."

Table 1. Respondents' Answers to How They Are Managing Financially by Age Group, 2017

Age	Finding It Difficult to Get By	Just Getting By	Doing Okay	Living Comfortably
18–24	10%	23%	44%	22%
25–34	9%	23%	41%	27%
35–44	9%	23%	41%	28%
45–54	9%	22%	41%	28%
55–64	8%	21%	39%	31%
65–74	6%	17%	39%	38%
65 and Older	5%	16%	39%	40%
75 and Older	5%	13%	39%	43%

Source: Board of Governors of the Federal Reserve Board, "Survey of Household Economics and Decisionmaking," 2024, https://www.federalreserve.gov/consumerscommunities/shed.htm.

Table 2. Respondents' Answers to How They Are Managing Financially, 2013–22

Age	Finding It Difficult to Get By	Just Getting By	Doing Okay	Living Comfortably
2013	12%	24%	38%	25%
2014	10%	24%	40%	25%
2015	9%	22%	41%	28%
2016	9%	21%	40%	29%
2017	7%	19%	40%	33%
2018	7%	18%	41%	34%
2019	6%	18%	39%	36%
2020	7%	18%	40%	35%
2021	6%	16%	39%	39%
2022	4%	13%	38%	44%

Source: Board of Governors of the Federal Reserve Board, "Survey of Household Economics and Decisionmaking," 2024, https://www.federalreserve.gov/consumerscommunities/shed.htm.

Table 3. Respondents' Answers to How They Are Managing Financially, Age 55–64 in 2013 and Age 65–74 in 2021

Age	Finding It Difficult to Get By	Just Getting By	Doing Okay	Living Comfortably
Age 55–64 in 2013	12%	24%	37%	26%
Age 65–74 in 2021	3%	13%	37%	48%
Change (Percentage Points)	–9	–11	0	22

Source: Board of Governors of the Federal Reserve Board, "Survey of Household Economics and Decisionmaking," 2024, https://www.federalreserve.gov/consumerscommunities/shed.htm.

The SHED survey also may provide insights on the transition from work into retirement. Table 3 reports results for the SHED financial security question for respondents age 55 to 64 in 2013, followed by respondents age 65 to 74 in 2021, a largely overlapping group. In 2013, 36 percent of those age 55 to 64 reported they were "finding it hard to get by" or "just getting by," versus only 16 percent of those age 65 to 74 in 2021. The share reporting they were "doing okay" was unchanged, while the share reporting they were "living comfortably" increased by 22 percentage points. If Americans nearing retirement in 2013 possessed inadequate savings, one might expect results nearly the opposite of those presented in Table 3.

Using the HRS, Susann Rohwedder, Michael Hurd, and Péter Hudomiet track self-reported financial security among the same birth cohorts over different ages.[3] From age 55 to 59 to age 85 and over, the share of individuals reporting themselves "somewhat satisfied" with their financial situation remains roughly stable at slightly under 40 percent of the population. The share of individuals reporting themselves "not satisfied" with their financial situation starts at around 43 percent from age 55 to 59 then declines over retirement to about 18 percent for individuals age 85 and over. Likewise, at age 55 to 59, only about 17 percent of individuals report themselves "very" or "completely satisfied" with their financial situation, rising to about 43 percent among 85-year-olds and above.

Retirement Fears Often Go Unrealized

How do we square most retirees reporting they are doing well with most Americans, including retirees, believing the nation faces a retirement crisis? Often it is assumed that if Americans fear a retirement crisis—and, quite clearly, they do—then there must be a retirement crisis to fear. And yet Americans' fears of a retirement crisis could be overstated.

For example, the Chapman University Survey on American Fears finds that 57 percent of Americans fear "not having enough money for the future," which clearly would overlap with specific fears for retirement income.[4] Fears for future finances rank fourth among 94 specific fears that, to varying degrees, Americans suffer from, placing between "pollution of drinking water" and "people I love becoming seriously ill." The most common fear, expressed by 74 percent of Americans, was "corrupt government officials."

For context, 44 percent of Americans fear oil spills, 32 percent government use of drones in the US, 29 percent sharks, and 19 percent volcanos. In other words, many Americans fear many things that, statistically speaking, they probably don't have to worry much about.

And we can prove that, at least in the past, many Americans' fears of a retirement crisis have proven to be unwarranted. Using data from the federally sponsored HRS, I analyzed how Americans' preretirement expectations matched up to postretirement reality. I looked at HRS data of Americans nearing retirement in 1992.[5]

The HRS survey respondents nearing retirement were asked whether, in retirement, they expected their standard of living to increase, stay the same, or decline. As might be expected, the answers were pessimistic: 41 percent of HRS respondents expected their standard of living to decline, 51 percent expected them to stay the same, and only 8 percent expected their standard of living to increase.

I then looked at the HRS survey conducted in 2002, analyzing how newly retired Americans described their experience so far. A full 48 percent stated that their retirement years were "better" than the years just before retirement, 37 percent said retirement was about the same, and only 15 percent said that retirement was "not as good" as their time just before retiring. Clearly, many pre-retirees' fears regarding retirement were not realized.

We can see the same phenomenon using Gallup data, which have been collected regularly for the past two decades. Each year, Gallup asks working-age Americans whether they expect to be able to afford to live comfortably in retirement. In 2002, 59 percent of working-age Americans expected they would be able to afford to live comfortably in old age. Fast-forward to 2023, the most recent data available. At that time, 77 percent of retirees said they had enough money to "live comfortably," a figure that is consistent over the past two decades.[6]

The key point is that many Americans who were of working age and worried in 2002 are now seniors living, by their own description, comfortably. Even if every 2002 respondent who predicted a comfortable retirement ended up retiring comfortably, roughly half the 2002 workers who predicted they would fall short in old age failed to do so.

Crisis? What Crisis?

Even the 2017 Vanguard survey, in which majorities of Americans declared their belief in a retirement crisis, found more encouraging news if we dig into the numbers. While Vanguard asked Americans if they believed the *country* faced a retirement crisis, respondents also were asked if they would describe their own financial situation as a retirement crisis. Here the figures differed considerably.

While 59 percent of near retirees agreed with the statement "I believe there is a national retirement crisis," only 10 percent of near retirees agreed that "I would describe my own retirement situation as a crisis." For retirees, 54 percent of whom believed a national retirement crisis exists, only 4 percent described their own retirement situation in those terms.

A similar "a crisis for thee, but not for me" is found in other countries as well. Residents of Australia, Canada, and the United Kingdom appear only slightly less concerned with the retirement prospects of their fellow citizens, but only the smallest number of retirees—between 1 and 8 percent of recent retirees—describe their own financial situation as a crisis.

In sum, public opinion data on retirement preparation show a much more nuanced picture than the media often portray. Yes, majorities of Americans—and indeed majorities of other countries' residents—will tell you that they believe in a retirement crisis. But historical data have shown that many of these fears turn out to be unjustified, as financial satisfaction consistently increases with age. Moreover, majorities of retirees consistently tell pollsters that they feel financially secure, while only tiny numbers describe their financial situation in terms that warrant the description of a crisis.

12

How Does the US Stack Up Globally Concerning Retirement?

Everyone likes to read rankings. Who's up, who's down, how do we compare? And that even goes for rankings of national retirement systems.

At first glance, the American retirement system does not fare well. But it pays to keep digging. The well-publicized rankings of different countries' retirement systems often include extraneous factors such as, believe it or not, biodiversity while ignoring issues that might seem more on point, such as how much people save, how high retirees' incomes are, and how financially secure seniors feel.

In this chapter, we dig through the studies and the data to produce a more accurate picture of how the United States' retirement system matches up to the best in the world. Will we end up standing on the podium at the Olympics of old-age security or sulking in the locker room?

First, the Bad News

The Mercer CFA Institute, created in collaboration with Monash University and the Victorian Government in Australia, created the Mercer CFA Institute Global Pension Index. The index includes 43 countries with two-thirds of the world's population. It ranks national retirement systems in terms of the adequacy of benefits, the sustainability of retirement programs, and the financial integrity and regulation of retirement plans.

In 2022, the Netherlands, Denmark, and Israel took gold, silver, and bronze. The US ended up only in the middle of the pack, ranking 19th of 43 countries analyzed. Worse, our rating has slipped for two years running. Overall, Mercer found, the US retirement system garners only a grade of C+, which denotes a "system that has some good features, but also has major risks and/or shortcomings that should be addressed; without these improvements, its efficacy and/or longterm sustainability can be questioned."[1] Not good.

The French firm Natixis's Global Retirement Index purports to provide a new ranking of "how well retirees live in 43 nations based on 18 measures of health, wealth, quality of life and material well-being that affect citizens' retirement security."[2] The measures include per capita income, health care costs, and longevity figures published by organizations that include the World Bank, the World Health Organization, and the Organisation for Economic Co-operation and Development (OECD). Once again, the US doesn't exactly lead the pack: In 2022, Natixis ranked the US 18th of 44 countries in terms of retirees' quality of life.[3]

These reports only reinforce the views of the typical financial reporter or policymaker that the US retirement system is effectively broken.

The Usual Studies Aren't Everything They Seem

It really pays to look at the details of these global rankings.

One might think, for instance, that a well-performing retirement system produces high retirement incomes. And the Mercer Index does argue that the US should increase the minimum benefits paid to the lowest-income retirees—which I agree with and stress in later chapters.

But the Mercer Index doesn't look closely at the amount of retirement savings or the level of incomes that typical retirees receive. Instead, it's a consultant's checklist that focuses on system policies. Consultants like "systems" that dictate most of how individuals will prepare for retirement. But Americans by and large don't like one-size-fits-all solutions—and our retirement system, such as it is, comprises a wide range of different vehicles and options that are supposed to come together to produce good results. What matters is whether the hodgepodge of retirement savings vehicles in the US works.

Mercer's criteria don't focus on whether the US retirement system produces good outcomes. For instance, the US was dinged for allowing preretirement withdrawals from 401(k) accounts—a practice that can reduce account balances but which some experts believe is essential for encouraging people to save in these plans in the first place. Certain aspects of preretirement withdrawals are uniformly set in federal law and thus difficult to test. However, the Government Accountability Office found that

> allowing borrowing increases participation among eligible employees, especially lower-income employees. Allowing pension-plan borrowing also significantly affects how much employees contribute. Participants in plans that allow borrowing contribute, on average, 35 percent more to their pension accounts than participants in plans that do not allow borrowing.[4]

For example, Alicia Munnell and her coauthors found that allowing employees to borrow against their 401(k) balances increases the contribution rate by 2.6 percentage points, nearly four times the effect of a plan having an employer match.[5]

The Mercer report also lowers the US score for not requiring that retirees annuitize part of their savings, even though Social Security benefits—which form the base of retirement income and the vast majority of it for the lowest-earning households—are already paid out as a life-long inflation-indexed annuity. Moreover, as discussed elsewhere, retirees may wish to retain liquidity to cover unexpected expenses, particularly for health care. In other words, the criteria by which Mercer ranks national retirement systems are, while hardly crazy, at least subjective.

The Natixis Index is subject to similar criticisms. The index measures retirement quality using variables such as life expectancy at birth, average income per capita for the entire population, unemployment, and income inequality. Each country's carbon emissions and biodiversity are in there as well.

But I would wager the typical reader is not thinking about that when they hear the US retirement system ranks poorly. Whatever these figures may be worth, Natixis's rankings don't say much about retirees' quality of life or a retirement system's capacity to help retirees' maintain their preretirement standard of living.

As we see, when it comes to two key factors—incomes and happiness—US retirees do well. I start by reviewing some of the hard data on retirement savings and retirement incomes around the world. Then I consider more subjective assessments—opinion surveys in which retirees from different countries tell us how they feel about certain issues.

Comparing Government Pension System Finances

Critics of America's retirement system often wish to change it so that retirees would rely less on their personal savings and more on government-provided benefits. We can't say for sure how that would turn out in the United States, but by turning to data on other developed countries, we can see how that model has fared abroad. The OECD compiles a detailed database of economic, demographic, and policy figures that help illustrate how different developed countries prepare for retirement and what the outcomes tend to be.[6]

I focus on high-income developed countries, excluding lower-income countries such as Turkey and Mexico along with countries that were once part of the Soviet Union's Eastern Bloc. I also exclude Luxembourg, a tiny but prosperous city-state–cum–tax haven in Europe. Including those countries does not change the results appreciably but makes it more difficult to focus on the countries most similar to the United States.

I begin with the generosity of US Social Security benefits relative to those of other developed countries: A lack of benefit generosity is at the root of many arguments against the current US retirement system. As progressive critics of the US retirement system allege, Social Security provides more modest benefits relative to preretirement earnings than the government pension system in the typical developed country.

Across the selection of OECD countries, the median country provides an average retirement benefit equal to 50 percent of the average wage of workers in the labor force at the time.[7] In the US, the average Social Security benefit as measured by the OECD is equal to only 39 percent of the national average wage, making US Social Security benefits about one-fifth less generous than in the typical OECD country when measured as a percentage of the wages of average workers at the time.[8]

However, the countries offering less generous pension benefits for middle-wage earners are hardly dystopian: These countries include

Figure 1. Pension Benefit for the Average Wage Earner as a Percentage of the National Average Wage, 2020

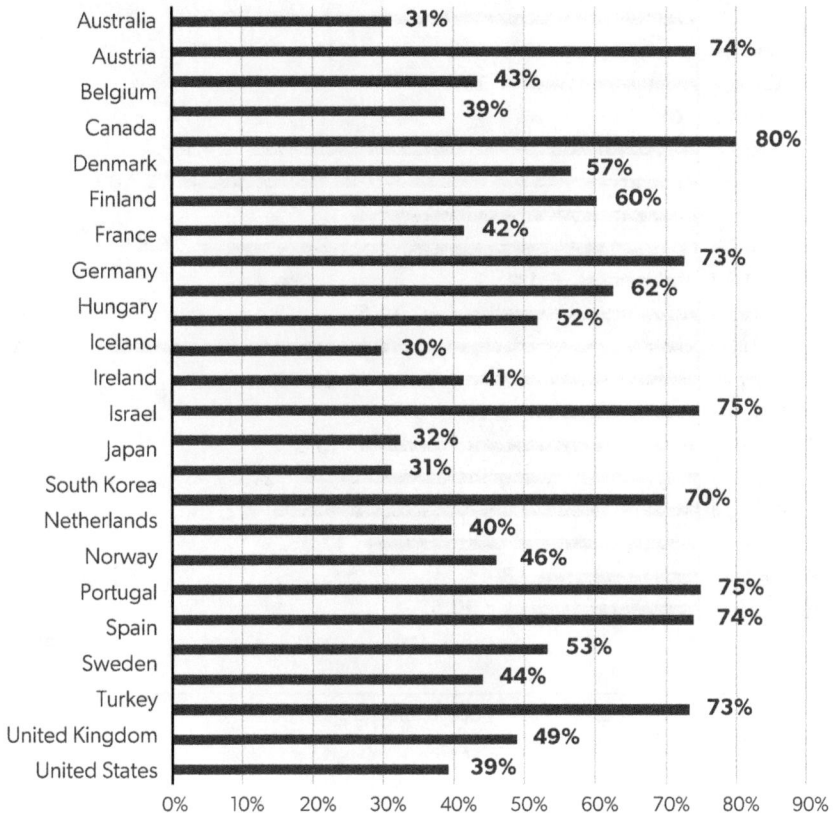

Source: Organisation for Economic Co-operation and Development.

Canada, with average pension benefits equal to 39 percent of the national average wage; Japan (32 percent); Australia (31 percent); South Korea (31 percent); and Ireland (30 percent) (Figure 1).

However, the less generous Social Security benefits found in the United States are funded with lower taxes, which leave more room for households to save for retirement on their own. The United States Social Security contribution rate for the Old-Age, Survivors, and Disability

Figure 2. Mandatory Public-Sector Contribution Rates, 2020

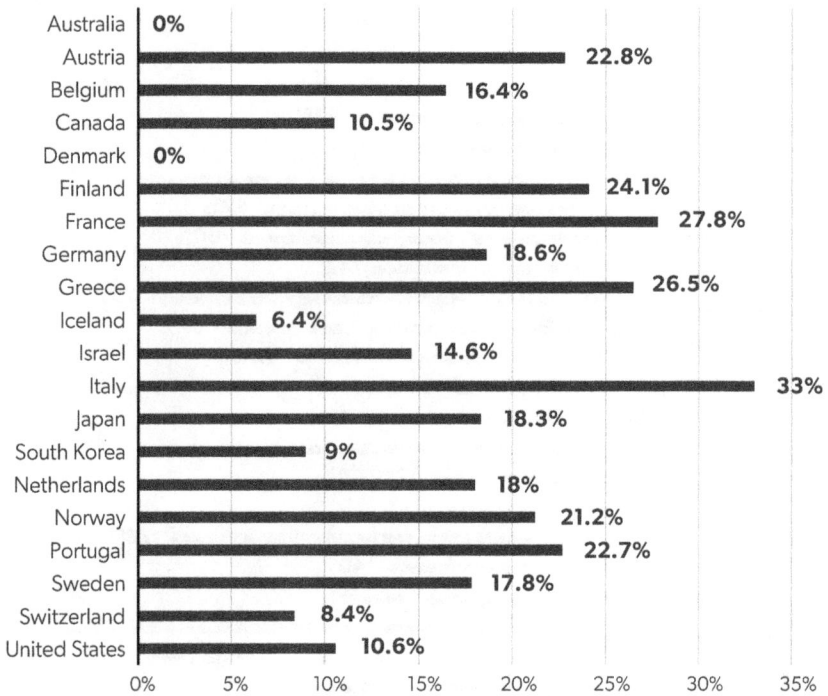

Source: Organisation for Economic Co-operation and Development.

Insurance program is 10.6 percent of wages, split between employer and employee. The OECD lists only this portion of the Social Security payroll tax, omitting the remaining 1.8 percent of pay dedicated to the Disability Insurance program.

The US contribution rate is well below the OECD median of 18.2 percent of pay for an average wage employee (Figure 2). Australia funds its Age Pension from general tax revenues, while Denmark has mandatory private pensions with a combined employer-employee contribution rate of 12 percent of pay.[9]

Nevertheless, these figures provide some context on America's required pension contributions relative to other high-income countries. While the US Social Security tax is well below those of continental European countries such as Italy, mandatory contributions in the US are on par with Canada, Iceland, South Korea, and Switzerland.

Next, I turn to the two major factors that affect the level and sustainability of retirement incomes. The first factor, which principally affects governmental retirement income programs, is a country's demographics. Most national pension plans are, like Social Security, funded on a pay-as-you-go basis, which means that taxes paid by today's workers are used to fund benefits for today's retirees.

As a result, the ratio of workers paying into pension programs to beneficiaries claiming funds from those programs directly drives the cost of paying any given level of benefits. The implicit cost of a pay-as-you-go program as a percentage of employee wages is equal to average benefits as a percentage of average wages divided by the ratio of workers to beneficiaries.

Figure 3 contains OECD projections of the ratio of working-age to over-65 residents for 2050. By midcentury, the median OECD country in my sample is projected to have just 1.9 working-age residents for each resident age 65 and over. The United States is projected to have 2.5 working-age residents for each senior, the second-highest ratio among the 24 countries examined.

By itself, America's demographic advantage allows the US to pay any given level of pension benefits at a cost that is roughly one-quarter lower than in the typical developed country. For example, a pension benefit equal to 40 percent of the national average wage would in 2050 cost the median OECD country's workers 21 percent of their wages, versus only 16 percent of pay in the United States. Compared to a country such as Japan, which in 2050 is projected to have only 1.2 working-age residents per senior, any given level of retirement benefits can be funded in the US at roughly half the cost as a percentage of worker's pay simply due to the US having more workers per retiree.

Demographically, the United States is substantially better prepared to maintain its government retirement program than is the typical developed country. More advantageous demographics put the United States' lower Social Security contribution in a more positive light, in that any given contribution rate can support higher benefits if there is a higher ratio of contributors to beneficiaries. That seems at least worth noting in comparing how residents of different countries can prepare for retirement.

Figure 3. Projected Ratio of Working-Age to Retirement-Age Residents by Country, 2050

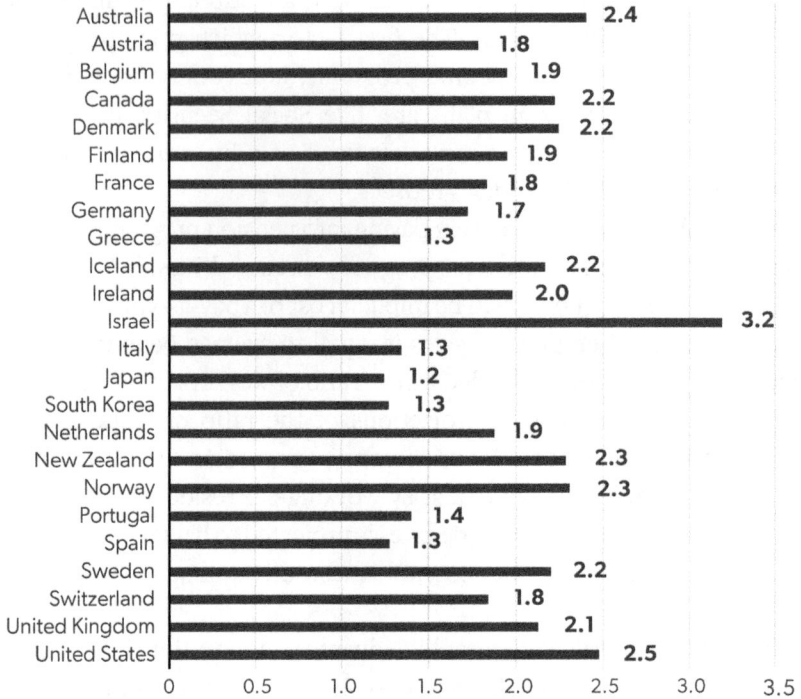

Source: Organisation for Economic Co-operation and Development.

Americans Are Actually Big Savers

The second major factor affecting a country's retirement income security is the level of retirement savings. Private retirement savings invested in real assets are significantly less subject to the effects of demographic changes than is a pay-as-you-go financed government retirement program. Having high levels of prefunded pension benefits provides protections against the costs of demographic changes.

Here again the US is in a strong position relative to many other developed countries. The median OECD country in 2020 held private and public retirement plan assets equal to 70 percent of gross domestic product

Figure 4. Public and Private Retirement Funds as a Percentage of GDP, 2020 or Latest Year Available

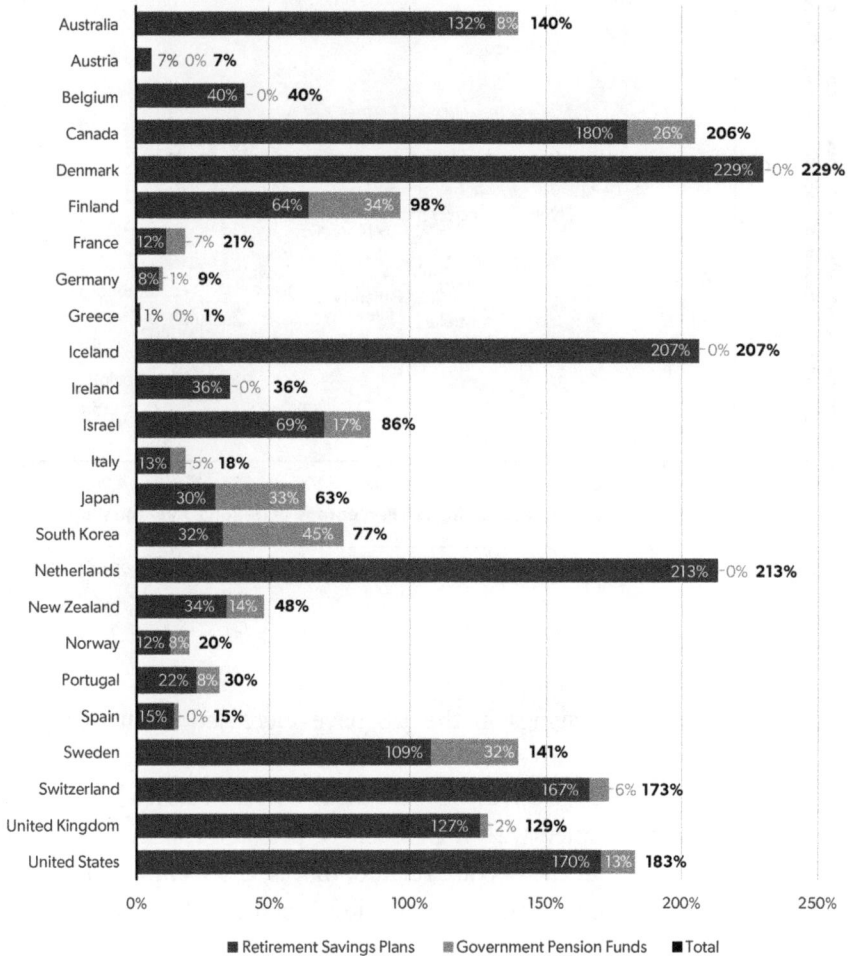

Country	Retirement Savings Plans	Government Pension Funds	Total
Australia	132%	8%	**140%**
Austria	7%	0%	**7%**
Belgium	40%	0%	**40%**
Canada	180%	26%	**206%**
Denmark	229%	0%	**229%**
Finland	64%	34%	**98%**
France	12%	7%	**21%**
Germany	8%	1%	**9%**
Greece	1%	0%	**1%**
Iceland	207%	0%	**207%**
Ireland	36%	0%	**36%**
Israel	69%	17%	**86%**
Italy	13%	5%	**18%**
Japan	30%	33%	**63%**
South Korea	32%	45%	**77%**
Netherlands	213%	0%	**213%**
New Zealand	34%	14%	**48%**
Norway	12%	8%	**20%**
Portugal	22%	8%	**30%**
Spain	15%	0%	**15%**
Sweden	109%	32%	**141%**
Switzerland	167%	6%	**173%**
United Kingdom	127%	2%	**129%**
United States	170%	13%	**183%**

■ Retirement Savings Plans ■ Government Pension Funds ■ Total

Source: Organisation for Economic Co-operation and Development.

(GDP). (See Figure 4.) In the US, combined private- and public-sector retirement funds were equal to 183 percent of GDP, over 2.5 times higher.

Some countries, such as France, Germany, Norway, and Spain, had retirement savings that were only a small fraction of those in the United States. This may not always have been the case, but, as discussed in other

Figure 5. Trade-Off Between Government Pension Benefits and Retirement Income from Personal Saving and Work, OECD Countries

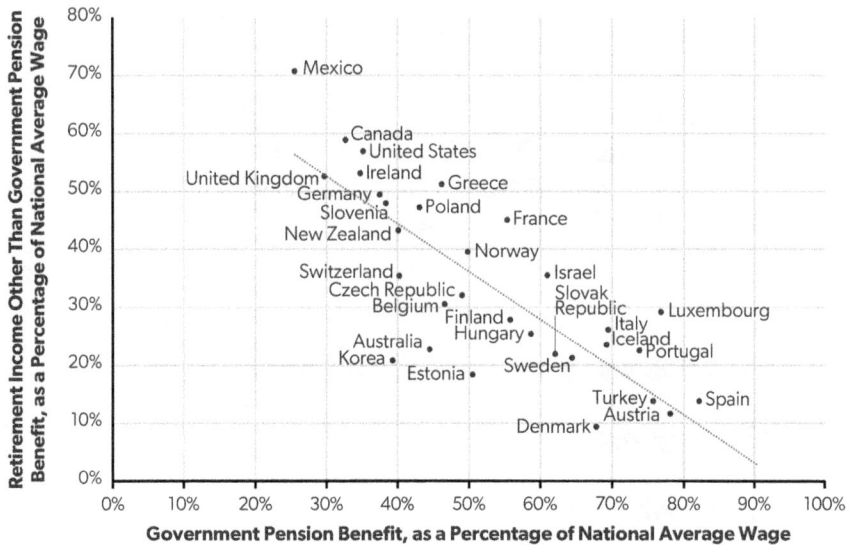

Source: Author's calculations using data from Organisation for Economic Co-operation and Development.

chapters, retirement savings in the US have increased dramatically in recent decades, even relative to the economy's size.

The combination of relatively low levels of Social Security benefits in the United States coupled with high levels of private retirement savings raises the prospect that the two are related; that is, the seemingly low levels of private retirement savings in many developed countries are causally related to higher levels of government pension benefits offered in these countries. If working-age households target any given level of retirement income, such as replacing 70 percent of their preretirement earnings, then increases in publicly provided pension benefits will tend to lead to lower levels of private savings.

Figure 5 compares the generosity of government pension benefits and the levels of retirement incomes that households provide through other sources, such as employer-sponsored retirement plans, personal savings, and work in retirement. Both pension benefits and non-pension sources of income are measured as a percentage of the average wage in the workforce at the time. Across developed countries, the inverse relationship between government pensions and other sources of retirement income is clear: For each dollar of retirement income provided via government pension benefits, retirement income from other sources declines by about 82 cents.

This evidence supports the conclusion that more generous government retirement benefits do not translate to more adequate total retirement incomes on anything approaching a dollar-for-dollar basis. The proponents of expanding the US Social Security program to match the generosity of European country programs must take seriously the idea that increasing Social Security benefits would lead to a meaningful reduction in the amounts that Americans save for retirement on their own.

Retiree Incomes Across the Globe

I now consider how government pension benefits, personal savings, and other sources of income in retirement total across countries. I illustrate levels of retirement savings in two ways. First, using OECD data, I calculate the average retirement incomes in a country as a percentage of the average incomes of residents of all ages. (See Figure 6.) This comparison is not a "replacement rate" in the conventional sense of comparing retirees' incomes to their own preretirement earnings. Instead, it captures the relative well-being of working-age and aged residents of the same country.

In the United States, the mean resident age 66 to 75 has an income equal to 102 percent of that of the total population mean income. The United States ratio of retiree to working-age incomes is the seventh highest among the 25 OECD countries examined here and above the median number of 95 percent. These figures indicate that American seniors today tend to be a better-off portion of the US population, while in some other countries, seniors continue to be a relatively poor segment of the population.

Next, I look at the median disposable income available to residents age 65 and over in dollar terms, with local currencies converted to US dollars using purchasing power parity (PPP), a method that accounts for

**Figure 6. Mean Incomes of Residents Age 66–75 as a Percentage of
Average Population Income, Latest Data Available**

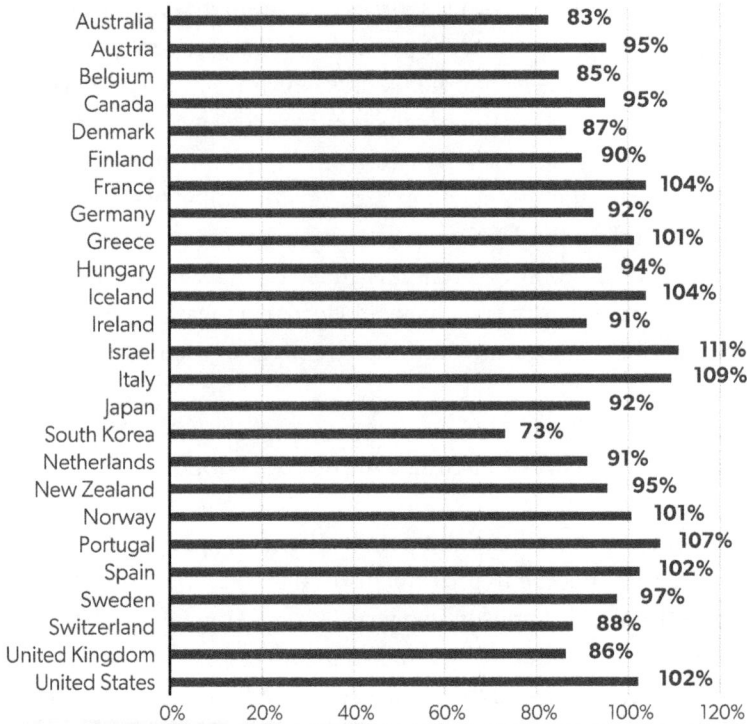

Country	Percentage
Australia	83%
Austria	95%
Belgium	85%
Canada	95%
Denmark	87%
Finland	90%
France	104%
Germany	92%
Greece	101%
Hungary	94%
Iceland	104%
Ireland	91%
Israel	111%
Italy	109%
Japan	92%
South Korea	73%
Netherlands	91%
New Zealand	95%
Norway	101%
Portugal	107%
Spain	102%
Sweden	97%
Switzerland	88%
United Kingdom	86%
United States	102%

Source: Organisation for Economic Co-operation and Development.

differences in local costs of living. Disposable income, according to the
OECD, "represents the money available to a household for spending on
goods or services."[10] It includes

> income from economic activity (wages and salaries; profits of
> self-employed business owners), property income (dividends,
> interests and rents), social benefits in cash (retirement pen-
> sions, unemployment benefits, family allowances, basic income
> support, etc.), and social transfers in kind (goods and services
> such as health care, education and housing, received either free
> of charge or at reduced prices).[11]

Figure 7. Median Disposable Incomes, Residents Age 65 and Over

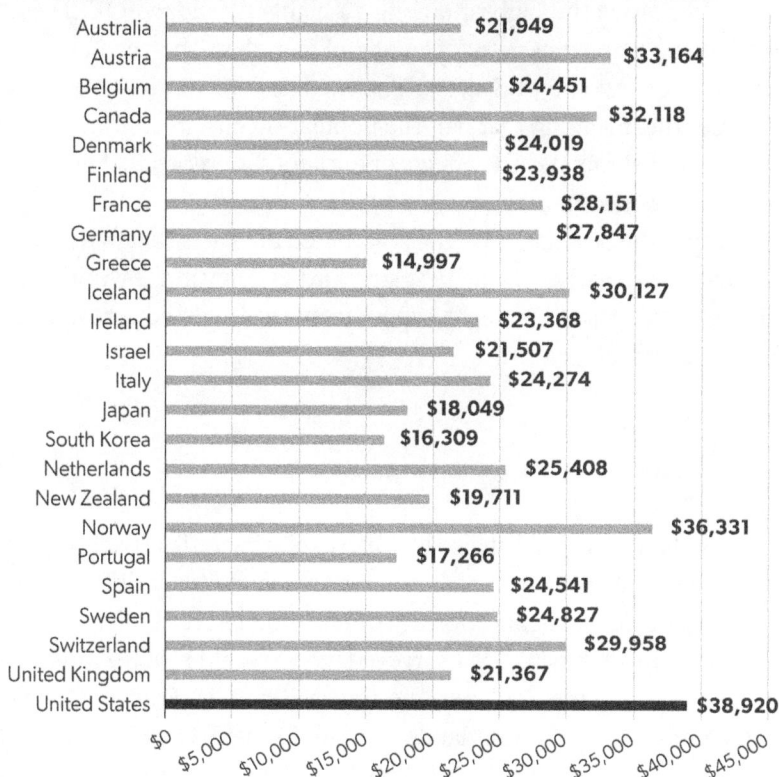

Australia	$21,949
Austria	$33,164
Belgium	$24,451
Canada	$32,118
Denmark	$24,019
Finland	$23,938
France	$28,151
Germany	$27,847
Greece	$14,997
Iceland	$30,127
Ireland	$23,368
Israel	$21,507
Italy	$24,274
Japan	$18,049
South Korea	$16,309
Netherlands	$25,408
New Zealand	$19,711
Norway	$36,331
Portugal	$17,266
Spain	$24,541
Sweden	$24,827
Switzerland	$29,958
United Kingdom	$21,367
United States	$38,920

Source: Organisation for Economic Co-operation and Development.
Note: The data in this figure are from 2019 or the most recent available year and are adjusted for PPP.

With regard to the provision of health care, which differs across countries, disposable income subtracts the taxes a country's residents pay—some of which are used to finance the government's health provision—but then adds the value of government-provided health coverage. Private health premiums, such as supplemental insurance to cover costs not provided for by Medicare, are not subtracted from disposable income, but the value of the health benefits purchased also are not added to disposable income. Moreover, the adjustment of disposable incomes for differences in local prices using PPP helps account for the fact that unit pricing of health services in the United States tends to be higher than in other developed countries.[12]

The US median disposable income of $38,920 for residents age 65 and over in 2019 is the highest among 24 highly developed OECD countries (Figure 7) and nearly 60 percent higher than the median OECD country retiree income of $24,363. The median looks at a person at the 50th percentile, meaning that half the population has greater income and half lesser, and eliminates the effects of outliers such as a small number of extremely high-income retirees.

Put simply, the best data the OECD gathered indicates that in real terms, the typical US retiree has the highest standard of living in the world. This is hardly the conclusion one might expect from reading media descriptions of the US retirement system.

What Do Retirees Have to Say?

While hard data are crucial, it also is worth exploring retirees' self-reported levels of financial security. These, too, tell a substantially different story from what a reader of media coverage of retirement issues might expect.

In 2019, the Dutch bank ING surveyed workers and retirees in 15 countries: Australia, Austria, Belgium, the Czech Republic, France, Germany, Italy, Luxembourg, the Netherlands, Poland, Romania, Spain, Turkey, the United Kingdom, and the United States. ING asked retirees to respond to the statement: "In retirement, my income and financial position let me enjoy the same standard of living that I had when working." Possible responses included "strongly agree," "agree," "neither agree nor disagree," "disagree," and "strongly disagree" (Figure 8).[13]

In the US, 47 percent of retirees either agreed or strongly agreed that they could maintain their preretirement standard of living. Only the prosperous city-state of Luxembourg was more successful, at 53 percent. Only 28 percent of European retirees agreed they could maintain their preretirement standard of living, including only 14 percent in France and 26 percent in Germany. Australia was in between, with 33 percent of retirees agreeing they could maintain their preretirement standard of living. Australia has a strong private retirement savings system, but, unlike in the US, Australia's system of employer-sponsored retirement plans largely replaces rather than supplements a government-provided benefit.

Figure 8. Percentage of Retirees Who Agree or Strongly Agree They Can Maintain Their Preretirement Standard of Living

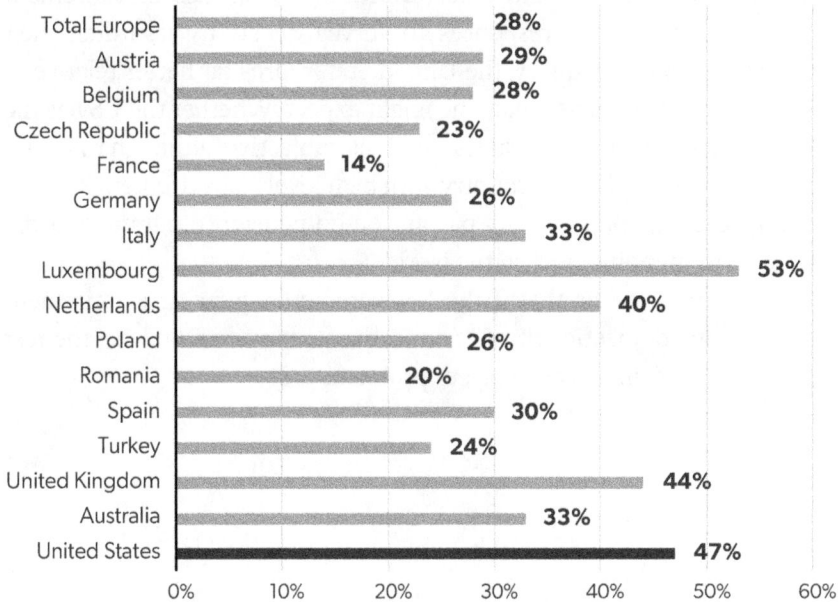

Country	Percentage
Total Europe	28%
Austria	29%
Belgium	28%
Czech Republic	23%
France	14%
Germany	26%
Italy	33%
Luxembourg	53%
Netherlands	40%
Poland	26%
Romania	20%
Spain	30%
Turkey	24%
United Kingdom	44%
Australia	33%
United States	47%

Source: ING, "ING International Survey Savings," February 2019, https://think.ing.com/uploads/reports/ING_International_Survey_Savings_Retirement_Saving_Challenges_2019_FINALv2.pdf.

It's a similar story when we look at retirees who strongly disagree with the statement "In retirement, my income and financial position let me enjoy the same standard of living that I had when working." These retirees are likely facing a true retirement crisis.

In the US, only 9 percent of retirees characterized their incomes in that way—again, second only to Luxembourg. In Europe as a whole, the share of retirees falling far short of maintaining their preretirement standard of living was 2.5 times higher at 23 percent. In France and Germany, nearly one-third of retirees say their incomes fall far short of what they need, 3.5 times the US rate.

Seniors in the Netherlands, which Mercer ranks the best retirement system in the world, report lower levels of retirement income adequacy than do retirees in the supposedly C+ United States. Perhaps a retirement system is more than the sum of the parts as assessed by a benefits consultant.

Whether we look at hard data on retirement savings or retirement incomes or on seniors' responses to survey questions regarding their retirement income adequacy, the United States fares far better relative to other developed countries than one might expect. Whether the US has the strongest retirement system in the world is subjective, although that case can certainly be made for a country with high levels of retirement savings, favorable demographics for its pay-as-you-go pension program, and the highest retirement incomes in the world.

What seems clear is that if the US were actually facing a retirement crisis, as many domestic critics of our retirement system believe, the rest of the world is facing an even bigger problem.

PART IV

13

Are Children Causing the Retirement Crisis?

I have a colleague who has, if I recall correctly, six children. When you have that many, perhaps even he can't recall correctly. I have just one. Let's assume that my colleague and I have the same annual salary. He obviously devotes a large portion of his salary to feeding, clothing, and educating his children, meaning he spends much less on himself and his spouse. My one son costs me far less, leaving me and my wife more to spend on ourselves.

So here is the question on which the retirement crisis depends: Does my colleague need the same income in retirement that I do? His preretirement earnings are the same as mine, so conventional financial planning would say that the two of us should aim for the same income in retirement—say, 70 percent of our preretirement pay. But his consumption during his working years will be far lower than mine, because so much of his preretirement earnings are devoted to raising his kids. That means he could maintain his preretirement standard of living, the goal that both the life-cycle model and conventional financial planning aim for, with a far lower retirement income than I could.

The difference between Americans facing a "retirement crisis" and a situation in which roughly nine in 10 households are well prepared for retirement hinges on how we answer that question.

Your children might eat you out of house and home. But will they deprive you of a secure retirement as well? That's what some researchers believe. As this chapter shows, there's a much more interesting and reassuring story to be told.

But how children affect parents' spending and saving needs has a broader lesson about how the adequacy of Americans' retirement savings is assessed. The typical news story or congressional hearing might start by citing some frightening but ultimately meaningless factoid regarding retirement savings: the median retirement account balance is this, only a certain percentage of Americans are participating in a 401(k), or so-and-so survey finds that Americans think there's a retirement crisis. It might then follow up by citing a statistic drawn from the Center for Retirement Research's National Retirement Risk Index (NRRI) or some similar study concluding that some alarming percentage of Americans will fall short of the income they need in old age.

The disconnect in these conversations is that the frightening factoids that begin the discussion have nothing to do with why a major study like the NRRI concludes that Americans are under-saving. So what *does* cause a study like the NRRI to project that Americans are dramatically underprepared for retirement?

The answer is precisely the topic this chapter discusses: How do children affect retirement income security? Claims that kids harm retirement security are central to predictions of a future "retirement crisis" for Americans. If it weren't for kids, or at least how some analysts think about children and retirement savings, the share of Americans at risk of an inadequate retirement income could be cut by two-thirds.

What Did I Get Myself in For?

Children are cute, much of the time. They're heartwarming. Having kids will get your parents and, better yet, your in-laws off your back about producing some grandchildren. But as any parent can tell you, children are expensive. From diapers to degrees, kids involve a near-constant outflow of money.

The US Department of Agriculture, drawing on data from the Consumer Expenditure Survey, finds that a middle-class household with two children spends nearly one-third of its $81,700 annual income keeping its children fed, clothed, cared for, and educated through high school graduation, with total child-rearing costs exceeding $235,000. A single-parent household with a lower income of $24,000 spends approximately 40 percent of its annual income on child-related costs.[1]

Much of this outlay of money takes place during the years in which parents have a second important task: saving for their own retirement. Indeed, various research from the US and abroad finds that parents do save less than nonparents do. Taken on its own, such data would point toward children being detrimental to parents' prospects for a satisfying and financially secure retirement.[2]

However, there is a countervailing point of view, which can be summed up by Dartmouth College economist Jonathan Skinner's "peanut butter theory":

> Parents are already used to getting by on peanut butter, given that a large fraction of their preretirement budget has been devoted to supporting children, so it's not difficult to set aside enough money to keep them in peanut butter through retirement.[3]

RAND Corporation economists describe the logic in more technical terms: "Holding constant lifetime earnings, households with (grown) children should consume less in retirement than households without children, and households with more children should consume less than households with fewer children." But, they point out, this lower level of spending "should not necessarily be taken to indicate worse economic preparation, yet it would be under the income replacement rate method."[4]

Imagine people who earned $50,000 per year during their working lives. One person has to support themselves and a child with that income, while a second doesn't. The reality is that the parent has a different standard of living over their working years than the nonparent does. And yet, if we don't take children into account, we'll assume they need to maintain the same standard of living in retirement.

Think about it this way: The life-cycle model's baseline prediction is that people wish to maintain their standard of living over time. If the costs of raising children leave parents with less money to spend on themselves during their working years, then they'll require less money to maintain that standard of living into old age. If the peanut butter theory is correct, parents would optimally save less for retirement than nonparents would, but in retirement, they report similar capacity to maintain their preretirement standard of living. Skinner himself was agnostic on whether the peanut butter theory of parental retirement saving is true, and subsequent research has not resolved the question.

But answering the question of how children affect parents' retirement saving is central to the broader question of how well Americans are saving for retirement. In a 2009 American Enterprise Institute study, I calculated retirement income replacement rates using a formula to estimate the share of a household's preretirement earnings that parents spend on themselves rather than on their children. Retirement income replacement rates were calculated based on retirees replacing their own preretirement spending, not the share of their incomes that were spent on their kids. The median replacement rate using this adjustment was 17 percentage points higher than when using non-adjusted figures, leading to a smaller share of households with retirement incomes falling short of any given benchmark for retirement income adequacy.[5]

Similarly, the authors of the NRRI estimated how accounting for child-rearing costs would affect the NRRI's projections of the shares of Americans with inadequate retirement savings. The NRRI doesn't account for the costs of raising kids, meaning it assumes that parents and nonparents with the same preretirement earnings require the same income in retirement, even if the parents spent a good chunk of their preretirement earnings raising their kids.

However, Alicia Munnell and her coauthors estimated that if the NRRI assumed that parents need to replace only the earnings they spent on themselves during their working years (excluding amounts consumed by their kids), the percentage of households age 51–61 in 2004 with insufficient retirement savings would drop from 35 percent to 12 percent.[6] In other words, in this projection at least, two-thirds of households that have inadequate retirement incomes wouldn't be where they are if it weren't for their kids!

Obviously, as the chapter assessing the retirement crisis research literature shows, a skeptic could pick other bones with the NRRI. My point here is that if the NRRI, one of the first and to this day most influential studies of retirement savings adequacy, led with the conclusion that 88 percent of Americans approaching retirement had sufficient savings, the retirement crisis narrative never would have taken off in the first place.

This simply illustrates how academic and public policy disagreements over Americans' retirement savings adequacy don't hinge on what you hear on TV or read in the newspaper. Disagreements often depend on tiny details of economic theory or modeling that almost no one gives the first thought to.

Getting to the Bottom of the Problem

I'm reasonably confident that most of the studies concluding that Americans face a retirement crisis didn't even consider how children affect retirement savings at the time the models were built. A model builder must prioritize many other factors. Moreover, most retirement savings rules of thumb from financial planners, such as recommended replacement rates or target ratios of retirement savings to final salaries, don't take children explicitly into account. Nevertheless, once the question is raised, researchers should try addressing it. And increasingly they have.[7]

That said, how children affect the need to save for retirement is a surprisingly difficult question to answer, because most government data aren't really set up to test it. To quantitatively analyze how children affect saving and spending, I needed to be able to follow people over time, to see how their spending patterns changed as children entered and, more important, left the household. Most governmental surveys contain data on a randomly selected sample of the population each year, with little or no overlap in the samples from one year to the next. This makes it more difficult to determine how a child entering or leaving the household affected that household's finances.

Only one dataset would let me follow households over time in the ways necessary to look at the question of children and retirement saving. The Panel Study of Income Dynamics (PSID) follows the same households over many years and measures how much households spend in different categories of expenditures.[8] The PSID also tracks how many children a household has. If I put all this together, I could see how children affect how much parents can and must save for retirement.

First, I looked at how much households spend at different ages, dividing households into those that would never have kids and those that would. Because the PSID follows households over time, I could look at how much parents spent even before they became parents.

Figure 1 shows that parents have different spending patterns over their working lifetimes than nonparents do. Both start at similar levels at age 25, when many people who become parents haven't actually had their kids yet. But as children enter the picture, total household spending rises

Figure 1. Total Household Spending by Age, Parents and Nonparents

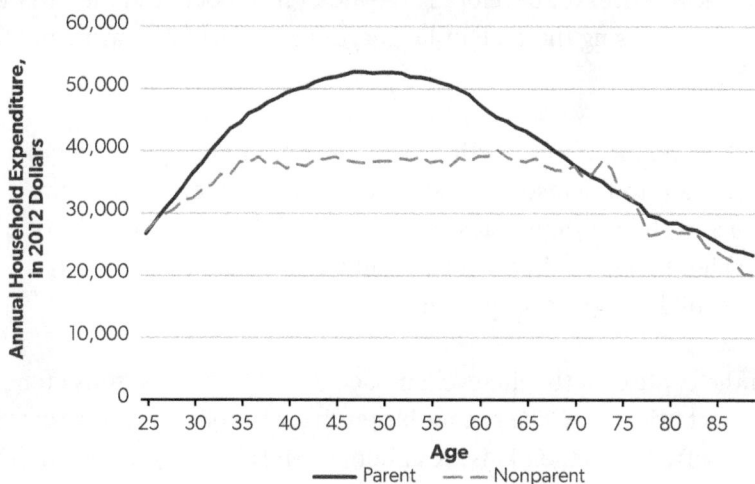

Source: Author's calculations from Panel Study on Income Dynamics.

so that by middle age, parental households are spending one-third more than nonparents are.

But then something happens. Around age 50, spending by parents peaks and starts to decline. By age 70, parents are spending about the same per year as nonparents are. And from age 70 onward, spending by both parents and nonparents declines significantly. This well-known pattern of spending is discussed in Chapter 10.

What this means is that, for the purposes of maintaining their preretirement standard of living, parents don't need to maintain their household's average level of spending over their lifetimes. Parents need only maintain the amounts they were spending on themselves. And those amounts are pretty well captured by how much they spend as they enter retirement, when most children have (parents hope) left the nest.

All this is consistent with an interpretation of the life-cycle model in which parents wish to maintain *their own* standard of living over time, not spend as much on themselves in retirement as they spent on themselves plus their kids during their working years. If they follow this pattern, then household spending will rise (and saving fall) when children are living at home, but spending will decline and savings increase once kids leave.

This is how Franco Modigliani, who won the Nobel Memorial Prize in Economic Sciences for developing the life-cycle model, read the situation. He predicted, using the type of language that Nobel Prize winners often use, that

> the amount of net worth accumulated up to any given age in relation to life resources is a decreasing function of the number of children and that saving tends to fall with the number of children present in the household and to rise with the number of children no longer present.[9]

In the context of the life-cycle model, it wouldn't make sense for parents to act otherwise. The peanut butter theory implies that if parents eat peanut butter when their kids are at home—and as a parent, trust me, they do—they should save so they can afford to eat peanut butter in retirement as well. But what if parents want to eat caviar in old age instead? Well, to do that they would have to spend less and save more while their kids are living at home, which means surviving on something even cheaper than peanut butter, if such a thing exists.

Now, as other chapters show, most retirees live comfortably in old age, and few report they are financially constrained. So perhaps caviar isn't off the menu after all. The point, though, is that people don't tend to aim for wildly different standards of living at different points in their lives. If so, then the peanut butter theory has something to tell us.

What Do Parents Spend Their Money On?

Now some doubt this narrative and think there's something else different between parents and nonparents besides the fact that one group has a swarm of demanding little rug rats. And surely there are other differences. But in a 2022 study published in the *Journal of Retirement*, I ran those traps.

I ran regression analyses that compared households both within a given year and across time while controlling for differences in age, income, employment status, education, race, and ethnicity. Still I concluded that when kids leave home, household spending drops, and household saving increases.[10]

But there's an easier way to check. In addition to data on total household spending, the PSID contains figures on what households are spending their money on. And these figures show that declines in spending for parental households in the years kids are leaving home are precisely in the categories you might think parents would spend less on as their children become economically independent: food, childcare, education, housing, and transportation.

So, while the fancy statistical analysis is nice, the picture in Figure 1 more or less tells the story. It's hard to tell a plausible story in which the decline in parental households' spending from middle age to retirement isn't driven by kids leaving home.

What Does Other Research Say?

Although children are viewed as the largest factor in assessing US households' retirement savings adequacy, there has been little research on the subject. But most of it supports the view that parents spend less as kids leave home, meaning parents enter retirement with a much lower level of household spending than they need to maintain in old age.

In a 1995 study using data from the United Kingdom, economists Orazio Attanasio and Martin Browning show that a hump-shaped age-expenditure profile is flattened considerably after accounting for changes to household size. This implies that late-career household expenditures will be more representative of the spending level that parents wish to maintain in retirement, versus a higher average expenditure level that occurred over longer periods in which the household contained children.[11]

Similarly, Browning and Mette Ejrnæs concluded that the number and age of children are important in determining the pattern of household consumption expenditures.[12] Attanasio and his coauthors in 1999 also conclude that household demographics are an important driver of age-expenditure patterns,[13] while Banks and his coauthors found that relative to childless households, households with children consume a greater share of their lifetime resources earlier in life, when children are present, and a smaller share in retirement.[14]

Still other studies look at how having children affects household savings. Sociologist Michelle Maroto, who relied on data from the National Longitudinal Survey of Youth (NLSY), finds that children are associated with lower wealth among low- and medium-wealth households but higher wealth among high-wealth households.[15] Laura Ravazzini and Ursina Kuhn find similar effects of children on savings for Australian, German, and Swiss households.[16]

Using a simulation model built on the NLSY data, Williams College economist David Love finds that

> wealth builds up gradually until around age 50, after which point it accelerates slightly to a peak near retirement age. The upturn in saving occurs right around the age at which children are exiting the household and finishing post-secondary schooling.[17]

Karl Scholz and Ananth Seshadri, using Health and Retirement Study data on households in their 50s, find that a middle-income household that had two children would approach retirement with a net worth 13 percent lower than a similar childless household. But Scholz and Seshadri conclude that lower saving by parents is consistent with a life-cycle model in which parents wish to smooth their own consumption, implying that parents enter retirement with approximately the same ability to maintain their standard of living as nonparents do.

The Smell Test

Throughout this book, I'm skeptical of statistical claims that don't seem to match up to the reality we see around us. This doesn't mean we should reject data. But factual claims should at least stand up to a smell test. If, for instance, children were pushing millions of retirees into having inadequate incomes in old age, as the models projecting a retirement crisis must presuppose for their overall claims to have validity, we should be able to find that retired parents express some greater level of dissatisfaction than childless retirees do.

But that just doesn't seem to be the case. In a 2006 study, the RAND Corporation's Susann Rohwedder used Health and Retirement Study data to analyze how retirees describe their own retirement income adequacy.[18] She examined survey questions regarding whether retirees worry about their incomes, report that their retirement years are worse than the years before retirement, or report that they are "not at all satisfied" with retirement. But after controlling for various characteristics, Rohwedder finds no statistically significant correlation between having had children and self-reported negative outcomes in retirement.

What Does This All Mean?

Parents can take some solace from this chapter. Yes, they're probably saving less for retirement than their childless friends are. But they're also spending less, and that lower level of spending will tend to carry through to retirement. There's no evidence from parents themselves that children lead to an unhappier or less financially secure retirement. So that's one less thing to worry about.

For policymakers, a realistic view of how children interact with their parents' spending and saving decisions means that, if we once thought America faced a retirement crisis, we shouldn't think that now. And that is because projections that large percentages of working-age Americans will retire with inadequate incomes *depend* on the assumption that parents, who spent much of their preretirement earnings on their kids, need precisely the same retirement incomes as nonparents who spent their preretirement incomes on themselves.

Adults who had different standards of living before retirement are assumed to need the same standard of living in retirement. If you don't assume this, the retirement crisis goes away.

14

Public Employee Pensions:
Mismeasurement Breeds Mismanagement

W hat gets measured gets managed, so the business saying goes. But what gets mismeasured gets mismanaged. The mismeasurement involved with state and local government employee pensions is severe and skews all sorts of conclusions: how expensive these pensions are, how pensions should invest, and how state and local government employee compensation compares to pay and benefits in the private sector.

Perhaps most important, in the real world, how public pension finances are measured causes pensions to be mismanaged, with pension sponsors contributing far less than they should and pensions taking increasing and inappropriate risks with their investments. These risks fall on not just employees who participate in these pension plans but taxpayers and the economy as a whole. Getting these answers right starts with getting the numbers right. But putting these answers into action will demand more than just that.

The Public Pensions Landscape

Around the world, traditional defined benefit pensions—which provide fixed, guaranteed retirement benefits—have given way to defined contribution plans, in which benefits are based on contributions and investment returns and the risk is borne by the employee. Currently, only around 15 percent of private-sector employees in the United States are offered a defined benefit pension, and many of these are either 401(k)-like "cash balance" plans or legacy pension plans that are not offered to newly hired employees.

But defined benefit plans continue to roam the earth in the public sector. Nearly all full-time employees at all levels of the US government are offered a traditional pension. Although supplemental defined contribution plans have become more common, most public employees continue to accrue most or all their retirement benefits from a defined benefit plan.

The cost and risk of defined benefit pensions have become pressing issues for US cities and states, where pension funding has suffered despite rising contributions and increased risk-taking of plan investments. Rising costs have placed pressure on government budgets, squeezing out resources available for other budget priorities such as education and health care.

An example is Oregon. In 2017, Oregon enacted a record increase in its public education budget, increasing spending by 11 percent. Nevertheless, a number of Oregon schools reported having to make staff reductions due to budget constraints.[1] This is because required contributions for the state's public employees' retirement system have increased faster than the resources available to schools and other agencies, leaving fewer resources available for non-pension functions.

Nationwide, the average actuarially determined contribution (ADC) for retirement systems increased from 6.8 percent of employee payroll in 2001 to 20.8 percent of wages in 2023. (See Figure 1.) The ADC formerly was quaintly referred to as the actuarially *required* contribution, until it became clear that the contribution in fact was not required and that many governments were not making these payments in full.

Even in 2022, state and local governments flush with federal pandemic aid fell slightly short of making their full contributions. But far worse were the five years following the Great Recession, when from 2009 through 2013, contributions fell an average of 17 percent short each year compared to what the plan actuaries had calculated.

Figure 1 represents the national average, which blends many plans whose sponsors make their full contributions annually with a smaller number of bad actors that regularly shortchanged their pensions and allowed these plans to become dangerously underfunded. The names are familiar to any newspaper reader: Illinois, Kentucky, New Jersey, and others. The national averages give the appearance that the well-funded plans will bail out the poor performers, which would almost certainly be untrue.

Figure 1. Average Actuarially Determined Contributions, as a Percentage of Employee Payroll

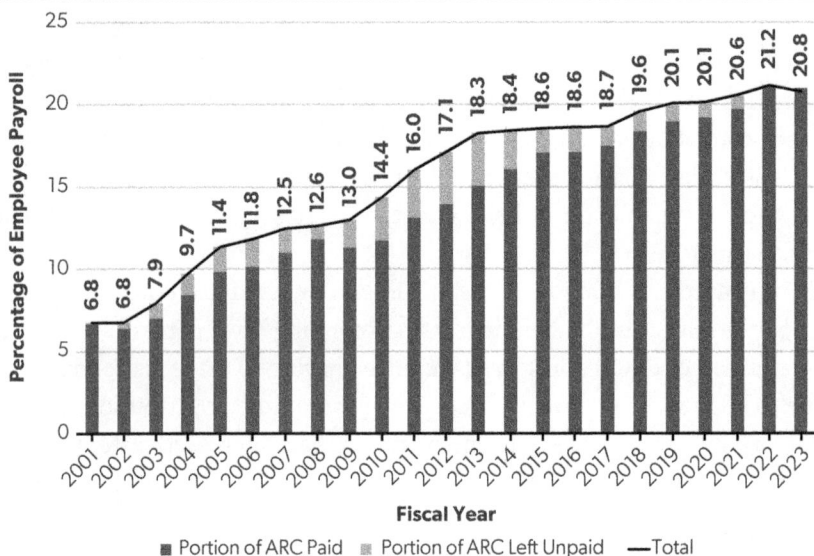

Source: Author's calculations using data from Public Plans Database, https://publicplansdata.org/api/?q=getchartdata&format=csv&chart=nationalarc.
Note: "ARC" stands for "annual required contribution."

How Pension Funding Works

Each year, the sponsor of a state or local employee pension must determine how much to contribute to the plan. Under the most common pension-funding practices, this annual contribution is composed of two parts. The first is to fund the "normal cost" (sometimes called the "service cost") of new pension benefits accruing to employees in the coming year as a result of their participation in the plan. The normal cost of the pension is what might be considered part of employee compensation for that year.

The second part of the pension contribution is an amortization payment the government makes to pay off unfunded liabilities accrued in prior years. Payments to address unfunded liabilities are not part of employees' current compensation, nor do employees contribute toward these contributions. Rather, the government makes the amortization payment to make up for funding shortfalls that arose either because of lower-than-expected investment returns or through the government's failure to make its full contribution in prior years. An amortization period of 20 to 30 years is now typical for public-sector plans, meaning unfunded liabilities from prior years are supposed to be fully paid off over that period.

In both cases, the necessary contribution is calculated using the present value of the future benefit liability. The present value is calculated by starting with the future nominal dollar amounts that must be paid by the plan then discounting these dollar amounts to the present using the interest rate that is assumed to be earned on the pension's portfolio of investments. In 2022, the median assumed interest rate was 7.0 percent.[2]

The chosen discount rate significantly affects the annual contributions a government must make to its pension plan. The effect of changing the discount rate used by a pension plan depends on how long in the future the benefit liability must be paid. For benefits that must be paid in the near future, the choice of discount rate does not matter much. But for benefits that will not be paid for several decades, the compounding effect of a lower or higher discount rate can be massive.

The average duration of already accrued pension liabilities (that is, liabilities already existing at the time) is generally about 13 years. That is to say, about half of accrued benefits will be paid in the coming 13 years, while half are paid beyond that point. The annual cost of amortizing unfunded liabilities would drop by about 11 percent for each percentage point increase in the assumed rate of return on plan investments.

The duration of newly accruing benefits is generally about 10 years longer. Because of the effects of different discount rates compounding over longer durations, the normal cost of new accruing benefits is more sensitive to changes in the discount rate. A 1 percentage point increase in the assumed investment rate of return would reduce the contribution toward normal costs by about 19 percent, assuming an average duration of liabilities of 23 years.

Unlike corporate defined benefit pensions, whose plan funding parameters are prescribed under federal law, state and local pension plans have great latitude over the discount rate they can apply to their liabilities and the period over which unfunded liabilities are amortized. Public plans operate under accounting standards established by the Government Accounting Standards Board (GASB), which sanctions the use of the expected return on pension assets to calculate the discounted present value of plan liabilities.

Investment Return Assumptions and Pension Risk-Taking

In 2023, the median assumed investment return among public plans nationwide was 7.0 percent, ranging from a low of 5.25 percent for Kentucky's Employee Retirement System (ERS) to a high of 7.55 percent for the Mississippi Public Employees Retirement System (PERS).[3] Different assumed investment returns can powerfully affect the measured value of a pension's liabilities.

To provide a simple illustration: If a plan owed a lump-sum payment of $1 million 15 years in the future, it would discount that dollar amount by its assumed return compounded over 15 years. The resulting present value would equal the plan's liability. Assuming a 7 percent return, the present value of $1 million in 15 years' time is about $349,938.[4]

But these present values are sensitive to the chosen investment return. Using the same $1 million payment owed in 15 years, the present value would range from a high of $464,000 if discounted using Kentucky ERS's 5.25 percent discount rate to a low of $336,000 if discounted using Mississippi PERS's 7.55 percent rate.

For state and local governments that are concerned with restraining the amounts they must contribute to their pensions each year, this discounting approach creates an obvious incentive to either exaggerate the expected return pension investments or increase the expected return by taking additional investment risk. As economists George Pennacchi and Mahdi Rastad write:

> Valuation using the GASB actuarial standard . . . leads to moral hazard incentives in the form of "accounting arbitrage": a pension plan has the incentive to invest in assets with high systematic risk in order to justify a higher discount rate that will reduce the actuarial valuation of its liabilities.[5]

And public plans in the United States have increased their risk-taking. In a 2023 study of teacher pension plans, I found that the median teacher plan shifted from holding 65 percent of its assets in risky investments in 2001 to 76 percent in 2019.[6] Looking at asset allocations over longer periods, the shift to risky investments such as common stocks, private equity, and hedge funds has been dramatic.

University of Amsterdam economist Aleksandar Andonov and his coauthors conclude that these accounting-based incentives explain the investment portfolios of US public plans, which take greater risk than either US corporate pensions or public employee plans in Canada, the United Kingdom, or the Netherlands, where different accounting standards mean such incentives do not exist.[7] These plans generally must discount their liabilities using a fixed interest rate, which does not vary based on the investment allocation the plan chooses.

The Valuation Debate

As a newly hired analyst at the American Enterprise Institute in 2009, I told my wife I had an op-ed coming out in the *Wall Street Journal*. "What is it about?" she asked.

"It's about how state and local government pensions are using the wrong discount rate to value their liabilities," I responded.[8]

"Good luck with that," she said.

And yet, since that time, great progress has been made in gaining a more accurate picture of how much public-sector pensions truly owe and how well funded they actually are.

Over the same 20 years in which state and local governments struggled with rising pension costs, an academic struggle took place as policy analysts, economists, and actuaries debated how best to measure the liabilities of public-sector pensions. The question comes down to what present value to ascribe to a payment that might not be paid until decades in the future. This is a debate over the appropriate discount rate that pensions should use to value their benefit liabilities.

The consensus among academic economists and independent government agencies is that even the high costs reported by public pensions today may be severely understated. This critique goes by a variety of names, including "financial economics," "fair market valuation," and the "market value of liabilities." All denote the same concepts.

As discussed earlier, the discount rates that state and local government pensions use are derived from the expected returns on the pensions' assets. By contrast, economists believe that the discount rate applied to a liability, including future pension benefits, should be derived from the risk of the liability itself, not to the risk and expected return of any assets that may be used to fund that liability.[9] This counterintuitive notion benefits from some explanation.

The basic logic is that pension payments are "bond-like." This means that, like a government bond, public-sector pensions offer a fixed, guaranteed payment extending for years in the future. In most cases in which things have been tested, government pension payments have turned out to be safer than government bonds.

In Detroit, Puerto Rico, and several California cities, bankrupt governments have defaulted on bonds before resorting to cuts to pension benefits. If pension benefits are (at least) as safe as bonds, it makes sense to discount future pension liabilities back to the present using the interest rates on government bonds.

The economics profession is essentially united in this view. As Donald Kohn, then vice chairman of the Federal Reserve Board, put it in a 2008 speech to a pension advocacy group:

> For all intents and purposes, accrued benefits have turned out to be riskless obligations. While economists are famous for disagreeing with each other on virtually every other conceivable issue, when it comes to this one there is no professional disagreement: The only appropriate way to calculate the present value of a very-low-risk liability is to use a very-low-risk discount rate.[10]

Similarly, writing in the flagship journal the *American Economic Review*, Jeffrey Brown of the University of Illinois and David Wilcox of the Fed wrote:

Nearly all state and local pension defined benefit pension plans compute the present value of their future liabilities using the expected return on the assets held in the pension trust. This practice contrasts sharply with finance theory, which is unambiguous that the appropriate discount rate is one that reflects the riskiness of the liabilities, not the assets.[11]

Boston College economist Alicia Munnell, often seen as a moderate on retirement issues, nevertheless was clear regarding how pension valuations should work: "Given their guaranteed status, state and local pension liabilities should be discounted at a riskless rate."[12]

Indeed, in a 2014 survey of distinguished professional economists conducted by the University of Chicago Booth School of Business, 96 percent agreed with the statement "By discounting pension liabilities at high interest rates under government accounting standards, many U.S. state and local governments understate their pension liabilities and the costs of providing pensions to public-sector workers."[13]

When pension liabilities are valued using a lower bond interest rate, unfunded liabilities explode upward and pensions' funded ratios plummet. For example, using discount rates based on the assumed returns on pension investments, pensions in 2020 reported total liabilities of about $5.8 trillion.[14] Given that these plans held around $4.2 trillion in assets at that time, in aggregate the plans were about 73 percent funded and had unfunded liabilities of around $1.6 trillion. Pension plans report these figures to their governmental sponsors based on GASB accounting standards and use them to calculate the levels of future contributions necessary to, over decades, return to 100 percent funding.

However, the Federal Reserve Board also calculates pension liabilities for use in the Financial Accounts of the United States. But instead of discounting future benefit payment using the assumed return on pension investments—again, currently around 7 percent—the Fed discounts liabilities using a corporate bond yield of 4 percent. Using the Fed's approach, unfunded liabilities in 2022 were measured at $3.9 trillion, and the funded ratio of state and local government pensions fell to only 57 percent.[15]

It is worth putting the $3.9 trillion figure for state and local government unfunded pension liabilities in 2022 into perspective. In 2022, the publicly held national debt was approximately $24 trillion, a concerning amount to be sure. But this figure covers all federal debt issued to the public for any reason to cover any governmental need, such as recessions, wars, and health care.

State and local governments have accrued an amount equal to 16 percent of the federal debt from one cause alone: a failure to fully fund one component of compensation for a set of employees who combined make up only 12 percent of the US workforce. It is a staggering level of debt for such a limited purpose and subset of the US population.

Moreover, even the averages the Federal Reserve calculated merge the well-funded plans with the poorly funded. For example, even using these stricter standards, the Fed found that Wisconsin's state pensions were 89 percent funded, South Dakota's 75 percent, and New York's 72 percent.[16] But on the other side of the distribution were New Jersey (31 percent funded), Illinois (35 percent), and Kentucky (38 percent).

Federal regulators would almost certainly shut down a corporate pension that was funded at these levels. But unlike private-sector pensions, state and local government pensions are effectively unregulated.

These differences aren't merely accounting abstractions. Public-sector plans aim to be fully funded over time, such that each generation of employees and taxpayers pays full freight for the benefits that current employees will receive when they retire. This concept is known as intergenerational or inter-period equity.

In the words of the GASB, intergenerational equity means "taxpayers of today pay for the services that they receive and the burden of payment for services today is not shifted to taxpayers of the future."[17] The GASB illustrates this concept with such phrases as "living within our means" and "fairness." Similarly, the American Academy of Actuaries states that "from an economic perspective, each generation of taxpayers ideally should pay for the compensation of the public employees who provide services to those taxpayers, including the funding of pension benefits that accrues during the period."[18]

State and local government pensions argue that intergenerational equity is best satisfied by discounting future benefit liabilities using the assumed return on the pension's investments. If those returns materialize, then contributions paid this year by taxpayers and employees will fully fund the future benefits that employees earn this year. Requiring pensions to use a lower assumed return would, in expectation at least, cause today's taxpayers and employees to overpay for their benefits, thereby violating intergenerational equity.

This would be perfectly reasonable if the returns on public pensions' investments were guaranteed. But the assumed returns on stocks, hedge funds, private equity, and the like are anything but guaranteed. Even over the long term, those investments carry significant risks. Long-term returns might be higher than currently assumed, but they also might be lower.

And when investment returns turn out to be lower than a pension plan assumed, as they have over the past several decades, taxpayers must make additional contributions to make up the difference. This contingent liability is the key difference between a defined contribution plan and a defined benefit pension.

In a defined contribution plan, the employer promises to provide a contribution that may or may not achieve some expected return in the future. In a defined benefit plan, the employer guarantees the benefit and must make all contributions necessary to ensure that benefit is paid, come what may. This contingent liability to make additional contributions in the future comes over and above the upfront contributions that pension sponsors make each year. But the value of this contingent liability is not measured in standard GASB-style public pension accounting.

The insight of the so-called financial economics critique of pension accounting standards is that the costs of protecting against low returns more than offset the benefits of receiving unexpectedly high returns. The reason is that low investment returns for a public-sector pension tend to be correlated with times when the economy is doing poorly, when tax revenues fall short, and when government obligations for other programs like unemployment and welfare increase.

As a risk assessment published in 2010 by Washington state's pension actuary stated, "Weak economic environments were correlated with weak investment returns. Lower investment returns created the need for increased contributions at a time when employers and members could least afford them."[19]

Pension Liabilities Don't Care What the Pension Invests In

The pushback against discounting pension liabilities using interest rates on safe government bonds is simple: Pensions don't invest in safe government bonds. They invest in a variety of assets of various risk levels that are designed to produce a total return that substantially exceeds what government bonds can produce.

For instance, Girard Miller—then columnist for *Governing* magazine and subsequently the chief investment officer of the Orange County Employees Retirement System—stated, "Pension funds are not going to invest their entire portfolio in 3 percent Treasury bonds right now—or ever—so the risk-free model is not even descriptive of reality and has little normative value."[20]

But this objection doesn't matter. Specifically, the value of the liability remains the same regardless of what the pension plan invests in—whether it is the safest bonds or the riskiest alternative investments available. We can illustrate this logic numerically using the pricing of financial products called put and call options.[21]

In simple terms, a *put option* sets a minimum price at which the holder can sell a financial asset—say, a stock—at some point in the future. For a stockholder, purchasing a put option acts as an insurance policy against low investment returns, since you can fall back on the put option if needed. The put option captures the value of the contingent liability for taxpayers to make supplemental contributions if the plan's investment returns fall short of the assumed rate of return.

A *call option* is the opposite: It gives the holder the option to purchase a financial asset at some given price in the future. By selling a call option, the holder of a stock in effect gives away investment returns above a stated level. In this example, a pension plan sells a call option giving away stock returns above a given level to finance the purchase of a put option protecting against returns below a given level.

Using a combination of put and call options, a pension plan accounts for not only its upfront contribution but also the contingent liability to make future as-needed payments. By using options prices, we can illustrate the cost of truly fully funding a future pension benefit liability without placing any cost burden on future generations—in other words, maintaining intergenerational equity.

Recall our illustration from earlier: Imagine that a pension plan owes a single, lump-sum payment of $1 million taking place 15 years in the future. If the pension assumes a 7.0 percent return on plan investments, as a typical plan does today, the contribution required to fund that liability would be $349,938; that's $1 million, discounted 15 years to the present at a 7.0 percent interest rate. That's the amount that a state or local pension would contribute today to "fully fund" the future payment.

But for today's taxpayers to *truly* fully fund the liability, they must ensure that tomorrow's taxpayers won't be put on the hook if the assumed 7 percent investment return doesn't pan out. That's the contingent liability issue.

To do this, the pension plan purchases a put option guaranteeing the plan's right to sell its $349,938 investment in 15 years' time for no less than $1 million. The price of a put or call option today depends on several factors: the risk of the underlying investment, measured as the standard deviation of annual returns; the length of time until the option can be exercised; the "strike price" of the option at the future date; and the return available on riskless investments.

For a typical portfolio held by a public-sector pension, it is reasonable to assume a standard deviation of annual returns of 12 percent. The standard deviation of annual returns is a measure of the riskiness of the investment portfolio. For example, a standard deviation of 12 percent implies that around two-thirds of annual returns will be within plus or minus 12 percentage points from the average return. The holding period is assumed to be 15 years, the strike price is $1 million, and, to maintain consistency with how the Federal Reserve currently measures pension liabilities, the safe return on bonds is assumed to be 4 percent.

The cost of a put option guaranteeing against future generations needing to bail out the pension plan would be $216,592. Combined with the $349,938 initial investment, this total cost of $566,529 would guarantee that the $1 million payment could be made *and* future taxpayers won't be the ones called on to pay it.

But what if the pension's investments end up returning more than 7.0 percent? That would produce a surplus, which would benefit future generations at the expense of the present. To address that risk, the pension plan today could sell a call option that would give away any ending fund balance above $1 million. The call option ensures that future generations don't profit at the expense of the current one, and the current generation can use the proceeds of the call option sale to offset the cost of the put option.

But here lies the rub: The proceeds from selling a call option only partially offset the cost of the put option. Using the same input parameters used to price the put option, the cost of the call option is only $17,718—a lot less than it costs to purchase the put option.

The call option is worth less because stock returns tend to be high in what economists call "states of the world" in which other things are going well—in particular, when the economy is strong and money is easy to come by. Even if we subtract the $17,718 proceeds from selling the call option, the total price of both guaranteeing the pension's $1 million payment and ensuring intergenerational equity comes to $548,812.

Now, having gone through all this discussion and number crunching, what is special about $548,812? It is precisely the figure we would have obtained simply by discounting the $1 million liability for 15 years at the 4 percent return that is assumed for safe bond investments.

In other words, the value of a pension liability does not depend on the risk or expected return of the assets the pension uses to fund that liability. It does not depend on the assumption that the pension invests only in government bonds. Had we run the same exercise assuming the pension invested entirely in stocks—say, with an expected return of 10 percent and standard deviation of annual returns of 18 percent—the results would have been the same, as they would had we assumed the pension held a less-risky, lower-returning portfolio of investments.

Moreover, it does not matter if the pension system does not actually purchase options protecting against below-assumed returns while giving away returns above the assumed level. The plan is carrying those costs in-house, but doing so does not make the costs disappear so much as simply making them less transparent to policymakers and the public.

Long Time Horizons Don't Reduce Investment Risk

The financial economics critique of public pension accounting standards and funding practices is that holding a risky investment portfolio doesn't make a guaranteed pension benefit cheaper. But pensions have a response: that their investments aren't so risky after all. One supposed advantage of traditional pensions over defined contribution plans is their greater ability to bear investment risk, based on the supposedly longer duration of their investments.

Dorothee Franzen of the Organisation for Economic Co-operation and Development describes the logic in this way:

> The main characteristics of DB [defined benefit] pension funds are the importance of liabilities and the long-term investment horizon. Pension funds are usually described as long-term investors. This conception provides the argument for higher investment in asset classes such as equity that are subject to higher volatility in the short-term but also reward higher returns in the long-term.[22]

Since traditional pensions tend to hold investments over long periods—for instance, contributions made when an individual begins employment at age 21 might be used to fund benefits the employee collects at age 100—they seemingly have less reason to fear market risk than other investors have and thus should logically take on more of it.

There seemingly is an underlying logic to this argument. It is well-known that the distribution of risky investment returns shrinks as the holding period for the investment increases. This relation is sometimes expressed via a "tulip graph," which tracks the distribution of annualized returns over time.

Figure 2 starts with an investment portfolio that has an assumed average annual return of 7.0 percent and a standard deviation of annual returns of 12 percent, broadly comparable to the typical state and local government pension portfolio in the United States today. As discussed earlier, the standard deviation is a measure of risk, of how much the typical year's return tends to be above or below the long-run average.

Using the standard deviation, I calculate the potential distribution of average annualized returns over different holding periods. I calculate returns at the 25th percentile—meaning the return over a given holding period is higher than 25 percent of outcomes and lower than

Figure 2. Investment Returns at 25th, 50th, and 75th Percentiles, over Varying Holding Periods

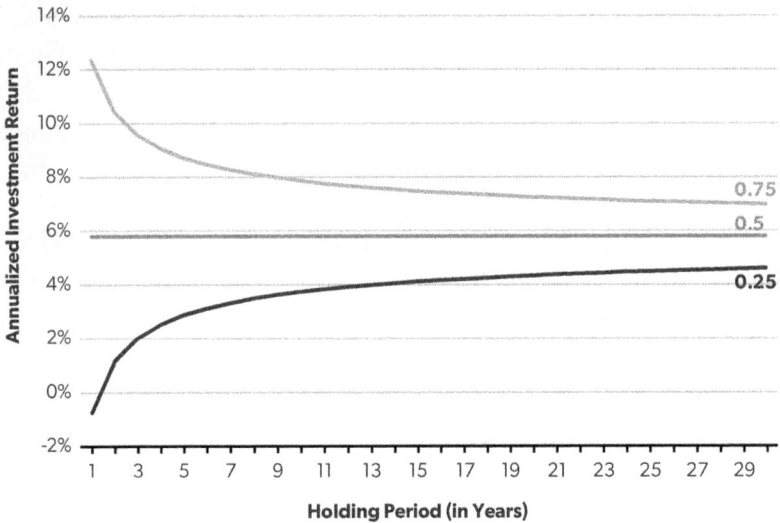

Source: Author's calculations.
Note: This figure assumes mean annual return of 7 percent and standard deviation of annual returns of 12 percent.

75 percent—the median or 50th percentile return, and the 75th percentile return, which is above 75 percent of outcomes and below 25 percent. Figure 2 looks like a tulip placed on its side.

Over short holding periods, the range of possible investment returns is extreme: Over one year, 25 percent of returns are over 15.1 percent, and another 25 percent are –1.1 percent or lower. But over time the distribution of annualized returns narrows, consistent with the view that risk declines over long holding periods.

Over 15 years, the 25th percentile return increases from an annual loss of 1.1 percent to an annualized gain of 4.8 percent. Over 30 years, the 25th percentile return rises to 5.5 percent. Seemingly, if a pension plan has long time horizons, it can reap the returns from holding stocks without bearing much of the risk.

But here is the problem: Over longer periods, the effects of compounding trump the effects of declining risk. That is to say, receiving an annualized return just a point or two below your assumed rate, compounded year

Figure 3. Compounded Value of $1 over Different Holding Periods and Percentiles

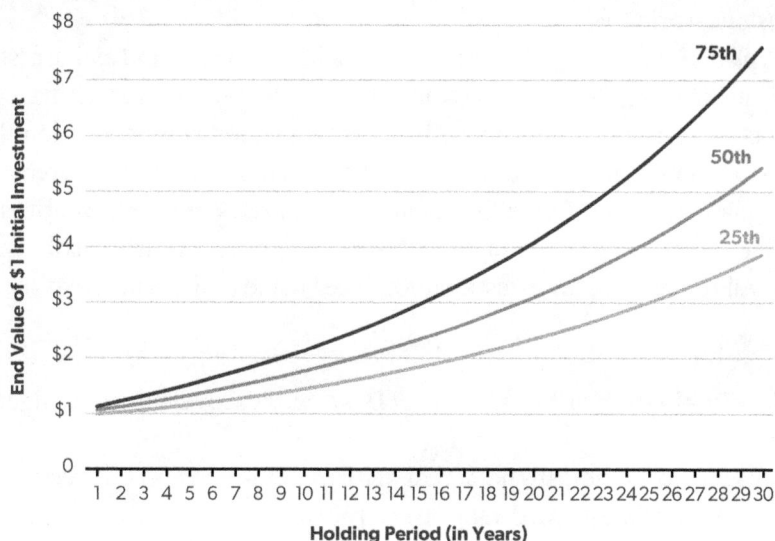

Source: Author's calculations.

after year after year, produces a crushing shortfall in the dollar value of the investment over time.

For instance, imagine that a pension invested $1 in a portfolio with an expected return of 7.0 percent and a standard deviation of annual returns of 12 percent. (See Figure 3.) After one year, the expected balance on the investment would be $1.07. The value of the investment at the 25th percentile of outcomes would be $0.99, while at the 75th percentile, the value after one year would be $1.15.

After a holding period of 30 years, the expected value of the initial $1 investment would be $7.61. At the 25th percentile, however, the value would be only $5.02, a 34 percent shortfall. At the 75th percentile, the investment would rise to be worth $11.49, which is 51 percent higher than the expected value. In contrast to the earlier tulip graph, this second illustration is often called the "trump chart."

This discussion shows that while the distribution of annual returns falls over longer holding periods, the distribution of the dollar values of investments grows wider. And pensions must pay dollars. While this is not a particularly complex point to convey, there is little incentive in the public pensions world to do so.

A plan's investment advisers want it to load up on risky and exotic assets, because that is how they make their money. The plan's actuaries have no incentive to convey this knowledge, since a defined benefit pension that fails to leverage the premium on risky investments is financially untenable. And plan trustees, often either political appointees or representatives of public-sector workers, are under pressure to keep near-term contributions low. All this adds up to investments choices made under faulty reasoning.

How Public-Sector Pensions Can Destabilize Government Budgets

As discussed earlier, if the actual returns on a pension's investments fall short of the assumed rate of return, the sponsor must make larger catch-up contributions in future years. These catch-up contributions increase the burden of pensions on government budgets. If contributions rise too high, governments may even skip making them. This alleviates the immediate budgetary burden but obviously only worsens the problem for the future.

This is true for any defined benefit pension system at any time. But the risks posed by public employee pensions to their sponsoring governments' budgets have increased significantly, due to two factors: Pension programs are larger today relative to their sponsors' budgets, and those pensions are taking greater investment risk. These factors multiply to increase pension plans' potential to cause havoc in the budgets of the governments that sponsor them.

The first factor is the sheer size of pension plans. In 1946, state and local government pensions held assets equal to 25 percent of annual state and local government expenditures.[23] Imagine, for simplicity, that the pension funds lost 10 percent in value and that the government was obliged to make up that loss in a single year. Doing so would cost the government revenues equal to 2.5 percent of its annual budget.

By 1980, state and local pension funds had grown to equal 58 percent of state and local expenditures. So making up a 10 percent investment loss in a single year would demand revenues equal to 5.8 percent of annual expenditures.

By 2023, state and local government pension funds had grown to equal 147 percent of state and local government expenditures. Making up a 10 percent asset loss in a single year would cost governments an amount equal to 14.7 percent of annual expenditures. The growing size of pensions by itself means that, while once an afterthought in governmental activities, pensions are now the 900-pound gorilla of public finance, throwing their weight around and forcing the rest of the budget to accommodate them.

But there is a second factor as well: Increasing risk-taking by public pensions makes the probability of a sizable investment loss increase. Due to falling interest rates over the past several decades, pensions have loaded up on risk to meet their investment return goals. While pensions once held bonds and commercial paper, today they focus on stocks, real estate, private equity, and hedge funds.

In a 2013 paper, I estimated the risk profile of a pension portfolio that would have an expected nominal return of 8.0 percent. In 1975, a plan could achieve 8.0 percent expected returns with a portfolio having a relatively low standard deviation of annual returns of just 3.7 percent. Such a portfolio would lose money in about one year out of 65.

By 1995, the standard deviation of returns of an investment portfolio with an expected return of 8.0 percent would have been about only 4.3 percent. By 2013, a pension plan aiming for an 8.0 percent expected return would need to take significantly greater risk, building a portfolio with a standard deviation of annual returns of around 14 percent.[24]

The 2013 paper also showed that when a larger pension size is multiplied by greater investment volatility, the risk public pensions pose to state and local government budgets increased by a factor of 10 from 1975 to 2013.[25] Given the increasing size and risk-taking of state and local government pensions over the past decade, pension budgetary risk has only increased.

One of the goals of public pension reforms should be to allocate and manage risk in such a way that the destabilizing effect pensions can have on public expenditures is reduced. Some governments have done this shifting partially or fully to defined contribution retirement plans, in which case employees bear the risk and reward.

Other governments, such as in Nevada, have instituted annual adjustments to employee and employer contributions, so that both share in the risk of pension investments. Still other places, such as Wisconsin and South Dakota, fine-tune annual cost-of-living adjustments based on the funded status of the retirement plan. What lawmakers cannot and should not do is ignore pension risk.

No, Public Pensions Do Not Grow the Economy

As state and local pension systems have come under criticism, pensions and their proxies have generated numerous defenses. One of the most active groups in this area has been the National Institute on Retirement Security (NIRS), an advocacy group that receives funding from pension plans, their financial advisers and actuaries, and others.

One of NIRS's most popular and long-running studies is titled "Pensionomics." The 2021 edition of the report concludes, "Retiree spending of pension benefits in 2018 generated $1.3 trillion in total economic output, supporting nearly seven million jobs across the nation. Pension spending also added nearly $192 billion to government coffers at the federal, state and local levels."[26] I have personally met with pension trustees who honestly believe these claims.

To be fair, the logic is seemingly simple and compelling. As NIRS illustrates:

> A retired firefighter uses his pension money to buy a new lawnmower. As a result of that purchase, the owner of the hardware store, the lawnmower salesman, and each of the companies involved in the production of the car all see an increase in income, and spend that additional income. These companies hire additional employees as a result of this increased business, and those new employees spend their paychecks in the local economy.[27]

Topping it all off, all those individuals pay taxes on their incomes. The tax revenue generated by pension benefits offsets much of their cost while creating millions of jobs in the process.

But these claims, which NIRS backs with impressive-seeming figures on where the economy grows and why certain types of jobs are created, are entirely fictitious. The argument isn't over the size of the "Keynesian multiplier," the degree to which a dollar of income is re-spent after being received. It is nothing as sophisticated as that.

Rather, "pensionomics's" magical conclusions depend on counting only one side of the equation: Pension benefits boost the economy, but the taxes and employee contributions necessary to fund those pensions—that is, billions of dollars that *can't* be spent because they're instead flowing into government pension plans—have no negative effect. In reality, while pension benefits may have a multiplier effect, pension contributions have a "divisor effect": Each dollar that can't be spent because it is contributed to public pensions reduces economic activity by more than $1.

If you count both sides of the equation, the rough effect of public-sector pensions on the overall economy is zero. NIRS, and the various retirement plans, unions, investment managers, and actuarial firms that support its work, should be embarrassed that this quality of work continues to be produced.

But NIRS should know this, because its own studies basically admit it. On the second-to-last page of the paper, NIRS finally acknowledges—however obliquely—that there's another side to the story:

> This study measures the gross economic impacts of pension benefit expenditures only, rather than the net economic impacts. Pension payments are a form of deferred compensation, meaning that employees and employers contribute to the pension trust over the course of an employee's career as a portion of the employee's total compensation. Had that employee received that compensation in another form—for example, a slight increase in gross pay each month—s/he would have seen higher disposable income, and presumably would have spent a portion of that income in the local economy at that time.[28]

In other words, the money paid into pension plans could have been used to stimulate the economy. NIRS defers from analyzing the net economic impact of pension benefit payments because, it says, doing so "would require a dynamic model and data that spans several decades."[29] But we can come to an easy approximation.

Pensions are an effectively closed system. All the money they pay out is derived from money that was paid in, plus interest. Over their careers, government employees and taxpayers paid money into their state's retirement system. That money otherwise would have been spent or saved. Had it been spent, it would have stimulated the economy in the past. Had it been saved, it would have stimulated the future economy by funding factories or research or investment in human capital.

We gave up that economic boost. Is there any reason to believe that the economic boost we're enjoying from pension benefits today is larger than the economic loss we experienced by giving up money to pension systems in the past? No. Why would it be?

If anything, public employee pensions may tend to worsen the economy. First, as economists Leora Friedberg and Anthony Webb show, traditional pensions encourage public employees to retire several years earlier than they otherwise might.[30] A smaller labor force reduces gross domestic product.

Moreover, the funding required to pay public pension benefits, which are significantly more generous than those afforded to private-sector employees, causes taxes to be higher than they otherwise might be. Higher taxes, all other things equal, tend to depress economic activity.

And yet the news media and interest groups that are the intended recipients of pensionomics are sufficiently credulous that the series has been annually reissued for more than a decade. Individual pension systems have commissioned their own pensionomics-style studies, and I can say from meeting with pension trustees and administrators that they actually believe they are running what amounts to financial perpetual motion machines. Programs that can destabilize public budgets and starve funds from education, health care, and public safety deserve a more rigorous treatment than this.

Victory for the Financial Economics Critique, in Theory

At the time the financial economics critique of pension valuation was made, the debate was fierce. The public pensions industry fought back: the pension plans themselves, the actuarial firms that serve those pensions plans, state treasurers who oversee the pension plans, and various industry groups such as NIRS, the National Conference of Public Employee Retirement Systems, and the National Association of State Retirement Administrators. Op-eds were written, and debates were held. I personally found myself on a Nixonian "enemies list" put together by a public-sector employees union in Texas.

Over time, others started to weigh in on public pensions.

In 2011, the Congressional Budget Office (CBO) reviewed the two approaches to pension liability valuation. The CBO deemed that the fair market value approach reflects "the cost of the risk to taxpayers that the rate of return on risky pension assets may not meet expectations."[31] As the CBO put it, "By accounting for the different risks associated with investment returns and benefit payments, the fair-value approach provides a more complete and transparent measure of the costs of pension obligations."[32]

Beginning in 2012, the bond ratings service Moody's rejected pension liability figures as reported using GASB standards and instead revalued those plans' own reported liabilities using a high-grade corporate bond yield.[33] This produced higher unfunded pension liabilities and lower pension funding ratios.

Starting in 2013, the two official accounts of the US economy—the Bureau of Economic Analysis's National Income and Product Accounts and the Federal Reserve's Financial Accounts of the United States—began measuring public-sector pension liabilities using a discount rate derived from the yield on corporate bonds.

In 2014, the Society of Actuaries' Blue Ribbon Panel on Public Pension Plan Funding, of which I was a member, recommended that state and local pensions report both plan liabilities and the normal cost of accruing benefits as valued using the yield on riskless securities such as US Treasury bonds.[34]

In 2016, the Actuarial Standards Board's Pensions Task Force concluded that "a market-based alternative liability measurement should be calculated and disclosed for all valuations of pension plans for funding purposes."[35]

In December 2021, the Actuarial Standards Board issued a revision to Actuarial Standard of Practice (ASOP) 4, which pertains to the measurement of pension plan obligations and the determination of pension contributions.[36] The revised ASOP 4 requires that beginning with reports covering pension activity after February 15, 2023, pension actuaries must include a market-consistent measurement of pension liabilities. This is defined by the board as

> an actuarial present value that is estimated to be consistent
> with the price at which benefits that are expected to be paid
> in the future would trade in an open market between a knowl-
> edgeable seller and a knowledgeable buyer.[37]

In practice, this implies that benefits must be discounted using an interest rate drawn from safe bonds, though the ASOP does not dictate precisely which interest rate pension actuaries should use.

Substantively, the debate over pension liability valuation is all but over, and those favoring a fair market valuation approach won.

The question is how much that victory matters in practice. To be sure, many involved in the debate simply wanted to get the numbers right. And there is progress in that direction, even if the GASB steadfastly continues to sanction accounting methods that seemingly every other government agency has rejected.

And yet, the real hope was that providing more informative pension liability figures would change how pensions acted. If state and local governments realized that their pension liabilities were substantially larger than previously thought, they might take stronger actions to fund those liabilities and enact reforms to make pensions cheaper down the road. Likewise, if pension plans realized that taking additional investment risk did not make their liabilities smaller, perhaps they would invest more prudently.

To date, neither has truly occurred. Pensions are taking more investment risk today than ever, leveraging the GASB accounting standards in which a plan that takes more risk immediately becomes "better funded" and immediately may reduce its annual contributions.

Likewise, while several pension plans undertook reforms in the wake of the Great Recession, those efforts were often modest in scope and still leave state and local government pensions far more costly to governments and generous to participants than their private-sector counterparts do. The normal cost of newly accruing state and local employee pension benefits as measured by the Federal Reserve has declined only slightly in recent years.

In a sense, however, much of this was to be expected. The pension accounting debate occurred when state and local governments found themselves squeezed by rising pension costs, which were calculated *using a methodology that significantly understated those costs*. These governments already were paying as much as they could pay or were willing to pay given other budgetary considerations. Convincing these governments that they should be paying even more would not change the broader financing constraints under which they are operating. In short, many state and local governments are in a pension funding box that is difficult to get out of.

Progress seemingly has been made in encouraging public plans to reduce their assumed investment returns. This was not done in explicit recognition of the merits of the financial economics critique; to acknowledge the truth of that critique would demand an immediate shift to a government bond yield, not an incremental downward adjustment to returns based on increasingly risky investments.

Nevertheless, from 2002 to 2021, the mean nominal return assumed by state and local plans fell from 8.1 percent to 7.1 percent, a seemingly meaningful move toward realism.[38]

And yet even this sign of progress is deceptive, because all the reduction in assumed nominal returns, and then some, came from plans reducing their assumed rates of inflation. Assumed real rates of return, which are more meaningful for plans that offer cost-of-living adjustments to benefits, rose from 2002 to 2021.

In 2002, the average plan assumed a real rate of return of 4.1 percent, rising to 4.6 percent by 2021. Making matters worse, in mid-2002, the inflation-adjusted yield on Treasury Inflation-Projected Securities (TIPS) with a duration of 10 years or more was about 3.2 percent, while in mid-2021, the real yield on TIPS was negative.

The same trend is shown when comparing nominal assumed pension returns to nominal yields on 30-year Treasury bonds: Bond yields have declined far more than assumed pension returns. This means pensions are today assuming they will receive a substantially larger risk premium over safe investments than they did in the past, on the order of an additional 2 percentage points of return. It is hard to view these practices as pension managers having learned their lesson.

For the financial economics approach to pension liability valuation to truly affect how pensions are managed, one of two things must happen.

First, public pensions must be required to not only disclose the market value of their liabilities but fund those liabilities using market-based interest rates as well. This is how pension regulation works in the private sector. A pension must discount its liabilities using a corporate bond yield, and it must make contributions to fund those liabilities while assuming a corporate bond yield paid on those contributions.

Now, this does not mean that private pensions may not invest in riskier assets such as stocks. They can, and they do. But what private pensions may not do is credit themselves with the returns on riskier assets before those returns materialize.

In other words, risky but higher-returning investments by private-sector pensions affect the funded ratio of the plan by increasing the plan's assets, not by reducing the plan's liabilities. This is how it should be.

If state and local government employee pensions were required to *fund* their liabilities as private pensions do, which includes not only a lower discount rate applied to liabilities and contributions but a shorter period in which to amortize unfunded liabilities, the average governmental pension contribution in 2016 would have risen from 24 percent of employee wages to 105 percent.[39] That would be an existential threat to defined benefit pensions in the public sector.

And, much like the private-sector employer response to the Employee Retirement Income Security Act of 1974, public-sector employers would likely respond to the requirement to truly fully fund their pensions by abandoning these plans in favor of defined contribution retirement accounts. Even if governments were willing and able to make these extremely high levels of pension contributions, nonpublic employees would likely rebel at the voting booth when they compared the amounts being contributed to public employees' pensions versus the employer matches they received for their 401(k) plans.

This sheds light on why the transition from defined benefit to defined contribution occurred in the private sector even as defined benefit pensions remain predominant in the public sector. Faced with the requirement to fully fund benefit liabilities and rapidly address unfunded liabilities, private-sector employers largely determined that defined benefit pensions were not worth their cost in terms of attracting and retaining employees, at least relative to other forms of pay and benefits. Defined benefit pensions continue in the public sector, but only because state and local governments are not required to fully fund future benefits and rapidly address funding shortfalls.

The second potential avenue to reform pensions is indirect. In theory, mere disclosure of the market value of pension liabilities could affect pension policy. When public-sector entities issue debt, they must produce disclosures for potential investors that detail the entity's other financial obligations, including pensions. And pensions should be of particular interest to bond investors, since in practice pensions are paid before bonds in times of fiscal distress.

To date, the pension liability values listed in such bond disclosures have been based on the GASB expected-return discount rates, producing lower dollar figures that imply a greater level of security for bonds issued by a state or local government. Were the Securities and Exchange Commission to require that state and local governments instead disclose the market-consistent liability figures that are now mandated by ASOP 4, those figures could affect how ratings agencies and investors view a bond issuance. Market pressure, via the interest rates that governments must pay on their borrowings, could create incentives for governments to reduce pension liabilities and fully fund the liabilities they do owe.

Such pressure is likely to be effective only in certain fringe cases. Bond investors and ratings agencies are concerned almost entirely with the risk of default. They do not care, for instance, if rising pension costs push out expenditures on schools, public safety, or infrastructure except to the degree that such cuts might increase the risk of a default on the government's debts. But citizens do care about these matters, which are crucial for the vitality and prosperity of their own communities.

And so, while mandating that state and local governments disclose the market value of public pension liabilities is a victory for good government, it was a long-fought and limited victory over a period in which unfunded public pension liabilities increased by over $1 trillion.

Reforming Public-Sector Pensions

The debate over pension liability valuation did not produce significant changes in how public employee pensions are either structured or funded. A number of pension reforms were implemented in the wake of the Great Recession, but these likely would have taken place regardless as state and local governments attempted to address their larger fiscal circumstances.

Yet the Bureau of Labor Statistics reports that in 2022, 39 percent of state and local government employees had access to a defined contribution plan, even if in many cases the defined contribution account is a supplement to rather than a substitute for a traditional pension.[40] About 19 percent of public employees currently participate in such a plan.

At the federal level, defined contribution plans were introduced for newly hired employees as part of 1980s-era reforms that established a new and less generous defined benefit that is coupled with the defined contribution Thrift Savings Plan. A mix of traditional pension accruals and retirement account savings is now taken for granted by most federal workers, who continue to have an attractive retirement package.

Reforms that reduce the cost of pensions for public employees might be possible so long as governments enacting the reforms shared the savings with the employees themselves via higher salaries. Defined contribution plans are better suited to cost reduction than defined benefit plans are, simply because so much of the cost of a traditional pension is embedded in the implicit guarantee against low future investment returns.

Defined contribution plans allow greater portability between jobs. For example, someone going into teaching might think they have a skill they could transfer effectively anywhere in the country. But an employee who shifts from one defined benefit pension to another midcareer leaves tens or even hundreds of thousands of dollars on the table.

The reason is that benefit accruals for traditional pensions are back-loaded: Benefits in retirement are equal to final salary *multiplied by* years of service. Both increase over an employee's career, but the multiplicative effect creates a nonlinear accrual of benefits over time.

A public employee may go through several decades of work accruing little in the way of future pension benefits then accrue hundreds of thousands of dollars in the final 10 or 15 years of work just before retirement. An employee who splits their career between two defined benefit programs will receive significantly lower benefits than an employee who spends a full career in one plan. Defined contribution retirement accounts do not suffer from these odd accrual patterns and are fully portable between jobs.

While the financial economics critique of pension valuation may not have reaped the immediate benefits its proponents might have hoped for in terms of improved pension funding and potential reforms to pension structures, they have achieved one important goal: putting state and local governments on notice of how precarious their pension funding health might be.

According to the nonprofit group Truth in Accounting, the state government of Illinois faces about $43 billion in explicit bonded debt but over $140 billion in unfunded pension liabilities, even using the forgiving GASB accounting standards.[41] The true value using market valuation methods is much higher.

All this means that, in the case of a true fiscal crisis, Illinois could default on the entirety of its explicit debt and still not have sufficient funds to pay what it owes to retirees. I have little doubt that in such a circumstance Illinois—or Connecticut, Kentucky, New Jersey, or one of many states with poorly funded pensions—would come to the federal government for assistance, requiring citizens of fiscally responsible states to bail out entities that have for decades systematically underfunded their retirement systems. It is important that the federal government can tell these states, "You knew."

15

The Retirement Savings Gap Is Really a Government Funding Gap

The retirement savings gap "is a critical financial issue that refers to the difference between the amount of money needed for a comfortable retirement and the actual savings accumulated by individuals," according to the financial education organization Finance Strategists.[1] And many say that difference may be huge. According to the National Institute on Retirement Security, "The collective retirement savings gap among working households age 25–64 ranges from $6.8 to $14 trillion."[2] "Without changes," CNBC reports, "the retirement-savings gap could create a $1.3 trillion economic burden through 2040."[3]

Responses to the retirement savings gap usually involve giving the government greater responsibility for retirement income provision—which makes sense, if you accept that most households aren't saving enough on their own. Multitrillion-dollar proposals to expand Social Security or establish an automatic individual retirement account plan set up by state governments are all solutions designed to address a retirement savings gap stemming from the behavior of ordinary Americans who just aren't up to the challenging task of preparing for retirement.

But what if the real retirement savings gap doesn't lie with citizens, despite all their foibles and failures? That's what this chapter addresses. The larger retirement savings gap, and potentially the *real* retirement crisis, rests with government retirement programs of all types—around the country and, indeed, around the world. Individuals and households saving for retirement are imperfect and make many errors along the way. But they have the incentive to get things right and to put aside enough money today to provide a decent standard of living tomorrow.

In the public sector, the levels of data and expertise available to administer publicly run retirement programs immensely surpass even the most sophisticated individual saving for retirement. But the incentives are all in the opposite direction. Politicians are rewarded for promising benefits today while leaving the paying for benefits part to the future. As a result, as we have seen in the previous two chapters, it is rare for a retirement program at any level of government to amass sufficient resources to meet its obligations.

Funding Shortfalls in Government-Run Retirement Plans

Federal, state, and local governments administer various plans that provide income in retirement. Some, such as Supplemental Security Income, are means-tested safety-net programs not designed to provide income for typical households that save for retirement. Others, however, are designed to and effectively provide retirement income even for many upper-income households.

Social Security is a near-universal program that replaces preretirement earnings on a progressive basis. Federal employees, the uniformed military, and state and local government employees all participate in retirement plans, generally defined benefit pensions, which together with Social Security should allow most workers to maintain their preretirement standard of living once they retire.

However, all these government-run retirement plans require adequate funding. In most cases, defined benefit pensions do not have assets currently on hand sufficient to fund all the benefits they have promised. In Social Security's case, neither current nor scheduled payroll tax rates will allow for the full payment of benefits past the early 2030s.

Thus, the retirement crisis is not merely a problem of insufficient household preparation. Indeed, funding shortfalls in the government sector could exceed retirement saving shortfalls by households. If so, we might conclude that the retirement saving problem could be considerably larger than is currently understood.

But it also may cast doubt on whether the government sector can be counted on to properly administer and fund programs designed to increase retirement benefits in light of perceived under-saving by households. Government programs have often focused on delivering near-term benefits while falling short on making benefit funding adequate over the long term. Although Social Security and state and local pensions are financed differently, they share this common shortcoming.

Social Security. The Social Security program offers retirement, survivor, and disability benefits to eligible individuals and their spouse and dependents. Social Security's funding shortfalls have been a matter of public attention and sporadic legislative efforts since the late 1980s, but no meaningful reforms have been enacted since 1983. Long-term funding shortfalls reappeared just one year following the 1983 reforms and have grown almost without pause every year since. As of 2023, Social Security was underfunded by about 20 percent over the next 75 years.[4]

That said, placing Social Security's funding shortfalls in terms that are comparable to a household retirement saving gap is difficult because of the way Social Security benefits are financed. Most retirement plans are intended to be prefunded, such that a plan's assets are sufficient to pay all the future benefits currently owed by the plan. Any shortfall of plan assets relative to plan liabilities is a funding gap. On that basis, Social Security's trust fund assets of roughly $2.8 trillion are far outstripped by the approximately $43 trillion in benefits the program has earned but not yet paid out.[5]

However, Social Security is financed mostly on a pay-as-you-go basis in which current taxes are used to pay current benefits. Since the Social Security Amendments of 1939, policymakers abandoned the notion of building Social Security assets to a level sufficient to pay full accrued benefits.

An alternative approach is to look at Social Security's 75-year funding shortfall inclusive of future payroll tax revenues. The funding shortfall is the dollar amount today that, earning interest and combined with taxes collected in the future, would be sufficient for Social Security to pay full scheduled benefits over the next 75 years. The 75-year period is designed to encompass the projected lifespans of nearly all employees currently covered by Social Security. Thus, the 75-year unfunded obligation in dollar terms is roughly equivalent to a personal retirement saving shortfall applied to the full working and retired population.

There are different projections of Social Security's long-term funding shortfall. The best-known figures are those calculated by the Social

Security Administration's actuaries based on demographic and economic assumptions made by the Social Security Board of Trustees. As of 2023, the trustees projected a 75-year actuarial deficit equal to 3.6 percent of the wages over the next 75 years, producing a present value funding gap of $23.7 trillion.

The Congressional Budget Office (CBO) makes its own projections of Social Security's finances. While the CBO does not disclose the dollar value of Social Security's projected funding shortfall, the agency does project a 75-year funding shortfall equal to 5.1 percent of taxable payroll, a substantially larger deficit than is projected by the Social Security trustees.[6] Assuming the same present value of taxable payroll over the next 75 years, this would result in a funding gap of about $33.6 trillion.

These Social Security Administration and CBO projections are, by their authors' own admission, imprecise. They are based on projections of myriad demographic and economic variables extending decades into the future. Nevertheless, these are the best guesses of the amounts by which promised Social Security benefits exceed the taxes currently available to pay them.

Federal Employee Pensions. Federal government employees participate in three retirement plans. Employees hired before 1987 participate in the Civil Service Retirement System (CSRS), a defined benefit pension plan. These employees do not participate in Social Security and receive their full retirement benefit via the CSRS.

The newer Federal Employees Retirement System (FERS) is a smaller defined benefit plan that has enrolled federal employees hired since 1987. In addition, FERS-covered employees participate in the Thrift Savings Plan (TSP). The federal government contributes 1 percent of employee pay to the TSP for all employees. Employees who choose to make their own contributions may receive a federal matching contribution up to 4 percent more of their salaries.

As a defined contribution plan, the TSP is always "fully funded" in the sense that it cannot have obligations in excess of its assets. As defined benefit plans, the CSRS and FERS must match assets to liabilities to ensure that the plans can pay full benefits as scheduled. In both cases, the plans' assets consist of special-issue government bonds similar to those issued to the Social Security trust funds. These bonds are assets to the CSRS and FERS programs, though they are equal and opposite liabilities to the US government and, by extension, the taxpayer. For these purposes, however, we ignore such distinctions.

As of its most recent actuarial valuation for fiscal year 2014, the CSRS is 18 percent funded and has an unfunded liability of $815 billion. The FERS program is 78 percent funded and has an unfunded liability of $209 billion. Total unfunded liabilities for the two federal employee plans equal $1.024 trillion.[7]

Military Retirements. The Military Retirement System (MRS) pays pension benefits to uniformed members of the US military who satisfy certain criteria, in particular a vesting period of 20 years of service before retirement. In addition, the MRS pays disability and survivor benefits to eligible military members and their families.

The MRS is a funded defined benefit pension plan. However, like FERS and the CSRS, the MRS is funded with special-issue government bonds, which means that from a budget-wide perspective, the plan is essentially funded on a pay-as-you-go basis. For these purposes, however, I analyze the plan on a freestanding basis and consider its fund's government bonds only as an asset to the plan. As of the end of fiscal year 2021, the MRS was 60 percent funded and had an unfunded liability of $745 billion.[8]

State and Local Government Employee Pensions. Although 401(k)-type defined contribution plans have taken over the private sector, state and local governments still generally provide defined benefit pensions for their employees. Unlike federal employee pensions, state and local government plans invest in nongovernmental assets such as stocks, corporate bonds, and alternative investments like hedge funds and private equity. However, state and local plans have, by their own admission, amassed fewer of these assets than is needed to pay the benefits they have promised.

How much state and local plans have fallen short is a matter of debate. As discussed in Chapter 13, the debate centers around the correct discount rate with which to calculate the present value of plan liabilities. State and local pensions operate under rules set by the Governmental Accounting

Standards Board (GASB), which dictates that pension liabilities should be discounted using the expected return on plan assets.

At present, the median plan assumes a nominal return of 7.0 percent.[9] Using that methodology, state and local plans in 2022 were about 73 percent funded and had unfunded liabilities of around $1.6 trillion.[10]

However, virtually the entirety of the rest of the pension world operates under rules in which pension benefits, which are almost sure to be paid, are discounted using interest rates that reflect the low risk of those liabilities. Moreover, the official ledger book of the federal government, the National Income and Product Accounts, does not accept the state and local pension liabilities as calculated under GASB standards. In accordance with international standards for calculating national accounts data, the Bureau of Economic Analysis (BEA) reports state and local pension liabilities as discounted using a corporate bond yield, with the current rate chosen by the BEA being 4.0 percent. Using these assumptions, unfunded liabilities in 2022 were measured at $3.9 trillion, and the funded ratio of state and local government pensions was at 57 percent.[11]

Summarizing Studies of the Household Retirement Savings Gap

In this section, I summarize the results of several studies that estimate the retirement savings gap among US households. The studies are analyzed in greater detail in Chapter 4. Here, I merely focus on tabulating the range of estimates of the amounts by which US households may have under-saved for retirement.

The National Institute on Retirement Security estimated in 2013 that households faced a retirement savings gap of between $6.8 and $14 trillion.[12] Similarly, as of 2019, the National Retirement Risk Index (NRRI) estimated that half of working-age households were at risk of an inadequate retirement income and the total retirement savings gap equaled $7 trillion.[13] The NRRI was revised to version 2.0 in 2023, but the new version finds a similar share of households to have under-saved for retirement.[14]

The Employee Benefit Research Institute (EBRI) maintains the Retirement Security Projection Model, which projects a variety of retirement income. The EBRI model projects that 43 percent of Americans are currently at risk of falling short of income in retirement. The total projected retirement saving shortfall under the EBRI's model as of 2020 was $3.68 trillion.[15]

Two influential studies on retirement saving have been coauthored by University of Wisconsin economists John Karl Scholz and Ananth Seshadri. The second study was coauthored with William Gale of the Brookings Institution.[16] While this latter study does not calculate the dollar value of a retirement savings gap, in a 2017 study, I estimated a value equal to about $615 billion.[17]

The RAND Corporation's Michael Hurd and Susann Rohwedder used Health and Retirement Study data to project the capacity of households nearing retirement to maintain their standard of living in old age.[18] Hurd and Rohwedder concluded that 71 percent of working-age households at the time were likely to be able to maintain their standard of living.[19]

It would be even more difficult to derive a dollar value from the Hurd and Rohwedder study than from either of the Scholz and Seshadri studies because Hurd and Rohwedder find that lack of preparation is highly concentrated among lower-income households. Because this group would tend to have less wealth even if adequately prepared, the dollar value of a retirement savings gap is likely to be lower than that estimated by Scholz and Seshadri and their coauthors. But any precise dollar figure would be speculative.

Totaling Up

Table 1 summarizes the figures outlined earlier, providing a range of low and high values when appropriate. For instance, the low value for Social Security's unfunded obligation is derived from the Social Security Administration, while CBO projections provide the high value. Similarly, the low value for the household retirement savings gap is $0.615 trillion, estimated from Scholz, Seshadri, and Gale, while the high estimate of $14.0 trillion is derived from the National Institute for Retirement Security.

In Table 1, the combined low value of funding gaps for federal, state, and local government retirement programs is $27.1 trillion, while the

Table 1. Funding Shortfalls in Federal, State, and Local Government Retirement Plans

	Low	High
Government Programs		
Social Security	$23.7	$33.6
Federal Employee Pensions	$1.0	$1.0
Military Pensions	$0.7	$0.7
State and Local Government Pensions	$1.6	$3.9
Total Funding Gap	*$27.1*	*$39.2*
Household Retirement Savings Gap	$0.615	$14.0

Source: Author's calculations from plan actuarial reports.

aggregated high value is $39.2 trillion. At the low values for both government funding gaps and the household retirement savings gap, government underfunding is 42 times greater than the household retirement savings gap. At the high end, the government funding gap exceeds the household retirement savings gap by a factor of 2.4.

Finally, if the low estimate for government underfunding is compared to the high estimate for the household retirement savings gap, even in this most favorable grouping for government stewardship of retirement plans, government underfunding is 86 percent greater than the household retirement savings gap.

Retirement Savings Gaps Around the World

In a 2017 study, the World Economic Forum examined the so-called retirement savings gap in eight countries around the world, claiming to document a worldwide retirement savings shortfall of nearing $70 trillion, with projections that the savings gap could rise to $400 trillion by midcentury.[20] The forum's study of retirement systems in Australia, Canada, China, India, Japan, the Netherlands, the United Kingdom, and the United States focused on the familiar litany of retirement savings problems including the "lack of easy access to pensions," "low levels of

Table 2. World Economic Forum Estimates of Retirement Savings Shortfalls by Source (2015 US Dollars, Trillions)

	Government and Public Employee Pensions	Corporate Pensions	Individual Retirement Savings	Total	Percentage of Gap from Government Underfunding
Australia	1.5	0	0	1.5	100%
Canada	2.5	0	0.1	2.7	96%
China	7.7	0	3	10.7	72%
India	1.3	0	2.1	3.5	38%
Japan	6.7	0.2	4.1	11	61%
Netherlands	1.7	0	0	1.7	100%
UK	5.9	0.1	2	8	74%
US	23.2	0.6	4.1	27.8	83%
Total	50.5	0.9	15.6	66.9	75%

Source: World Economic Forum, *We'll Live to 100—How Can We Afford It?*, May 26, 2017, https://www.weforum.org/publications/we-ll-live-to-100-how-can-we-afford-it.

financial literacy," "inadequate savings rates," and the "high degree of individual responsibility to manage pension[s]."[21] (See Table 2.)

The forum proposed the familiar list of policy solutions, including adapting pensions to the changing workforce, reducing gender imbalances in retirement savings, and sharing various retirement saving risks more collectively. All these are worth considering.

But the forum ignored its own figures as to the source of retirement savings gaps around the world. In all but one of the eight countries examined, the majority of the retirement savings gaps was accounted for by government. In the median country, 75 percent of the total savings gap derived from government underfunding. It is puzzling that a survey of retirement savings gaps ignores the main sources of those gaps and instead turns to various policies to help households save their way out of governments' poor stewardship of their own retirement programs.

Conclusions

An obvious but important point is that the total problem facing future retirees is the sum of household and government savings shortfalls, meaning that the financial challenges facing future retirees remain potent. If undersaving households are confronted with underfunded government plans, a true retirement crisis could occur.

However, households' apparent advantage should inform policymakers' choices regarding marginal changes in the sector from which retirement income is generated. The relative sizes of household and governmental under-saving should give pause to those who believe that government should properly take on a greater role in retirement income provision. On a population-wide basis, it is difficult to understand why responsibility should be shifted from the household sector, which is doing a better job of saving for retirement, to the government sector, which unquestionably is doing a poorer job.

This is particularly so when one considers the potential causes of under-saving. No one suggests that households wish to impoverish themselves in retirement. Rather, household saving tends to fall short for practical reasons.

Some households lack the opportunity to save because they are not offered a retirement plan at work. Others that might wish to save lack the financial sophistication, such that they are scared off from saving or choose inappropriate or costly investments. Still others have such low incomes that they cannot afford to reduce current spending. Most of the problems households face are a matter of either plan design or basic economic constraints.

In the public sector, by contrast, the principal problem is not plan design. Presidents and Congress have known since the mid-1980s that Social Security requires another round of reforms as baby boomers retire and lifespans increase. Underfunding in state and local government pensions has been increasing for the past two decades. Inaction on both Social Security and public-sector pensions is attributable entirely to political motivations, which are unlikely to disappear in the foreseeable future.

The core problem with retirement plan underfunding at the governmental level isn't plan design but human nature: Voters wish to be promised things without being asked to pay for them, and elected officials are often willing to oblige them.

PART V

16

Social Security:
The History and the Challenge

The chief actuary of the Social Security Administration has declared that Social Security—which is the federal government's largest spending program, most workers' largest tax expense, and most retirees' largest income source—is "not in close actuarial balance."[1] In other words, Social Security is running out of the money needed to pay full benefits. To most Americans who follow the news, that may not be surprising.

But that declaration came not today but in 1990, more than three decades ago.[2] In 1991, the program's trustees first called for action to address Social Security's long-term finances. By 1997, that call was issued with even greater urgency, noting the need to address "problems soon to allow time for phasing in any necessary changes and for workers to adjust their retirement plans to take account of those changes."[3]

Since then, Congress and various presidential administrations have accomplished precisely nothing to make the Social Security program fiscally sustainable and more responsive to 21st-century Americans' needs. Today, Social Security faces a long-term funding shortfall exceeding $23 trillion, and the program's combined trust funds are projected to run out in the mid-2030s.[4]

The only Social Security reform legislation under active consideration is from congressional progressives. These elected officials argue that, due to the failures of the US private retirement saving system, the only solution to a future retirement crisis is to expand Social Security benefits for rich and poor alike, financed by higher taxes on rich and poor alike.

The Social Security 2100 Act, originally cosponsored by nearly nine in 10 House Democrats, would phase out the current ceiling on wages subject to Social Security taxes, which was $160,200 in 2023. This would raise the effective top marginal tax rate on earned income by 12 percentage points, giving the United States one of the highest top marginal tax rates in the developed world.[5]

According to the Tax Policy Center, the top federal tax rate on labor income in the US was 46 percent in 2018. Adding state income taxes, the marginal rate under current law could rise as high as 59 percent in California. Applying the 12 percent Social Security tax would raise the top effective tax rate to over 70 cents on the dollar.

For their part, Republicans and conservatives have been adrift on how to address the program's looming insolvency since the failure of President George W. Bush's 2005 Social Security reform. At the time, the newly reelected Bush made Social Security reform the major domestic initiative of his second term in office, staking on the effort the political capital he had built during his victory in the 2004 presidential campaign.

Bush promoted voluntary personal retirement accounts to which a worker could divert a portion of the existing Social Security payroll tax in return for accepting a lower Social Security benefit at retirement. This would be combined with a broader progressive reduction in future benefits that exempted the bottom third of workers from benefit changes but froze the growth of benefits for high-earning workers. But Bush's investment of political capital came to naught: Despite Republicans having control of the Senate and House, Bush's proposal never even received a vote.

Since that time, many right-leaning officials have reverted to denial: wishing to neither increase Social Security taxes nor reduce benefits but not yet internalizing that those are the only two options available.

Just how is Social Security financed? And how do changing demographics both increase the program's costs and make it a poorer deal for current and future Americans? In the pages that follow, I answer those questions.

I also discuss some good news: During a period when nothing has been done to fix Social Security, private retirement savings for Americans have skyrocketed, and retirement incomes have reached new highs. In combination, these two trends point to solutions that make Social Security more affordable and effective: reforms to truly guarantee against poverty in old age while gradually scaling down Social Security retirement benefits for middle and high earners, which will build a more limited but more robust safety net.

In conjunction, private retirement saving would be scaled up by making on-the-job retirement plans accessible to all workers and using incentives, nudges, and potentially a mandate to ensure that all US employees save some minimum amount for retirement. This approach, modeled on systems in countries such as Australia, New Zealand, and the United Kingdom, could pave the way for a more affordable Social Security program without sacrificing Americans' retirement income security.

Understanding Social Security

Social Security provides a retirement income base on which most Americans must build with personal savings, employer-sponsored retirement plans, and earnings in retirement. The Social Security program was created in the 1930s under the Franklin D. Roosevelt administration. "We can never insure one hundred percent of the population against one hundred percent of the hazards and vicissitudes of life," Roosevelt said, "but we have tried to frame a law which will give some measure of protection to the average citizen and to his family against the loss of a job and against poverty-ridden old age."[6]

All this seems reasonable. But if we recall the discussions of the life-cycle theory of spending and saving, it makes sense for individuals to save for retirement as a way to smooth their standard of living and maximize their well-being over their lifetimes. If that's true, why do we need a Social Security program in the first place? Won't people save for retirement on their own?

Nearly every developed country has a program that broadly resembles Social Security even if, as we shall see, the details may differ considerably. Governments establish such programs for three main economic reasons.

The first rationale for a public Social Security–like program is to overcome failures in private markets. Private insurance markets may not offer health or disability plans to individuals who appear to be at greater risk of accessing such plans. A universal program that includes all citizens can avoid these market failures.

This rationale applies to Social Security's disability and survivors programs. But it has considerably less application to the mass of benefit obligations, valued in the trillions of dollars, that are owed to members of the middle- and upper-income households who could in theory save those amounts on their own.

A second reason for social insurance plans like Social Security is paternalism: Some people may fail to save for retirement even if it is in their interests to do so, and it benefits both them and the rest of society if these households are forced to save. As economist Larry Kotlikoff put it, "There seems to be an unstated belief that, left to their own devices, a sizeable fraction of households would inadequately save and insure."[7] In these cases, government must either allow these myopic individuals to fall into poverty in old age or compel other citizens to supplement them using their own taxes.

Bailing out non-savers piles new disincentives to save on top of the lack of foresight that caused some households not to save in the first place. Compulsory saving protects both individuals who lack foresight and responsible citizens who might otherwise be called up to assist them. Indeed, as Louis Kaplow writes, "Paternalistically motivated forced savings constitutes an important, and to some the most important, rationale for social security retirement systems."[8]

Finally, social insurance programs can include an element of redistribution that private programs do not. Social Security's benefit formula favors low-earning individuals in ways that a private retirement savings plan could not.

Most Americans share these reasonable economic goals, and the US Social Security program broadly accomplishes them. But, as we will see, Social Security does so through a funding and benefits mechanism that, while understandable in the context of the time in which the program was developed, would not be the most efficient or effective means for accomplishing those goals if the program were being devised today.

Social Security's Defining Policy Features

The Social Security program has several defining features that were introduced in 1935 and continue to this day. First, it is a contributory social insurance program, meaning employees pay into Social Security from their wages. Roosevelt saw the worker contribution as generating earned benefits, not mere welfare to those who failed to provide for themselves.

In 1935, the Social Security payroll tax was 2 percent of the first $3,000 in earnings, split evenly between employers and employees. In 2024, employees and employers pay a combined 12.4 percent of employee wages to Social Security, with the tax levied up to a maximum of $168,600 in annual earnings.

Second, while Social Security is contributory, it is also progressive. Benefits for high earners are greater in dollar terms than for low earners, but benefits do not rise proportionally with wages. That is to say, retirement benefits as a percentage of preretirement earnings—the so-called replacement rate provided by Social Security—are highest for low-earning workers and decline as earnings increase. The Congressional Budget Office calculates that for retirees who were born in the 1960s, Social Security benefits will replace 78 percent of the career-average inflation-adjusted earnings of individuals in the lowest fifth (quintile) of the lifetime earnings distribution, 49 percent for retirees in the middle quintile, and 31 percent for retirees in the highest earnings quintile.[9]

Financial planners often recommend a retirement income equal to 70 percent of preretirement earnings. Many low earners approach or even exceed that replacement rate through Social Security alone, while high earners must save substantial amounts on top of Social Security to get there. That fact alone helps explain vast inequalities in private retirement savings.

Third, Social Security is funded on a "pay-as-you-go" basis, meaning that current taxes fund current benefits. Pay-as-you-go financing allowed the program to pay benefits soon after it was established, rather than waiting a full working generation before full benefits could be paid. Over time, however, pay-as-you-go funding entails two significant downsides, which lie at the root of the financial problems that Social Security faces.

First, a pay-as-you-go system pays huge windfalls to early generations of retirees, who receive full retirement benefits after contributing for only a few years. Unlike a traditional funded pension system, a pay-as-you-go program like Social Security can begin paying benefits almost as soon as taxes start being collected. Social Security began collecting taxes in 1937 and paid its first benefit in 1940, just three years later.

Now, for Americans participating in Social Security at the time, receiving a more-or-less full Social Security benefit after just three years of contributions was a great deal—made even better by the fact that the first workers covered by Social Security paid a combined employer-employee tax of just 2 percent of their earnings, one-sixth the 12.4 percent tax rate we pay today.

Social Security analysts generally measure the relative generosity of the program using so-called money's worth ratios, which divide the Social Security benefits a person can expect to receive over their lifetime by the lifetime Social Security taxes they paid. Both figures are expressed in discounted present value dollars, meaning the value of lifetime taxes is increased to account for the interest those taxes could have earned and the value of lifetime benefits is reduced, because a benefit paid at age 85 is less valuable than a benefit paid at age 65. A money's worth ratio greater than one implies that the participant received more in benefits than they paid in taxes, even including interest earned on their taxes.

The Social Security Administration's Dean Leimer has done the most extensive research work exploring how Social Security has treated Americans in different generations. In research published in 2004, Leimer calculated money's worth ratios for early generations of Social Security participants.[10]

Americans born before 1885, who would have been 55 or older when Social Security began paying benefits in 1940, received an almost indescribably good deal from the program. Their lifetime benefits were on average over 16 times greater than the lifetime Social Security taxes they paid. (See Figure 1.) Even Americans retiring around 1970 received on average five times in benefits what they paid in taxes.

For those who prefer to think in terms of annual rates of return, Leimer showed that the earliest retirees received a more than 35 percent annual return on their taxes.[11] It's no wonder that Social Security was so popular.

Now, how does this affect Social Security's finances today? Well, consider that any pension system can ultimately pay out only what it has taken in. That is, the value of contributions, plus interest, must ultimately equal the value of benefit payments.

When early generations of Social Security participants received more in benefits than they paid in taxes, that left less money to pay benefits for future Americans—otherwise known as "us." Had the initial cohorts of Social Security participants received back only what they had paid in,

Figure 1. Ratio of Lifetime Benefits to Lifetime Taxes, by Year of Birth

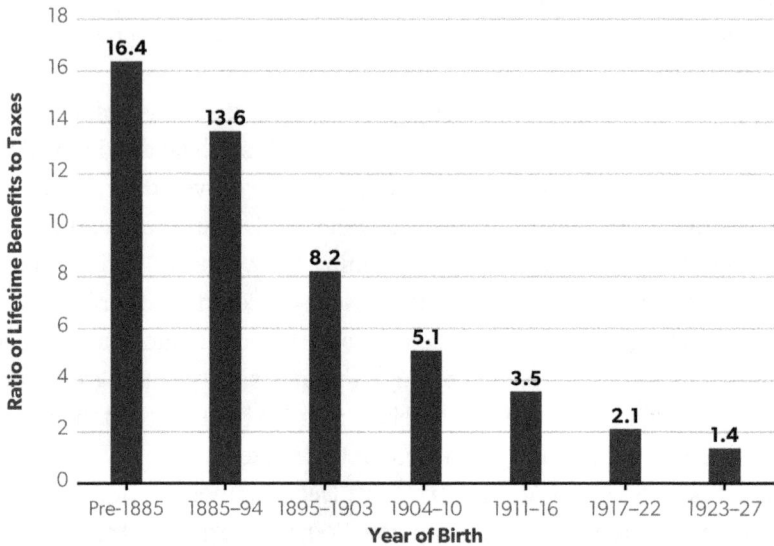

Source: Dean R. Leimer, "Historical Redistribution Under the Social Security Old-Age and Survivors Insurance and Disability Insurance Programs" (working paper, Social Security Administration, Office of Policy, Office of Research, Evaluation, and Statistics, February 2004).

Social Security's trust fund would have built up a balance of tens of trillions of dollars that could be called upon to pay future benefits.[12]

As with any good deal, it was too good to last. As Social Security matured, Americans spent a greater share of their working lives paying into it. Moreover, the Social Security payroll tax increased—from 2 percent of earnings from 1937 to 1949, to 6 percent of pay in 1960, to 8.4 percent in 1970, to 10.2 percent in 1980, and to the current 12.4 percent rate beginning in 1990.[13]

More years paying a higher tax rate makes Social Security a worse deal. And, unquestionably, Social Security is not as good a deal for today's and tomorrow's Americans as it was for generations past.

These Social Security windfalls to early generations of beneficiaries are in one sense easy to justify. Social Security was enacted during the Great Depression, when poverty was a truly crushing nationwide problem and the elderly in particular were at risk for penury.

Certainly, extra payments to keep the elderly out of poverty during the Depression and the years following were worthwhile even if they put a dent in Social Security's finances in future years. The problem, however, is that most of those early generation windfalls didn't go to the poor.

Economists Sylvester Schieber and John Shoven have calculated the dollar value of Social Security windfalls to early generations of participants.[14] Americans of all earnings levels did well under Social Security, but the largest windfalls went to the highest earners. For example, a low-wage male worker retiring in 1940 received $29,958 more in benefits than he had paid in taxes. But a worker earning the maximum taxable wage, also retiring in 1940, received a windfall of $58,780, almost twice as large.

Does this mean that Social Security was not progressive? No. Low-wage workers received higher replacement rates than high-wage workers did, meaning that their benefits replaced a larger portion of their preretirement earnings.

Likewise, the rate of return that low-wage workers received on their payroll taxes was higher than that for high-wage workers. But *everyone* received high rates of return in the early years of Social Security. The large dollar value windfalls for high-wage workers came precisely because they "invested" more in a program that was paying above-market returns.

Yet this created a seesaw effect: Since Social Security is a pay-as-you-go program, the benefits paid out ultimately must equal the taxes paid in. If early generations of retirees received far more in benefits than they paid in taxes, later generations must pay more in taxes than they will receive in benefits.

This explains why Social Security's rate of return has fallen, such that many future retirees will get less from the system than they paid into it. In fact, every penny of Social Security's nearly $18 trillion funding shortfall is a function of early generations of retirees receiving windfalls from the system. However Social Security's funding gap is fixed, whether through tax increases or benefit reductions, it will never again be as good a deal for Americans as it was in its early decades of existence.

And yet, what's done is done. Regardless of whether we think those early generation windfalls were good policy, they're *done* policy. We can't go back and change anything. So policymakers today must decide how to dig themselves out of a hole that was dug for them by way of decisions made nearly a century ago.

Pay-as-you-go funding creates an additional financing issue for Social Security. In a program that simply transfers money from workers to beneficiaries, the ratio of workers to beneficiaries is crucial. A theme of this chapter is that policymakers need to make Social Security work better, not merely make Social Security solvent.

Yet it would be irrational to ignore the reason Social Security reform is on the table at all: In little more than a decade, the program's trust funds will be exhausted, and over the next 75 years, Social Security has promised some $23 trillion more in benefits than it will take in through taxes. While making Social Security solvent is not a sufficient criterion for a successful Social Security reform, solvency is hardly a trivial consideration. An insolvent system cannot afford to pay the benefits it has promised, and that security is the role a social insurance program is designed to play.

Social Security is a pay-as-you-go transfer program, with a small trust fund originally designed simply to smooth fluctuations in cash flows from one year to next. Even these "legacy debts" caused by early generations of participants would not have doomed Social Security's financing had it not also been for changing demographics.

Again recall that a pay-as-you-go program like Social Security collects taxes from workers and transfers the money to retirees and other beneficiaries. Given that structure, the number of workers and beneficiaries is crucial. Here's an easy way to understand the math.

In 2023, Social Security will pay about $1.3789 trillion in benefits to 65.9 million beneficiaries, for an average benefit of about $20,849.[15] Similarly, in 2023, about 180.9 million workers paid taxes into Social Security, and together they earned about $9.6 trillion, for an average wage of $52,951. So the average benefit is equal to about 39.4 percent of the average wage.

Likewise in 2023, there were about 2.7 workers for each Social Security beneficiary. Divide the 39.4 percent benefit as a percentage of the average wage by 2.7 workers for each beneficiary and you find that the "cost rate" of Social Security benefits is equal to 14.6 percent of the average worker's wage. If you look in the Social Security trustees report, it is almost precisely the 14.5 percent cost rate calculated by Social Security's actuaries.

In other words, if you know the average benefit as a percentage of the average wage—which doesn't change much over time—and you know the ratio of workers to beneficiaries, you can easily figure out how much the program will cost.

This means you also can easily figure out how changing demographics will affect Social Security's finances in years to come. The story of the aging of America's population is well-worn: Longer lifespans increase the number of beneficiaries collecting benefits, while lower birth rates reduce the relative number of workers paying into Social Security. Over time, those demographic changes have reduced the ratio of workers to beneficiaries and increased the cost to each worker of funding Social Security, even if benefits remain unchanged.

In 1960, there were 5.1 workers per beneficiary. If the average Social Security benefit were equal to 39.4 percent of the average wage, then a tax of 7.7 percent of each employee's wages would be enough to keep benefits paid. But if the worker-to-beneficiary ratio declines to 2.1, as Social Security's trustees project will happen over the long term, the cost of the very same benefit increases to 18.8 percent of pay.

While the phrase "population aging" makes a reader focus on the increasing number of seniors, the falling birth rate is actually the more powerful force affecting Social Security's finances. From 1940 to 1970, the fertility rate averaged just over three children per woman. Had that fertility rate remained steady into the future, Social Security would likely remain solvent regardless of the windfalls to early generations and regardless of the rising number of beneficiaries.

But birth rates fell, to roughly two children per woman in the 1990s and to about 1.7 in 2019. A birth rate of 1.7 children per woman means a future population of workers paying into Social Security that's barely over half the size of the workforce that would exist if birth rates remained at 3.0. That's a big factor affecting Social Security's finances.

There's little that policymakers can do to change the nation's demographics. Which means that ultimately, we must bring Social Security's costs and revenues in line with one another. That means higher taxes or lower benefits, at least relative to what we have been promised. Breaking lifelong promises made by the largest federal government program is difficult, but the simple mathematics of Social Security leave policymakers little choice in the matter.

Why It Paid (Some People) to Delay Reform

Since the mid-1980s, Americans have been told that, lacking additional revenues, Social Security will be unable to pay full benefits past the mid-2030s. By 1992, Social Security's trustees urged in their annual report that "appropriate options to strengthen the long-range financing of the program should be developed."[16] Presidents Bill Clinton and George W. Bush both tried to reform Social Security.

Compared to issues with reforming Medicare or improving education, Social Security reform presents some remarkably straightforward choices. And yet, nearly 40 years and $23 trillion of unfunded benefit obligations later, nothing has been done. Why has Congress waited four decades to fix Social Security, when common sense says it's easier to act sooner than later?

The answer is that common sense is wrong: Americans nearing retirement played a game of chicken with Congress for decades, refusing to support the additional taxes needed to keep Social Security solvent while daring their representatives to cut their benefits when Social Security's trust fund runs out in 2035. Older Americans will almost certainly win that game, since neither political party has the will to cut Social Security.

The reality is that reforming Social Security, and other long-term governmental programs for that matter, is in the hands of both citizens and politicians who benefit precisely from not reforming them.

There is no magic to Social Security reform. We either must increase revenues or reduce benefit outlays. Early action on Social Security reform would spread tax increases or benefit cuts over multiple generations, making reform less painful and economically harmful than lumping all the changes on a single group of Americans.

However, Social Security policy is governed by Americans wishing to benefit not all generations but mostly their own. Yes, today's workers—or for that matter, workers at any time over the past four decades—could have secured their future Social Security benefits by paying higher Social Security taxes to keep the program solvent.

And yet, if a future Congress will not cut Social Security benefits even in the case of insolvency, then present taxpayers rationally should oppose raising taxes to fund those benefits. And historically they have: In 2005, for example, only 37 percent of Americans told Gallup they supported raising Social Security's 12.4 percent payroll tax rate to maintain the program's solvency.[17]

Politicians similarly benefit by dodging Social Security's $23 trillion-plus funding shortfall: Why take a political hit for advocating unpopular reforms when you can pass the problem on to a future Congress?

For past and present workers, the financial gains from delaying reform can be considerable. Imagine that when long-term Social Security funding shortfalls reappeared in the late 1980s, Congress incrementally raised taxes as needed to maintain the program's 75-year solvency.

For example, in 1983, Social Security was projected to remain solvent for 75 years. But in 1984, the program's 75-year actuarial balances were estimated as a deficit equal to 0.06 percent of payroll. Congress, if it had acted, would have increased the payroll tax rate in 1984 by that amount. As long-term deficits widened in following years, the payroll tax rate would have inched upward.

Had that responsible approach been taken, Social Security today would be solvent for 75 years, and the threat of benefit cuts would be off the table. But here's the downside: An average-wage worker retiring in 2035 would have paid nearly $125,000 in additional payroll taxes over their career relative to the tax rates currently in place.[18] A worker earning the maximum salary subject to Social Security payroll taxes—$162,200 in 2023—would have paid more than $350,000. Delaying Social Security reform pays significant financial dividends to workers, so long as benefits won't be cut when the trust funds run dry.

And almost certainly benefits will not be cut, at least not in any way proportionate to the financial shortfalls facing the program beginning in the mid-2030s. Nearly every elected Democrat at the federal level is on record not only opposing any benefit cuts, even for the rich, but in support of expanding the program.

President Donald Trump opposed any Social Security cuts, and his influence, along with the rising number of Republican-voting seniors, has pushed that party to the left on Social Security.[19] Ambitious senators such as Josh Hawley, angling to be Trump's heir, argue that Republicans should abandon any "fiddling" with Social Security.[20] Personally, I will turn age 65 in 2033, and I have little fear that my own Social Security benefits will be cut.

Of course, delaying Social Security reform does not make its costs disappear. It just makes those costs more expensive and shifts them to younger Americans. Come 2035, working-age Americans will pay roughly $350 billion annually on top of their existing payroll taxes to fund Social Security benefits that seniors insist they "earned" yet never got around to fully paying for. Reluctance either to raise taxes or reduce benefits makes these programs a great financial deal for past and present retirees but an equal and opposite poor deal for future Americans.

This political dynamic is unlikely to change. Social Security reform might incorporate two solutions.

The first is to require annual automatic adjustments to the program to maintain long-term funding health, just as federal law requires of private-sector pensions. Each year, Social Security's actuaries would estimate the plan's funding shortfall, and, automatically, payroll taxes would increase or future benefits be reduced to address it. The Swedish pension system has such automatic stabilizers.[21] Even if we disagree about whether to balance Social Security by tax increases or benefit cuts, future generations benefit if we stop current generations' decades-long strategy of foisting the bill onto their children and grandchildren.

The second is to enact reforms today that are forecasted with great certainty to be financially sustainable. In other words, not simply a fifty-fifty chance that Social Security will remain solvent, but reforms in which there is little chance of revenues falling short of promised benefits. Then, in future years, Congress may decide to either increase benefits or reduce the tax rate, depending on Americans' needs and preferences at the time.

The worst approach would be to continue to promise benefits that would require tax rates that Americans have shown themselves over many years to be unwilling to pay. Decades of kicking the can down the road, policy wise, have not been helpful to Social Security or Americans' retirement planning. Social Security reform in the 21st century should not make the same mistake again.

Can We Party Like It's 1983?

As policymakers consider reforming Social Security to avert the trust funds' insolvency in the mid-2030s, it is not uncommon for them to look backward to the Social Security reforms of 1983, which averted a trust fund insolvency that was just months away. The 1983 experience would indicate that Congress need not tackle Social Security reform *today*, so long as it is willing to come together in a bipartisan fashion at some point before the trust funds run dry. Is that a model that would work to fix Social Security in the 2030s?

Despite similarities between the experience of 1983 and what policymakers face today, there are some important differences. First, while Social Security's looming insolvency in the 2030s will be demographically driven, the 1983 funding crisis was caused by economics.

Before the 1983 reforms, the Social Security trust fund was a modest device used to balance small year-to-year differences in revenues or outlays. But due to severe inflation and lower-than-expected wages in the early 1980s, Social Security trust funds were at immediate risk of not being able to pay scheduled benefits in 1983. This funding problem came upon Social Security rapidly: As late as 1979, Social Security was projected to remain solvent for decades to come.

And yet, while sudden, the problems facing Social Security in 1983 were actually much more modest than what the program faces today. The reason is that, even if Social Security had become insolvent in 1983, the benefit cuts involved would have been small and temporary.

From 1983 through 1989, Social Security revenues would have fallen short of benefit costs by less than 4 percent. And in 1990, the program was projected to return to solvency and continue running payroll tax surpluses until 2015, with trust fund assets built up during that period adding years of solvency thereafter. While the bipartisan group of policymakers who constructed the 1983 reforms deserves great credit for thinking about the program's long-term solvency, the short-term funding gap they faced at the time would have been small and short-lived.

Today, Social Security faces an entirely different set of problems. Social Security's pending insolvency in the 2030s is almost entirely driven by population aging, not high inflation or slow economic growth. Congress has known for nearly four decades that Social Security would require additional reforms to remain solvent. However, were insolvency to arrive, it would be a much larger crisis than what Social Security faced in 1983.

Instead of the 1983 scenario of benefit cuts of less than 4 percent lasting for seven years, retirees and the disabled would face benefit cuts of 20 percent or more that would last indefinitely were the trust funds to run dry in the 2030s. The idea that Congress could easily come together to address Social Security shortfalls that dwarf those the program faced in 1983 seems optimistic.

And yet it is worth looking back at how Congress and Republican President Ronald Reagan constructed a reform proposal in 1983. While many in Congress today argue that Social Security's solvency should be addressed entirely through increased taxes, tax increases played a relatively modest role in the 1983 reforms. Those reforms accelerated an already-scheduled increase in the combined employee and employer payroll tax rate from 10.8 to 12.4 percent, which previously had been scheduled to take place by 1990. This, the main tax increase in the reform package, increased payroll tax rates modestly and for only six years.

Most of the heavy lifting was done on the benefit side of the ledger. The reforms delayed the 1984 cost-of-living adjustment (COLA) by six months, a step that amounted to a onetime but permanent reduction in current benefits of about 1.75 percent. The COLA delay, along with the accelerated implementation of the payroll tax rate increase, addressed trust fund solvency in the short term.

Long-term solvency was improved by scheduling a two-year increase in the full retirement age, from 65 to 67, to take place between 2000 and 2022. This amounted to a benefit reduction of over 13 percent. In addition, the reforms made half of Social Security benefits subject to income taxes for beneficiaries with incomes above $25,000 in nominal terms, with the revenues funneled back to Social Security. Benefit taxation is an implicit means test of benefits for higher-income retirees. But because the dollar threshold at which benefits are taxable was not adjusted each year, either for inflation or wage growth, benefit taxation will affect a larger share of retirees over time.

The reforms also broadened the participation base for Social Security by including newly hired federal employees and employees of nonprofits and by prohibiting state or local governments that already participated in Social Security from withdrawing. Overall, about 22 percent of the 1983 reforms' improvement to Social Security's funding derived from tax increases, about 58 percent from benefit reductions, and about 20 percent from broadening the participant base.

Interestingly, the reform process itself revealed some of the preferences of elected officials at the time. The 1983 reforms were outlined by the National Commission on Social Security Reform, but the commission itself could not agree on a full set of reforms to make Social Security solvent for 75 years.[22] When the House of Representatives considered the legislation, two amendments were offered to bring Social Security to full 75-year solvency.

The first amendment would have increased the full retirement age from 65 to 67 from 2000 to 2022, while the second would have increased the Social Security payroll tax from 12.4 to 13.46 in 2010. Despite Democrats holding a 100-seat majority in the House, the amendment to increase the retirement age passed by a vote of 228 to 202, while the amendment to increase the payroll tax rate failed overwhelmingly, falling by a vote of 132 to 296.[23]

While the politics of Social Security have changed over time as the number of retirees has increased, the 1983 reforms do not instill confidence that Congress would pass a one-sided reform relying overwhelmingly on revenue increases.

Why Not Simply Increase Taxes?

Raising taxes is never popular. Nevertheless, given the importance Americans place on their Social Security benefits, why not simply tell Americans they need to pay more?

The first reason is that, as important as Social Security benefits were to retirees in the program's early years, as Americans grow progressively richer and financial markets become easier to access, one might expect that individuals could rely more on their own savings and less on tax-and-transfer benefits financed by younger generations.

To understand, we need to look at Social Security's benefit formula both vertically and horizontally. A vertical view looks at how the program treats participants with different levels of preretirement earnings who retire in the same year. Social Security pays a high replacement rate to a new retiree who had low earnings, on the assumption that they could not have saved adequately for retirement given their low level of pay during their working years. That is perfectly reasonable.

It also is perfectly reasonable to assume that a high earner does not require the same Social Security replacement rate, since they had the extra income available to build retirement savings on top of Social Security.

But now think about how Social Security's benefit formula works horizontally, across time. One might reasonably think that as Americans' earnings rise over time, they will become increasingly able to save for retirement on their own. Certainly the data discussed in earlier chapters showing rising retirement savings in every income group support that conclusion.

So one might also reasonably conclude that, as we grow progressively richer, Social Security need not grow quite as fast as our earnings do. That is, as fewer Americans face the kind of material want that faced millions of retirees at the time Social Security was established, Social Security could focus its resources more on those in need while Americans with higher incomes would be expected to take a larger role in preparing for retirement.

And yet, that's not how the Social Security benefit formula works. Imagine a person who retired in 1979 having average preretirement earnings of $96,000 per year (in today's dollars).[24] The Social Security benefit rules in place at the time would have awarded that retiree an annual Social Security benefit of about $19,220. That was deemed to be sufficient, such that based on the retiree's past earnings, he or she could save enough outside of Social Security to maintain their standard of living in old age.

But now take a person with precisely the same preretirement earnings who will retire in 2039. That person will receive a Social Security benefit of about $34,560 per year, again in today's dollars. Why? If $19,220 was good enough for a $96,000 earner in 1979, why must a $96,000 earner retiring in 2039 receive nearly twice as much—financed, of course, by higher payroll taxes during their working years?

The reason Social Security promises ever-increasing benefits to Americans with precisely the same preretirement earnings is that the current Social Security benefit formula works largely in relative terms. That is to say, a "low earner" isn't a person with earnings of approximately $30,000 per year. Instead, a low earner is someone who earns, say, half the national average wage, no matter how high that average wage might rise.

What this means is that, as Americans' wages and salaries increase over time, a high earner in dollar terms gradually becomes a middle earner and then gradually becomes a low earner. No matter how rich we become, at no point does Social Security see the need to pay an average benefit equal to about 40 percent of the national average wage.

But this approach wasn't built into Social Security from the beginning. Social Security's original benefit formula wasn't indexed for wage growth the way the current formula is. That doesn't mean that benefits never increased; Congress adjusted benefits as needs and resources allowed. But Social Security wasn't on autopilot.

The current benefit formula grew out of the Social Security Amendments of 1977. These changes, passed by Congress and signed by President Jimmy Carter, put the program on autopilot for the future. But, of course, autopilot means a path to insolvency.

Importantly, the benefit formula changes adopted as part of the 1977 amendments were opposed by an expert panel convened to provide recommendations on how to adjust the Social Security benefit formula. The Consultant Panel on Social Security was chaired by Harvard economics Professor William C. Hsiao and included the future Nobel Prize–winning economist Peter Diamond. It recommended a more modest approach for Social Security.

Instead of increasing benefits year over year, regardless of need, the panel said that benefits should rise at a slower and more affordable rate of growth. It should, the panel recommended, be left to "future Congresses [to] determine the extent to which benefits can be increased beyond the levels reached automatically, in the light of needs of the beneficiaries and willingness of the workers to pay the necessary taxes."[25]

Had the panel's recommendations been adopted, Americans with the same earnings but retiring in different years would have received the same benefits and the same replacement rate of preretirement earnings. That is, a person with a given level of real, inflation-adjusted earnings—say, $30,000 per year—would not be considered rich, then middle class, and then poor as the national average wage rose over time.

And under the panel's approach, as national average earnings increased, the cost of benefits relative to earnings—what Social Security's actuaries call the program's "cost rate"—would decline, and Social Security could be expected to remain solvent in perpetuity. Congress could still increase benefits as needed, but the baseline would be a system that would be affordable under current law tax rates regardless of the nation's changing demographics.

But it was not to be. When the 1977 amendments were passed, they locked in a benefit formula that put Social Security on a path for longer-term insolvency. Just as important, the automatic nature of the benefit formula implemented in 1977 meant that Congress was no longer in active control of Social Security benefit levels, as it had been over the first four decades of the program's history.

Politically speaking, it is one thing for Congress to periodically increase benefits as affordable, as it did before the amendments. It is another thing entirely when Congress must claw back benefits to an affordable level, as it must do under the post-1977 benefit formula.

A second reason to consider Social Security solvency options based on benefit restraint rather than tax increases is that Social Security benefits are an easy substitute for personal retirement savings, and vice versa. While people aren't perfectly rational, many—particularly middle- and high-income households—plan for retirement holistically, thinking of how much they need to save to supplement the benefits they will receive from Social Security or other sources.

As a result, higher Social Security benefits will lead to lower personal savings, and lower benefits will lead to higher savings. Put another way, a $1 reduction to future Social Security benefits could be expected to result in a less than $1 reduction to retirees' total incomes.

Because changes to Social Security's tax and benefit rules have been so infrequent, research in this area often looks elsewhere for evidence.

For instance, the Brookings Institution's William Gale examined households' substitution between personal savings and the benefits they expect to receive from a traditional defined benefit pension. He found that households with greater education or that have retirement savings accounts (both are largely proxies for income) reduce their personal savings by 70 percent or more of the amount they expect to receive in pension benefits.[26]

Gary Engelhardt of Syracuse University and Anil Kumar of the Federal Reserve looked at substitutions between traditional pensions and personal savings among US households, finding that each dollar of pension wealth is on average associated with a 45- to 60-cent decline in non-pension wealth. Again, lower-income households don't seem to react much, but higher earners reduce saving by 70–100 cents for each dollar of pension benefits they expect to receive.[27]

Rob Alessie and his coauthors looked at various European countries. They found that, overall, households reduce savings by 50 to 60 cents for each dollar (or euro) of pension benefits they expect to receive.[28] Less-educated individuals don't appear to alter their personal saving at all based on the amount they expect to receive from government pension plans, but more educated workers reduce personal savings roughly one-for-one for what they'll receive from the government.

Marta Lachowska and Michał Myck, writing in the *American Economic Journal*, analyzed a 1998 pension reform in Poland that reduced benefits for people in certain younger birth cohorts but exempted people born before a specific given date. They found that college-educated households saved to make up basically 100 percent of the benefit cut, but those without college educations made up only 14 to 40 percent of the benefit reduction.[29]

Italian economists Orazio Attanasio and Agar Brugiavini looked at 1992 pension reforms in Italy that reduced future benefits for certain types of households based on age, earnings, and other factors while leaving other households' benefits unchanged. They found that, on average, households increased their saving by 30 to 40 percent of the size of the pension benefit cuts, but the effects differed among households. Among middle-aged households, personal savings replaced close to 100 percent of the benefit cut, indicating that these households saw government pensions and personal savings as close substitutes.[30]

Attanasio and RAND's Susann Rohwedder analyzed pension reforms in the United Kingdom that reduced benefits. They found that for people over age 31, personal savings offset about 70 percent of the change in government-provided retirement benefits.[31]

Perhaps the most interesting study, by Isen Gelber and his coauthors, analyzes Americans who were affected by what came to be called the Social Security "notch."[32] Amendments to the Social Security Act passed in 1972 were designed to protect beneficiaries against rising inflation. However, the 1972 amendments inadvertently "double indexed" the benefit formula such that high inflation would create dramatic increases in the benefits to which retirees were entitled.

This quickly would have led to Social Security's insolvency. The 1977 amendments addressed the double-indexing issue but grandfathered individuals born through January 1, 1917. Americans born after January 1, 1917—and therefore turning 65 beginning in 1982—received "sharply lower Social Security benefits . . . under the new formula."

According to data in the Social Security trustees report, over only five years, replacement rates for new retirees fell across the board by about 20 percent.[33] The replacement rate represents Social Security benefits as a percentage of preretirement earnings.

This legislative change provided a sharp break that the researchers could employ to assess how Social Security benefits affected Americans' earnings. Using Social Security Administration data, Gelber and his coauthors were able to analyze individuals born just before and just after the notch threshold date in 1917 to determine how their earnings would react to a change in Social Security benefits.

The researchers had access to Social Security Administration earnings data from 1978, when the first notch-affected cohorts would have been age 61, through 2012, when they would have reached age 95. The compelling fact in this study is that it follows Americans who already were close to retirement age. Nevertheless, the data indicated that the notch cohorts increased their earnings from age 61 onward by enough to make up for at least 61 cents of each dollar of lost Social Security benefits.

The authors concluded that a $1 reduction to future Social Security benefits would improve Social Security's finances by more than $1: Not only would Social Security save $1 in benefit costs, but the extra earnings individuals would generate in response would increase payroll tax revenues to the program.

A similar dynamic would likely hold for proposals that would expand Social Security and increase retirement benefits. In other words, relative to the notch cohorts, who received lower retirement benefits, Americans retiring just before them reduced their earnings in retirement by 61 cents for each dollar of additional benefits they received. Thus, $1 of additional Social Security benefits would cost the program more than $1, due to the loss of payroll tax revenues through reduced earnings.

An analysis of one prominent piece of Social Security expansion legislation, the Social Security 2100 Act, points toward some of these costs. The Social Security 2100 Act was first introduced into the House by Representative John Larson in 2014 and has been periodically updated and reintroduced since.

The Penn Wharton Budget Model project, based at the University of Pennsylvania's Wharton School of Business, uses a sophisticated dynamic economic model to analyze the budgetary and economic effects of various public policies.[34] Analyzing the 2019 iteration of the Social Security 2100 Act, which would expand benefits for all recipients financed by increases in both the payroll tax rate and the wage ceiling on which taxes are levied, the Penn Wharton Budget Model concluded that the act would reduce both labor supply and saving. Moreover, by 2049, gross domestic product would be about 1.1 percent lower than under a baseline in which the federal government simply borrowed to pay full Social Security benefits. Compared to a reform plan that achieved solvency through progressive benefit reductions and tax increases, gross domestic product in 2049 under the Social Security 2100 Act would be nearly 6.4 percent lower.

That personal savings and Social Security benefits are close substitutes, at least for middle- and high-income households, stands in contrast to Medicare, as it is more difficult for working-age households to build personal savings to protect against health costs in old age. Health costs in old age can vary considerably from person to person and year to year, making a savings approach generally less effective than one based on insurance principles.

The US health care system is also complex and includes both government and health insurers, such that a typical consumer does not typically pay for a health procedure in the same way they might purchase a television or an automobile. If tax dollars are to be reserved for one entitlement program, Medicare appears to be the one that ought to take priority. Of the two programs, Social Security benefits appear far more amenable to replacement by personal savings than do the complex and variable benefits that seniors receive from Medicare.

So Make the Rich Pay

One common Social Security reform is to increase or eliminate the "cap" on earnings subject to Social Security taxes, which was $160,200 in 2023. The cap applies both to earnings subject to taxes and to earnings used to calculate benefits. Thus, a person earning over the payroll tax ceiling neither pays taxes nor earns benefits on earnings above that level.

A common rationale for increasing the payroll tax ceiling is that the share of total earnings subject to taxes has declined over the past several decades. There is some truth to this claim. In 2022, 82 percent of total earnings were taxed by Social Security.[35] The highest rate of coverage was 92 percent when Social Security taxes began in 1935, and coverage hit 90 percent of total earnings in 1982 and 1983 because of an increase in the payroll tax ceiling passed as part of the Social Security Amendments of 1977.

And yet those figures also are selective. From 1937 to 2022, an average of 83 percent of total earnings have been subject to Social Security taxes. (See Figure 2.) The lowest rate of coverage was 71 percent in 1965.

The standard story behind the decline in the share of earnings covered by Social Security is that earnings inequality has increased; the rich are earning more while the less than rich are earning less. In some technical sense, this must be true. And, indeed, rising earnings for a small number of extremely well-paid individuals have caused the share of earnings subject to payroll taxes to shrink.

But there is a second cause of earnings inequality that does not play into the rich-versus-poor narrative favored by many Social Security reformers. It is well-known that, over time, the amounts that employers have paid for employee health coverage have increased.

Figure 2. Social Security Taxable Earnings as a Percentage of Total Covered Earnings, by Year

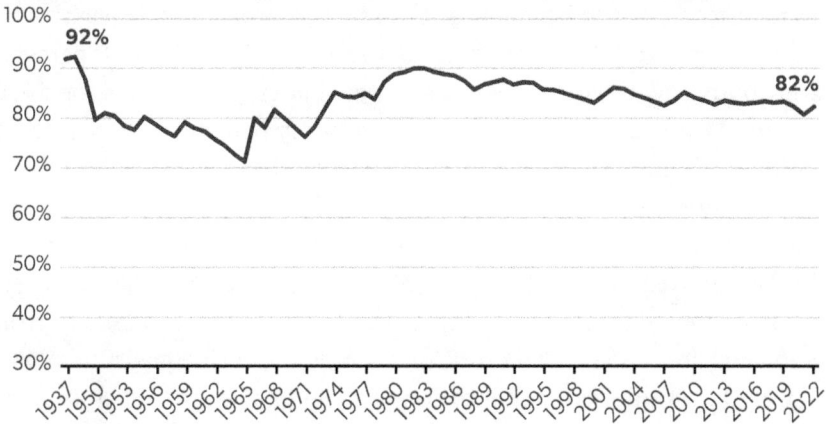

Source: Social Security Administration, *Annual Statistical Supplement to the Social Security Bulletin, 2023,* Table 4.B, November 2023, https://www.ssa.gov/policy/docs/statcomps/supplement/2023/supplement23.pdf.

Somewhat less well-known is that when employee benefit costs increase, employers tend to cover their increased costs by holding back on wage increases for employees. In this way, rising health costs have eaten away at employee wages. If health costs borne by employers had not risen so quickly, wages today would be higher.

But health costs do not eat away at wages equally for every employee. While salaries may differ wildly among different employees, the costs paid by their employers for health care are much more similar. This implies that health costs are a larger share of the compensation package for low earners than for high earners. This in turn implies that, when health costs rise faster than other forms of compensation, the squeeze on wages is larger for low earners than high earners.

All this means that, even if total compensation for low- and high-earning employees rose at the same rate over time, wages would rise faster for higher earners than low earners. And, as a result, a greater share of total wages would fall above the Social Security payroll tax ceiling.

In a 2014 article written with my American Enterprise Institute colleague Mark Warshawsky, we outlined what Bureau of Labor Statistics

(BLS) data showed even over the relatively brief period from 1999 through 2006.[36] In the BLS National Compensation Survey, low-income workers saw their total pay and benefits rise by 41 percent from 1999 through 2006. And yet these workers' wages and salaries increased by only 28 percent, barely outpacing inflation. The reason was that employer costs for these workers' health costs nearly doubled, from 6.5 percent to 12.2 percent of their compensation, eating up money that otherwise could have gone toward salaries.

Now consider a "one-percenter" who earns $250,000 or more a year. The BLS data showed that total compensation for these workers rose by 36 percent from 1999 through 2006. That's actually a lower rate of growth than for low-income workers, indicating that compensation inequality may have decreased over this period. But the one-percenter's health costs rose from just 4 percent of compensation in 1999 to only 4.3 percent in 2006. It's not that their health costs didn't rise in dollars terms, but simply that health benefits are a much smaller part of high earners' total pay and benefits.

As a result, salaries for the one-percenters grew by 35 percent, a faster rate than for low-wage workers. In other words, while compensation inequality may have decreased, earnings inequality increased. And it is earnings inequality that receives the focus in the Social Security reform discussion.

Other research, published by Gary Burtless and Sveta Milusheva of the Brookings Institution, reached similar conclusions. Using different data sources and analyzing the period from 1996 to 2008, the two authors concluded that "because employer health insurance contributions represent a much higher percentage of compensation below the taxable maximum, health insurance cost trends exerted a disproportionate downward pressure on money wages below the taxable maximum."[37] Extrapolating from their 1996 to 2008 data, they project that had employer health costs grown no faster than wages, payroll tax revenues collected by Social Security in 2020 would have been about 3.8 percent higher.

Some have argued for increasing Social Security's maximum taxable salary to cover 90 percent of total earnings. Doing so would roughly double the current law payroll tax ceiling to about $350,000. A great deal of earnings reside between $160,000 and $350,000, and taxing these earnings would reduce Social Security's long-term funding shortfall by about one-quarter.

At the same time, lifting the payroll tax ceiling to $350,000 would be a substantial tax increase on Americans in that income range, increasing their effective marginal tax rate by approximately 12 percentage points. Higher taxes would reduce labor supply and encourage earners to shelter income from taxes, such as by forming S corporations and converting earnings into nontaxed investment income. While policymakers must consider and balance the pros and cons, adjusting the payroll tax ceiling to cover the same share of earnings as it did at Social Security's inception is not out of step with the program's original design.

Others argue for going further, either by eliminating or phasing out the payroll tax ceiling. In the context of considering what it means for "the rich to pay their fair share," few countries fund their government pension program with an uncapped tax on earnings. In fact, the current US payroll tax ceiling of $160,200 is well *above* that of the typical developed country.

In the United Kingdom, the National Insurance tax that funds the state pension and a number of other programs is equal to 12 percent of wages up to around $64,000 in annual earnings, with a 2 percent continuing tax on earnings above that amount. In Canada, the 11.9 percent tax for the Canada Pension Plan applies only to about the first $49,000 in earnings.

In Figure 3, I calculate what the US Social Security payroll tax ceiling would be if it were set using the rules followed by a number of other developed countries. Specifically, I rely on Organisation for Economic Co-operation and Development (OECD) data that express each country's maximum taxable salary as a multiple of the average salary in that country. I then apply those multiples to the average US salary to produce the dollar figures shown in Figure 3.

Only Japan would have a higher payroll tax ceiling than the US, exceeding the US level by about 4 percent. But Belgium, Canada, France, Germany, Japan, Korea, Luxembourg, the Netherlands, Norway, Sweden, and Switzerland all have payroll tax ceilings that are approximately half those of the US Social Security program.

While subjecting all earnings to Social Security payroll taxes is often portrayed as a commonsense idea, the reality is that doing so is inconsistent with both Social Security's history and how other countries around the world fund their Social Security–like pension programs.

Figure 3. Maximum Salary Subject to Social Security Taxes If the US Followed Rules in Other Developed Countries

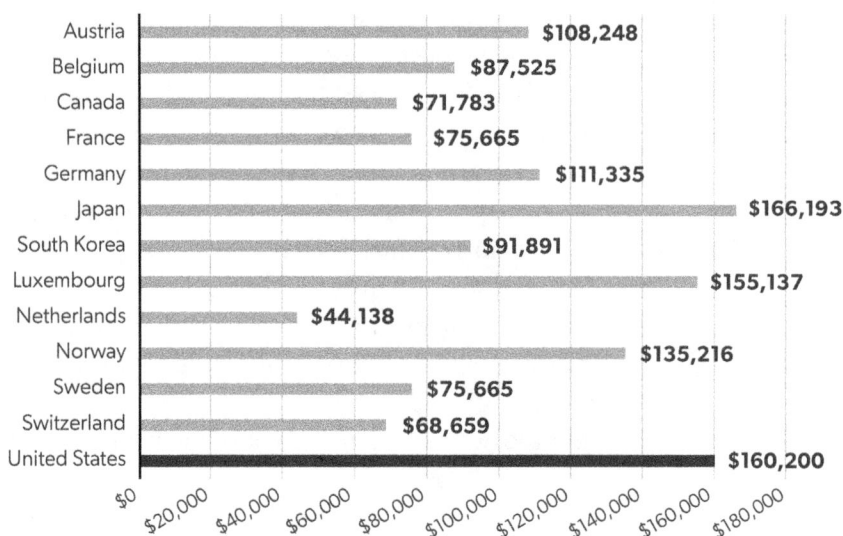

Austria	$108,248
Belgium	$87,525
Canada	$71,783
France	$75,665
Germany	$111,335
Japan	$166,193
South Korea	$91,891
Luxembourg	$155,137
Netherlands	$44,138
Norway	$135,216
Sweden	$75,665
Switzerland	$68,659
United States	$160,200

Source: Author's calculations from Organisation for Economic Co-operation and Development data.

OK, So Make the Really Rich Pay

However, in recent years there has been declining enthusiasm for the "commonsense" traditional revenue raiser of increasing the Social Security payroll tax rate, which, as was noted, began in 1935 at 2 percent of wages and has risen over time to the current 12.4 percent rate. There is even reduced support for lifting the $160,200 payroll tax ceiling. For example, President Joe Biden pledged not to increase taxes in any way on Americans who earned less than $400,000 annually. This placed the vast majority of workers off-limits for Social Security tax increases. Kamala Harris, Biden's vice president and the Democratic Party's nominee for president in 2024, reiterated that pledge.[38]

In response, proposals to use tax increases to make Social Security solvent, or even to expand benefits, have increasingly relied on tax increases targeted at Americans earning $400,000 or more. That group, which makes up less than one-half of 1 percent of the labor force, would be called on to address a roughly 20 percent funding gap in the federal government's largest spending program. But to do so would be a challenge.

Recent proposals in both the US House and Senate would increase taxes on high earners in two ways. First, these plans would impose the Social Security payroll tax on earnings over $400,000, creating a "donut hole" between the payroll tax ceiling of $160,200 in 2023 and the new $400,000 threshold. However, the $400,000 threshold would be maintained in nominal dollar terms, while the current-law payroll tax ceiling increases each year along with nominal wage growth. Thus, over about 25 years, the donut hole would disappear, and all earnings would be subject to taxes.

Second, progressive reformers have increasingly turned to taxes on investment income as prospects for payroll tax rate increases have politically faded. Legislation in both the House and Senate would impose a 12.4 percent tax on investment earnings for Americans with incomes over $400,000. This tax would act as a supplement to the current capital gains tax. A revised version of the Social Security 2100 Act in the House and Senator Sheldon Whitehouse's Medicare and Social Security Fair Share Act share both these tax parameters.

As appealing as these targeted tax increases may be to some, they come with two significant weaknesses. First, both the United States and other developed countries have moved away from imposing extremely high tax rates on high-income citizens. According to OECD data for 2019, the top marginal tax rate in the US was 48.4 percent. That figure includes federal income and payroll taxes and an assumed state income tax rate of 2.4 percent. This placed the US slightly above the median among 35 developed countries.

If we add the 12.4 percent combined payroll tax that the Social Security Expansion Act would impose on higher earners, the top marginal tax *effective* rate would increase to 60.8 percent,[39] placing the United States top marginal tax rate among the top five of 35 OECD countries. Due to the concentration of high earnings in a small number of states where top state income tax rates may significantly exceed the 2.4 percent state income tax rate assumed by the OECD, the true top tax rate could be even higher.

For example, the maximum state and local income tax is 14.8 percent for a resident of New York City, 13.3 percent in California, 10.8 percent in New

Jersey, and 9.0 percent in Massachusetts. Policymakers will be faced with a prudential question of whether to impose such high marginal tax rates for the sake of a single federal government program when other pressing needs exist.

Under the investment income taxes considered by some reformers, the United States also would face a less internationally competitive situation with regard to investment taxes. Figure 4 shows maximum capital gains tax rates by country, based on OECD data. The current maximum rate in the United States is 29.2 percent, a figure that includes the formal capital gains tax, the 3.8 percent net investment income tax for high-income earners, and the average capital gains tax imposed by states. If the Social Security Expansion Act's 12.4 percent additional tax were applied, the US rate would increase to 42 percent, matching Denmark for the highest rate in the world.

Cumulatively, these progressive Social Security reform proposals would impose tax increases of a size that occurs only rarely. Based on a Tax Foundation analysis of the revenue effects of major legislation relative to the size of the economy, either the Social Security 2100 Act or the Medicare and Social Security Fair Share Act would likely be the largest peacetime tax increase in US history.[40]

A reasonable question facing a progressive Social Security reformer is, given the rare opportunity for a once-in-a-generation tax increase, whether the proceeds should be entirely devoted to a single program whose primary beneficiaries—seniors—already have the highest incomes and lowest incidence of poverty on record. Progressives appear to favor many other policies more than giving higher benefits to an already high-income group, such as providing universal health care and free college education. The tax increases necessary to fund Social Security expansion plans make these other policies all but impossible to achieve.

But there is a second, more philosophical concern with proposals that would address Social Security's financing shortfalls entirely on the backs of a small number of high-income Americans. Since its inception in 1935, Social Security has balanced the two pillars of "individual equity" and "social adequacy." Individual equity means that each American is provided a fair rate of return on the contributions they pay into Social Security. As the Consultant Panel on Social Security put it, "The Social

Figure 4. Maximum Tax Rate on Capital Gains by Country, with Supplement for the Social Security Expansion Act

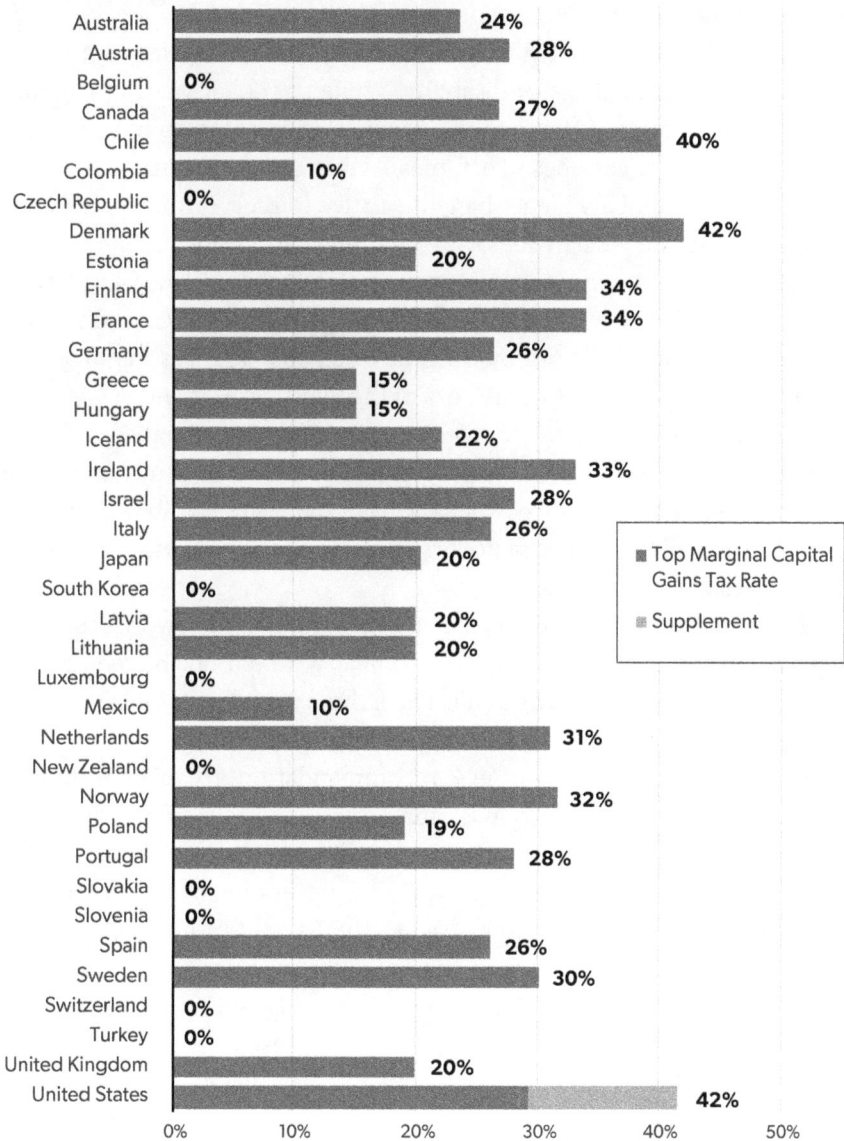

Australia	24%
Austria	28%
Belgium	0%
Canada	27%
Chile	40%
Colombia	10%
Czech Republic	0%
Denmark	42%
Estonia	20%
Finland	34%
France	34%
Germany	26%
Greece	15%
Hungary	15%
Iceland	22%
Ireland	33%
Israel	28%
Italy	26%
Japan	20%
South Korea	0%
Latvia	20%
Lithuania	20%
Luxembourg	0%
Mexico	10%
Netherlands	31%
New Zealand	0%
Norway	32%
Poland	19%
Portugal	28%
Slovakia	0%
Slovenia	0%
Spain	26%
Sweden	30%
Switzerland	0%
Turkey	0%
United Kingdom	20%
United States	42%

Legend:
- ■ Top Marginal Capital Gains Tax Rate
- ▨ Supplement

Source: Tax Foundation.

Security system has created strong expectations among its participants that they will receive retirement benefits that are reasonably related to their lifetime earnings."[41]

Social adequacy tilts the benefit formula in favor of low earners to reduce poverty in old age or disability. While the dollar value of benefits rises with the earnings level of the beneficiary, benefits do not rise proportionately with earnings. That means that a low-earning participant receives a substantially higher benefit relative to their earnings—a higher "replacement rate"—than does a high-earning participant.

From the beginning, Social Security was designed *not* to soak the rich. In 1934, President Roosevelt established the cabinet-level Committee on Economic Security, chaired by Secretary of Labor Frances Perkins. The committee developed the framework of the Social Security Act, which was passed the following year. Roosevelt's committee recommended that participating in the Social Security program be mandatory for any employee earning less than $3,000 per year, which translates to about $63,000 adjusted for inflation to 2024 dollars or about $215,000 if we account for the growth of average wages.

But here is the important part: Under the original framework for Social Security, anyone earning above $3,000 in 1935 would not be required to participate in Social Security at all. Thus, there would have been *no* redistribution from high earners to low and middle earners.

In practice, the committee's recommendation to exempt higher earners from Social Security was impractical; an individual with multiple jobs, for example, could have exceeded the committee's ineligibility threshold, but each of the employee's employers might be unaware of that fact. Thus, when Congress passed the Social Security Act in 1935, high earners contributed up to the $3,000 maximum salary threshold and received benefits calculated on their earnings up to that threshold, but neither paid taxes nor received benefits based on earnings above that amount. The maximum salary subject to payroll taxes has increased, from $3,000 in 1935 to $160,200 in 2023, but that practice has continued through today.

Years ago, when asked about eliminating the ceiling on wages subject to Social Security payroll taxes, a conservative (by today's standards) politician replied:

There may be an argument for raising the income [threshold] some because of inflation and because a lot more people have moved into higher income brackets in the last five years. But . . . let's suppose you took it off altogether. You say, "What do I care about some baseball player making $10 million a year," right? But if you think about it, what would happen is you would be putting people in a position of paying over the course of their lifetime 50, 60, 100 times more than they would ever draw out of the Social Security system. And you can say, "Well, they owe it to society." But these people also pay higher income taxes, and the rates are still pretty progressive for people in very high rates. . . .

You would really have tremendously changed the whole Social Security system. You would have basically said, "If you get to where you make $70,000 or more a year, we're going to soak you, and you're never going to get anything out of this compared to what you're putting in."[42]

That "conservative" was President Clinton, speaking in 1998.

And yet, the policy of "soaking the rich" in which, in President Clinton's words, "you're never going to get anything out of this compared to what you're putting in" is now embraced by many members of both the House and the Senate.

In the final chapter, I argue for an approach to Social Security reform that would indeed place the burden of funding the program more squarely on high-income Americans. But that approach explicitly incorporates a change in philosophy for the Social Security program. It is another matter entirely to pose as a Social Security traditionalist, speaking of "earned benefits" that Americans "paid for," while proposing policies that would do the opposite.

17

What About Other Solutions to Funding Social Security?

A common policy proposal to address Social Security solvency is to further increase the so-called normal or full retirement age—that is, the age at which a participant can receive unreduced retirement benefits. From Social Security's inception in 1935 through 2000, the full retirement age was set at 65. As legislated in the 1983 reforms, the retirement age began increasing in 2000, rising to age 67 by 2022. Various proposals would increase the retirement age further, either by an explicit number of years or by indexing the retirement age to improvements in longevity.

Increasing the retirement age has much to say for it. As Marc Goldwein of the Committee for a Responsible Federal Budget has argued, an increased retirement age would strengthen Social Security's finances, increase economic growth by encouraging longer work lives, and even boost seniors' financial, physical, and mental health.[1] Various research has found that those who delay retirement are in better mental and physical health than those who retire early and that even mandatory delays in retirement appear to improve health and longevity.

When other countries have increased their retirement ages, the death rate for individuals forced to delay retirement declined. Similarly, economists Maria Fitzpatrick and Timothy Moore found that mortality increased at age 62, when Social Security retirement benefits first become available.[2] In other words, offering Social Security appears to cause those who take early benefits to die earlier than they otherwise would have.

Yet even a large increase in the retirement age would not restore Social Security's solvency by itself. One proposal, from the late Representative Sam Johnson, would have increased the normal retirement age by three months per year beginning in 2022, until reaching age 69 in 2030. This kind of dramatic change in the retirement age is required to put a meaningful dent in Social Security's long-term funding gap.

But even dramatic increases in the retirement age would have only modest effects on Social Security's long-term funding gap. According to Social Security's actuaries, the rapid three-year increase in the normal retirement age to 70 that Johnson proposed would resolve only 29 percent of Social Security's 75-year funding gap.[3] Anyone who simultaneously believes that increasing the retirement age is a draconian change and that Social Security's funding gap is modest needs to reconcile their views.

Moreover, it is important to understand what an increase in the normal retirement age is and is not. It is *not* an increase in the age at which an individual may claim Social Security retirement benefits. It *is* an increase in the age at which an individual can claim full unreduced retirement benefits.

Under current law, an individual may claim Social Security retirement benefits beginning at the early retirement age of 62. Benefits are increased if the participant chooses to delay claiming, by about 7 percent per year up through age 70. After age 70, there is no credit for delayed claiming.

This description should make several things clear. Most importantly, a change in the Social Security normal retirement age does not alter *when* you can claim benefits, but it does alter *how much* you would receive at any age at which you claim.

For example, imagine that the Social Security normal retirement age were changed from 67 to 70. A worker could still claim at age 62 but would be subject to a larger benefit reduction for doing so because instead of claiming five years before the normal retirement, that worker would be claiming seven years early. As a result, that worker would receive two additional years of early claiming penalties, resulting in benefits about 21 percent lower than had the normal retirement age remained at age 67.

And that same approximately 21 percent reduction holds for everyone, regardless of when they claim benefits. People who claim benefits at age 62 will get roughly 21 percent less when the normal retirement age is 70 than when it was 67, as would the person who claims at 67 and the person who claims at 70. That person retiring at 70, instead of receiving three years of credit for delaying retirement past 67, would not receive those additional payments. *Everyone* receives the same uniform benefit cut.

This fact belies claims that increasing the retirement age is discriminatory against lower-income Americans because they tend not to live as long. The Government Accountability Office (GAO) released a report that looked at how increasing the Social Security retirement age might affect different groups of Americans.[4]

After reviewing evidence regarding differential longevity by income, which finds that higher-income households live and collect Social Security benefits longer than low earners do, the GAO stated, "Our analysis indicates that one frequently suggested change to address Social Security's financial challenges, raising the retirement age, would further reduce projected lifetime benefits for lower-income groups proportionally more than for higher-income groups."[5] The popular media agree: *Los Angeles Times* columnist Michael Hiltzik declared, "This implication is simply ignored by those who declare that raising the retirement age is a simple fix for Social Security."[6]

But these claims are wrong. If the retirement age goes up by a year, then every retiree—rich and poor, long-lived and short-lived—receives about 7 percent less in retirement benefits than they otherwise would have. They receive 7 percent less in each year they retire, so they receive about 7 percent less over their lifetimes. The GAO's analysts surely understand this.

So how did the GAO conclude that raising the Social Security retirement age would disproportionately hurt low-earning, shorter-lived retirees? By packaging an increase in Social Security's "normal retirement age"—currently age 67, which is the retirement age policy that's actually "frequently suggested" in the GAO's terms—with another policy that's rarely suggested and that doesn't contribute to fixing Social Security's solvency problem: raising the *early* retirement age of 62, when people can first claim retirement benefits.

Unlike raising the normal retirement age, raising the early retirement age *is* regressive because those who die between 62 and the new early retirement age, say 64 or 65, would not receive benefits. Because of differential mortality by income, those individuals would be disproportionately poor. Yet plenty of Social Security reform proposals raise the normal retirement age but don't touch the early retirement age. The GAO unfairly maligned those plans as harming the poor.

In fact, other, higher-quality research shows that increasing the Social Security retirement age is in fact slightly *progressive*. The Congressional Budget Office (CBO) analyzed the distributional effects of a range of policy options to address Social Security financing, measuring how different policies would affect taxes or benefits for low-, middle-, and high-earning Americans.[7]

Low earners were defined as those in the bottom fifth (or quintile) of the lifetime earnings distributions, middle earners were in the middle quintile, and high earners were in the top quintile. One option analyzed was to increase the normal retirement age from 67 to 70. For Americans born in 1980, the CBO's model determined that lifetime benefits would decline by 10 percent for low earners, 13 percent for middle earners, and 16 percent for high earners. This result is precisely the opposite of what the GAO and news media accounts claim.

What accounts for the difference? Well, a three-year increase in the Social Security retirement age has the same percentage effect on everyone's retirement benefits. But low earners are more likely to claim Social Security Disability Insurance benefits. A disabled worker is awarded Social Security benefits calculated as if they had worked to the normal retirement age, whatever that age is. So for a worker who claims Social Security disability benefits, whether the normal retirement age is 67, 70, or 100 won't affect their benefits.

Now, does all this mean that policymakers should increase the Social Security retirement age? I am open to the idea, so long as additional protections are put in place for low earners. Moreover, an increase in the normal retirement age acts as not only a benefit cut but also a signal regarding the "right" age to retire. Likely part of the increase in the age of claiming Social Security that has taken place over the past several decades was the result of the signaling effect of the normal retirement age rising from 65 to 67.

If We're Living Longer, Why Not Increase the Retirement Age?

At the same time, there is an argument based on fairness and causality that increasing the retirement age is discriminatory toward low earners—though not for the reasons that the GAO and news columnists claim. We all know the familiar story that Social Security faces insolvency because Americans are living longer. This story makes an increase in the retirement age appear reasonable: If we're living longer and that's costing the program more, then we all should work a bit longer as well.

And it is true that, on average, we're living longer. When Social Security began paying benefits in 1940, the average male age 65 could expect to survive and collect benefits for an additional 12.7 years.[8] Today, an average 65-year-old male will survive an additional 19.1 years, collecting benefits 50 percent longer than a retiree did in 1940. By 2060, a 65-year-old male can expect to survive 21.6 more years. There's no way around the fact that this increases costs for the Social Security program and exacerbates Social Security's solvency problem.

And yet, not everyone is living longer. US Treasury Department economist Hilary Waldron found that, among Americans born in 1912, those in the top half of the lifetime earnings distribution lived on average 1.2 years longer than those in the bottom half.[9] But for Americans born in 1941, differences widened: Those in the top half outlived those in the bottom half by an average of 5.8 years. More recent studies have found similar results.

And so, when an increase in the Social Security retirement age is proposed as a response to increasing lifespans and rising benefit costs, low earners might reasonably ask whether they are being asked to pay for a problem they didn't cause. It isn't them living longer and collecting more benefits but a uniform increase in the retirement age that is causing them to pay for part of the problem via lower benefits.

Now, as I noted earlier, no plausible increase in the Social Security retirement age is sufficient to address the program's full funding shortfall. So a package of reforms will be necessary. That package could increase the retirement age, both to reduce rising costs for middle and high earners driven by longevity and to signal a desire for longer work lives, coupled with specific provisions that would enhance benefits for low earners so they are not punished for a longevity problem they did not cause.

Nevertheless, even for a well-designed reform package to succeed, it must be clearly communicated why different provisions are introduced and who those provisions are targeted toward.

But I Paid for Those Benefits! Actually, You Didn't.

Social Security's status as an "earned benefit" adds a moral component to discussions of reform, making any potential change to Social Security benefits an emotionally charged issue. It is one thing to alter a level of future welfare benefits, a transfer funded by one part of the population (higher earners) to benefit another part (lower earners). However important a welfare benefit may be to those who receive it, it is uncommon to hear that higher-income Americans have a moral or legal obligation to fund those benefits and low-income Americans have a moral or legal obligation to receive them.

But Social Security is a different matter entirely, because the program was structured intentionally to resemble a private-sector pension or insurance plan, not a government welfare program. When Social Security was developed, some of President Franklin D. Roosevelt's advisers wanted to fund the program using progressive general tax revenues. Roosevelt disagreed, not because he opposed a progressive funding source but because he believed it crucial to give Americans a sense of ownership in their benefits. Roosevelt said,

> I guess you're right on the economics, but those taxes were never a problem of economics. They are politics all the way through. We put those pay roll contributions there so as to give the contributors a legal, moral, and political right to collect their pensions.... With those taxes in there, no damn politician can ever scrap my Social Security program.[10]

To date, Roosevelt has proven to be correct. Even today, progressive-leaning elected officials—and, indeed, increasing numbers of conservative politicians—rail against efforts to cut Americans "earned benefits," the benefits they paid for through a lifetime of work.

Except, that's not always the case. For instance, consider Americans born during the 1960s, who will enter retirement in the years leading up to the Social Security trust funds insolvency. Obviously, one solution to Social Security's financing shortfall would be to cut these Americans' benefits—precipitously—when the trust funds run dry. But would this not deprive these Americans of benefits they had rightfully paid for and deserve to receive?

Not according to the CBO, which has calculated Social Security "money's worth ratios" for Americans of different ages and earnings levels. The

Table 1. Ratio of Lifetime Benefits to Lifetime Taxes, Individuals Born in the 1960s

	Average	Lowest	Second	Middle	Fourth	Highest
		———Quintile of Lifetime Earnings———				
Scheduled Benefits	1.40	2.76	1.86	1.57	1.35	0.97
Payable Benefits	1.11	2.36	1.53	1.25	1.05	0.82

Source: Congressional Budget Office, "CBO's 2021 Long-Term Projections for Social Security: Additional Information," July 8, 2021, https://www.cbo.gov/publication/57342.
Note: Benefits and taxes are measured in present value terms, adjusting for interest.

CBO finds that the average American born in the 1960s is promised lifetime Social Security benefits equal to 1.4 times their lifetime taxes, even after accounting for interest.[11] This means that average Americans retiring around the time the trust fund is scheduled to run dry are promised 40 percent more in benefits than they paid in taxes.

No wonder the trust fund is running dry! Low-earning Americans, in the bottom fifth (or quintile) of the lifetime earnings distribution, are promised 2.76 times more in taxes than they'll pay in benefits. Even the highest-earning quintile falls just a bit short of getting their taxes back, with interest: They are promised a money's worth ratio of 0.97. (See Table 1.)

Now consider what Americans would receive under a "payable benefits" scenario, in which benefits are cut by 20 percent or more when the Social Security trust funds are exhausted. Even then, the average American born in the 1960s would receive 1.1 times more in benefits than they paid in taxes. The CBO's numbers show that even the crudest way of making Social Security solvent would not deprive Americans of benefits they had truly earned and paid for.

That isn't to say that an overnight 20 percent or more cut in benefits for all retirees and disabled workers, rich and poor alike, is the best way to fix Social Security. Regardless of whether Americans actually paid for the benefits they are entitled to, they have gone through most of their lives believing they have because they've been told they have, and they have made their retirement plans based on those beliefs.

The point remains, however, that the deeply embedded idea that Americans have truly earned and paid for their benefits is untrue. Even today, most Americans are promised more in benefits than they will pay in taxes, and that imbalance helps explain why Social Security as currently structured is financially unsustainable.

Could Investing in Stocks Be the Answer?

To make Social Security solvent requires either higher taxes or lower benefits. Or does it? For decades, policymakers have been attracted to a third option that promises to avoid those politically painful options. That option is to earn a higher rate of return on Social Security dollars by investing those funds in the stock market—and it remains as alluring today as it did in the late 1990s.

But—and I say this as someone who previously advocated for adding personal accounts to Social Security that could invest in stocks—the siren song of saving Social Security through the stock market is ultimately a dead end. This seeming blanket rejection of investing Social Security funds in stocks does not mean that private investment is bad. But the stock market does not solve the problems that Social Security faces.

As economists John Geanakoplos, Olivia Mitchell, and Stephen Zeldes wrote in an early and influential explanation of these issues:

> Many advocates of Social Security privatization argue that rates of return under a defined contribution individual account system would be much higher for all than they are under the current social security system. This claim is false. The mistake comes from ignoring accrued benefits already promised based on past payroll taxes, and from underestimating the riskiness of stock investments.[12]

Reading their paper more than two decades ago marked an important shift in how I thought about Social Security reform.

But more than two decades later, the key issues remain misunderstood. Even today, elected officials propose investing Social Security funds in the stock market as a way to avoid tax increases or benefit reductions. So it is worth discussing these questions in greater detail.

The allure of investing Social Security in stocks is straightforward. Social Security itself pays a fairly low rate of return. For instance, Social Security's actuaries estimate that a single male with medium earnings and retiring in 2029 will receive a 2.16 percent real rate of return on his and his employer's Social Security payroll taxes.[13] This return is lower than the 2.33 percent real rate of return paid by the Social Security trust fund's bonds from 1960 through 2020—and far below the 6.4 percent real rate of return paid by the S&P 500 stock index over that same period.

Moreover, the 2.16 percent return promised by Social Security cannot be paid, due to the insolvency of the program's trust funds projected for the mid-2030s. If Social Security benefits were reduced when the trust funds ran dry, as they would be under a literal interpretation of current law, then Social Security's seemingly meager 2.16 percent real return would be reduced to only 1.64 percent. How could private investments *not* improve on that situation?

The answer has two parts. First, to receive the higher returns paid by stocks and bonds, one must have the money to invest in stocks and bonds. And Social Security does not have such money: As a pay-as-you-go program in which current taxes pay for current benefits, all of Social Security's revenues are currently allocated to keep benefit checks arriving in seniors' mailboxes—or, more correctly these days, electronically transferred to their bank accounts.

Where would this extra money to invest in the stock market come from? And if we have a source of extra money, why not simply use it to fill Social Security's funding gaps in the short term rather than investing that money for the future, leaving the short-term gap unaddressed?

Second, part of the higher return paid by stocks is simply a compensation for the extra risk that stocks carry. Wall Street and the financial services industry are not in the business of giving away free money. That stocks have higher expected returns than bonds is simply another way of saying that, for any given amount of expected dividend or interest payments expected from a stock or bond in future years, investors won't pay as much for a stock as they will for a bond.

That lower price paid for stocks today drives up the expected return on the investment in future years. But the reason investors won't pay as much for a stock as they will for a bond is precisely because the stream of dividends a stock pays to its owner is far riskier than the stream of interest payments a bondholder receives. Put another way, $1 of stocks is worth the same as $1 of bonds: They may have different expected returns, but they also carry different levels of risk.

The reality is that the basic premise—that Social Security pays a low return while private investments pay a high return—isn't really correct. The reason goes back to Social Security's pay-as-you-go financing.

As discussed earlier, a pay-as-you-go system like Social Security can begin paying full benefits immediately, while a funded pension system must wait a complete working generation before full benefits can be paid. That's a long time during which Social Security would pay a substantially higher return than a private pension system would. As the Social Security Administration's Dean Leimer showed, the earliest Social Security beneficiaries received a nearly 30 percent annual return on their contributions.[14]

Now, once Social Security has matured and workers are contributing throughout their careers, it will pay a lower return than a funded system would. The implicit rate of return on a mature pay-as-you-go system is the rate of growth of the tax base. That is the growth rate of the labor force, which the Social Security trustees project at 0.45 percent annually, plus the growth of average wages, which is projected to be 1.25 percent above inflation over the long term, for a total annual return of about 1.7 percent above inflation.

By contrast, the Social Security trustees project that the government bonds held in the program's trust funds will yield about 2.3 percent above inflation over the long term. But while Social Security pays a lower return in future years, it paid participants a much higher return over its first several decades.

But still, some ask whether there is some way around this problem. A recent Social Security reform proposal spearheaded by Senator Bill Cassidy has attempted to square this circle. Under Cassidy's plan, the federal government would borrow several trillion dollars over about five years, with the proceeds invested in a fund containing stocks, private equity, and other risky but high-returning investments. The fund would not be touched for 75 years, after which annual interest on the fund would be sufficient along with payroll tax revenues to keep Social Security solvent indefinitely. While the Cassidy proposal would contain several other provisions, reportedly it is the borrow-to-invest element of his plan that garnered the most bipartisan interest in the Senate.

This approach has several problems. First, and most obviously, building an investment fund that won't be touched for 75 years doesn't do anything to address Social Security's funding shortfalls between today and the 75th year, which top $23 trillion. In other words, while the appeal of the borrow-to-invest plan is that it avoids the choice between tax increases and benefit cuts, in reality this plan doesn't.

Second, as discussed previously, the higher return paid on stocks—on which all else in this plan depends—is simply a compensation for increased risk. And holding stocks collectively does not make that risk go away. Just ask state and local governments, which have loaded up their public employee retirements with risky assets using precisely the same reasoning as Cassidy's plan and have found that fluctuating returns result in wildly varying annual contributions that must be made to these plans. If the Social Security fund returned just a little less each year than projected, the final balance 75 years hence could be dramatically smaller.

And there is reason to believe that the plan's assumed stock market returns could fall short. If the federal government shows up with $1.5 trillion looking to purchase stocks, the only way it can convince current stockholders to part with their equities would be to pay more for them. My American Enterprise Institute colleague Mark Warshawsky estimated that Cassidy's borrow-to-invest plan would boost the initial value of the stock market by about 10 percent.[15]

This initial bump in stock prices would reduce the average annual stock return over the next 75 years by about 0.14 percentages points. This lower return would not only cause the Social Security fund to fall about 9 percent short of its assumed value but reduce the returns that Americans receive on their 401(k)s, individual retirement accounts (IRAs), and other stock investments.

No financial planner would recommend that a person who reached midlife with insufficient retirement savings should take out a loan and invest the money in the stock market. By contrast, the borrow-to-invest

Social Security plan most closely resembles what is called a "pension obligation bond" issued by state or local governments to fund their employee retirement systems.

The governments issue debt then invest the proceeds in risky assets, hoping to profit off the difference. Sometimes this works, and sometimes it doesn't, but in general, pension obligation bonds are regarded as one of the worst practices of state and local government pensions. But a pension obligation bond is also something that prudent advisers don't recommend.

In 2015, the Government Finance Officers Association, which represents public finance officials throughout the United States and Canada, approved a resolution putting the issue in simple terms: "State and local governments should not issue POBs [pension obligation bonds]."[16] It would be a sad irony if the one practice that Social Security derived from other pension systems is generally considered to be one of the least responsible.

Third, even if the proposal does work as planned, it's not a free lunch. Wharton School economist Kent Smetters has shown that investing the trust fund in stocks is economically equivalent to the government imposing a capital gains tax on stock investments.[17] In each case, if the stock market goes up, the government takes a slice of the gains; if stock returns fall short, it shoulders some of the losses.

This gets at a more fundamental problem with the borrow-to-invest plan: It doesn't increase national saving, grow the economy, or result in a larger future gross domestic product. It simply finds another way to extract an additional slice of the economic pie and dedicate those funds to Social Security.

Even if investing stocks truly were low-risk and offered high returns over the long term, what works for one investor can't work for everyone. A single investor with a superior investment strategy earns higher returns, but these come at the expense of other, less-astute investors. But when a single massive entity is investing trillions of dollars on behalf of the entire US population, it's a zero-sum game.

If individuals must ultimately bear the risk of Social Security investments in stocks, it makes sense to view the pros and cons of those investments in the same way that individuals might. And from that perspective, investing the Social Security trust fund in stocks—or, for that matter, establishing personal retirement accounts holding equities—doesn't make much of a difference.

Here's why. Most Americans will have two main sources of retirement income. The first is Social Security, which pays a low rate of return but is safe. The second is personal savings, such as an IRA or 401(k) in which, importantly, the saver can choose the mix of risk and return they desire. Between low-risk, low-return Social Security and adjustable-risk, adjustable-return personal retirement savings, Americans would have an overall mix of risk and return that suits their preferences.

Even if you think that stocks are a much better deal than bonds, offering much higher long-run returns at lower risk, Americans already have decided on the portfolio allocation that works best for them. Adding more risk to the Social Security portion of their retirement savings package doesn't make them better off if they already have the mix of risk and return they prefer.

The same concerns found in Social Security investing in the stock market arise with proposals for personal retirement accounts embedded in Social Security. To fund these accounts would require additional resources, since every dollar of Social Security taxes already is spoken for. And to the degree that personal account investment in stocks produced higher returns, this is a benefit that most Americans could already obtain simply by shifting their 401(k) and IRA accounts toward riskier investments.

The political controversy embedded in any proposal to invest Social Security funds in the stock market would make doing so a heavy lift from a legislative point of view while doing precious little to address the program's multitrillion-dollar funding shortfalls. Those funding shortfalls will themselves be a heavy lift politically, so it seems unwise to increase the load. Instead, as I discuss in the following chapter, policymakers should work together to facilitate additional retirement savings outside the Social Security program.

18

Social Security Reform:
What's Been Tried

Social Security reform is motivated by this: The program is significantly underfunded going forward. So most reform proposals focus on funding. They start with current tax and benefit formulas, which leave the program insolvent over the long term, and adjust them so Social Security moves toward solvency, greater progressivity, or whatever goals the policymaker desires. Different proposals place different weights on increasing taxes versus reducing benefits, but most reforms give little thought to Social Security as a program rather than a funding problem: They assume Social Security works well, except it is underfunded.

The federal government treats almost no other program this way. Medicare and Medicaid are regularly reassessed and adjusted to produce better outcomes at lower costs. Welfare programs are reformed to improve social protections while reducing downsides, such as disincentives to work and marry. Education policy is continually reevaluated to improve outcomes. Yet Social Security is often treated as if its tax and benefit formulas were handed down on tablets from on high.

This way of thinking about Social Security comes with considerable downsides when implementing Social Security reform, which depends crucially on public understanding and support.

I have on my home office wall a framed copy of a 2005 *Doonesbury* comic strip, drawn by the progressive cartoonist Garry Trudeau. This comic strip consisted of a near-verbatim repetition of a speech given by President George W. Bush in which he explained the Social Security benefit formula. These speeches were given as part of a massive second-term effort by the Bush administration to enact Social Security reform. I worked in the Bush administration and supported those reforms. And yet the cartoon serves as a reminder that with Social Security, clarity is crucial.

The joke of the *Doonesbury* comic is that the president's statements, all of which are technically correct, are comically indecipherable to all but the small coterie of analysts versed in the minutiae of the program's financing. I recall at the time, while working in the Bush White House, receiving a telephone call from a congressional staffer who worked for a leading proponent of Social Security reform. The staffer told me that no one on Capitol Hill had any idea what the White House was talking about.

I then asked which nuance of the reforms they could use help with. No, I was told: They literally cannot understand what you all are saying. They don't know what you all are talking about. If no one can understand what you are saying, it isn't unreasonable to expect them to assume the worst.

Part of this problem stemmed from the inherent complexity of the Social Security program, which nearly no one, including members of Congress, understands at any level of detail. I would wager that not one person in 100 could accurately—or even reasonably accurately—describe how Social Security benefits are calculated.

But much of the problem, I believe, comes from how the Bush reforms and many other Social Security plans have been developed in the first place. Here I ask you to follow my best efforts to explain President Bush's proposed reform, called "progressive price indexing." But if you cannot follow the explanation, that merely proves my point.

The current Social Security benefit formula is "wage indexed," which means that the initial benefits for successive cohorts of new retirees rise each year at the rate of average wage growth in the economy. This wage indexing does not refer to cost-of-living adjustments that are paid after retirement, but rather to the initial benefit that a new retiree receives this year versus the benefit paid to new retirees in the prior year.

Wage indexing instead refers to Social Security's so-called bend points, which are dollar amounts of monthly preretirement earnings that are replaced at either 90 percent, 32 percent, or 15 percent. Those dollar amounts are increased each year along with national average wage growth. This results in real, inflation-adjusted benefits offered by Social Security that rise year after year, automatically and without input from Congress.

Some reformers have argued that Social Security benefits should instead be "price indexed," which implies that benefits for new retirees next year will rise only with inflation relative to those paid to this year's new retirees.[1] Using price indexing, Social Security's bend points would be increased each year with inflation, rather than at the higher rate of wage growth. While never quite explained in this way, price indexing would be an inflation-adjusted freeze on future benefits. Price indexing would reduce future benefit outlays without cutting benefits in real terms and would contribute a great deal to restoring Social Security's solvency.

However, price indexing also would successively reduce the "replacement rates" offered by Social Security, meaning retirement benefits as a percentage of the retirees' preretirement earnings. The reason is that average preretirement earnings would continue to increase by about 1 percent per year above inflation while average inflation-adjusted benefits would remain constant, meaning that Social Security's replacement rates would tend to drop by about 1 percent per year.

To avoid reducing replacement rates for low earners, President Bush adopted "progressive price indexing," which retained wage-indexed benefits for workers at the 30th percentile of the earnings distribution and below while paying only price-indexed benefits to the highest-earning workers. Those with earnings between the 30th percentile and the maximum taxable wage would receive a mix of wage-indexed and price-indexed benefits.

To accomplish this, the lower two of the Social Security benefit formula's three replacement factors—which for a person retiring in 2020 replaced 90 percent of monthly earnings up to $1,024, 32 percent of earnings between $1,024 and $6,172, and 15 percent of earnings from $6,172 up to the maximum taxable wage—would each year be multiplied by a factor that is slightly less than one, thereby reducing benefits for higher-earning retirees.

Got it? Of course not. Almost no one outside of a few policy wonks got it. And more important, even they didn't *really* get it because, even if they could explain the technicalities of the benefit formula, they didn't give much thought to where it would all end up: with every retiree above the 30th percentile of the earnings distribution receiving approximately the same benefit. No one ever mentioned that end point, since most people weren't aware of it.

But they didn't mention the end point because the end point wasn't their intent. Their intent was simply to steer the large and ungainly

SS *Social Security* away from the iceberg and in a more financially sustainable direction without unduly reducing benefits for low earners. What they lacked was a clear view of the program's ultimate destination, much less a clear way to communicate that view.

As it happened, President Bush's Social Security reforms did not come close to passing Congress, even with the House and Senate both under Republican control. Part of the failure lay with the proposal's incorporation of voluntary personal retirement accounts, which would allow workers to divert a portion of their payroll tax to a 401(k)-like account in exchange for accepting a lower traditional benefit in retirement. Congressional Democrats and philosophically aligned think tanks and advocacy groups bitterly opposed these accounts.

Moreover, Republicans had come to believe that personal accounts, by investing in supposedly higher returning stocks, would obviate the need for benefits cuts. Discovering that not to be a fact caused some confusion among Republican members of Congress and reduced their enthusiasm to take on a politically difficult issue. At the same time, President Bush's own political capital had been sapped by the seeming lack of progress in the war in Iraq.[2]

But part of the failure, I believe, is attributable to the fact that a typical American, much less a typical member of Congress, had difficulty understanding what was being proposed and why. Given the choice between a system they know but have doubts about and a new reform about which they understand little, many Americans will opt for the status quo. The same, I might add, applies to current proposals to expand Social Security through substantial tax increases.

The Social Security 2100 Act, for example, was first introduced by Representative John Larson in 2014 and eventually garnered cosponsorship from nearly nine in 10 Democratic House members. And yet, even during Democrats' unified control of Congress and the presidency in 2021 and 2022, the Social Security 2100 Act never was passed through the Ways and Means Committee, much less receive a vote on the floor of the House. Social Security reform is simply an extremely difficult issue to tackle, and policymakers wishing to do so must think carefully about how they present their ideas.

The Blank-Slate Approach to Social Security Reform

In the years since the failure of Bush's efforts, I have thought carefully about Social Security reform—not merely what it should look like, but at a more fundamental level how one might develop a reform proposal. Instead of the conventional approach of starting with the current program and making incremental technical changes each year, we could instead ask what kind of retirement system we would like to give Americans who will retire, say, 50 years from now.

These Americans have not paid a penny into Social Security, nor does the system owe them a penny. In a sense, Congress can give them any Social Security program it wants. And once Congress decides on what the best plan for future Americans might look like, the technical folks can design the rules and formulas for getting from here to there.

Part of this approach is that whatever is decided would be phased in over time. An individual just entering the workforce today would receive benefits entirely based on the new program that the blank-slate process devised. An individual retiring today would receive benefits based on the current Social Security formula. And individuals retiring in intervening years would receive a blend of the two.

This blank-slate approach allows policymakers to ask much broader questions: What protections should Social Security offer to future retirees? What should we demand that working Americans pay in return for those protections? What level of retirement benefits should be mandated, encouraged, and simply left to individuals' preferences? What is the appropriate mix between Social Security benefits and income from household retirement savings?

Different people will have different ideas of what that ideal Social Security program might look like. Yet those who honestly perform this thought experiment are unlikely to answer: "Exactly like the current Social Security program." And that is because the world has changed dramatically in the 85 years since Social Security was designed.

When Social Security was originally contemplated, widespread individual-level participation in capital markets for retirement saving was difficult to foresee. Practically no mutual funds were available, and those that existed were costly. There was no internet to help manage plan administration and guide investment choices.

Americans were not merely financially illiterate but in many cases had difficulty even reading. The concepts of behavioral economics that guide many retirement plan structures today were unknown. Social Security was constructed as it was largely because there was little other option.

But 21st-century America is different. And in 21st-century America, I believe, many Americans would likely agree with the following framework. First, the government should protect against penury in old age, and it should do that job well. Gaps in the existing safety net should be filled.

Second, to generate income on top of that government-provided protection, Americans should adopt greater responsibility to save for retirement on their own. After all, if every American saved assiduously for retirement, Social Security's role could understandably be more limited. That may not have been possible in 1935, but there is nothing preventing it in 2035 and beyond.

These basic ideas point toward a division of labor in providing income in retirement. Government has a natural advantage in redistributing income from rich to poor, identifying those in need, and directing resources toward them. So the safety net against poverty in old age is an appropriate role for government.

But there is far less pressing need for the federal government to provide substantial retirement benefits to middle- and high-earning households that could, should, and would save for retirement on their own. Today, Social Security provides over $80,000 in annual retirement benefits to a couple that together earned well over $300,000 annually during their working career. Under current Social Security benefit rules, the government will pay substantially more to such high earners in the future.

Even two medium-wage workers retiring in 2023 will together receive a combined Social Security benefit of over $56,000, placing them at nearly three times the elderly poverty threshold before touching even a penny of their own retirement savings. It is difficult to see that someone creating an ideal government pension program from scratch in the 21st century, especially knowing resources will be in short supply, would provide generous benefits for middle- and upper-income households that can easily save for retirement on their own.

Now, one might reasonably suppose that in a 21st-century federal retirement policy, government should facilitate household retirement saving; it might go further to automatically enroll workers in retirement plans, or it could go the final step toward mandating that individuals save for retirement outside of Social Security. But dividing the labor between government-sponsored poverty protection and household-managed personal retirement saving allows each sector to operate at its best.

As we have seen elsewhere, governments around the world are poor at ensuring promised retirement benefits are fully funded, while household retirement savings have increased manyfold. Given that track record, while poverty protection should be the government's focus, it would seem foolhardy to task the government with adequately funding trillions of dollars in benefits for members of households who are at no risk of poverty in old age.

How Other Countries Do It

It is worth illustrating how this framework might play out by examining the retirement systems of similar countries, including Australia, Canada, New Zealand, and the United Kingdom. I selected these countries not because they are the only countries available, but because they are similar to the United States in many respects—except the way they structure income provision for the elderly. This exercise demonstrates how much might be accomplished by modeling policy after countries that share the United States' tradition of social protections for the poor coupled with robust private financial markets.

Australia starts with a means-tested minimum retirement pension called the Age Pension, which is provided by the government and funded through general tax revenues. This base benefit is coupled with a requirement that all full-time private-sector employees participate in an employer-provided retirement plan with a minimum contribution level.

Australia's Age Pension provides a retired couple with no assets or other income sources a benefit equal to about USD 1,900 per month. However, that government-provided minimum benefit is means-tested: It decreases by 50 cents with each dollar the couple earns over about USD 450 per month. Benefits also decrease based on retirees' assets, including their home value.

The Australian means test acts as an implicit tax on personal saving for retirement, but Australia seeks to overcome that disincentive to save by requiring all full-time workers to participate in a retirement plan. Each employee is enrolled in a retirement plan funded by an amount equal to 9.5 percent of employee wages, contributed by their employer. The contribution rate is scheduled to increase to 12 percent by 2025. About half of Australian retirees receive the full means-tested benefit, about one-quarter receive a reduced benefit, and about one-quarter lose their benefit via the means test.[3]

To judge how well Australia's Age Pension works, it is worth comparing retirement incomes in the United States to Australia. Relying on Organisation for Economic Co-operation and Development (OECD) data, in 2018 the median US senior had a disposable income of $36,050, far exceeding the $21,892 median (in US dollars) in Australia. So the typical American senior is better off than the typical Australian over age 65.

And yet, at the 10th percentile of the income distribution, representing the poorest retirees, Australian seniors have an annual disposable income of $14,595, while US seniors at the bottom of the income distribution have incomes of just $12,431. As social insurance, Australia's targeted, means-tested Age Pension appears to provide better protections against poverty in old age than does Social Security.

Moreover, Australia's pension system is far cheaper. The 2020 cost of Australia's means-tested benefit was 2.5 percent of gross domestic product (GDP). Over time, as savings grow in employer-sponsored retirement plans, government outlays on the means-tested benefit are projected to decline to about 2.3 percent of GDP in 2060. And this falling cost will occur despite a decline in Australia's ratio of workers to beneficiaries, which ordinarily increases the costs of pay-as-you-go retirement programs.[4] Over that same period, US government expenditures on Social Security are projected to increase from 5.3 percent to 6.1 percent of GDP.[5]

In short, the US will be spending over twice as much while having fewer protections for our lowest-income seniors. Australia's clear division of labor—a robust but limited government benefit to guarantee against poverty coupled with universal private retirement savings plans to supplement the government benefit—matches well with the blank-slate thought process outlined earlier.

New Zealand offers a similar model to Australia, but with an important twist. New Zealand pays a flat-dollar pension benefit to nearly all retirees, regardless of past earnings or years in the labor force. For a retired couple, the New Zealand Superannuation benefit is equal to about USD 1,800 per month.[6] In contrast to Australia, however, New Zealand's flat-dollar benefit is not reduced based on other retirement savings, though it is subject to taxes.

The lack of a means test makes New Zealand's Superannuation benefit more expensive than a means-tested program such as Australia's Age Pension, but it also reduces the need to mandate personal retirement saving on top of what the government provides. New Zealand's supplemental KiwiSaver accounts, introduced in 2007, feature automatic enrollment and a government and employer match. But, unlike Australia, there is no requirement to save.

Like Australia, New Zealand's approach appears to work well as social insurance against poverty in old age. Despite having median disposable retirement incomes that are barely half those of the United States, New Zealand seniors at the 10th percentile have incomes that slightly exceed their US counterparts. New Zealand's model also is consistent with what a blank-slate approach to Social Security policy might arrive at.

The United Kingdom's programs for retirement income provision have undergone substantial reforms in recent years that should strengthen retirement security in decades to come. The UK's main benefit program for the elderly is called the New State Pension. Unlike Social Security, in which benefits are based on lifetime earnings, the New State Pension offers benefits based on years in the labor market. A couple that has spent at least 35 years in the labor force would each receive the full New State Pension benefit of about USD 1,800 per month.[7] The State Pension is not means-tested, though it is subject to income taxes.

Basing benefits on years in the workforce embodies a "You do your part, we'll do our part" philosophy that might appeal to many Americans. If a person goes to work each day throughout their career, they will receive the full benefit available from the New State Pension, whether they earned a little or a lot at their job.

But to maintain their standard of living in retirement, middle- and upper-income Britons would need to save well beyond what the New State Pension will provide. To increase personal retirement savings, in 2012 the United Kingdom introduced the National Employment Savings Trust (NEST). NEST automatically enrolls all employees who earn a minimum of about USD 10,000 per year in a defined contribution retirement account if they are not already offered a retirement plan at work.

Participation is voluntary, but if the employee continues in the plan, their employer must contribute at least 3 percent of their pay, and the employee must contribute at least 5 percent of their salary. Most employees, however, receive a government credit that reduces their cost to about 4 percent of their salary. Neither NEST nor the New State Pension have been in place long enough for OECD data to reflect how well they will prepare UK residents for retirement.

Canada's government retirement system has two tiers. Canada's Old Age Security (OAS) benefit is a base benefit to prevent poverty, similar to the US Supplemental Security Income (SSI) program. The OAS benefit is paid on a flat-dollar basis and prorated based on years of residency in the country. The benefit and means-testing formulas are complex, but a retired couple with no other income sources would receive about USD 910 per month in OAS benefits.

The maximum SSI benefit for a US retiree couple in 2023 is $1,371 per month. However, like SSI, the OAS benefit is means-tested. It can decrease if a retiree has other income sources, including from the Canada Pension Plan (CPP).

The CPP provides benefits on top of the OAS and is sometimes viewed by Americans as comparable to the US Social Security program. However, there are important differences. First, unlike US Social Security, the CPP benefit formula is not progressive. Each retiree receives a benefit equal to 33 percent of their average preretirement earnings, whereas Social Security can replace up to 90 percent of preretirement earnings for very low-earning individuals. Nearly all the redistribution in Canada's public retirement programs occurs through the means-tested Old Age Pension program.

Second, CPP tax and benefit formulas are applied to a much lower level of earnings than are Social Security's. In the US, Social Security payroll taxes were levied on earnings up to $160,200 in 2023, while in Canada taxes are levied and benefits calculated based only on earnings up through about $65,000 per year. As a result, the average new Canadian retiree in 2021 received a CPP benefit of about $562 per month versus over $1,600 in US Social Security benefits for an average new retiree that year.

On top of the OAS and CPP, Canadians may participate in employer-sponsored retirement plans similar to those offered in the US. Canada has neither mandatory participation in retirement plans like Australia nor automatic enrollment as in New Zealand and the United Kingdom. Participation in employer-sponsored retirement plans appears to be significantly lower in Canada than in the US.

The government agency Statistics Canada reports that, while retirement plan coverage was nearly universal in Canada's public sector in 2021, only 22 percent of private-sector employees participated in a retirement plan.[8] Participants were split roughly evenly between defined benefit and defined contribution retirement plans.

Canada does not go as far as the other countries in fleshing out what I would see as a blank-slate approach to retirement security, at least insofar as facilitating private savings to supplement its relatively modest government benefits. At the same time, Canada's outcomes for retiree incomes are not poor: Canada's median disposable income for residents age 65 and over of $31,967 approaches the US median of $36,050, while its 10th percentile income of $17,759 exceeds the US figure of $12,431 by a substantial margin. That said, Canada also has lower levels of income inequality in the years before retirement, which presumably would lead to a tighter distribution of incomes in old age.

We can clearly see the difference in focus between the United States and these other four Anglo countries by looking at the maximum benefits their state pension systems pay to a new retiree. (See Figure 1.) In 2021, a single worker who earned the maximum taxable salary for at least 35 years and claimed benefits at the normal retirement age would receive an annual Social Security benefit of $42,849. That amount dwarfs what a retiree in the other four countries would receive.

In 2021, the New Zealand Superannuation benefit paid to all retirees was equal to USD 11,456. The maximum Age Pension in Australia was USD 13,150, and because the benefit is means-tested, a truly high-income

Figure 1. Maximum Annual Benefit from Government Retirement Program (US Dollars, 2021)

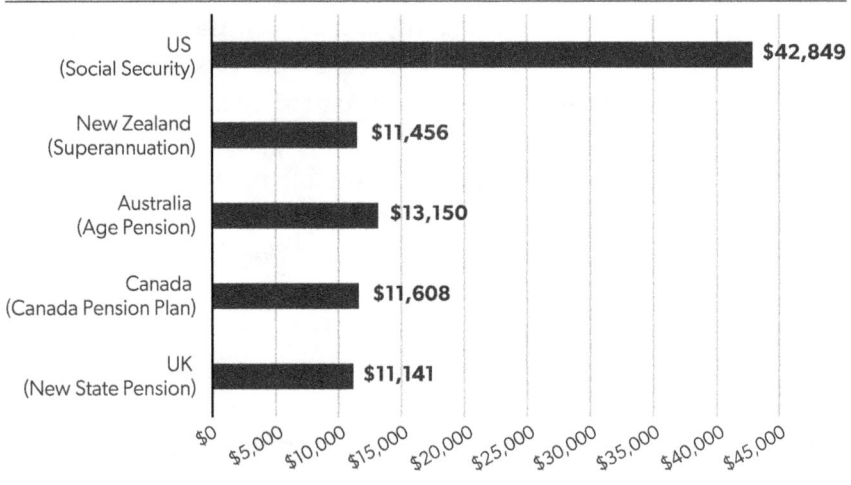

Source: Author's calculations from governmental sources.
Note: Adjusted for exchange rate differences as of July 2022.

retiree might receive nothing. The maximum CPP benefit in 2021 was just $11,608; CPP benefits are based on salaries with a much lower ceiling than is applied in the US.

Finally, the maximum New State Pension in the United Kingdom, paid to a retiree with at least 35 years in their work history, was USD 11,141. In sum, the maximum Social Security benefit paid to US retirees is about 3.5 times higher in real terms than is paid in Australia, Canada, New Zealand, or the United Kingdom—all countries that Americans sometimes claim are more "socialist" than the United States.

One objection to the far lower maximum retirement benefits paid in other Anglo countries might be that, while reducing costs for their respective programs, the inadequacy of benefits leaves a typical retiree unprepared for old age. And yet that is not how seniors in these countries describe their financial situations. In a 2017 Vanguard survey, 4 percent of US seniors agreed with the statement, "I would describe my own retirement situation as a crisis." In Australia, the share of retirees calling their financial situation a crisis was 8 percent; in Canada, 6 percent; and in the United Kingdom, 1 percent.[9]

However politically sacrosanct US policymakers might consider Social Security's tax and benefit formulas to be, there are other ways to attain retirement income security that are compatible with the United States' basic political and economic traditions. Australia, Canada, New Zealand, and the United Kingdom each have fully functioning free-market economies and democracies that provide well for their seniors, all while structuring their retirement systems significantly differently from the US Social Security program. These examples should open policymakers' minds to a wider range of Social Security reform options, given the US political system's repeated failures to enact reforms over the past several decades.

19

A Social Security Reform Plan That Works

L et's build a Social Security reform plan. I'll use the blank-slate
approach to designing a retirement package and the general philosophies of retirement programs in the four countries discussed in the previous chapter.

In this reformed Social Security program, retirees would receive a
government-provided benefit equal to 28 percent of the national average
wage for single retirees and 41 percent of the average wage for couples, as
is done in Australia. For 2024, given that the Social Security trustees projected the national average wage would be $68,628, this would produce a
guaranteed minimum benefit of $19,216 for single retirees and $28,137 for
couples.[1] In each case, these benefits exceed the federal poverty threshold, ensuring that no American retires into poverty.[2]

Moreover, the minimum benefit would increase in future years at the
rate of average wage growth, whereas the federal poverty threshold rises
only with inflation. Thus, the income protection offered by the flat benefit
would increase over time.

Using 2024 parameters, in which approximately 55 percent of retiree
households are married, 45 percent are single, and there are 2.7 workers
for each beneficiary, these benefits would cost approximately 8.8 percent
of employee wages. On top of this cost would be expenditures for Social
Security's disability and survivor's insurance benefits, which together
would cost about 3.0 percent of payroll.

Thus, total benefit costs would be approximately 11.8 percent of payroll
if applied to the 2024 population of beneficiaries, versus the current cost
rate of about 14.5 percent of wages. In an apples-to-apples comparison,
this reform outline is about one-fifth less expensive than current-law
Social Security.

Obviously, the costs of this reformed system would rise as changing demographics caused the population to age. Assuming a worker-to-
beneficiary ratio of two to one, the cost of the retirement benefits would

rise to about 11.8 percent of wages; adding survivors and disability benefits would push the total cost to about 15 percent of taxable payroll.

However, these cost estimates assume the benefit is paid without a means test, as in New Zealand. Doing so results in higher costs than a means-tested retirement benefit but allows policymakers to avoid the difficult question of whether to mandate private retirement savings on top of Social Security. Whether to means test the reformed Social Security benefit involves a trade-off between financial costs to the taxpayer and giving individuals the personal autonomy to prepare (or not prepare) for retirement as they choose.

If lawmakers were willing to mandate retirement plan participation, the cost of this reformed Social Security program could be reduced while maintaining the guarantee against poverty in old age. In Australia, the government-provided benefit is subject to a means test that eliminates benefits for roughly the richest quarter of the retiree population, reduces them for another quarter, and leaves them unchanged for approximately half of retirees.

A similar means test in the United States would reduce the cost of the minimum benefit by approximately 38 percent, reducing the long-term cost of the retirement plan from 11.1 percent of wages to about 7.1 percent and making retirement, survivors, and disability benefits affordable within the current 12.4 percent payroll tax rate.

However, a means test acts as an effective tax on retirement savings. For that reason, Australia mandates both that all employers offer a retirement plan and that all employees must participate. In Australia, contributions are funded by employers alone at an amount equal to 12 percent of employee wages, up to a maximum annual wage of about USD 178,000. Together, mandatory personal retirement savings coupled with a means-tested government benefit reduce the cost of Australia's government retirement system without also reducing protections against poverty in old age.

A Simpler Benefit

The advantage of a traditional defined benefit pension like Social Security over defined contribution retirement accounts is predictability. A person planning for retirement must decide how much to save on their own and at what age they can afford to retire. That is difficult to do if you don't know how much income you will receive from sources other than your own savings.

In many cases, such calculations are simple. A public-sector employee with a traditional pension that pays a benefit equal to 2 percent of final salary multiplied by the employee's number of years of service has a fairly predictable benefit. Employees know roughly how much their salaries grow each year, so they can estimate the benefits they would receive at any given retirement age.

In many countries, government pensions are similarly easy to calculate. In the Anglo countries I discussed in the previous chapter, the benefit formulas, while differing from each other, are not difficult to understand.

Social Security is far more complex, as we have seen. Estimating one's benefit involves a series of calculations that would be challenging even for many numerate Americans. And even that is just part of the problem.

For example, a lower-earning spouse—traditionally the wife, though Social Security's rules are gender-neutral—may qualify for a benefit based only on their own earnings or may qualify for a supplemental benefit if their benefit would be less than half the benefit received by the higher-earning spouse. This requires the lower-earning spouse to calculate both their own and their spouse's benefits.

Using data from the Health and Retirement Study (HRS), I found that even Americans on the verge of retirement have difficulty predicting what they will receive from Social Security. The HRS survey operates in waves, such that the same household is interviewed multiple times. Households that have yet to retire are asked what they believe they will receive from Social Security, while households already retired are asked what benefit they actually receive. By looking at households just before and after retirement, I was able to compare near retirees' predicted benefits with the benefits they ended up receiving.

In the HRS, nearly one-quarter of near retirees could not even hazard a guess as to their Social Security benefits. While many responses—nearly 25 percent—are centered close to the true value of realized benefits, many others miss the mark by large margins. One-quarter of respondents underestimated their benefits by more than 22 percent, and a tenth underestimated them by more than 50 percent.

Likewise, one-quarter of respondents overestimated their benefits by more than 21 percent, and a tenth overestimated their benefits by more than 100 percent. Moreover, the Social Security benefit estimates statements produced by the Social Security Administration have not seemed to improve the ability of near retirees to predict their future benefits.[3]

While defined contribution retirement plans such as 401(k)s carry market risk, the complex Social Security benefit formula is embedded with predictability risk: A person who overestimates their Social Security benefit by 20 percent suffers the same type of loss as a person whose 401(k) account drops by 20 percent on the eve of retirement and never recovers. In other words, while Social Security has the disadvantages of a traditional defined benefit pension, in particular the tendency toward underfunding, the complexity of the Social Security benefit formula undermines one of its principal strengths.

The flat-benefit approach I propose is far simpler. The benefit paid to new retirees today would be well-known, since every new retiree receives the same amount. Since the base benefit would be indexed to wage growth—and the Social Security trustees project that wages will grow about 1 percent faster than inflation each year—a person retiring 20 years from today could easily estimate that their base benefit will be about 20 percent higher in real terms than the benefit paid to new retirees today.

For example, if the base benefit for a single retiree in 2024 were $19,216, the benefit for a new retiree 20 years from now would be about $24,447. The Social Security Administration could easily calculate and publicize these values to inform Americans in their retirement planning.

A means test does introduce additional complexity, but even with a means test, the flat-benefit approach is far simpler than current Social Security. Moreover, for low- or middle-earning workers, the means test offers protection against a market downturn close to retirement, which means that a fall in the value of their retirement savings would not result in a dollar-for-dollar decline in their income in old age.

Objections to the Flat-Benefit Plan

There is no working around the fact that the flat, means-tested benefit I am proposing is different from how Social Security functions today and how it has functioned throughout its history. So it is worth considering several common, reasonable objections to the type of reforms I have argued for.

The first objection pertains to shifting from an earnings-based system, in which benefits rise with earnings and contributions, to a flat-benefit system, in which every retiree receives the same amount. This approach is indeed foreign to the United States. But it is worth considering how the United States Social Security program came to have the kind of benefit structure it does when other Anglo countries generally provide a smaller but more focused benefit aimed at preventing poverty in old age.

The story is that Americans won't support targeted benefit programs; as they say, "A program for the poor is a poor program."[4] Many in the US policy community take this dictum as if it were handed down from on high, but it's a testable hypothesis. And as such, it has failed the test of subsequent history.

In 1972, the federal government spent slightly less than 1 percent of gross domestic product (GDP) on programs targeted toward low-income households. By 2012, means-tested federal programs had nearly quadrupled in size to 3.8 percent of GDP, with further increases projected for the future.[5]

But perhaps we can put a finer point on the history of the Social Security benefit formula and why it differs from other Anglo countries. As the Manhattan Institute's Chris Pope has documented, while the Franklin D. Roosevelt administration staff that developed Social Security was on the progressive wing of American politics, the two congressional committee chairs charged with shepherding the legislation through Congress were Southerners, both of whom had fathers who fought in the Civil War. And not for the winning side.[6] The New Deal coalition of Northern progressives and Southern segregationists was, in the political scientist Ira Katznelson's terms, the "strange marriage of Sweden and South Africa."[7]

There was not a great deal of enthusiasm at the time for policies that would disproportionately benefit black Americans, as a British-style flat benefit would. Edwin Witte, the executive director of the Committee on

Economic Security that drafted the Social Security program, noted that the administrative difficulties of establishing a program to track every worker's wages and calculate their benefits

> would be materially lessened if we had a flat-benefit system like that of England. This would eliminate the necessity of keeping track of individual earnings, which is half of the total problem. But flat benefits, without regard to earnings, do not appeal to many Americans who are accustomed to wide differentials between urban and rural areas and in different parts of the country and between occupations and races.[8]

The Jackson, Mississippi, *Daily News* wasn't quite so oblique:

> The average Mississippian can't imagine himself chipping in to pay pensions for able-bodied Negroes to sit around in idleness on front galleries, supporting all their kinfolks on pensions, while cotton and corn crops are crying for workers to get them out of the grass.[9]

In other words, the issue wasn't necessarily so much a program for the poor as a program for poor blacks, and that helps explain why Social Security doesn't pay a universal flat retirement benefit similar to other Anglo countries. It is not clear why policymakers should treat the current benefit formula as if it's sacred when its origins may be anything but.

A second objection applies not to the fact that the flat benefit would be flat but that, under an Australian-style implementation at least, it would be means-tested based on other sources of income in retirement.

Now, to be clear, Social Security benefits *already* are partially means-tested. Beginning with the 1983 reforms, and extended with the congressional budget legislation passed in 1993, Social Security benefits are partially subject to federal income taxes. The higher a retiree's income, the more tax they are likely to pay on their Social Security benefits. And the proceeds of those taxes flow directly back to the Social Security trust funds.

Over one-quarter of the improvement to Social Security's long-term financing accomplished through the 1983 reforms was attributable to the introduction of income taxes on benefits. This provision is no different from an explicit means test in which, based on a retiree's income, benefits were reduced from the start.

That said, even under current-law benefit taxation rules, no one can or will lose their entire Social Security benefit—nor should they, given that they accrued these benefits under a set of rules in which those benefits would not be explicitly means-tested. But it was easy to oppose means-tested benefits when Social Security began in 1935 because, due to favorable demographics, the program was so inexpensive to begin with. But Social Security today is far more expensive, and without changes to benefit rules, it will grow even more so in future decades.

Americans do not face a future in which they pay a given tax rate and Social Security benefits either are or are not means-tested. Rather, they can pay a higher tax rate to finance non-means-tested benefits, or they could pay approximately 60 percent as much to finance benefits that would be subject to a means test. That is to say that means tests come with advantages and disadvantages, and Americans should weigh them both.

A final and seemingly compelling objection is simply that this flat-benefit plan isn't what Americans appear to want. No one is crying out for a radical transformation of Social Security that would force middle- and high-earning households to rely more on their own savings in retirement, even if such a plan would guarantee against poverty in old age.

At the same time, no one is crying out to pay higher taxes either. This cognitive dissonance, coupled with a political and financing system for Social Security that allows those inconstant views to coexist, helps explain the decades-long delay in reforming Social Security.

I would suggest that perhaps the question simply has not been framed correctly. In 2020, I authored a question in the RAND Corporation's American Life Panel, an ongoing survey of a representative sample of US households.[10] The question asked was straightforward and intentionally devoid of framing or spin:

> Some Americans are concerned about not having enough income once they retire. If you wished to increase your future retirement income, would you prefer to: Pay higher Social Security taxes while working and receive a higher Social Security

Table 1. Survey Respondents' Preference for Receiving Higher Retirement Income

	Pay More into Social Security	Save More on My Own
Gender, Male	28%	72%
Gender, Female	25%	75%
Age, 21–34	20%	85%
Age, 35–64	29%	71%
Age, 65 and Older	28%	72%
Race, White	26%	74%
Race, Black	28%	72%
Race, Asian	27%	73%
Ethnicity, Hispanic	28%	73%
Education, High School Graduate	31%	69%
Education, BA or More	21%	79%
Urban	27%	73%
Rural	18%	82%
Family Income Less Than $35,000	36%	64%
Family Income $35,000–$99,999	26%	74%
Family Income $100,000 or More	18%	82%
All	26%	74%

Source: RAND Corporation, "Well Being 534—ALP Omnibus Survey," February 2020, https://alpdata.rand.org/index.php?page=data&p=showsurvey&syid=534.

benefit when you retire? Or make higher contributions to a private retirement account such as an IRA or 401(k) and receive higher income from that account when you retire?[11]

This is in fact the question facing Americans over Social Security. The program cannot afford to pay all the benefit it has promised in the future. If Americans do not wish to accept lower incomes in old age, they must either pay more into Social Security or save more for retirement on their own.

The survey's results, shown in Table 1, indicate a strong preference for increased personal saving versus paying more in Social Security taxes in exchange for receiving higher Social Security benefits. Overall, 76 percent of respondents favored increased personal saving versus 26 percent who favored a pay-more get-more deal with Social Security.

These results are remarkably consistent across various demographic groups. There was no subgroup in which less than 64 percent of respondents favored saving more on their own versus paying more into Social Security. If, realistically, Americans will ultimately face this choice, it makes sense to present them with that choice.

Establishing Retirement Plans for All

Congress could not reasonably shift greater responsibility to individuals to save for retirement if it also did not make greater efforts to facilitate retirement savings. While, as discussed in earlier chapters, private-sector retirement plan coverage, contributions, and savings have increased, not every employee currently has access to a retirement plan at work. And researchers find that workplace retirement plans are significantly more effective at facilitating savings than do-it-yourself plans such as individual retirement accounts (IRAs).

According to the Bureau of Labor Statistics, 72 percent of all US workers had access to a workplace retirement plan in 2022, but only 54 percent of Americans working at establishments with 50 or fewer employees were offered a retirement plan at work. While the retirement plan coverage gap is smaller than many claim, a Social Security program that is more tightly focused on preventing poverty in old age cannot succeed if millions of workers do not have easy access to a plan with which to build savings on their own.

Some states already are taking steps to close the coverage gap through so-called automatic IRA plans. California, Connecticut, Illinois, Oregon, and other states are establishing structures that would open IRAs for any employee who is not offered a workplace retirement plan such as a 401(k). Employees would automatically be enrolled in these new IRA accounts, with contribution rates typically about 5 percent of wages.

Employers' duties would be limited: Under federal law, employers cannot contribute to IRA accounts. These state auto IRA plans also are not subject to the Employees Retirement Income Security Act, the federal law that regulates private-sector pensions and imposes a number of duties on employers that offer such plans. Employers would be required to report to their state if they did not offer a workplace plan and to cooperate with enrolling employees, but in general costs for employers are small.[12]

These state plans do have certain significant disadvantages due to being implemented at the state rather than the federal level. First, it is difficult to conceive that Congress would enact a Social Security reform that depended on universal access to workplace retirement plans if such access also depended on the policy decisions of state lawmakers, many of whom have not embraced the idea of state auto IRAs. Second, because auto IRAs were established by states without federal cooperation, many interact with means-tested federal benefit programs in ways that can be financially punishing for low earners who save.

Most major federal welfare benefits carry either income or asset tests, many of which can be triggered by savings held in an IRA plan.[13] A federally designed version of the state auto IRA could more carefully consider how mandatory or automatic enrollment retirement savings accounts should be counted against such benefits, many of which are designed to be paid to working-age households.

To date, enthusiasm for universal access to workplace retirement plans has been most strong among Democratic elected officials, which is ironic given that many criticize 401(k) plans as poor vehicles for retirement savings. Congressional Republicans, for their part, have been coy about strong measures to promote expanded workplace access to retirement savings.

Republican members of Congress have generally opposed not only mandates for employers to offer retirement plans but even mandates that employers that do offer such plans automatically enroll their employees, which is today regarded as a best practice. The so-called Setting Every Community Up for Retirement Enhancement 2.0 Act, which bipartisan majorities in Congress passed and President Joe Biden signed into law in 2023, would mandate only that newly formed retirement plans established by larger employers automatically enroll employees, a limitation that would delay for decades anything close to universal automatic enrollment.

Political conservatives are understandably wary of governmental mandates. And yet they should consider that Social Security's insolvency is looming just a decade in the future. Without providing every American worker a meaningful alternative by which to save for retirement, the prospect of higher Social Security taxes seems all but assured. And, whatever one may think of a government mandate to offer a retirement plan or automatically enroll employees in it, taxes are not voluntary either.

A reasonable compromise might empower the federal government to establish auto IRAs or similar accounts that would be either centrally administered by a government agency or allocated to regulated private providers. The latter approach might help overcome opposition from the financial industry, which could be considerable and powerful in Congress.

In the United Kingdom, the financial services industry has learned to coexist alongside the recently introduced National Employment Savings Trust retirement accounts for employees who aren't offered a retirement plan at work. Moreover, during the decade in which the UK's new account plan has been in place, participation rates among all private-sector workers have risen from 42 percent to 86 percent.[14] That is nothing to sneeze at and should be possible in the United States.

These supplement accounts should be designed to keep costs low for both employees and their employers, bypassing most of the reasonable concerns a skeptical elected official might have. While a default contribution rate could be a matter for discussion, Australia's selection of a 12 percent contribution rate does not appear unreasonable.

How to Pay for It All

Policymakers also should consider how to finance both the new government-provided flat benefit and ongoing costs for the current Social Security program, which would continue more or less on its current course for several decades as the new flat benefit was phased in.

Social Security is funded by a payroll tax on wages. Although there is no explicit legal link between taxes paid and the benefits to which a person becomes entitled, payroll tax financing was designed to make Social Security more closely resemble a private retirement savings plan. That makes sense given lawmakers' intent at the time Social Security was introduced.

But if policymakers shifted Social Security's focus toward a flat benefit more squarely focused on preventing old-age poverty, they might also consider altering how benefits are financed. In Australia, Canada, and New Zealand, benefits aimed at preventing poverty in retirement are funded by general tax revenues, which in a US context means mostly income taxes. The Canada Pension Plan, which provides nonprogressive benefits on top of the means-tested Old Age Security, is funded via a payroll tax.

The United Kingdom, by contrast, continues to fund its flat retirement benefit with an explicit tax on earnings, similar to Social Security's payroll tax. That may be because the UK's National Insurance tax funds not only the New State Pension but also a range of other benefits.

If the new flat retirement benefit for the US were funded via general tax revenues, the system would be far more progressive overall than the current Social Security program, leaving low earners with both higher benefits and lower taxes than under current law Social Security. Costs would be shifted to higher-earning households that pay most income taxes, but the total costs of the program would be significantly lower than current-law Social Security.

However, even if the new flat benefit were affordable under the current 12.4 percent payroll tax rate in the long term, in the shorter term, Social Security still faces insolvency. Even if the flat benefit were phased in over less than a full working career, Social Security's trust funds could unlikely be prevented from running dry.

Additional revenues almost certainly will be required. That is the cost of delaying Social Security reform for so many decades. Benefit adjustment policies that once might have sustained solvency permanently, such as the proposal discussed in the George W. Bush administration to "price index" the growth of initial benefits, no longer would be enough. And the more dramatic benefit changes that are needed to maintain solvency without increased revenues are politically unpalatable.

It is one thing to legislate a two-year increase in the normal retirement age in 1983 and have that change fully implemented four decades later. It is another thing to increase the retirement age by another two to three years in under a decade. Even this would not be sufficient to keep the trust funds from being exhausted.

So additional revenues are almost certainly on the table. Some see higher taxes as a total solution. I see additional revenues as a necessary bridge to a better and more sustainable Social Security program. As with any policy that must deliver additional revenues, the key is to produce that money in a way that is as unharmful as possible to Americans and the American economy.

Rolling Back the Retirement Contributions Tax Preference

To produce the short-term revenues needed to keep Social Security afloat while gradually implementing reforms to benefit levels, policymakers could look to the current tax preference for retirement savings.[15] Under current law, contributions to 401(k), IRA, and certain other retirement plans are not counted as income in the year the contributions are made, so they are not subject to federal income taxes. In addition, employer contributions to retirement plans are exempt from Social Security and Medicare payroll taxes. Income taxes are levied on retirement plan contributions, however.

The tax break paid on retirement savings is intuitively attractive and, some might even argue, crucial to building retirement income security. In fact, however, most research finds that the retirement tax preference does relatively little to increase total savings. Moreover, even if seen as a simple subsidy rather than an incentive, the tax preference flows overwhelmingly to well-off households that face little risk of inadequate incomes in retirement.

The retirement savings tax preference is widely misunderstood, so it helps to clarify precisely how savers benefit from the tax preference and how it reduces revenues received by the federal government (and by states that levy income taxes, which piggyback off the federal tax code for calculating income subject to taxes). Contributions to employer-sponsored retirement plans and IRA accounts are exempted from income taxes in the year the contributions are made. That reduces a person's income taxes that year and reduces federal tax revenues.

However, when individuals retire, their withdrawals from retirement plans are subject to income taxes. Fiscally speaking, this deferred taxation more or less compensates the federal budget for the initial loss of income tax revenue, plus interest. The "plus interest" part is important, because the loss of income tax revenues when contributions are made increases the federal deficit and debt, and the federal government must pay interest on that debt.

Income tax revenues may not balance out precisely, because retirees typically pay lower income tax rates than do working-age households. But, over the long term, income tax collections from retirement plans compensate for much of the additional revenue loss, plus interest.[16]

However, applying income taxes to retirement plan withdrawals does not make up for lost capital gains tax revenues, which ordinarily would have been levied in addition to income taxes. In effect, as economist Peter Brady of the Investment Company Institute points out, the tax preference effectively sets the capital gains tax rate on retirement plan assets to zero.[17]

The Congressional Budget Office (CBO) reports that the net present value of the retirement income tax preference for both income taxes and payroll taxes in 2019 was $276 billion, or 1.3 percent of GDP. About three-quarters of that cost was attributable to lost income taxes, with the remainder due to lost payroll taxes on employer contributions to retirement plans.

The $276 billion net present value reported by the CBO is equal to the cost of forgone tax revenues on retirement plan contributions in 2019 minus the present value of the future taxes that will be collected when those contributions plus interest are withdrawn in retirement. So, even counting the eventual taxes levied on retirement benefits, the cost to the federal budget is massive. The US Treasury produces a similar figure.

For context, as of 2023, the CBO projects a long-term Social Security funding shortfall equal to 1.7 percent of GDP, meaning that eliminating the retirement savings tax preference could address about three-quarters of Social Security's funding gap. Even a scaling back and limiting of the tax preference could provide stopgap funding for Social Security while longer-term reforms focused on limiting the growth of benefits were phased in.

The usual objection to the retirement savings tax preference is that it is regressive: A high earner who pays a high federal income tax rate receives a larger break on their taxes in a given year than a low earner who pays little or no federal income taxes. Gene Sperling, a prominent policymaker in the Clinton and Obama administrations, wrote in the *New York Times* that

> the federal government's use of tax deductibility to encourage savings turns our progressive structure for taxing income into a regressive one: While earners in the highest income bracket get a 39.6 percent deduction for savings, the hardest-pressed workers, those in the lowest tax bracket, get only a 10 percent deduction for every dollar they manage to put away.[18]

Similarly, Monique Morrissey of the left-leaning Economic Policy Institute declares that "for the same dollar contribution to a 401(k), high-income taxpayers in the 35 percent tax bracket get a tax break that's three-and-a-half times larger than the tax break received by moderate-income taxpayers in the 10 percent bracket."[19]

But that's not actually true. What Sperling and Morrissey are describing is a tax *deduction*, similar to the federal mortgage interest deduction, not a tax *deferral*. Their depictions are incorrect because they ignore that contributions are taxable when withdrawn.

If the individual pays the same income tax rate in retirement that they did when they contributed to their retirement plan, the tax paid on withdrawal exactly offsets the tax benefit received on the contribution, including interest. Assuming that income tax rates remain the same from work into retirement, the federal retirement contributions tax preference is equivalent to if a worker invested a given amount of after-tax income without any taxes on investment gains.

Now, the capital gains element of the retirement tax preference *is* regressive. Under current law, married couples with incomes below $94,000 in 2024 pay no taxes on long-term capital gains. Couples with incomes between $94,000 and $584,000 pay a 15 percent long-term capital gains rate, while those with incomes above $584,000 pay a 20 percent rate.

According to the US Census Bureau's most accurate estimates, the median income of households age 65 and older in 2018 was $55,610.[20] Even assuming substantial growth since that time, a large number of retirees would not have paid capital gains taxes on their savings, significantly degrading the value of the federal retirement tax preference. In other words, the tax incentive to save is indeed lower for the low-income households that presumably policymakers most wish to encourage to save, albeit for reasons that differ from the common perception of how the retirement tax break functions.

Of course, there's more to it than this. The main reason that high-income households receive a greater share of the retirement preference is simply that high earners contribute far more dollars to retirement plans than do low earners, because Social Security's progressive benefit formula does much less for the rich than the poor. So if they wish to have a sufficient income in retirement, high earners contribute more to retirement plans.

The CBO finds that households in the bottom fifth of the lifetime earnings distribution receive Social Security benefits equal to about 80 percent of their career-average preretirement earnings, adjusted for inflation; an individual in the highest fifth of lifetime earnings receives a Social Security replacement rate of about 31 percent.[21] If, for example, both groups desired a total retirement income equal to 70 percent of their preretirement earnings, the highest earnings quintile would need to save a great deal on top of Social Security, while the low earners would need to save nothing at all. Anyone wondering why household retirement savings are distributed so unequally should start by looking at the similarly unequal, but opposite, distribution of Social Security replacement rates.

The most important question from a policy perspective, however, is whether the retirement tax preference significantly increases retirement savings. And the best evidence indicates that it does not. All this bears some explanation.

At first glance, it would seem obvious that reducing the effective capital gains tax on savings would encourage people to save more. Tax economists call this the "substitution effect": Just as a lower tax on labor income encourages people to substitute more for less leisure, so a lower tax on savings should cause people to save more and consume less. Increasing savings isn't merely intended to be good for the individual involved but also increases the productivity of the economy as a whole by providing more capital for factories, equipment, research, and so forth.

In fact, the economic theory behind the retirement tax incentive is much more complex. First, lowering the tax rate on retirement savings has two effects: The substitution effect encourages households to save more by increasing the effective after-tax rate of return on retirement savings. But that same increase in the after-tax rate of return on savings means that a household can reach any given retirement savings goal with lower, not higher, levels of contributions.

For example, in the introduction to this book, I noted that some people refer to a "retirement number," a dollar goal for their retirement savings. Anyone targeting such a retirement savings goal would likely save *less* for retirement due to the federal tax preference, because that preference makes it easier to hit such a goal.

Second, we know from behavioral economics that many people don't do what economic theory says they should. Despite the tax incentive, only around three-quarters of private-sector workers who are offered a 401(k) enroll in that plan. Seemingly, this is leaving money on the table. And yet, when employees are automatically enrolled in a retirement plan, most will continue to participate. The success of automatic enrollment involves employees who simply aren't paying much attention to the retirement tax incentive.

Likewise, economist John Beshears and his coauthors found that, in a program in which employees were automatically enrolled at a 3 percent contribution rate and could maximize the employer matching contribution by contributing 6 percent of their pay, over half of employees contributed at precisely a 3 percent or 6 percent rate.[22] Clearly, these employees aren't reacting to the tax preference.

Moreover, in 2022, only 16 percent of Vanguard 401(k) participants contributed the maximum amount that is eligible for the federal tax preference.[23] None of this is what one would predict if the federal tax preference were highly effective in encouraging Americans to increase their saving.

Third, it is easy for many households to reap the benefits of federal tax preference without increasing their savings. They can do so by saving more inside tax-favored retirement accounts while saving less in taxable accounts. The CBO finds that 58 percent of the combined value of the retirement contributions tax preference for both income and payroll taxes flows to households in the top fifth of the income distribution.[24]

These households typically have substantially more investments *outside* of retirement plans than inside of them. These households also tend to be financially literate or use the services of accountants or financial planners.

It would be strange indeed if these households did not strategically allocate their savings to minimize their taxes.

And numerous studies find this to be the case. One highly regarded 2014 study focused on changes to retirement tax preferences in Denmark, using a massive government data sample that included high-quality data on households' income and assets. The study examined a reduction in the tax preference for retirement savings among high-income households.

The study concluded that most high-income households did not even respond to the change in the tax preference. And among those that did respond, the main change was to switch assets between different investment accounts, not to reduce total savings. The study also concluded that each dollar of government tax incentives increased savings by only around one penny. That's not a great deal for the taxpayer.

Other studies reach similar conclusions. University of California, Los Angeles, economist Daniel Benjamin estimates that only about one-quarter of 401(k) balances represent net savings to the economy as a whole.[25] For each dollar of savings inside 401(k) accounts, about 25 cents is offset by the cost of the federal tax incentive, which is financed by government borrowing, and about 50 cents is offset by lower household savings in other areas, such as taxable investment accounts.

Other studies are even more pessimistic. Karen Pence of the Federal Reserve Board concluded that total savings of 401(k) participants change little at all.[26] Yale economist Orazio Attanasio and his coauthors analyzed how household finances changed when households enrolled in IRA accounts.[27] Household spending did not decline, which implies that household saving did not increase.

Moreover, assets in ordinary taxable accounts fell by approximately the amounts that went into IRA accounts. In other words, these households received the tax preference, but they didn't save more.[28] Attanasio and his coauthors found similar results for tax-favored accounts in the United Kingdom, while other studies concurred regarding retirement tax preferences in Italy,[29] Latvia,[30] and Spain.[31]

Now, even if the retirement tax preference did not increase retirement savings, one might nevertheless support it as a simple subsidy to help buttress retirement incomes for those who need it the most. But, from that perspective, the tax preference is almost precisely upside down:

According to the CBO, 63 percent of the income tax preference flows to the highest-income fifth of households, with 40 percent going to the richest tenth. By contrast, the bottom 60 percent of households receive just 13 percent of the total tax break. Truly low-income households receive practically nothing.

So, in sum, the federal tax preference for retirement savings neither significantly increases savings nor benefits Americans at risk of an inadequate income in old age. Not to mention, it costs a great deal of money at a time when money will be increasingly short in the federal budget.

While this outcome may not be what policymakers hoped for, it opens up possibilities to fund Social Security reform that might otherwise not have existed.

Eliminating the retirement tax preference outright would increase long-run income tax revenues by about 0.7 percent of GDP each year. Eliminating the tax preference would also increase Social Security and Medicare payroll tax revenues by about 0.6 percent of GDP.[32]

Moreover, revenues would increase by even more in the coming few decades. This is because retirement benefits currently being paid would continue to be subject to income taxes, while current retirement plan contributions would no longer receive the tax break. Over time, as the new tax regime was phased in, the increase in federal revenues would fall to a steady-state improvement of about 1.3 percent of GDP.

Thus, repealing the federal retirement tax preference would bring in additional money in the short term, when it will be needed the most, while providing breathing room for other changes to Social Security to be phased in.

Yes, rolling back the retirement tax preference would be a tax increase. Most Americans, and in particular Americans to the right of the political center, don't like tax increases. Here I would make two points.

First, this is about the smallest tax increase necessary to keep Social Security solvent, because—in my reform proposal—it is coupled with the largest reductions in long-term benefit costs. Those who would oppose this tax increase would also need to propose even larger benefit reductions to avoid it. I am not aware of any who have done so, and indeed, in the Donald Trump–era Republican Party, many claim to oppose any Social Security benefit reductions at all.

This points to the benefits of everyone putting their cards on the table and making their plans explicit. It is fine to oppose benefit reductions if you also are willing to propose the necessary tax increase to fund full benefits in perpetuity. If you are unwilling to do so, then you lack a serious Social Security platform.

Moreover, this is the type of tax increase that, under the economic logic that both conservative and progressive experts tend to adhere to, might well increase economic growth. It helps to start with an example of how income tax rates might affect incentives to work, which are commonly discussed in public policy.

As discussed previously, a tax change can have both income and substitution effects: An across-the-board cut to income tax rates would reduce both a person's average tax rate, thereby increasing their income and reducing incentives to work, and their marginal tax rate, which increases incentives to work. The overall effect of the tax cut is the net of the income and the substitution effects.[33] Generally, the substitution effect is held to be more important, so an across-the-board tax cut would tend to increase labor supply, but the overall effects are dampened by the income effect.

Reducing the tax preference for retirement savings would have a different effect, however. Since the households that receive most of the tax preference already have other investments on top of their retirement accounts, their marginal incentive to save would not change. Each dollar of additional savings is already taxed at the capital gains rate of up to 20 percent and would continue to be following repeal of the tax preference.

However, repealing the tax preference would have a negative income effect on these households, because they would need to save more to reach any given savings goal. If your "retirement number" is $1 million, you'll need to save more to get there. That income effect will tend to increase savings.

Alternatively, if we frame repeal of the tax preference in terms of income taxes paid in any given year, high-income households would in general pay a higher average tax rate but not a higher marginal tax rate. That points to those households working more, not less.

The common alternative sources of additional revenues would almost certainly reduce incentives to work. Raising the 12.4 percent payroll tax rate paid by most workers by several percentage points would reduce the rewards to work. Increasing or eliminating the payroll tax ceiling would have even greater negative effects, because marginal tax rates for individuals would rise significantly while their average tax rates would increase by substantially less.

Consider someone earning just above the 2024 maximum wage subject to Social Security payroll taxes of $168,600. Eliminating the payroll tax ceiling would minimally affect their average tax rate and thus produce no incentive to work more. But a 12 percentage point increase in their marginal tax rate would generate steep incentives not to work.

So, Social Security reformers who dislike the idea of rolling back the retirement tax preference must grapple with the difficult choice between tax increases that are likely even more economically damaging or reducing benefits even further so that additional revenues are not needed.

Obviously, rolling back a large tax preference that has been in place for decades would be politically challenging. But so would increasing the Social Security payroll tax, the largest tax that most workers pay; eliminating the cap on wages subject to taxes, which would impose the largest tax increase in history on a small slice of the population; or sharply reducing Social Security benefits, on which millions of retirees and disabled workers depend. Limiting the tax preference for retirement plan contributions isn't an *easy* way to find revenues for Social Security. It simply may be an easier way than the alternatives.

The Future of Retirement Income Security

The United States needs innovative thinking on a range of public policy issues, including Social Security and retirement savings. Unfortunately, anyone advocating a more focused Social Security program and increased private retirement savings will likely be accused of wishing to "privatize" the program. But Australia, Canada, New Zealand, and the United Kingdom clearly demonstrate ways to address retirement security that reduce budgetary costs and increase private retirement savings while agreeing with our political and economic traditions.

Reforming Social Security to focus on low-earning Americans could eradicate old-age poverty while making the program financially sustainable.

The nation should reform its private retirement savings system to close coverage gaps and automatically enroll employees in retirement plans.

Compared to other public policy challenges facing the United States, such as health care and education, Social Security and retirement savings are eminently solvable—but only if policymakers willingly step up with creative solutions to politically difficult issues.

About the Author

Andrew G. Biggs is a senior fellow at AEI, where he studies Social Security reform, state and local government pensions, and public-sector pay and benefits.

Before joining AEI, Biggs was the principal deputy commissioner of the Social Security Administration (SSA), where he oversaw the SSA's policy research efforts. In 2005, as an associate director of the White House National Economic Council, he worked on Social Security reform. In 2001, he joined the staff of the President's Commission to Strengthen Social Security. Biggs has been interviewed on radio and television as an expert on retirement issues and public- versus private-sector compensation. He has published widely in academic publications and daily newspapers such as the *New York Times*, *Wall Street Journal*, and *Washington Post*. He has also testified before Congress on numerous occasions. In 2013, the Society of Actuaries appointed Biggs co–vice chair of a blue ribbon panel tasked with analyzing the causes of underfunding in public pension plans and how governments can securely fund plans in the future. In 2014, *Institutional Investor* magazine named him one of the 40 most influential people in the retirement world. In 2016, President Barack Obama appointed Biggs to be a member of the financial control board overseeing reforms to Puerto Rico's budget and the restructuring of the island's debts, to which he was reappointed by Presidents Donald Trump and Joe Biden.

Biggs holds a bachelor's degree from Queen's University Belfast in Northern Ireland, master's degrees from Cambridge University and the University of London, and a PhD from the London School of Economics and Political Science.

Notes

Chapter 1

1. Heather Gillers et al., "A Generation of Americans Is Entering Old Age the Least Prepared in Decades," *Wall Street Journal*, June 22, 2018, https://www.wsj.com/articles/a-generation-of-americans-is-entering-old-age-the-least-prepared-in-decades-1529676033.

2. Tara Siegel Bernard, "'Too Little Too Late': Bankruptcy Booms Among Older Americans," *New York Times*, August 5, 2018, https://www.nytimes.com/2018/08/05/business/bankruptcy-older-americans.html.

3. Rachel Siegel, "Social Security Recipients Will See a Small Increase in 2020," *Washington Post*, October 10, 2019, https://www.washingtonpost.com/business/2019/10/10/social-security-recipients-will-see-small-increase.

4. Ben Steverman, "Half of Older Americans Have Nothing in Retirement Savings," *Bloomberg*, March 26, 2019, https://www.bloomberg.com/news/articles/2019-03-26/almost-half-of-older-americans-have-zero-in-retirement-savings.

5. Ben Steverman, "World's Retirees Risk Running Out of Money a Decade Before Death," *Bloomberg*, June 13, 2019, https://news.bloomberglaw.com/employee-benefits/worlds-retirees-risk-running-out-of-money-a-decade-before-death.

6. John Manganaro, "U.S. Heading from Retirement 'Crisis' to Retirement 'Catastrophe': Allianz," ThinkAdvisor, June 1, 2023, https://www.thinkadvisor.com/2023/06/01/u-s-heading-from-retirement-crisis-to-retirement-catastrophe-allianz.

7. Joe Johnston, dir., *Captain America: The First Avenger* (Hollywood, CA: Paramount Pictures, 2011).

8. Tyler Bond et al., "Retirement Insecurity 2021—Americans' Views of Retirement," National Institute on Retirement Security, February 2021, https://tinyurl.com/2bpnmxyw.

9. Anna Madamba and Stephen P. Utkus, "Retirement Transitions in Four Countries," Vanguard, January 2017, https://www.firstlinks.com.au/uploads/whitepapers/Vanguard-retirement-transitions-Jan-2017.pdf.

10. Nora Colomer, "Most Seniors Say the US Is Suffering a Retirement Crisis and Many Are Struggling to Save: Survey," Fox Business, March 14, 2023, https://www.foxbusiness.com/personal-finance/seniors-say-us-suffering-retirement-crisis-inflation-struggling-to-save.

11. American Advisors Group, "AAG Retirement Savings Crisis Survey Results," February 15, 2023, https://www.aag.com/retirement-savings-crisis.

12. Bond et al., "Retirement Insecurity 2021."

13. Allianz Life, "Americans Facing a New Retirement Reality," press release, May 31, 2023, https://www.allianzlife.com/about/newsroom/2023-press-releases/americans-facing-a-new-retirement-reality.

14. Madamba and Utkus, "Retirement Transitions in Four Countries."

15. Transamerica Center for Retirement Studies, "The Current State of Retirement: Pre-Retiree Expectations and Retiree Realities," December 2015, https://www.transamericacenter.org/docs/default-source/retirees-survey/retirees_survey_2015_report.pdf.

16. Amy Resnick, "Americans' Retirement Expectations Remain Fluid," Planadviser, July 19, 2022, https://www.planadviser.com/americans-retirement-expectations-remain-fluid.

17. Principal, "Inside Your Client's Mind: Thinking, Saving, and Planning for Retirement," 2022, https://landing.principal.com/retirement-transition/inside-your-clients-mind.

18. Megan Brenan, "U.S. Retirees' Experience Differs from Nonretirees' Outlook," Gallup, May 18, 2021, https://news.gallup.com/poll/350048/retirees-experience-differs-nonretirees-outlook.aspx.

19. Jim Norman, "Healthcare Once Again Tops List of Americans' Worries," Gallup, April 1, 2019, https://news.gallup.com/poll/248159/healthcare-once-again-tops-list-americans-worries.aspx.

20. Rich Prisinzano and Sophie Shin, "The Social Security 2100 Act: Updated Analysis of Effects on Social Security Finances and the Economy," University of Pennsylvania, Penn Wharton Budget Model, September 24, 2019, https://budgetmodel.wharton.upenn.edu/issues/2019/9/24/the-social-security-2100-act-updated-analysis-of-effects-on-social-security-finances-and-the-economy.

21. James J. Choi, "Popular Personal Financial Advice Versus the Professors," *Journal of Economic Perspectives* 36, no. 4 (2022).

Chapter 2

1. Albert Ando and Franco Modigliani, "The 'Life Cycle' Hypothesis of Saving: Aggregate Implications and Tests," *American Economic Review* 53, no. 1 (1963).

2. Brian J. O'Connor, "Americans' Magic Number for Retirement Rises to $1.27 Million," SmartAsset, July 2, 2023, https://smartasset.com/retirement/americans-retirement-number-rises.

3. Julie Pinkerton, "Is $1 Million Enough? How Advisors Can Help Clients Set Better Retirement Goals," *US News & World Report*, June 17, 2022, https://money.usnews.com/financial-advisors/articles/is-1-million-enough-how-advisors-can-help-clients-set-better-retirement-goals.

4. Lorie Konish, "Americans Think They Will Need Nearly $1.3 Million to Retire Comfortably, Study Says. How to Calculate Your Own 'Magic Number,'" CNBC, June 26, 2023, https://www.cnbc.com/2023/06/26/americans-think-they-need-nearly-1point3-million-retire-comfortably-study.html.

5. Charles Schwab, "2023 401(k) Participant Study," August 2023, https://content. schwab.com/web/retail/public/about-schwab/schwab_2023_401k_participant_survey_ findings.pdf.

6. Fidelity Investments, "How Much Do I Need to Retire?," August 21, 2024, https://www.fidelity.com/viewpoints/retirement/how-much-do-i-need-to-retire.

7. Teresa Ghilarducci, "Our Ridiculous Approach to Retirement," *New York Times*, July 21, 2012, https://www.nytimes.com/2012/07/22/opinion/sunday/our-ridiculous-approach-to-retirement.html.

8. Martin Browning and Thomas F. Crossley, "The Life-Cycle Model of Consumption and Saving," *Journal of Economic Perspectives* 15, no. 3 (2001).

9. The life-cycle model can tell us about more than simply individual behavior. When we sum up the results of millions of individual saving decisions, it can tell us about the economy as a whole. Indeed, the life-cycle theory initially was employed for macroeconomic analysis of the whole economy as much as for microeconomic analysis of individual spending and saving decisions.

10. Jason S. Scott et al., "The Life-Cycle Model Implies That Most Young People Should Not Save for Retirement," *Journal of Retirement* 10, no. 3 (2023).

Chapter 3

1. As mentioned in Chapter 2, the life-cycle hypothesis generating a prediction of constant consumption from year to year depends on several common simplifying assumptions, such as that the rate of time preference equals the interest rate available on savings and that the individual's or household's ability to derive utility from consumption is the same at every age. That said, it is common to assume for analytical purposes that retirees desire the same level of spending they had before retirement and desire that level to remain constant throughout old age.

2. Social Security Administration, *The Future of Social Security*, January 2004, http://igmlnet.uohyd.ac.in:8000/InfoUSA/society/socwelf/10055.pdf.

3. Social Security Administration, *The Future of Social Security*.

4. Social Security Trustees, *The 2023 Annual Report of the Board of Trustees of the Federal Old-Age and Survivors Insurance and Federal Disability Insurance Trust Funds*, Social Security Administration, March 31, 2023, https://www.ssa.gov/oact/TR/2023/tr2023. pdf.

5. Social Security Administration, "Report of the National Commission on Social Security Reform," January 1983, https://www.ssa.gov/history/reports/gspan.html.

6. Dean R. Leimer, *The Role of the Replacement Rate in the Design of the Social Security Benefit Structure* (Government Printing Office, 1979).

7. Bonnie-Jeanne MacDonald et al., "How Accurately Does 70% Final Employment Earnings Replacement Measure Retirement Income (in) Adequacy? Introducing the Living Standards Replacement Rate (LSRR)," *ASTIN Bulletin: The Journal of the IAA* 46, no. 3 (2016).

8. Michael J. Boskin and John B. Shoven, "Concepts and Measures of Earnings Replacement During Retirement," in *Issues in Pension Economics* (University of Chicago

Press, 1987); and Andrew J. Rettenmaier and Thomas R. Saving, "How Generous Are Social Security and Medicare?," National Center for Policy Analysis, October 2006, https://www.ncpathinktank.org/pdfs/st290.pdf.

9. Social Security Trustees, *The 2023 Annual Report of the Board of Trustees of the Federal Old-Age and Survivors Insurance and Federal Disability Insurance Trust Funds*.

10. Here I describe the three steps in greater details. First, while the SSA methodology begins with the age-earnings profile outlined earlier in the chapter, the SSA increases earnings in each year by 21.6 percent. For instance, if a typical worker earned $30,000 in a given year, the SSA would assume a worker instead earned 21.6 percent more, or $36,480. This step increases inflation-adjusted average earnings over the final 35 years of employment to $56,423. These nearly 22 percent higher earnings result in a Social Security retirement benefit that, due to Social Security's progressive benefit formula, increases by only about 13 percent to $28,204. This reduces the replacement rate to 50 percent. The reason for this 21.6 percent upward adjustment to annual nominal earnings is discussed more in this chapter.

Next, the SSA replacement-rate methodology "wage indexes" the stylized worker's earnings rather than adjusting them for inflation. Wage indexing is an unfamiliar term and process for most readers. Inflation adjustment increases the value of earnings from the year the earnings occurred to retirement age by the rate of growth of prices, thereby adjusting for changes in the value of money and expressing those past dollars in terms of their current purchasing power. Wage indexing, by contrast, adjusts earnings upward by the growth of national average wages. That is, nominal earnings in a given year—meaning, the actual dollar value on an employee's paycheck—are multiplied by the ratio of the national average wage in the year before retirement to the national average wage in the year the earnings took place.

As long as real wage growth is positive, meaning that national average wages grow faster than inflation, wage-indexed earnings will always be higher than inflation-indexed earnings. And, since this calculation applies only to how replacement rates are measured, not to how benefits are calculated, benefits don't change. As a result, replacement rates measured relative to wage-indexed replacement rates will be lower than replacement rates measured relative to the same earnings adjusted for inflation. Wage indexing increases the measure of the medium earner's final 35 years of earnings to $65,664. Since the earner's benefit remains unchanged at $28,204, wage indexing the denominator of the replacement-rate calculation reduces the calculated replacement rate to 43 percent.

Finally, the SSA replacement-rate calculation expresses career-average earnings not as the final 35 years of earnings but as the highest 35 years of earnings. This step marginally increases the measured value of career-average earnings to $66,015. Again, since retirement benefits are unaffected, the measured replacement rate declines to 42.6 percent, the value published in the Social Security trustees report.

11. This figure is obtained by dividing the $28,204 annual benefit for a medium-wage worker claiming benefits in 2023 by the 42.6 percent reported replacement rate for that worker. See Social Security Administration, "Table V.C7.—Annual Scheduled Benefit Amounts for Retired Workers with Various Pre-Retirement Earnings Patterns," https://www.ssa.gov/oact/tr/2023/lr5c7.html.

12. Olivia Mitchell and John W. R. Phillips note that in other parts of the world, incomes for seniors are sometimes compared to the incomes of working-age households. See Olivia S. Mitchell and John W. R. Phillips, "Social Security Replacement Rates for Alternative Earnings Benchmarks" (working paper, Michigan Retirement Research Center, 2006).

13. An ancillary issue noted by Dean Leimer is that when the population is aging, average wages will grow more quickly than wages in any birth cohort. See Leimer, *The Role of the Replacement Rate in the Design of the Social Security Benefit Structure.*

14. Stephen Goss et al., "Replacement Rates for Retirees: What Makes Sense for Planning and Evaluation?," Social Security Administration, July 2014, https://www.ssa.gov/oact/NOTES/pdf_notes/note155.pdf.

15. Alicia H. Munnell, "Yes, There Is a Retirement Crisis," Next Avenue, August 7, 2014, https://www.nextavenue.org/yes-there-retirement-crisis/.

16. Social Security Trustees, *The 2013 Annual Report of the Board of Trustees of the Federal Old-Age and Survivors Insurance and Federal Disability Insurance Trust Funds*, Social Security Administration, May 31, 2013, https://www.ssa.gov/OACT/TR/2013.

17. Andrew G. Biggs and Glenn R. Springstead, "Alternate Measures of Replacement Rates for Social Security Benefits and Retirement Income," *Social Security Bulletin* 68 (2008). Even relative to wage-indexed earnings, Andrew Biggs and Glenn Springstead found higher replacement rates than were published in the trustees report, likely because that study looked at middle wageworkers rather than the trustees' stylized above-average wageworker, whose earnings would be higher and replacement rate lower. The Biggs and Springstead study also includes auxiliary benefits for spouses and widows, while the Social Security Administration's stylized worker examples do not.

18. Charles Jeszeck et al., *Retirement Security: Better Information on Income Replacement Rates Needed to Help Workers Plan for Retirement*, Government Accountability Office, March 1, 2016, https://www.gao.gov/products/gao-16-242.

19. Congressional Budget Office, "CBO's 2014 Long-Term Projections for Social Security: Additional Information," December 18, 2014, https://www.cbo.gov/publication/49795.

20. Congressional Budget Office, "Social Security Replacement Rates and Other Benefit Measures: An In-Depth Analysis," April 16, 2019, https://www.cbo.gov/publication/55038.

21. Patrick J. Purcell, "Income Replacement Ratios in the Health and Retirement Study," *Social Security Bulletin* 72, no. 3 (2012).

22. Albert Ando and Franco Modigliani, "The 'Life Cycle' Hypothesis of Saving: Aggregate Implications and Tests," *American Economic Review* 53, no. 1 (1963).

23. Social Security Trustees, *The 2009 Annual Report of the Board of Trustees of the Federal Old-Age and Survivors Insurance and Federal Disability Insurance Trust Funds*, Social Security Administration, May 12, 2009, https://www.ssa.gov/OACT/TR/2009/tr09.pdf.

24. C. Eugene Steuerle et al., *Do Analysts Use Atypical Workers to Evaluate Social Security?*, Urban Institute, March 15, 2000, https://www.urban.org/sites/default/files/publication/62091/309429-Do-Analysts-Use-Atypical-Workers-to-Evaluate-Social-Security-.PDF.

25. See Orlo R. Nichols et al., *Internal Real Rates of Return Under the OASDI Program for Hypothetical Workers* (Social Security Administration, 2001); and Alicia Haydock Munnell and Mauricio Soto, "What Replacement Rates Do Households Actually Experience in Retirement?," Center for Retirement Research, August 3, 2005, https://crr.bc.edu/what-replacement-rates-do-households-actually-experience-in-retirement.

26. Barbara A. Butrica et al., "This Is Not Your Parents' Retirement: Comparing Retirement Income Across Generations," *Social Security Bulletin* 72, no. 1 (2012).

27. All figures are based on current trustees report data and trustees projections for future growth of the average wage index.

28. Butrica et al., "This Is Not Your Parents' Retirement."

29. Christian E. Weller and Edith Rasell, "Getting Better All the Time: Social Security's Ever-Improving Future," Economic Policy Institute, March 30, 2000, https://www.epi.org/publication/issuebriefs_ib140.

30. Dean Baker et al., "Asset Returns and Economic Growth," Brookings Institution, 2005, https://www.brookings.edu/wp-content/uploads/2005/01/2005a_bpea_baker.pdf.

Chapter 4

1. American Advisors Group, "The Retirement Savings Crisis Is Real—and How Seniors Are Coping," February 15, 2023, https://www.aag.com/retirement-savings-crisis; and Darwin Correspondence Project, letter to Alexander Stephen Wilson, 1879, https://www.darwinproject.ac.uk/letter/DCP-LETT-11820.xml.

2. Tyler Bond et al., "Retirement Insecurity 2021—Americans' Views of Retirement," National Institute on Retirement Security, February 2021, https://tinyurl.com/2bpnmxyw.

3. Anna Madamba and Stephen P. Utkus, "Retirement Transitions in Four Countries," Vanguard, January 2017, https://intl.assets.vgdynamic.info/intl/australia/documents/retirement-centre/retirement-transitions.pdf.

4. Edward N. Wolff, "Retirement Insecurity: The Income Shortfalls Awaiting the Soon-to-Retire," Economic Policy Institute, 2002, https://www.epi.org/publication/books_retirement_intro.

5. Moreover, there is good reason to believe that even these levels of old-age poverty are overstated, due to the Current Population Survey—the data source for the official poverty rate—undercounting income from retirement plans such as traditional pensions and retirement accounts. See Adam Bee et al., *National Experimental Wellbeing Statistics: Version 1*, US Census Bureau, February 2023, https://www2.census.gov/library/working-papers/2023/adrm/ces/CES-WP-23-04.pdf.

6. Peter J. Brady et al., "Using Panel Tax Data to Examine the Transition to Retirement" (paper presented at the Proceedings Annual Conference on Taxation and Minutes of the Annual Meeting of the National Tax Association, 2016).

7. See note 15 in Jack VanDerhei and Craig Copeland, "Can America Afford Tomorrow's Retirees: Results from the EBRI-ERF Retirement Security Projection Model," Employee Benefit Research Institute, November 1, 2003, https://www.ebri.org/content/can-america-afford-tomorrow's-retirees-results-from-the-ebri-erf-retirement-security-projection-model-182.

8. John Gist, *Retirement Security Across Generations: Are Americans Prepared for Their Golden Years?*, Pew Charitable Trusts, May 2013, https://www.pewtrusts.org/~/media/legacy/uploadedfiles/pcs_assets/2013/EMPRetirementv4051013finalFORWEBpdf.pdf.

9. Jack VanDerhei, "EBRI Retirement Security Projection Model® (RSPM)–Analyzing Policy and Design Proposals," Employee Benefit Research Institute, May 31, 2018, https://www.ebri.org/content/ebri-retirement-security-projection-model-(rspm)-analyzing-policy-and-design-proposals.

10. VanDerhei and Copeland, "Can America Afford Tomorrow's Retirees."

11. Nari Rhee, "The Retirement Savings Crisis: Is It Worse Than We Think?," National Institute on Retirement Security, June 2013, https://www.nirsonline.org/reports/the-retirement-savings-crisis-is-it-worse-than-we-think.

12. Nancy Folbre, "Rowboats for Retirement," *New York Times*, June 24, 2013, https://economix.blogs.nytimes.com/2013/06/24/rowboats-for-retirement.

13. Jason Scott et al., "The Life-Cycle Model Implies That Most Young People Should Not Save for Retirement," *Journal of Retirement* 10, no. 3 (2023).

14. Unless the gradient by income of replacement-rate needs for total retirement incomes matched the gradient of Social Security replacement rates, the National Institute on Retirement Security analysis may misstate retirement savings adequacy.

15. See Financial Accounts of the United States, "Table L. 117 (A)," 2023.

16. For instance, even in the cases of government insolvencies, as in Detroit and Puerto Rico, nearly all accrued benefits were honored. In the case of underfunded multiemployer pensions, not only were accrued benefits honored but, thanks to a federal bailout of the plans, new benefits will continue to be accrued.

17. Tyler Bond and Frank Porell, *Examining the Nest Egg: The Sources of Retirement Income for Older Americans*, National Institute on Retirement Security, January 2020, https://www.nirsonline.org/wp-content/uploads/2020/01/Examining-the-Nest-Egg-Final-1.pdf.

18. Helaine Olen, "Sanders Is Right: Biden Is Vulnerable to Trump on Social Security," *Washington Post*, January 12, 2020, https://www.washingtonpost.com/opinions/2020/01/14/sanders-is-right-biden-is-vulnerable-trump-social-security.

19. Bond and Porell, *Examining the Nest Egg*.

20. Irena Dushi et al., "The Importance of Social Security Benefits to the Income of the Aged Population," *Social Security Bulletin* 77, no. 2 (2017).

21. Irena Dushi and Brad Trenkamp, "Improving the Measurement of Retirement Income of the Aged Population" (working paper, Social Security Administration, Office of Policy, Office of Research, Evaluation, and Statistics, Office of Retirement and Disability Policy, January 2021), https://www.ssa.gov/policy/docs/workingpapers/wp116.html.

22. Adam Bee and Joshua Mitchell, "Do Older Americans Have More Income Than We Think?," *Proceedings. Annual Conference on Taxation and Minutes of the Annual Meeting of the National Tax Association* 110 (2017): 1–85.

23. Jan E. Mutchler et al., "The Elder Economic Security Standard Index™: A New Indicator for Evaluating Economic Security in Later Life," *Social Indicators Research* 120, no. 1 (2014).

24. Mutchler et al., "The Elder Economic Security Standard Index™."

25. Alicia H. Munnell et al., "A New National Retirement Risk Index," Center for Retirement Research, June 2006, https://crr.bc.edu/wp-content/uploads/2019/12/IB_48.pdf.

26. Alicia H. Munnell et al., "The National Retirement Risk Index: An Update," Center for Retirement Research, October 2012, https://crr.bc.edu/wp-content/uploads/2019/12/IB_12-20.pdf.

27. Alicia H. Munnell, "The Case of the Missing Replacement Rates," MarketWatch, August 6, 2014, http://blogs.marketwatch.com/encore/2014/08/06/the-case-of-the-missing-social-security-data.

28. James S. Duesenberry, *Income, Saving, and the Theory of Consumer Behavior* (*Economic Studies: No. 87*) (Harvard University Press, 1949).

29. John Burnett et al., "Measuring the Adequacy of Retirement Savings," *Review of Income and Wealth* 64, no. 4 (2018).

30. Alicia H. Munnell et al., "National Retirement Risk Index: How Much Longer Do We Need to Work?," Center for Retirement Research, June 19, 2012, https://crr.bc.edu/national-retirement-risk-index-how-much-longer-do-we-need-to-work.

31. Amish Gandhi, *Investing in (and for) Our Future*, World Economic Forum, June 2019, https://www3.weforum.org/docs/WEF_Investing_in_our_Future_report_2019.pdf.

32. Ben Steverman, "Retirees Risk Running Out of Money a Decade Before Death," *Bloomberg*, June 13, 2019, https://news.bloomberglaw.com/employee-benefits/worlds-retirees-risk-running-out-of-money-a-decade-before-death.

33. Gandhi, *Investing in (and for) Our Future*.

34. Congressional Budget Office, "CBO's 2021 Long-Term Projections for Social Security: Additional Information," July 8, 2021, https://www.cbo.gov/publication/57342.

35. Charles A. Jeszeck et al., "Retirement Security: Most Households Approaching Retirement Have Low Savings, an Update," March 26, 2019, https://www.gao.gov/products/gao-19-442r.

36. Adriana Diaz, "Millions of US Workers near Retirement Age Have Zero Money Saved: Report," *New York Post*, August 4, 2023, https://nypost.com/2023/08/04/millions-of-us-workers-near-retirement-age-with-zero-savings.

37. Aimee Picchi, "Millions of Older Workers Are Nearing Retirement with Nothing Saved," CBS News, August 3, 2023, https://www.cbsnews.com/news/retirement-low-wage-older-workers-no-savings.

38. Picchi, "Millions of Older Workers Are Nearing Retirement with Nothing Saved."

39. Pew Charitable Trusts, "State Automated Retirement Programs Would Reduce Taxpayer Burden from Insufficient Savings," 2023, https://www.pewtrusts.org/en/research-and-analysis/articles/2023/05/11/state-automated-retirement-programs-would-reduce-taxpayer-burden-from-insufficient-savings.

40. Kate Dore, "A Retirement-Savings Gap May Cost the Economy $1.3 Trillion by 2040. How State-Run Programs Can Fix It," May 12, 2023, CNBC, https://www.cnbc.com/2023/05/12/how-state-run-programs-can-fix-the-retirement-savings-gap.html; Carrie McCabe, "What About America's $1.3 Trillion Retirement Crisis?," *Forbes*, October 26, 2023, https://www.forbes.com/sites/carriemccabe/2023/10/26/americas-13-trillion-retirement-crisis/?sh=6588978e4e65; Suzanne Woolley and Steven Crabill, "Retirement Savings Shortfall in US Will Cost $1.3 Trillion," Bloomberg Tax, May 12,

2023, https://news.bloombergtax.com/daily-tax-report/retirement-savings-shortfall-in-us-will-cost-1-3-trillion; Margarida Correia, "Americans' Lack of Retirement Savings Could Cost Governments $1.3 Trillion—Pew," *Pensions & Investments*, May 12, 2023, https://www.pionline.com/retirement-plans/americans-lack-retirement-savings-could-cost-governments-13-trillion-pew; and National Conference of State Legislatures, "State and Federal Impacts of Insufficient Retirement Savings," July 17, 2023, https://www.ncsl.org/labor-and-employment/state-and-federal-impacts-of-insufficient-retirement-savings.

41. See Bee and Mitchell, "Do Older Americans Have More Income Than We Think?"

42. Pew Charitable Trusts, "State Automated Retirement Programs Would Reduce Taxpayer Burden from Insufficient Savings."

43. Bee et al., *National Experimental Wellbeing Statistics*.

44. Pew Charitable Trusts, "State Automated Retirement Programs Would Reduce Taxpayer Burden from Insufficient Savings."

45. Congressional Budget Office, "Medicaid," May 2022, https://www.cbo.gov/system/files/2022-05/51301-2022-05-medicaid.pdf.

46. Congressional Budget Office, "Supplemental Nutrition Assistance Program," May 2022, https://www.cbo.gov/system/files/2022-05/51312-2022-05-snap.pdf.

47. Anne Tergesen, "Millennials on Better Track for Retirement Than Boomers and Gen X," *Wall Street Journal*, October 3, 2023, https://www.wsj.com/personal-finance/retirement/millennials-on-better-track-for-retirement-than-boomers-and-gen-x-1aebf00.

48. Fu Tan et al., *The Vanguard Retirement Outlook: A National Perspective on Retirement Readiness*, Vanguard, 2023, https://institutional.vanguard.com/content/dam/inst/iig-transformation/insights/pdf/2023/the-vanguard-retirement-outlook.pdf.

49. Susann Rohwedder et al., "Explanations for the Decline in Spending at Older Ages" (working paper, National Bureau of Economic Research, September 19, 2022).

50. Michael D. Hurd and Susann Rohwedder, "Spending Trajectories After Age 65 Variation by Initial Wealth," RAND Corporation, June 27, 2023, https://www.rand.org/pubs/external_publications/EP70132.html.

51. Peter J. Brady and Steven Bass, "When I'm 64 (or Thereabouts): Changes in Income from Middle Age to Old Age," Investment Company Institute, May 10, 2023, https://www.ici.org/system/files/2023-05/when-im-64-brady-bass-2305.pdf.

52. John Karl Scholz et al., "Are Americans Saving 'Optimally' for Retirement?," *Journal of Political Economy* 114, no. 4 (2006).

53. Michael D. Hurd and Susann Rohwedder, "Economic Preparation for Retirement" (working paper, National Bureau of Economic Research, 2011).

54. Michael D. Hurd and Susann Rohwedder, "Economic Preparation for Retirement," in *The Routledge Handbook of the Economics of Aging*, ed. David E. Bloom, Alfonso Sousa-Poza, and Uwe Sunde (Routledge, 2023).

55. Barbara A. Butrica et al., "This Is Not Your Parents' Retirement: Comparing Retirement Income Across Generations," *Social Security Bulletin* 72, no. 1 (2012).

Chapter 5

1. David Certner, "Examining Pathways to Build a Stronger, More Inclusive Retirement System," testimony before the House Committee on Education and Labor, Subcommittee on Health, Employment, Labor and Pensions, June 23, 2021, https://democrats-edworkforce.house.gov/imo/media/doc/CertnerDavidTestimony0623211.pdf.

2. Teresa Ghilarducci, "Employers Can't Provide Retirement Plans. Let's Stop Pretending They Can," Forbes, April 14, 2020, https://www.forbes.com/sites/teresaghilarducci/2020/08/14/employers-cant-provide-retirement-planslets-stop-pretending-they-can.

3. Teresa Ghilarducci et al., "Trends in Employer-Sponsored Retirement Plan Access and Participation Rates: Reconciling Different Data Sources," Schwartz Center for Economic Policy Analysis, January 2021, https://www.economicpolicyresearch.org/insights-blog/trends-in-employer-sponsored-retirement-plan-access-and-participation-rates.

4. Ghilarducci, "Employers Can't Provide Retirement Plans."

5. Teresa Ghilarducci, "Guaranteed Retirement Accounts: Toward Retirement Accounts," Economic Policy Institute, March 3, 2008.

6. John Scott and Andrew Blevins, "State Automated Retirement Programs Would Reduce Taxpayer Burden from Insufficient Savings," May 11, 2023, https://www.pewtrusts.org/en/research-and-analysis/articles/2023/05/11/state-automated-retirement-programs-would-reduce-taxpayer-burden-from-insufficient-savings.

7. Econsult Solutions, The Cost of Doing Nothing: Federal and State Impacts of Insufficient Retirement Savings, May 5, 2023, https://econsultsolutions.com/pew-federal-and-state-impacts-of-insufficient-retirement-savings.

8. Alan L. Gustman et al., "Do Workers Know About Their Pension Plan Type? Comparing Workers' and Employers' Pension Information," in Overcoming the Savings Slump: How to Increase the Effectiveness of Financial Education and Saving Programs (University of Chicago Press, 2009).

9. US Bureau of Labor Statistics, "National Compensation Survey: Employee Benefits in the United States, March 2021," 2021, https://www.bls.gov/ebs/publications/september-2021-landing-page-employee-benefits-in-the-united-states-march-2021.htm.

10. Center for Retirement Research, Oregon Market Research Report, July 2016, https://www.oregon.gov/treasury/financial-empowerment/Documents/ors-board-meeting-minutes/Undated/ORSP-Market-Analysis-13JULY2016.pdf.

11. By July 31, 2023, all employers of any size are required to register with Oregon-Saves, but Child Protective Services data covering this period were not available at the time of writing.

12. Sellwood Consulting, "OregonSaves Program Monthly Dashboard," Oregon-Saves, 2023, https://www.oregon.gov/treasury/financial-empowerment/Documents/ors-board-meeting-minutes/2023/2023-06-Program-Report-OregonSaves-Monthly.pdf.

13. John Chalmers et al., Auto-Enrollment Retirement Plans in OregonSaves, Michigan Retirement and Disability Research Center, September 2021, https://mrdrc.isr.umich.edu/publications/papers/pdf/wp425.pdf.

14. US Department of Labor, Employee Benefits Security Administration, *Private Pension Plan Bulletin*, September 2024, https://www.dol.gov/sites/dolgov/files/ebsa/researchers/statistics/retirement-bulletins/private-pension-plan-bulletins-abstract-2022.pdf.

15. Irena Dushi and Howard M. Iams, "The Impact of Response Error on Participation Rates and Contributions to Defined Contribution Pension Plans," *Social Security Bulletin* 70, no. 1 (2010).

16. Dushi and Iams, "The Impact of Response Error on Participation Rates and Contributions to Defined Contribution Pension Plans."

17. Craig Copeland, "The Effect of the Current Population Survey Redesign on Retirement-Plan Participation Estimates," *EBRI Notes* 36, no. 12 (2015).

18. Craig Copeland, "Current Population Survey: Checking In on the Retirement Plan Participation and Retiree Income Estimates," Employee Benefit Research Institute, May 30, 2019, https://www.ebri.org/content/current-population-survey-checking-in-on-the-retirement-plan-participation-and-retiree-income-estimates.

19. Craig Copeland, "Retirement Plan Participation and the Current Population Survey: The Impact of New Income Questions on These Estimates," Employee Benefit Research Institute, January 30, 2020, https://www.ebri.org/content/retirement-plan-participation-and-the-current-population-survey-the-impact-of-new-income-questions-on-these-estimates.

20. An establishment is the work location; a large employer may have multiple establishments.

21. Irena Dushi et al., "Retirement Plan Coverage by Firm Size: An Update," *Social Security Bulletin* 75, no. 2 (2015).

22. Internal Revenue Service, "Table 1.5. All Returns: Sources of Income, Adjustments, and Tax Items, by Age, Tax Year 2020 (Filing Year 2021)," 2021, https://www.irs.gov/statistics/soi-tax-stats-individual-income-tax-returns-complete-report-publication-1304-basic-tables-part-1.

23. Ric Edelman's proposal is at root a play on the risk premium paid to stocks, an issue that elsewhere is discussed in greater detail with reference to proposals for Social Security to invest in the stock market. Mark Schoeff, "Ric Edelman Proposes Social Security Fix: Allot $7,000 for Each Baby," InvestmentNews, April 19, 2017, https://www.investmentnews.com/ric-edelman-proposes-social-security-fix-allot-7000-for-each-baby-71135.

24. Jill Schlesinger, "Jill on Money: The Odd Couple of Retirement," *Mercury News*, September 20, 2021, https://www.mercurynews.com/2021/09/20/jill-on-money-the-odd-couple-of-retirement.

25. Congressional Budget Office, "CBO's 2021 Long-Term Projections for Social Security: Additional Information," July 8, 2021, https://www.cbo.gov/publication/57342.

26. Congressional Budget Office, "CBO's 2021 Long-Term Projections for Social Security."

27. Jason S. Scott et al., "The Life-Cycle Model Implies That Most Young People Should Not Save for Retirement," *Journal of Retirement* 10, no. 3 (2023).

28. Scott et al., "The Life-Cycle Model Implies That Most Young People Should Not Save for Retirement."

29. In addition, the authors point to low interest rates prevalent at the time and that in the life-cycle model, saving will make less sense when interest rates are low.

30. Internal Revenue Service, "Table 1.5."

31. Irena Dushi and Howard M. Iams, "Pension Plan Participation Among Married Couples," *Social Security Bulletin* 73, no. 3 (2013).

32. That is, 81 percent/90 percent = 89 percent.

33. David Joulfaian and David Richardson, "Who Takes Advantage of Tax-Deferred Saving Programs? Evidence from Federal Income Tax Data," *National Tax Journal* 54, no. 3 (2001).

34. Joshua Gotbaum, "De-Risking: Plan Sponsor & Participant Perspectives & Actions," International Centre for Pension Management, June 5, 2016.

35. Edwin Newman, dir., *Pensions: The Broken Promise* (New York: National Broadcasting Co., 1972).

36. Newman, *Pensions.*

37. Senate Committee on Labor and Public Welfare, Subcommittee on Labor, "Statistical Analysis of Major Characteristics of Private Pension Plans (Pursuant to S. Res. 235, Section 41, 92d Congress, 2d Session)," September 1, 1972, https://www.govinfo.gov/content/pkg/CPRT-92SPRT82399O/pdf/CPRT-92SPRT82399O.pdf.

38. Lenore A. Epstein, "Income of the Aged in 1962: First of the 1963 Survey of the Aged," *Social Security Bulletin* 27, no. 3 (1964).

39. Christine Irick, "Income of New Retired Workers by Social Security Benefit Levels: Findings from the New Beneficiary Survey," *Social Security Bulletin* 48, no. 5 (1985).

40. Craig Copeland, "Retirement Plan Participation: Survey of Income and Program Participation (SIPP) Data, 2012," *EBRI Notes* 34, no. 8 (2013).

41. Stephanie Aaronson and Julia Lynn Coronado, "Are Firms or Workers Behind the Shift away from DB Pension Plan?," Federal Reserve Board, May 6, 2005, https://doi.org/10.2139/ssrn.716383.

42. US Bureau of Labor Statistics, "Employer Costs for Employee Compensation," 2023, https://www.bls.gov/ecec/home.htm.

43. Seth D. Harris, "Retirement for Middle-Class Americans Is Crumbling," Biden Forum, September 26, 2018, https://bidenforum.org/retirement-for-middle-class-americans-is-crumbling-9bf0d5b680fc.

44. Government Accountability Office, *The Nation's Retirement System: A Comprehensive Re-Evaluation Is Needed to Better Promote Future Retirement Security*, October 2017, https://www.gao.gov/assets/d18111SP.pdf.

45. Federal Reserve Board, Financial Accounts of the United States, 2023, https://www.federalreserve.gov/feeds/z1.html.

46. Peter J. Brady and Steven Bass, "When I'm 64 (or Thereabouts): Changes in Income from Middle Age to Old Age," Investment Company Institute, May 10, 2023, https://www.ici.org/system/files/2023-05/when-im-64-brady-bass-2305.pdf.

Chapter 6

1. Vanguard, *How America Saves 2023*, 2023, https://corporate.vanguard.com/content/dam/corp/research/pdf/how_america_saves_2023.pdf.

2. Andrew G. Biggs, "How Much Should the Poor Save for Retirement? Data and Simulations on Retirement Income Adequacy Among Low-Earning Households," in *Remaking Retirement: Debt in an Aging Economy*, ed. Olivia S. Mitchell and Annamaria Lusardi (Oxford University Press, 2019).

3. Robert J. Myers, *Social Security*, 4th ed. (Pension Research Council, 1993).

4. Charles A. Jeszeck et al., "Retirement Security: Shorter Life Expectancy Reduces Projected Lifetime Benefits for Lower Earners," Government Accountability Office, March 2016, https://www.gao.gov/assets/gao-16-354.pdf.

5. Quoted in Charles D. Ellis et al., *Falling Short: The Coming Retirement Crisis and What to Do About It* (Oxford University Press, 2014).

6. Kyle Burkhalter and Daniel Nickerson, *Unfunded Obligation and Transition Costs for the OASDI Program*, Social Security Administration, March 2023, https://www.ssa.gov/oact/NOTES/ran1/index.html.

7. Natalie Sabadish and Monique Morrissey, *Retirement Inequality Chartbook: How the 401(k) Revolution Created a Few Big Winners and Many Losers*, Economic Policy Institute, September 6, 2013, https://www.epi.org/publication/retirement-inequality-chartbook.

8. Olivia S. Mitchell, "A Review of Tito Boeri, Lans Bovenberg, Benoît Coeuré, and Andrew Roberts's *Dealing with the New Giants* and Peter J. Orszag, Mark Iwry, and William G. Gale's *Aging Gracefully*," *Journal of Economic Literature* 46, no. 4 (2008).

9. Andrew G. Biggs, *Changes to Household Retirement Savings Since 1989*, American Enterprise Institute, May 8, 2020, https://www.aei.org/research-products/report/changes-to-household-retirement-savings-since-1989.

10. John Sabelhaus and Alice Henriques Volz, "Are Disappearing Employer Pensions Contributing to Rising Wealth Inequality?," Federal Reserve Board of Governors, February 1, 2019, https://www.federalreserve.gov/econres/notes/feds-notes/are-disappearing-employer-pensions-contributing-to-rising-wealth-inequality-20190201.html.

11. Sabelhaus and Henriques Volz, "Are Disappearing Employer Pensions Contributing to Rising Wealth Inequality?"

12. Sabelhaus and Henriques Volz, "Are Disappearing Employer Pensions Contributing to Rising Wealth Inequality?"

13. Sabelhaus and Henriques Volz, "Are Disappearing Employer Pensions Contributing to Rising Wealth Inequality?"

Chapter 7

1. CalTech, "Deciphering the Mystery of Bee Flight," November 29, 2005, https://www.caltech.edu/about/news/deciphering-mystery-bee-flight-1075.

2. Drystan Phillips and Teresa Ghilarducci, *Older Workers Claim Social Security While Working, Upending Beliefs About Raising the Retirement Age*, Schwartz Center for Economic Policy Analysis, July 11, 2023, https://www.economicpolicyresearch. org/resource-library/research/older-workers-claim-social-security-while-working-upending-beliefs-about-raising-the-retirement-age.

3. Gila Bronshtein et al., "The Power of Working Longer," *Journal of Pension Economics & Finance* 18, no. 4 (2019).

4. Gary V. Engelhardt et al., "Early Social Security Claiming and Old-Age Poverty: Evidence from the Introduction of the Social Security Early Eligibility Age," *Journal of Human Resources* 57, no. 4 (2020).

5. Social Security Administration, *Annual Statistical Supplement to the Social Security Bulletin, 2022*, December 2022, https://www.ssa.gov/policy/docs/statcomps/supplement/2022/supplement22.pdf.

6. Social Security Administration, "Increasing the Social Security Retirement Age: Workers in Physically Demanding Occupations or in Ill Health," *Social Security Bulletin* 49, no. 10 (1986).

7. Eugene Steuerle et al., "Can Americans Work Longer?," *Proceedings of the National Academy of Sciences* 94 (1999).

8. Richard Johnson and Gordon Mermin, "Will Changing Job Demands Boost Older Workers' Prospects?," Urban Institute, September 2008, https://www.urban. org/sites/default/files/publication/32021/411757-Will-Changing-Job-Demands-Boost-Older-Workers-Prospects-.PDF.

9. Richard Johnson, "Trends in Job Demands Among Older Workers, 1992–2002," *Monthly Labor Review* 127 (July 2004).

10. Johnson, "Trends in Job Demands Among Older Workers, 1992–2002."

11. Monique Morrissey, "Many Older Workers Have Difficult Jobs That Put Them at Risk: Working Longer Is Not a Viable Solution to the Retirement Crisis," Economic Policy Institute, May 17, 2023, https://www.epi.org/publication/older-workers-difficult-jobs.

12. Specifically, a physically demanding job was defined as one that involved one or more of "carrying/moving heavy loads," "lifting/moving people," or "tiring/painful positions" at least one-quarter of the time.

13. Jeff Brown, "Nearly 50 Years of Occupational Safety and Health Data," *Beyond the Numbers* 9, no. 9 (2020).

14. Wilbur J. Cohen and William L. Mitchell, "Social Security Amendments of 1961: Summary and Legislative History," *Social Security Bulletin* 24 (1961).

15. Social Security Administration, *Annual Statistical Supplement to the Social Security Bulletin, 2022*.

16. Social Security Administration, *Annual Statistical Supplement to the Social Security Bulletin, 2022*.

17. Adam Bee and Joshua Mitchell, "Do Older Americans Have More Income Than We Think?," *Proceedings. Annual Conference on Taxation and Minutes of the Annual Meeting of the National Tax Association* 110 (2017): 1–85.

18. David Neumark, Ian Burn, and Patrick Button, "Experimental Age Discrimination Evidence and the Heckman Critique," *American Economic Review* 106, no. 5 (2016).

19. David Neumark and Joanne Song, "Do Stronger Age Discrimination Laws Make Social Security Reforms More Effective?," *Journal of Public Economics* 108 (2013).

20. Joanna Lahey, "State Age Protection Laws and the Age Discrimination in Employment Act," *Journal of Law and Economics* 51, no. 3 (2008).

21. David H. Greenberg et al., "A Meta-Analysis of Government-Sponsored Training Programs," *ILR Review* 57, no. 1 (2003).

22. Legally, this is not how Social Security actually works. In fact, payroll taxes are based on wages, and benefits are calculated on wages subject to taxes, but there is no direct legal link between taxes paid and the benefits to which a participant is entitled. This structure relates back to constitutional arguments that took place at the time of Social Security's founding.

23. For discussion of these issues, see Andrew G. Biggs et al., *The Consequences of Current Benefit Adjustments for Early and Delayed Claiming*, Center for Retirement Research, January 20, 2021, https://crr.bc.edu/the-consequences-of-current-benefit-adjustments-for-early-and-delayed-claiming.

24. Gayle L. Reznik et al., "Social Security and Marginal Returns to Work near Retirement," Social Security Administration, April 2009.

25. Lucie Schmidt and Purvi Sevak, "Taxes, Wages, and the Labor Supply of Older Americans," *Research on Aging* 31, no. 2 (2009).

26. Congressional Budget Office, *Labor Supply and Taxes*, January 10, 1996, https://www.cbo.gov/publication/13598.

27. John Laitner and Dan Silverman, "Consumption, Retirement and Social Security: Evaluating the Efficiency of Reform That Encourages Longer Careers," *Journal of Public Economics* 96, no. 7–8 (2012).

28. Eric French, "The Effects of Health, Wealth, and Wages on Labour Supply and Retirement Behaviour," *Review of Economic Studies* 72, no. 2 (2005).

29. Andrew G. Biggs, *A New Social Security "Notch"? Bad News for People Born in 1947*, Center for Retirement Research, May 2010, https://crr.bc.edu/a-new-social-security-notch-bad-news-for-people-born-in-1947.

30. Gopi Shah Goda et al., "A Tax on Work for the Elderly: Medicare as a Secondary Payer" (working paper, National Bureau of Economic Research, 2007).

Chapter 8

1. Here I borrow from Tomasz Tunguz, "The Cost of Bad Data Is the Illusion of Knowledge," January 29, 2013, https://tomtunguz.com/cost-of-bad-data-1-10-100.

2. *Protecting and Improving Social Security: Enhancing Social Security to Strengthen the Middle Class*, hearing before the Subcommittee on Social Security of the House Committee on Ways and Means, 116th Cong. 5 (2019) (statement of John Larson, chairman of the House of Representatives Subcommittee on Social Security).

3. National Academy of Social Insurance, "The Role of Benefits in Income and Poverty," 2022, https://www.nasi.org/learn/social-security/the-role-of-benefits-in-income-and-poverty-2.

4. Adam Bee and Joshua Mitchell, "The Hidden Resources of Women Working Longer: Evidence from Linked Survey-Administrative Data," in *Women Working Longer: Increased Employment at Older Ages* (University of Chicago Press, 2017).

5. Social Security Administration, *Income of the Population 55 or Older, 2010*, March 2012, https://www.ssa.gov/policy/docs/statcomps/income_pop55/2010/index.html; Social Security Administration, *Income of the Population 55 or Older, 2000*, February 2002, https://www.ssa.gov/policy/docs/statcomps/income_pop55/2000/index.html; and Social Security Administration, "Income of the Aged Chartbook, 1996," May 1998, https://www.ssa.gov/policy/docs/chartbooks/income_aged/1996/index.html.

6. Bee and Mitchell, "The Hidden Resources of Women Working Longer."

7. Lenore E. Bixby, "Income of People Aged 65 and Older: Overview from 1968 Survey of the Aged," *Social Security Bulletin* 33 (1970).

8. US Census Bureau, "About Income & Poverty," November 21, 2021, https://www.census.gov/topics/income-poverty/about.html.

9. Sylvester J. Schieber and Andrew G. Biggs, "Biggs and Schieber: Retirees Aren't Headed for the Poor House," *Wall Street Journal*, January 23, 2014, https://www.wsj.com/articles/andrew-biggs-and-sylvester-schieber-retirees-aren8217t-headed-for-the-poor-house-1390522110.

10. Monique Morrissey, "Is the Retirement Crisis a Mirage?," Economic Policy Institute, February 18, 2014, https://www.epi.org/blog/retirement-crisis-mirage.

11. Morrissey, "Is the Retirement Crisis a Mirage?"

12. Adam Bee and Joshua Mitchell, "Do Older Americans Have More Income Than We Think?," *Proceedings. Annual Conference on Taxation and Minutes of the Annual Meeting of the National Tax Association* 110 (2017): 1–85.

13. These are not true replacement rates, in that Adam Bee and Joshua Mitchell compare the incomes of retirees at a given percentile of the earnings distribution to those of pre-retirees at the same percentile of the income distribution. A true replacement rate compares a retiree's income to their own preretirement earnings, which the figures presented by Bee and Mitchell do not do. To the degree that retirees in a given income percentile resided in a different earnings percentile before retirement, their individual replacement rates could be lower or higher than the figures represented in Table 3.

14. Irena Dushi and Brad Trenkamp, "Improving the Measurement of Retirement Income of the Aged Population" (working paper, Social Security Administration, Office of Policy, Office of Research, Evaluation, and Statistics, Office of Retirement and Disability Policy, January 2021), https://www.ssa.gov/policy/docs/workingpapers/wp116.html.

15. University of Chicago, Harris School of Public Policy and Notre Dame University, Wilson Sheehan Lab for Economic Opportunities, "Consumption and Income Poverty Dashboard," 2022, http://povertymeasurement.org/dashboard.

16. Adam Bee et al., *National Experimental Wellbeing Statistics: Version 1*, US Census Bureau, February 2023, https://www2.census.gov/library/working-papers/2023/adrm/ces/CES-WP-23-04.pdf.

Chapter 9

1. Congressional Budget Office, *The Distribution of Household Income,* 2018, 2021, https://www.cbo.gov/publication/57061.

2. The CBO presents data for households headed by an individual under age 65 in two categories: those with and without children. I produce a weighted average of the two data for these comparisons.

3. Adam Bee and Joshua Mitchell, "Do Older Americans Have More Income Than We Think?," *Proceedings. Annual Conference on Taxation and Minutes of the Annual Meeting of the National Tax Association* 110 (2017): 1–85.

4. The CBO reports income data in a range of categories that would be overwhelming for most readers. These include wages, employee's contribution for deferred compensation, employer's contribution for health insurance, employer's share of payroll taxes, federal unemployment tax, the corporate tax borne by labor, business income, capital gains, tax-exempt interest, taxable interest, positive rental income, dividend income, the corporate tax borne by capital, and other market income, the vast majority of which is benefits paid by private retirement plans. To simplify, I consolidate these sources of market income into these categories: Social Security benefits; retirement plan benefits; earnings; nonretirement plan investment and business income; means-tested benefits, unemployment insurance, and workers' compensation benefits (the latter two of which provide only tiny amounts of income on average); Medicare benefits, which are a service provided by the government but which the CBO (and international agencies such as the Organisation for Economic Co-operation and Development) includes in calculations of disposable income; and federal income and payroll taxes, which subtract from income.

5. For individuals who retired since 2000, the gradual increase in Social Security's normal retirement age has reduced Social Security replacement rates, although this reduction has been partly offset by increases in the average age at which individuals claim Social Security benefits.

6. Author's calculations from US Bureau of Labor Statistics, Current Population Survey.

Chapter 10

1. Michael D. Hurd and Susann Rohwedder, "Spending Trajectories After Age 65 Variation by Initial Wealth," *Journal of the Economics of Ageing* 26 (October 2023).

2. James J. Choi et al., "The Evolution of Late-Life Income and Assets: Measurement in IRS Tax Data and Three Household Surveys" (working paper, National Bureau of Economic Research, 2020).

3. Peter J. Brady and Steven Bass, *When I'm 64 (or Thereabouts): Changes in Income from Middle Age to Old Age,* Investment Company Institute, May 10, 2023, https://www.ici.org/system/files/2023-05/when-im-64-brady-bass-2305.pdf.

4. David A. Love et al., "The Trajectory of Wealth in Retirement," *Journal of Public Economics* 93, no. 1–2 (2009).

5. Chris Browning et al., "Spending in Retirement," *Journal of Financial Planning* 29, no. 2 (2016): 42–53.

6. Sudipto Banerjee, "Asset Decumulation or Asset Preservation? What Guides Retirement Spending?," Employee Benefit Research Institute, April 3, 2018, https://www.ebri.org/content/asset-decumulation-or-asset-preservation-what-guides-retirement-spending.

7. Banerjee, "Asset Decumulation or Asset Preservation?"

8. Cerulli Associates, "The $70 Trillion Dollar Opportunity: Understanding the Implications of Multigenerational Wealth Transfer," 2021, https://image.marketing.cerulli.com/lib/fe3411737164047c7d1072/m/1/158ef2ff-f113-4195-b998-65d01c49656f.pdf.

9. Jeffrey R. Brown et al., "Do Required Minimum Distribution Rules Matter? The Effect of the 2009 Holiday on Retirement Plan Distributions," *Journal of Public Economics* 151 (2017).

10. B. Douglas Bernheim et al., "What Accounts for the Variation in Retirement Wealth Among US Households?," *American Economic Review* 91, no. 4 (2001).

11. James Banks et al., "Is There a Retirement-Savings Puzzle?," *American Economic Review* 88, no. 4 (1998): 769–88.

12. Mark Aguiar and Erik Hurst, "Consumption Versus Expenditure," *Journal of Political Economy* 113, no. 5 (2005).

13. Mark Aguiar and Erik Hurst, "Lifestyle Prices and Production," Federal Reserve Bank of Boston, July 2005, https://www.bostonfed.org/publications/public-policy-discussion-paper/2005/lifecycle-prices-and-production.aspx.

14. Michael Hurd et al., "Explanations for the Decline in Spending at Older Ages," Michigan Retirement and Disability Research Center, 2021.

15. Mariacristina De Nardi et al., "Why Do the Elderly Save? The Role of Medical Expenses," *Journal of Political Economy* 118, no. 1 (2010).

16. Ann Carrns, "Retiree Medical Costs Are Expected to Moderate, but Still High," *New York Times*, June 30, 2023, https://www.nytimes.com/2023/06/30/your-money/retiree-health-care-costs.html.

17. Andrew Osterland, "Aging Baby Boomers Raise the Risk of a Long-Term-Care Crisis in the U.S.," CNBC, November 8, 2021, https://www.cnbc.com/2021/11/08/aging-baby-boomers-raise-the-risk-of-a-long-term-care-crisis-in-the-us.html.

18. Susann Rohwedder et al., "Risk of Large Medical Expenditures at Older Ages and Their Impact on Economic Well-Being," Michigan Retirement and Disability Research Center, 2022.

19. Rohwedder et al., "Risk of Large Medical Expenditures at Older Ages and Their Impact on Economic Well-Being."

20. Rohwedder et al., "Risk of Large Medical Expenditures at Older Ages and Their Impact on Economic Well-Being."

21. Rohwedder et al., "Risk of Large Medical Expenditures at Older Ages and Their Impact on Economic Well-Being," 22.

22. Kirsten J. Colello, "Who Pays for Long-Term Services and Supports? A Fact Sheet," Congressional Research Service, June 15, 2022.

23. Internal Revenue Service, "Table 1.5. All Returns: Sources of Income, Adjustments, and Tax Items, by Age, Tax Year 2020 (Filing Year 2021)," 2021, https://www.

irs.gov/statistics/soi-tax-stats-individual-income-tax-returns-complete-report-publication-1304-basic-tables-part-1.

24. Jeffrey R. Brown and Amy Finkelstein, "Supply or Demand: Why Is the Market for Long-Term Care Insurance So Small?" (working paper, National Bureau of Economic Research, 2004).

25. Leora Friedberg et al., "New Evidence on the Risk of Requiring Long-Term Care," Center for Retirement Research, November 2014, https://crr.bc.edu/wp-content/uploads/2014/11/wp_2014-12.pdf; and Leora Friedberg et al., *Medicaid and Crowd-Out of Long-Term Care Insurance*, Network for Studies on Pensions, Aging and Retirement, October 2014.

26. James Poterba and Steven Venti, "Financial Well-Being in Late Life: Understanding the Impact of Adverse Health Shocks and Spousal Deaths" (paper presented at the 19th Annual Joint Meeting of the Retirement Research Consortium, Washington, DC, August 2017).

27. Thomas Davidoff, "Home Equity Commitment and Long-Term Care Insurance Demand," *Journal of Public Economics* 94, nos. 1–2 (2010).

28. Axel Börsch-Supan, "Saving and Consumption Patterns of the Elderly," *Journal of Population Economics* 5, no. 4 (1992).

29. Malene Kallestrup-Lamb et al., "Health, Retirement and Consumption," Society for Economic Dynamics, 2017.

30. Frederick Vettese, "How Spending Declines with Age, and the Implications for Workplace Pension Plans," C. D. Howe Institute, June 16, 2016, https://www.cdhowe.org/public-policy-research/how-spending-declines-age-and-implications-workplace-pension-plans.

31. Cesira Urzi Brancati et al., "Understanding Retirement Journeys: Expectations vs. Reality," UK International Longevity Centre, November 2015.

32. James Banks et al., "Life-Cycle Consumption Patterns at Older Ages in the United States and the United Kingdom: Can Medical Expenditures Explain the Difference?," *American Economic Journal: Economic Policy* 11, no. 3 (2019).

33. Amy Finkelstein et al., "What Good Is Wealth Without Health? The Effect of Health on the Marginal Utility of Consumption," *Journal of the European Economic Association* 11, no. suppl_1 (2013).

34. Kallestrup-Lamb et al., "Health, Retirement and Consumption."

35. Hurd et al., "Explanations for the Decline in Spending at Older Ages."

36. Alicia Munnell et al., "Are Retirees Falling Short? Reconciling the Conflicting Evidence," Center for Retirement Research, 2014.

37. Hurd and Rohwedder, "Spending Trajectories After Age 65 Variation by Initial Wealth."

Chapter 11

1. Megan Brenan, "Americans' Outlook for Their Retirement Has Worsened," Gallup, May 25, 2023, https://news.gallup.com/poll/506330/americans-outlook-retirement-worsened.aspx.

2. Board of Governors of the Federal Reserve Board, "Survey of Household Economics and Decisionmaking," 2024, https://www.federalreserve.gov/consumerscommunities/shed.htm.

3. Susann Rohwedder et al., "Explanations for the Decline in Spending at Older Ages" (working paper, Michigan Retirement and Disability Research Center, June 2022), https://sussexretirement.co.uk/wp-content/uploads/2022/09/20220926-Michigan-explanations-for-the-decline-in-spending-at-older-ages.pdf.

4. Christopher Bader, L. Edward Day, and Ann Gordon, "Survey of American Fears Wave 5," Chapman University, 2018, https://www.chapman.edu/wilkinson/research-centers/babbie-center/survey-american-fears.aspx.

5. Unfortunately, 1992 was the only survey year in which this question was asked.

6. Brenan, "Americans' Outlook for Their Retirement Has Worsened."

Chapter 12

1. David Knox, "Mercer CFA Institute Global Pension Index 2022," Mercer, October 11, 2022, https://www.mercer.com/en-fi/insights/investments/market-outlook-and-trends/mercer-cfa-global-pension-index.

2. Natixis Investment Managers, "2022 Global Retirement Index," September 11, 2022, https://www.im.natixis.com/us/research/2022-global-retirement-index.

3. Natixis Investment Managers, "2022 Global Retirement Index."

4. Government Accountability Office, *401(k) Pension Plans: Loan Provisions Enhance Participation but May Affect Income Security for Some*, October 1997, https://www.gao.gov/assets/hehs-98-5.pdf.

5. Alicia H. Munnell et al., "What Determines 401(k) Participation and Contributions?," *Social Security Bulletin* 64, no. 3 (2001).

6. Figures relying on OECD data are drawn from Organisation for Economic Co-operation and Development, OECD.Stat, 2023, https://stats.oecd.org.

7. The OECD often refers to this figure as a "replacement rate," which is interpreted to mean pension benefits as a percentage of a retiree's own past earnings. However, this interpretation depends on an unusual approach to measuring preretirement earnings, in which past nominal earnings are indexed not for inflation (to capture purchasing power) but for the growth of national average earnings. This method makes the preretirement earnings of a worker who earned the national average wage each year of their career equal to the national average wage in the labor force at the time of their retirement. See Andrew G. Biggs, "The Life Cycle Model, Replacement Rates, and Retirement Income Adequacy," *Journal of Retirement* 4, no. 3 (2017).

8. The OECD calculates benefits using a stylized middle-income worker, which produces slightly different results than when the true average benefit is compared to the average wage.

9. Likewise, New Zealand is not included on this list as its only government-provided retirement benefit, a flat benefit paid to all retirees, is funded from general tax revenues. The United Kingdom is excluded because the UK's National Insurance tax funds not only retirement but health and other benefits.

10. Organisation for Economic Co-operation and Development, Better Life Index, "Income," 2022, https://www.oecdbetterlifeindex.org/topics/income.

11. Organisation for Economic Co-operation and Development, Better Life Index, "Income."

12. The adjustment for health costs via PPP is not complete, however, because PPP adjustments are based on population-wide purchasing patterns, while seniors in the US tend to spend more on health care.

13. ING, "ING International Survey Savings," February 2019, https://think.ing.com/uploads/reports/ING_International_Survey_Savings_Retirement_Saving_Challenges_2019_FINALv2.pdf.

Chapter 13

1. Mark Lino et al., *Expenditures on Children by Families, 2015*, US Department of Agriculture, Center for Nutrition Policy and Promotion, January 2017, https://fns-prod.azureedge.us/sites/default/files/resource-files/crc2015-march2017.pdf.

2. Alicia H. Munnell et al., *The Impact of Raising Children on Retirement Security*, Center for Retirement Research, September 12, 2017, https://crr.bc.edu/the-impact-of-raising-children-on-retirement-security.

3. Jonathan Skinner, "Are You Sure You're Saving Enough for Retirement?," *Journal of Economic Perspectives* 21, no. 3 (2007): 59–80.

4. Michael D. Hurd and Susann Rohwedder, "Economic Preparation for Retirement," in *The Routledge Handbook of the Economics of Aging*, ed. David E. Bloom, Alfonso Sousa-Poza, and Uwe Sunde (Routledge, 2023).

5. Andrew G. Biggs, *Will You Have Enough to Retire On?*, American Enterprise Institute, February 11, 2009, https://www.aei.org/research-products/report/will-you-have-enough-to-retire-on.

6. Alicia H. Munnell et al., *Are Retirees Falling Short? Reconciling the Conflicting Evidence*, Center for Retirement Research, November 19, 2014, https://crr.bc.edu/are-retirees-falling-short-reconciling-the-conflicting-evidence.

7. For instance, in 2022, I coauthored a study with Alicia Munnell and Anqi Chen of the Center for Retirement Research at Boston College, which developed the NRRI. The study was inconclusive, in that it found that parents did spend less and save more of their incomes when kids left home, but it could not establish that household wealth rose. I believe I addressed some of those issues in a later study published in the *Journal of Retirement*, on which this chapter is based. For the joint study, see Andrew G. Biggs et al., *Do Households Save More When the Kids Leave? Take Two*, Center for Retirement Research, March 15, 2022, https://crr.bc.edu/do-households-save-more-when-the-kids-leave-take-two.

8. The Health and Retirement Study (HRS) is another dataset that follows households over time. However, the HRS contains only households age 50 and over, by which time many children have already left home.

9. Franco Modigliani, "Life Cycle, Individual Thrift, and the Wealth of Nations," *Science* 234, no. 4777 (1986).

10. Andrew G. Biggs, "Children and Retirement Income Adequacy," *Journal of Retirement* 10, no. 2 (2022).

11. Orazio P. Attanasio and Martin Browning, "Consumption over the Life Cycle and over the Business Cycle," *American Economic Review* 85, no. 5 (1995).

12. Martin Browning and Mette Ejrnæs, "Consumption and Children," *Review of Economics and Statistics* 91, no. 1 (2009).

13. Orazio P. Attanasio et al., "Humps and Bumps in Lifetime Consumption," *Journal of Business & Economic Statistics* 17, no. 1 (1999).

14. James Banks et al., "Life-Cycle Expenditure Allocations and the Consumption Costs of Children," *European Economic Review* 38, no. 7 (1994).

15. Michelle Maroto, "Saving, Sharing, or Spending? The Wealth Consequences of Raising Children," *Demography* 55, no. 6 (2018).

16. Laura Ravazzini and Ursina Kuhn, "Wealth, Savings and Children Among Swiss, German and Australian Families," in *Social Dynamics in Swiss Society* (Springer, Cham, 2018).

17. David A. Love et al., "The Trajectory of Wealth in Retirement," *Journal of Public Economics* 93, nos. 1–2 (2009).

18. Susann Rohwedder, "Self-Assessed Retirement Outcomes: Determinants and Pathways" (working paper, Michigan Retirement Research Center, 2006).

Chapter 14

1. Gordon R. Friedman, "Oregon Schools Cut Staff and Programs Despite Big Budget Increases," *The Oregonian*, August 11, 2017, https://www.oregonlive.com/politics/2017/08/oregon_schools_cut_staff_and_p.html.

2. National Association of State Retirement Administrators, *NASRA Issue Brief: Public Pension Plan Investment Return Assumptions*, March 2023, https://www.nasra.org/content.asp?contentid=120.

3. National Association of State Retirement Administrators, "Latest Investment Return Assumptions," July 2023, https://www.nasra.org/latestreturnassumptions.

4. To be consistent with an options-pricing exercise in a later section, this present value is calculated using continuous-time discounting. Using more typical discounting with annualized returns, the present value would be slightly higher.

5. George Pennacchi and Mahdi Rastad, "Portfolio Allocation for Public Pension Funds," *Journal of Pension Economics & Finance* 10, no. 2 (2011).

6. Andrew G. Biggs, "The Long-Term Solvency of Teacher Pension Plans: How We Got to Now and Prospects for Recovery," *Educational Researcher* 52, no. 2 (2023).

7. Aleksandar Andonov et al., "Pension Fund Asset Allocation and Liability Discount Rates," *Review of Financial Studies* 30, no. 8 (2017).

8. Andrew G. Biggs, "Public Pensions Cook the Books," *Wall Street Journal*, July 6, 2009, https://www.wsj.com/articles/SB124683573382697889.

9. Robert Novy-Marx and Joshua D. Rauh, "The Liabilities and Risks of State-Sponsored Pension Plans," *Journal of Economic Perspectives* 23, no. 4 (2009).

10. Donald L. Kohn, "The Economic Outlook" (paper presented at the National Conference on Public Employee Retirement Systems Annual Conference, New Orleans, LA, May 20, 2008).

11. Jeffrey R. Brown and David W. Wilcox, "Discounting State and Local Pension Liabilities," *American Economic Review* 99, no. 2 (2009).

12. Alicia H. Munnell et al., *Valuing Liabilities in State and Local Plans*, Center for Retirement Research, June 2010, https://crr.gnaritas.com/wp-content/uploads/2010/06/slp_11-508.pdf.

13. University of Chicago Booth School of Business, Kent A. Clark Center for Global Markets, "U.S. State Budgets (Revisited)," August 26, 2014, http://www.igmchicago.org/igm-economic-experts-panel/poll-results?SurveyID=SV_7ajlg33Q5PfJoZ7.

14. Author's calculations based on data from Public Plans Data, https://publicplansdata.org/.

15. Federal Reserve Board, Financial Accounts of the United States, 2023, https://www.federalreserve.gov/feeds/z1.html.

16. Federal Reserve Board, "State and Local Government Pension Funding Ratios, 2002–2020," December 16, 2022, https://www.federalreserve.gov/releases/z1/dataviz/pension/funding_ratio/map/#year:2020.

17. Governmental Accounting Standards Board, "Interperiod Equity and What It Means to You," June 2009.

18. American Academy of Actuaries, *Objectives and Principles for Funding Public Sector Pension Plans*, February 2014, https://www.actuary.org/sites/default/files/files/Public-Plans_IB-Funding-Policy_02-18-2014.pdf.

19. Office of the State Actuary, *2010 Risk Assessment: Moving Beyond Expectations*, August 31, 2010, https://leg.wa.gov/osa/presentations/Documents/RiskAssessment/2010RA.pdf.

20. Girard Miller, "Pension Puffery," *Governing Magazine*, January 5, 2012.

21. The discussion here draws on Andrew G. Biggs, "An Options Pricing Method for Calculating the Market Price of Public Sector Pension Liabilities," *Public Budgeting & Finance* 31, no. 3 (2011).

22. Dorothee Franzen, "Managing Investment Risk in Defined Benefit Pension Funds" (working paper, Organisation for Economic Co-operation and Development, 2010).

23. Author's calculations from Federal Reserve Board, Financial Accounts of the United States.

24. Andrew G. Biggs, *The Multiplying Risks of Public Employee Pensions to State and Local Government Budgets*, American Enterprise Institute, December 19, 2013, https://www.aei.org/research-products/report/the-multiplying-risks-of-public-employee-pensions-to-state-and-local-government-budgets.

25. Biggs, *The Multiplying Risks of Public Employee Pensions to State and Local Government Budgets*.

26. Ilana Boivie and Dan Doonan, *Pensionomics 2021: Measuring the Economic Impact of DB Pension Expenditures*, National Institute on Retirement Security, January 2021, https://www.nirsonline.org/reports/pensionomics21.

27. Boivie and Doonan, *Pensionomics 2021*.

28. Boivie and Doonan, *Pensionomics 2021*.

29. Boivie and Doonan, *Pensionomics 2021*.

30. Leora Friedberg and Anthony Webb, "Retirement and the Evolution of Pension Structure," *Journal of Human Resources* 40, no. 2 (2005).

31. Congressional Budget Office, *The Underfunding of State and Local Pension Plans*, May 2011, https://www.cbo.gov/publication/22042.

32. Congressional Budget Office, *The Underfunding of State and Local Pension Plans*.

33. Moody's Investors Services, *Adjustments to US State and Local Government Reported Pension Data*, April 27, 2013, https://www.nasra.org/Files/Topical%20Reports/Credit%20Effects/Moodysfinal1304.pdf.

34. Blue Ribbon Panel on Public Pension Plan Funding, *Report of the Blue Ribbon Panel on Public Pension Plan Funding*, Society of Actuaries, February 2014.

35. Pension Task Force, *Report of the Pension Task Force of the Actuarial Standards Board*, Actuarial Standards Board, February 29, 2016.

36. Actuarial Standards Board, *Measuring Pension Obligations and Determining Pension Plan Costs or Contributions*, December 2021, http://www.actuarialstandardsboard.org/asops/asop-no-4-measuring-pension-obligations-and-determining-pension-plan-costs-or-contributions.

37. Actuarial Standards Board, *Measuring Pension Obligations and Determining Pension Plan Costs or Contributions*.

38. National Association of State Retirement Administrators, "Latest Investment Return Assumptions."

39. Andrew G. Biggs, "How Much Would It Cost for State and Local Governments to Actually Fully Fund Their Pensions?," *Forbes*, April 1, 2016, https://www.forbes.com/sites/andrewbiggs/2016/04/01/how-much-would-state-and-local-governments-spend-on-pensions-if-they-were-actually-funding-them.

40. David Zook, "How Do Retirement Plans for Private Industry and State and Local Government Workers Compare?," *Beyond the Numbers* 12, no. 1 (2023).

41. Truth in Accounting, *Financial State of the States 2022*, October 24, 2022, https://www.truthinaccounting.org/news/detail/financial-state-of-the-states-2022.

Chapter 15

1. True Tamplin, "Retirement Savings Gap," Finance Strategists, July 11, 2023, https://www.financestrategists.com/retirement-planning/retirement-income-planning/retirement-savings-gap.

2. Nari Rhee, *The Retirement Savings Crisis: Is It Worse Than We Think?*, National Institute on Retirement Security, June 2013, https://www.nirsonline.org/reports/the-retirement-savings-crisis-is-it-worse-than-we-think.

3. Kate Dore, "A Retirement-Savings Gap May Cost the Economy $1.3 Trillion by 2040. How State-Run Programs Can Fix It," CNBC, May 12, 2023, https://www.cnbc.com/2023/05/12/how-state-run-programs-can-fix-the-retirement-savings-gap.html.

4. Social Security Trustees, *The 2023 Annual Report of the Board of Trustees of the Federal Old-Age and Survivors Insurance and Federal Disability Insurance Trust Funds*,

Social Security Administration, March 31, 2023, https://www.ssa.gov/oact/TR/2023/tr2023.pdf.

5. Kyle Burkhalter and Daniel Nickerson, "Unfunded Obligation and Transition Costs for the OASDI Program," Social Security Administration, March 2023, https://www.ssa.gov/OACT/NOTES/ran1.

6. Congressional Budget Office, "CBO's 2021 Long-Term Projections for Social Security: Additional Information," July 8, 2021, https://www.cbo.gov/publication/57342.

7. Office of Personnel Management, *Civil Service Retirement and Disability Fund Annual Report, Fiscal Year Ended September 30, 2021*, 2022.

8. US Department of Defense, Office of the Actuary, *Valuation of the Military Retirement System, September 30, 2021*, February 2023, https://media.defense.gov/2023/Mar/20/2003182809/-1/-1/0/FY%202021%20MRF%20VALRPT%20FINAL.PDF.

9. National Association of State Retirement Administrators, "NASRA Issue Brief: Public Pension Plan Investment Return Assumptions," March 2023.

10. Author's calculations using data from Public Plans Data, https://publicplansdata.org/.

11. Federal Reserve Board, Financial Accounts of the United States, 2023, https://www.federalreserve.gov/feeds/z1.html.

12. Rhee, *The Retirement Savings Crisis*.

13. Alicia H. Munnell et al., *How Would More Saving Affect the National Retirement Risk Index?*, Center for Retirement Research, October 22, 2019, https://crr.bc.edu/how-would-more-saving-affect-the-national-retirement-risk-index.

14. Yimeng Yin et al., *The National Retirement Risk Index: Version 2.0*, Center for Retirement Research, May 9, 2023, https://crr.bc.edu/the-national-retirement-risk-index-version-2-0.

15. Jack VanDerhei, *The Impact of Adding an Automatically Enrolled Loan Protection Program to 401(k) Plans*, Employee Benefit Research Institute, February 24, 2022, https://www.ebri.org/content/the-impact-of-adding-an-automatically-enrolled-loan-protection-program-to-401(k)-plans.

16. William Gale, John Karl Scholz, and Ananth Seshadri, "Are All Americans Saving 'Optimally' for Retirement?" (working paper, Michigan Retirement Research Center, 2009).

17. Andrew G. Biggs, *Is There a Retirement Crisis? Examining Retirement Planning in the Household and Government Sectors*, George Mason University, Mercatus Center, September 21, 2017, https://www.bls.gov/cex/research_papers/pdf/is-there-a-retirement-crisis-examining-retirement-planning-in-the-household-and-government-sectors.pdf.

18. Michael D. Hurd and Susann Rohwedder, "Economic Preparation for Retirement" (working paper, National Bureau of Economic Research, July 2011).

19. In personal communication, the authors indicate that current projections based on the most recent Health and Retirement Study data produce qualitatively similar results. Michael Hurd and Susann Rohwedder, email to Andrew G. Biggs, October 2021.

20. World Economic Forum, *We'll Live to 100—How Can We Afford It?*, May 26, 2017, https://www.weforum.org/publications/we-ll-live-to-100-how-can-we-afford-it.

21. World Economic Forum, *We'll Live to 100—How Can We Afford It?*

Chapter 16

1. Social Security Trustees, *1990 Annual Report of the Federal Old-Age and Survivors Insurance and Disability Insurance Trust Funds*, Social Security Administration, April 1990, https://www.ssa.gov/oact/TR/historical/1990TR.pdf.

2. Social Security Trustees, *1990 Annual Report of the Federal Old-Age and Survivors Insurance and Disability Insurance Trust Funds.*

3. Social Security Trustees, *The 1997 Annual Report of the Board of Trustees of the Federal Old-Age and Survivors Insurance and Disability Insurance Trust Funds*, Social Security Administration, April 1997, https://www.ssa.gov/oact/TR/TR97/tr97.pdf.

4. Social Security Trustees, *The 2023 Annual Report of the Board of Trustees of the Federal Old-Age and Survivors Insurance and Federal Disability Insurance Trust Funds*, Social Security Administration, March 31, 2023, https://www.ssa.gov/oact/TR/2023/tr2023.pdf.

5. Author's calculation using Organisation for Economic Co-operation and Development, "Table I.7. Top Statutory Personal Income Tax Rates," https://stats.oecd.org/index.aspx?DataSetCode=TABLE_I7.

6. Franklin D. Roosevelt, "Franklin Roosevelt's Statement on Signing the Social Security Act," Franklin D. Roosevelt Presidential Library and Museum, August 14, 1935, http://docs.fdrlibrary.marist.edu/odssast.html.

7. Laurence J. Kotlikoff, "Justifying Public Provision of Social Security," *Journal of Policy Analysis and Management* 6, no. 4 (1987): 674–96.

8. Louis Kaplow, "Myopia and the Effects of Social Security and Capital Taxation on Labor Supply," *National Tax Journal* 68, no. 1 (2015): 7–32.

9. Congressional Budget Office, "CBO's 2021 Long-Term Projections for Social Security: Additional Information," July 8, 2021, https://www.cbo.gov/publication/57342.

10. Dean R. Leimer, "Historical Redistribution Under the Social Security Old-Age and Survivors Insurance and Disability Insurance Programs" (working paper, Social Security Administration, Office of Policy, Office of Research, Evaluation, and Statistics, February 2004).

11. Dean R. Leimer, "Cohort-Specific Measures of Lifetime Net Social Security Transfers" (working paper, Social Security Administration, Office of Policy, Office of Research, Evaluation, and Statistics, December 2007).

12. This is, of course, ignoring the separate but significant question of whether the Social Security trust fund should be considered "real" from an economic and budgetary standpoint.

13. Social Security Administration, "Social Security Tax Rates," accessed July 25, 2023, https://www.ssa.gov/oact/progdata/oasdiRates.html.

14. Sylvester J. Schieber and John B. Shoven, *The Real Deal: The History and Future of Social Security* (Yale University Press, 1999).

15. Social Security Trustees, *The 2023 Annual Report of the Board of Trustees of the Federal Old-Age and Survivors Insurance and Federal Disability Insurance Trust Funds.*

16. Social Security Trustees, *1992 Annual Report of the Federal Old-Age and Survivors Insurance and Disability Insurance Trust Funds,* Social Security Administration, April 1992, https://www.ssa.gov/oact/TR/historical/1992TR.pdf.

17. Gallup, "Social Security," 2005, https://news.gallup.com/poll/1693/social-security.aspx.

18. This figure represents the sum of additional payroll taxes plus interest at the rate paid to the Social Security trust funds.

19. *New York Daily News,* "Full Transcript of Donald Trump's 2016 Presidential Announcement," April 27, 2017, https://www.nydailynews.com/2017/04/27/full-transcript-of-donald-trumps-2016-presidential-announcement.

20. Josh Hawley, "The GOP Is Dead. A New GOP Must Listen to Working People.," *Washington Post,* November 18, 2022, https://www.washingtonpost.com/opinions/2022/11/18/josh-hawley-oped-republican-party-working-people.

21. Ole Settergren and Boguslaw D. Mikula, "The Automatic Balance Mechanism of the Swedish Pension System," National Social Insurance Board, August 20, 2001.

22. National Commission on Social Security Reform, *Report of the National Commission on Social Security Reform,* Social Security Administration, January 1983, https://www.ssa.gov/history/reports/gspan.html.

23. John A. Svahn and Mary Ross, "Social Security Amendments of 1983: Legislative History and Summary of Provisions," *Social Security Bulletin* 46, no. 3 (1983).

24. The figures herein are drawn from Steve Robinson, "Focus on Social Security Replacement Rates," US Senate Budget Committee, October 6, 2015, https://www.budget.senate.gov/imo/media/doc/Social%20Security%20BB100615[2].pdf.

25. Senate Committee of Finance and House Committee on Ways and Means, "Report of the Consultant Panel on Social Security to the Congressional Research Service," 94th Cong., 2nd sess. (1976).

26. William G. Gale, "The Effects of Pensions on Household Wealth: A Reevaluation of Theory and Evidence," *Journal of Political Economy* 106, no. 4 (1998): 706–23.

27. Gary V. Engelhardt and Anil Kumar, "Pensions and Household Wealth Accumulation," *Journal of Human Resources* 46, no. 1 (2011): 203–36.

28. Rob Alessie et al., "Pension Wealth and Household Savings in Europe: Evidence from SHARELIFE," *European Economic Review* 63 (2013): 308–28.

29. Marta Lachowska and Michal Myck, "The Effect of Public Pension Wealth on Saving and Expenditure," *American Economic Journal: Economic Policy* 10, no. 3 (2018): 284–308.

30. Orazio P. Attanasio and Agar Brugiavini, "Social Security and Households' Saving," *Quarterly Journal of Economics* 118, no. 3 (2003): 1075–119.

31. Orazio P. Attanasio and Susann Rohwedder, "Pension Wealth and Household Saving: Evidence from Pension Reforms in the United Kingdom," *American Economic Review* 93, no. 5 (2003): 1499–521.

32. Alexander M. Gelber, Adam Isen, and Jae Song, "The Effect of Pension Income on Elderly Earnings: Evidence from Social Security and Full Population Data" (working paper, National Bureau of Economic Research, May 2016).

33. Social Security Trustees, *The 2023 Annual Report of the Board of Trustees of the Federal Old-Age and Survivors Insurance and Federal Disability Insurance Trust Funds.*

34. Rich Prisinzano and Sophie Shin, "The Social Security 2100 Act: Updated Analysis of Effects on Social Security Finances and the Economy," Penn Wharton Budget Model, September 24, 2019.

35. Social Security Administration, *Annual Statistical Supplement to the Social Security Bulletin, 2022*, December 2022, https://www.ssa.gov/policy/docs/statcomps/supplement/2022/supplement22.pdf.

36. Mark J. Warshawsky and Andrew G. Biggs, "Income Inequality and Rising Health-Care Costs," *Wall Street Journal*, October 6, 2014, https://www.wsj.com/articles/mark-warshawsky-and-andrew-biggs-income-inequality-and-rising-health-care-costs-1412568847.

37. Gary Burtless and Sveta Milusheva, "Effects of Employer-Sponsored Health Insurance Costs on Social Security Taxable Wages," *Social Security Bulletin* 73 (2013): 83.

38. For instance, see Kamala Harris (@KamalaHarris), "I will not raise taxes on anyone making less than $400,000 a year," X, October 23, 2024, 10:18 p.m., https://x.com/KamalaHarris/status/1849274250303074357.

39. I stress the *effective* tax rate, because in nominal terms the employee tax rate would increase by only 6.2 percent, the employee share of the Social Security payroll tax. However, it is the standard view of economists, and the Social Security Administration and the Congressional Budget Office, that employers fund increased payroll tax obligations by holding back on employee wages. That is, a 6.2 percent increase in the employer payroll tax would result in a commensurate reduction in wages paid to affected employees. As a result, the net return to earning $1 of additional wages would be reduced approximately as if the employee tax rate increased by 12.4 percentage points.

40. Garrett Watson, "Placing the House Build Back Better Act Tax Increases in Historical Context," Tax Foundation, October 4, 2021, https://taxfoundation.org/blog/house-democrats-tax-increases-historical-context.

41. Senate Committee of Finance and House Committee on Ways and Means, "Report of the Consultant Panel on Social Security to the Congressional Research Service."

42. Bill Clinton, "Remarks in a Panel Discussion at a National Forum on Social Security in Kansas City," American Presidency Project, https://www.presidency.ucsb.edu/documents/remarks-panel-discussion-national-forum-social-security-kansas-city.

Chapter 17

1. Committee for a Responsible Federal Budget, "The Case for Raising the Social Security Retirement Age," July 26, 2023, https://www.crfb.org/blogs/case-raising-social-security-retirement-age.

2. Mara D. Fitzpatrick and Timothy J. Moore, "The Mortality Effects of Retirement: Evidence from Social Security Eligibility at Age 62," *Journal of Public Economics* 157, no. C (2018): 121–37.

3. Social Security Administration, Office of the Chief Actuary, "Description of Proposed Provision: C1.7: After the Normal Retirement Age (NRA) Reaches 67 for Those

Attaining Age 62 in 2022, Increase the NRA by 3 Months per Year Starting for Attaining Age 62 in 2023 Until It Reaches 69 for Those Attaining Age 62 in 2030," accessed July 27, 2023, https://www.ssa.gov/OACT/solvency/provisions/charts/chart_run225.html.

4. Charles A. Jeszeck et al., *Retirement Security: Shorter Life Expectancy Reduces Projected Lifetime Benefits for Lower Earners*, Government Accountability Office, March 2016, https://www.gao.gov/assets/gao-16-354.pdf.

5. Jeszeck et al., *Retirement Security*.

6. Michael Hiltzik, "Here's Why Raising the Retirement Age for Social Security Is a Terrible Idea," *Los Angeles Times*, April 11, 2016, https://www.latimes.com/business/hiltzik/la-fi-hiltzik-retirement-age-20160411-snap-htmlstory.html.

7. Congressional Budget Office, *Social Security Policy Options*, December 2015, https://www.cbo.gov/sites/default/files/114th-congress-2015-2016/reports/51011-SSOptions_OneCol-2.pdf.

8. Social Security Trustees, *The 2023 Annual Report of the Board of Trustees of the Federal Old-Age and Survivors Insurance and Federal Disability Insurance Trust Funds*, Social Security Administration, March 31, 2023, https://www.ssa.gov/oact/TR/2023/tr2023.pdf.

9. Hilary Waldron, "Trends in Mortality Differentials and Life Expectancy for Male Social Security–Covered Workers, by Average Relative Earnings" (working paper, Social Security Administration, Office of Policy, Office of Research, Evaluation, and Statistics, October 2007).

10. Martha Derthick, *Policymaking for Social Security* (Brookings Institution Press, 1979).

11. Congressional Budget Office, "CBO's 2021 Long-Term Projections for Social Security: Additional Information," July 8, 2021, https://www.cbo.gov/publication/57342.

12. John Geanakoplos et al., "Would a Privatized Social Security System Really Pay a Higher Rate of Return" (working paper, National Bureau of Economic Research, May 2000).

13. Michael Clingman et al., "Internal Real Rates of Return Under the OASDI Program for Hypothetical Workers," Social Security Administration, April 2022, https://www.ssa.gov/oact/NOTES/ran5/index.html.

14. Dean R. Leimer, "Historical Redistribution Under the Social Security Old-Age and Survivors Insurance and Disability Insurance Programs" (working paper, Social Security Administration, Office of Policy, Office of Research, Evaluation, and Statistics, February 2004).

15. Mark J. Warshawsky, "Senator Cassidy's Social Security Solvency Proposal Is a Tax on Pension Investments," AEIdeas, June 12, 2023, https://www.aei.org/economics/public-economics/senator-cassidys-social-security-solvency-proposal-is-a-tax-on-pension-investments.

16. Government Finance Officers Association, "Pension Obligation Bonds," January 1, 2015, https://www.gfoa.org/materials/pension-obligation-bonds.

17. Kent A. Smetters, "The Equivalence of the Social Security's Trust Fund Portfolio Allocation and Capital Income Tax Policy" (working paper, National Bureau of Economic Research, May 2001).

Chapter 18

1. John F. Cogan and Olivia S. Mitchell, "Perspectives from the President's Commission on Social Security Reform," *Journal of Economic Perspectives* 17, no. 2 (2003).

2. For a more in-depth and nuanced discussion of the George W. Bush administration's efforts on Social Security reform, see Charles Blahous, *Social Security: The Unfinished Work* (Hoover Institution Press, 2013).

3. Julie Agnew, "Australia's Retirement System: Strengths, Weaknesses, and Reforms," Center for Retirement Research, April 2013, https://crr.bc.edu/wp-content/uploads/2013/04/IB_13-5-508.pdf.

4. Australia Department of the Treasury, *Retirement Income Review: Final Report*, July 2020, https://treasury.gov.au/sites/default/files/2021-02/p2020-100554-udcomplete-report.pdf.

5. Social Security Trustees, *The 2023 Annual Report of the Board of Trustees of the Federal Old-Age and Survivors Insurance and Federal Disability Insurance Trust Funds*, Social Security Administration, March 31, 2023, https://www.ssa.gov/oact/TR/2023/tr2023.pdf.

6. Work and Income New Zealand, "New Zealand Superannuation and Veterans Pension Rates (Current)," 2023, https://www.workandincome.govt.nz/map/deskfile/nz-superannuation-and-veterans-pension-tables/new-zealand-superannuation-and-veterans-pension-ra.html.

7. Age UK, "The New State Pension," July 18, 2023, https://www.ageuk.org.uk/information-advice/money-legal/pensions/state-pension/new-state-pension.

8. Statistics Canada, "Table 2. Percentage of Paid Workers Covered by a Registered Pension Plan," June 23, 2023, https://www150.statcan.gc.ca/n1/daily-quotidien/230623/t002b-eng.htm.

9. Anna Madamba and Stephen P. Utkus, *Retirement Transitions in Four Countries*, Vanguard, January 2017, https://www.firstlinks.com.au/uploads/whitepapers/Vanguard-retirement-transitions-Jan-2017.pdf.

Chapter 19

1. Social Security Trustees, *The 2023 Annual Report of the Board of Trustees of the Federal Old-Age and Survivors Insurance and Federal Disability Insurance Trust Funds*, Social Security Administration, March 31, 2023, https://www.ssa.gov/oact/TR/2023/tr2023.pdf.

2. US Census Bureau, "Poverty Thresholds," September 5, 2024, https://www.census.gov/data/tables/time-series/demo/income-poverty/historical-poverty-thresholds.html.

3. Andrew G. Biggs, "Does the Social Security Statement Improve Americans' Knowledge of Their Retirement Benefits?," *Insight*, no. 4 (December 8, 2010), https://www.rand.org/pubs/working_briefs/WB108.html.

4. Martha Derthick, *Policymaking for Social Security* (Brookings Institution Press, 1979).

5. Congressional Budget Office, *Growth in Means-Tested Programs and Tax Credits for Low-Income Households,* February 2013, https://www.cbo.gov/publication/43934.

6. Chris Pope, "Jim Crow's Welfare State," *RealClearPolicy,* April 3, 2023, https://www.realclearpolicy.com/articles/2023/04/03/jim_crows_welfare_state_891434.html.

7. Thomas J. Sugrue, "The Hundred Days War: Histories of the New Deal," *The Nation,* April 8, 2009, https://www.thenation.com/article/archive/hundred-days-war-histories-new-deal.

8. Edwin Emil Witte, *Social Security Perspectives: Essays* (University of Wisconsin Press, 1962).

9. Pope, "Jim Crow's Welfare State."

10. For details on the panel, see Michael S. Pollard and Matthew D. Baird, "The RAND American Life Panel: Technical Description," RAND Corporation, July 26, 2017, https://doi.org/10.7249/RR1651.

11. RAND Corporation, "Well Being 534—ALP Omnibus Survey," February 2020, https://alpdata.rand.org/index.php?page=data&p=showsurvey&syid=534.

12. For more details on state automatic individual retirement account plans, see William G. Gale and David C. John, "State-Sponsored Retirement Savings Plans: New Approaches to Boost Retirement Plan Coverage," in *How Persistent Low Returns Will Shape Saving and Retirement,* ed. Olivia S. Mitchell, Robert Clark, and Raimond Maurer (Oxford University Press, 2018), 173.

13. Andrew G. Biggs, "How Hard Should We Push the Poor to Save for Retirement?," *Journal of Retirement* 6, no. 4 (2019).

14. UK Department for Work & Pensions, "Workplace Pension Participation and Savings Trends of Eligible Employees: 2009 to 2022," November 22, 2023, https://www.gov.uk/government/statistics/workplace-pension-participation-and-savings-trends-2009-to-2022/workplace-pension-participation-and-savings-trends-of-eligible-employees-2009-to-2022.

15. This section draws on Andrew G. Biggs et al., *The Case for Using Subsidies for Retirement Plans to Fix Social Security,* Center for Retirement Research, January 16, 2024, https://crr.bc.edu/the-case-for-using-subsidies-for-retirement-plans-to-fix-social-security-2.

16. The exception is that income tax rates are on average lower in retirement than during a person's working years, which reduces taxes collected even on a long-term basis. However, this can differ from person to person. Moreover, if income tax rates rise in the future as a means to address the federal deficit and debt, today's workers could face higher rates in retirement.

17. Peter Brady, *How America Supports Retirement: Challenging the Conventional Wisdom on Who Benefits* (Investment Company Institute, 2016).

18. Gene B. Sperling, "A 401(k) for All," *New York Times,* July 22, 2014, https://www.nytimes.com/2014/07/23/opinion/a-401-k-for-all.html.

19. Monique Morrissey, "Fixing Upside-Down Tax Breaks Should Be a No-Brainer, But . . .," Working Economics Blog, September 16, 2011, https://www.epi.org/blog/refundable-tax-credits-retirement-brainer.

20. See Adam Bee et al., *National Experimental Wellbeing Statistics: Version 1,* US Census Bureau, February 2023, https://www2.census.gov/library/working-papers/2023/adrm/ces/CES-WP-23-04.pdf.

21. Congressional Budget Office, "CBO's 2021 Long-Term Projections for Social Security: Additional Information," July 8, 2021, https://www.cbo.gov/publication/57342.

22. See John Beshears et al., "The Importance of Default Options for Retirement Saving Outcomes: Evidence from the United States," in *Social Security Policy in a Changing Environment*, ed. Jeffrey B. Liebman. Jeffrey R. Brown, and David A. Wise (University of Chicago Press, 2009).

23. Vanguard, *How America Saves 2023*, 2023, https://corporate.vanguard.com/content/dam/corp/research/pdf/how_america_saves_2023.pdf.

24. Congressional Budget Office, *The Distribution of Major Tax Expenditures in 2019*, October 2021, https://www.cbo.gov/system/files/2021-10/57413-TaxExpenditures.pdf.

25. Daniel J. Benjamin, "Does 401(k) Eligibility Increase Saving? Evidence from Propensity Score Subclassification," *Journal of Public Economics* 87, nos. 5–6 (2003).

26. Karen M. Pence, *401(k)s and Household Saving: New Evidence from the Survey of Consumer Finances*, Federal Reserve Board of Governors, December 2001.

27. Orazio P. Attanasio et al., "Effectiveness of Tax Incentives to Boost (Retirement) Saving: Theoretical Motivation and Empirical Evidence" (working paper, Institute for Fiscal Studies, 2004), https://www.econstor.eu/handle/10419/71528.

28. Attanasio et al., "Effectiveness of Tax Incentives to Boost (Retirement) Saving."

29. Monica Paiella and Andrea Tiseno, "Evaluating the Impact on Saving of Tax-Favored Retirement Plans," *Journal of Pension Economics & Finance* 13, no. 1 (2014).

30. Ludmila Fadejeva and Olegs Tkacevs, "The Effectiveness of Tax Incentives to Encourage Private Savings," *Baltic Journal of Economics* 22, no. 2 (2022).

31. José-Ignacio Antón et al., "Supplementary Private Pensions and Saving: Evidence from Spain," *Journal of Pension Economics & Finance* 13, no. 4 (2014).

32. Under the current Social Security benefit formula, part of that revenue gain would be offset by higher future Social Security benefit payments, though Medicare payments would not increase significantly. However, under the flat-benefit reform discussed here, Social Security benefits would increase by significantly less.

33. For background, see Congressional Budget Office, *How the Supply of Labor Responds to Changes in Fiscal Policy*, October 25, 2012, https://www.cbo.gov/publication/43674.

Index